Praise for

IRON EMPIRES

"Ambition, greed, corruption, 'creative destruction,' and a bit of conscience—Michael Hiltzik's vivid account of the railroad barons in the Gilded Age shows us the workings of unbridled capitalism at its zenith (or nadir, as the case may be). The names Morgan, Harriman, Pullman, Hill, Villard, and Rockefeller will forever be associated with creating America's first great infrastructure and making America 'modern.'"

—Gordon H. Chang, author of *Ghosts of Gold Mountain:*
The Epic Story of the Chinese Who Built the Transcontinental Railroad

"A grand story well told."   —*Washington Independent Review of Books*

"Were the railroad barons of the nineteenth century great entrepreneurs in the American spirit who built a remarkable network of railroads? Or were they robbers who fleeced local people and passengers alike? In this superb and comprehensive book, Hiltzik lets you decide, with the help of a few hints."

—Christian Wolmar, author of the *The Great Railroad Revolution:*
The History of Trains in America

"Lively storytelling and accessible writing makes Hiltzik's work suitable for all types of readers interested in railroad history."   —*Library Journal*

"This prodigiously researched book tells the fascinating stories of the railroad barons who did so much to build America, not only through their vision and genius, but also through their cunning and ruthlessness. Hiltzik's brilliant narrative—of power and plutocrats—often bears uncanny parallels to what's happening in America today."

—Steven Greenhouse, author of *Beaten Down, Worked Up:*
The Past, Present, and Future of American Labor

IRON EMPIRES

ROBBER BARONS, RAILROADS,
and the
MAKING OF MODERN AMERICA

MICHAEL HILTZIK

MARINER BOOKS
HOUGHTON MIFFLIN HARCOURT
BOSTON   NEW YORK

First Mariner Books edition 2021
Copyright © 2020 by Michael Hiltzik

For information about permission to reproduce selections from this book,
write to trade.permissions@hmhco.com or to Permissions,
Houghton Mifflin Harcourt Publishing Company,
3 Park Avenue, 19th Floor, New York, New York 10016.

hmhbooks.com

Library of Congress Cataloging-in-Publication Data
Names: Hiltzik, Michael A., author.
Title: Iron empires : robber barons, railroads, and the making of modern America /
Michael Hiltzik.
Description: Boston : Houghton Mifflin Harcourt, 2020. |
Includes bibliographical references and index.
Identifiers: LCCN 2019033911 (print) | LCCN 2019033912 (ebook) |
ISBN 9780544770317 (hardcover) | ISBN 9780544770348 (ebook) |
ISBN 9780358567127 (pbk.)
Subjects: LCSH: Railroads—United States—History—19th century. | Industrialists—United
States—History—19th century. | Capitalists and financiers—United States—History—19th
century. | Big business—United States—History—19th century. | United States—Economic
Conditions—1865–1918. | United States—History—1865–1921.
Classification: LCC HE2751 .H425 2020 (print) | LCC HE2751 (ebook) |
DDC 385.0973/09034—dc23
LC record available at https://lccn.loc.gov/2019033911
LC ebook record available at https://lccn.loc.gov/2019033912

Book design by Helene Berinsky

Maps by Mapping Specialists, Ltd.

Printed in the United States of America

1 2021
4500828663

For Deborah, Andrew, and David

Contents

PART III: THE GHOST DANCE

Introduction:
Agents of Transformation

FOR TWO WEEKS in deep summer, westbound passengers on a Union Pacific train encountered a tubercular Scot whose conversation, dripping with literary grandiloquence, had earned him the nickname "Shakespeare." Pale, thin, and wracked by coughing fits, he seemed not long for this world. Generally he could be found seated at one end of a car, propping open the door with his foot as though hoping the rush of air might soothe his unremitting fever.

It was 1879, a mere decade after the Union Pacific and Central Pacific lines had met at Promontory Summit in what was then Utah Territory, completing the first transcontinental railroad. The passenger was Robert Louis Stevenson, at twenty-eight still several years shy of the worldwide fame he would acquire with the publication of *Treasure Island* in 1883 and *Kidnapped* and *The Strange Case of Dr. Jekyll and Mr. Hyde* in 1886. An object of pity among his fellow travelers and occasional abuse by railroad personnel, he would mine the journey for an account of rail travel as seen from the lower depths, published in 1892 as *Across the Plains*.

Stevenson's fellow travelers were emigrants, lured west by lavish propaganda in which the railroads promised them access to the bounty of the plains and the golden riches of distant California. According to these reports, the climates of Minnesota and Montana were endowed with "the power of healing any malady." The Northern Pacific declared that "prosperity, freedom, independence, manhood in its highest sense, peace of mind and all the comforts and luxuries of life are awaiting you." The Union Pacific predicted that "a $50 lot may prove a $5,000 investment."

The first thing Stevenson noticed upon embarking on his transcontinental trip was the contempt with which railroad personnel treated the emigrants (not excepting himself). They herded the passengers like cattle into plain wooden cars that had all the creature comforts of packing crates, equipped with benches too short to accommodate anyone but a small child, and lamps that "shed but a dying glimmer even while they burned." Dining cars still being almost unknown on American railways, the train would stop at intervals for the travelers to take their meals at trackside hostels—and often stole away without even a whistle blast of warning. "You had to keep an eye upon it even while you ate," Stevenson reported.

Stevenson described his companions as "mostly lumpish fellows, silent and noisy, a common combination." Their conversation "ran upon hard times, short commons [the scarcity of food, water, land for farming], and hope that moves ever westward." The one sentiment they all seemed to share, which Stevenson judged "the most stupid and the worst," was scorn for the Chinese passengers, who were sequestered in their own car. Stevenson's compatriots, mostly immigrants of European descent like himself, harbored the conviction that "it was the Chinese waggon, and that alone, which stank." In truth, he wrote, as the train made its way west the atmosphere in the others became steadily more rank—the Chinese car was the exception, "and notably the freshest of the three."

Along the way there were indications that for the passengers, the benefits of the westbound journey might fall short of what they had been promised: Trains as crowded as their own were passing them, headed back East. At every platform where they met, eastbound passengers cried to them through the windows "in a kind of wailing chorus, to 'Come back.' On the plains of Nebraska, in the mountains of Wyoming, it was still the same cry, and dismal to my heart, 'Come back!'"

But there was to be no turning back, for the railroads had already etched themselves into the American landscape and American culture.

That had become clear after the momentous meeting at Promontory.

In 1871 Charles Francis Adams Jr., then America's most perceptive analyst of this new industry, had described the transformation underway. "Here," he wrote, "is an enormous, an incalculable force practically let loose suddenly upon mankind."

A muckraking journalist and politician, the grandson of one US president and great-grandson of another, Adams perceived that the burgeoning industry would exercise "all sorts of influences, social, moral and political; precipitating upon us novel problems which demand immediate solution; banishing the old before the new is half matured to replace it; bringing the nations into close contact before yet the antipathies of race have begun to be eradicated; giving us a history full of changing fortunes and rich in dramatic episodes." The railroad, he concluded, would be "the most tremendous and far-reaching engine of social change which has ever blessed or cursed mankind."

As Adams foretold, the railroad industry's influence would penetrate every corner of American life, bringing ever more change to a country that, at the moment when the driving of a ceremonial golden spike marked the transcontinental railroad's completion, was still struggling to come to terms with the wrenching events of the Civil War.

In the ensuing decades, the railroads would visit upon America violent clashes among powerful entrepreneurs fighting for the prize of monopoly rights; strikes that would remake the relationship between management and labor; boom times and depressions; and stock market frenzies, panics, and crashes. Investors would be rooked, whole communities defrauded, tycoons created and others bankrupted, family fortunes established for generations and others destroyed by a single heir's folly. Cartels would be assembled and shattered, politicians suborned.

The railroads would also give American farmers and manufacturers access to lucrative new markets for their produce and goods. Hamlets would be transformed into prosperous towns, towns into thriving cities, and the vacant territories of half a continent filled with homesteaders, very like the emigrants with whom Stevenson shared his cramped traveling quarters.

IT IS TEMPTING to view the railroad as an elemental, impersonal force, driving all before it. But of course it was the creation of human beings: the surveyors and engineers who mapped out the lines' routes, the laborers who cleared the terrain and laid the rails, and ultimately the business leaders whose individual personalities, ambitions, determination, and morals commanded the others' fates. The most notable among the latter group were Cornelius Vanderbilt, Jay Gould, J. Pierpont Morgan, and Edward H. Harriman. Each would play his hour upon the great stage of the railroad industry, attended by a host of supporting characters. Placed end to end, so to speak, they formed a continuum that for more than four decades, from the Civil War through the first years of the twentieth century, transformed America's railroads from a patchwork of short lines waging constant self-destructive war with one another into a titanic enterprise that could justly be considered America's first big business.

Historians have considered the role of outstanding individuals in shaping the fortunes of humankind ever since Thomas Carlyle codified his great man theory in a series of 1840 lectures on heroes: "They were the leaders of men, these great ones; the modellers, patterns, and in a wide sense creators, of whatsoever the general mass of men contrived to do or to attain," he wrote.

Historians were soon engaging Carlyle's argument, debating the extent to which even the most consequential figures of an age were responsible for shaping historical events: Were they like vessels in a river, making their way under their own power; or builders bending the river to their intentions or altering its course; or merely logs following the path the waters dictated for them? Today it is acknowledged, as the philosopher Sidney Hook wrote in his 1943 book *The Hero in History*, that history is a "balance between the part men played and the conditioning scene which provided the materials, sometimes the rules, but never the plots of the dramas of human history." The question is where to strike the balance.

It is a question that pertains to the main figures in this book, a pageant of visionaries, speculators, bankers, and manipulators. In these pages they will be seen in their changing relationships as partners, competitors, allies, and enemies, until the two surviving players, Morgan and Harriman, confront each other in a battle of wills and capital that serves as a defining moment for the entire era, indeed, for the nineteenth century. Morgan and Harriman's ferocious two-man contest for supremacy over the railroad industry would shake the nation's financial markets, cost thousands of small investors their hard-won nest eggs, and produce dramatic, lasting changes in the relationship of business and government.

The actions of these powerful figures greatly influenced the shifting attitudes of the American public toward the railroads. At the moment of the first transcontinental railroad's completion, Americans viewed the project as an emblem of the United States' muscular capitalism and a symbol of its limitless possibilities. No other nation on earth had girded such a vast expanse with iron and steel rails; none so relied on its railroads as agents of economic growth and territorial expansion; none invited hosts of foreigners to its shores to cultivate millions of fallow acres. What struck visitors from abroad about the America emerging from the chaos of civil war was its enormous potential energy. When visitors came to take the measure of the New World, they traveled by rail to see it.

The completion of the transcontinental railroad in 1869 marked a new chapter in the American narrative. Despite its label, the road did not traverse the continent, running only from the Missouri River to Sacramento, nearly a hundred miles short of the coast. But the railroad frenzy it triggered was a real phenomenon. Total rail mileage in the United States soared every decade, despite occasional recession-related slumps—from fewer than 30,000 miles in 1860, to nearly 88,000 in 1880 and 163,500 in 1890.

The defining characteristic of the railroads was their size. America's largest industrial enterprises in the 1850s, the business historian Alfred Chandler observed, were the textile mills of New England. The largest of these, the Pepperell Mills of Biddeford, Maine, had expenditures higher than $300,000 only once during that decade. In 1855, however, the cost of operating the New York & Erie Railroad reached $2.8 million. By 1862 the cost of running the Pennsylvania Railroad was $12.2 million. The Pepperell Mills employed eight hundred laborers; by the 1880s the Pennsylvania's workforce numbered fifty thousand.

Just as the railway companies developed into the nation's first big industry, their chieftains became the first business leaders to acquire social and cultural eminence. They would be lionized as a new American aristocracy—more so since they held their positions not by the chance of birth but by the exercise of intelligence and will. "The railway kings are among the greatest men, perhaps I may say are the greatest men, in America," was the effusive judgment of Viscount James Bryce, a Scottish diplomat whose 1888 book, *The American Commonwealth*, updated Alexis de Tocqueville's *Democracy in America*, a half century on. As Bryce wrote:

> They have wealth, else they could not hold the position. They have fame, for everyone has heard of their achievements; every newspaper chronicles their movements. They have power, more power—that is, more opportunity of making their personal will prevail—than perhaps anyone in political life. . . . When the master of one of the greatest Western lines travels towards the Pacific on his palace car, his journey is like a royal progress. Governors of states and Territories bow before him; legislatures receive him in solemn session; cities and towns seek to propitiate him, for has he not the means of making or marring a city's fortunes?

To less respectful observers these industrialists would become known as the robber barons, the period of their reign lampooned as "the Gilded Age" by Mark Twain and Charles Dudley Warner in an 1873 novel of that title. At the dawn of the new century they would come under attack—first by Theodore Roosevelt, who after taking office as president assailed the railroad magnates as "malefactors of great wealth," and subsequently by congressional investigators who laid bare the secrets of what was then known as the "money trust" of Wall Street. By then Vanderbilt and Gould had passed on. But J. Pierpont Morgan and Edward Harriman still survived among the members of the caste of railway kings so admired by Bryce, and they became the Trustbuster's targets.

The first of the railroad tycoons, Cornelius Vanderbilt, was a proprietor. His goal was to bring railroad companies together under his personal ownership. Vanderbilt's sometime partner in this enterprise was the speculator Daniel Drew. Drew's goal was to squeeze whatever gains he could from investors in railroad securities without ever having to build the actual roads. Vanderbilt and Drew were succeeded in the continuum by Jay Gould, whose method was to build an empire by accumulating smaller railroads, positioning himself at the fulcrum of the transactions in order to siphon the profits into his own pockets.

The last of the tycoons in this pageant, Harriman and Morgan, harbored genuine ambitions to convert the fragmented American rail network into a consolidated, stable, profitable industry that could serve the country, without skimping on profits for themselves.

In this, Morgan and Harriman defined themselves, consciously or not, in opposition to the men who came before them. The Vanderbilts in particular would come to represent for Pierpont Morgan all that was disreputable and self-destructive about the railroads' leaders in the first decades after the Civil War. He would make it his business to tame the unruly industry—eventually with Harriman as his last surviving adversary—but he would not relish the scale of the task bequeathed him. In his view his predecessors, like characters out of Trollope, were indifferent to whether or not a railroad was built, for fortunes were best made not by the construction of a railway, but by the floating of railway shares. Their attitude seemed to be that if these fortunes could be made "before a spadeful of earth had been moved," how much more convenient. For the duration of his professional career, Morgan would strive to conduct himself as their polar opposite.

Morgan was a quintessential capitalist who liked to depict himself as chiefly an agent of shareholders. "*Your* roads," he is said to have crisply informed an uncooperative railroad president, "belong to *my* clients." Vanderbilt's goal was to stifle competition affecting his own railroads; Morgan's goal was to stifle *all* competition, so that the investments owned by his clients would have no headwinds interfering with greater profitability. Harriman's goal was to demonstrate that the best path to profitability was to invest in his railroads' quality until they could meet the demands of their customers.

By the end of the century, a profound revisionism with respect to America's first big business had asserted itself. The United States had become industrialized, urban, imperial, and modern. But Americans were asking whether the drive for modernity had come at too great a cost, or made some individuals too rich and powerful for the good of the nation.

"The question might be asked how the railroad companies for many years in succession have been able to . . . pursue a policy so detrimental to the best interests of the public," observed William Larrabee, a former governor of Iowa, in 1893, during the second of two successive economic depressions linked to the overbuilding and overinflated financing of the industry.

The simple answer was "their great wealth and power." They deployed both to produce more of the same, subordinating every moral principle, every goal, every instinct to the getting of wealth and power alone, and to do so at every level of government and society. "Their influence," Larrabee wrote,

> extends from the township assessor's office to the national capital, from the publisher of the small cross-roads paper to the editorial staff of the metropolitan daily. It is felt in every caucus, in every nominating convention and at every election. Typical railroad men draw no party lines, advocate no principles, and take little interest in any but their own cause; they are, as Mr. [Jay] Gould expressed it, Democrats in Democratic and Republicans in Republican districts. . . . Their favors, their vast armies of employes [sic] and attorneys and their almost equally large force of special retainers are freely employed to carry into execution their political designs, and the standard of ethics recognized by railroad managers in these exploits is an exceedingly low one.

Henry David Thoreau, who could hear the passing New England trains from his refuge on the shore of Walden Pond, viewed the railroads as carriers of the disease of speed, and placed them among civilization's distracting "pretty toys," totems of a deluding modernity. To Thoreau the railroads went hand in hand with a second technology with which they were inextricably bound, the telegraph. "They are but improved means to an unimproved end," he wrote in *Walden*, "an end which it was already but too easy to arrive at; . . . We are in great haste to construct a magnetic telegraph from Maine to Texas; but Maine and Texas, it may be, have nothing important to communicate." He foresaw the oppression, physical and spiritual, that would come in the wake of progress. "We do not ride on the railroad," he wrote; "it rides upon us."

The wealth created by the railroad industry was prodigious, but unevenly bestowed. A railroad magnate's decision about where to lay his tracks could turn a prairie hamlet of shacks into a great metropolis, or a thriving city into a ghost town. Decisions about how to raise capital and deploy it could filter riches to middle-class investors or turn their railroad securities from gilt to dross. The railroads were seen at first as providers of jobs, and good ones—jobs requiring skills that could be ported from location to location and road to road; by the 1880s, however, after the first punishing rounds of wage cuts and layoffs, they were regarded as exploiters of labor, becoming the targets of some of the first mass strikes in American history. Meanwhile, the mergers designed to eliminate what railroad owners called "excess" competition were condemned by their customers as instruments of monopoly allowing the roads to charge "excessive freight and passenger tariffs [operating] most injuriously to the best interest of the farming class," and "extortionate charges" levied on merchants.

The nineteenth-century economist Henry George, a scold of inequality amid abundance, anticipated from his vantage point in San Francisco the railroad's capacity to bring wealth to a few and poverty to the many. "A great change is coming over our State," he wrote with trepidation only a few months before the transcontinental railroad's completion. "The California of the new era will be greater, richer, more powerful than the California of the past; but will she be still the same California whom her adopted children, gathered from all climes, love better than their own mother lands? . . . She will have more wealth; but will it be so evenly distributed? . . . Will she have such general comfort, so little squalor and misery; so little of the grinding, hopeless poverty that chills and cramps the souls of men, and converts them into brutes?"

George saw how this story would unfold. "The completion of the railroad and the consequent great increase of business and population will not be a benefit to all of us, but only to a portion. . . . Those who *have* it will make wealthier; for those who *have not,* it will make it more difficult to get. . . . Can we rely upon sufficient intelligence, independence and virtue among the many to resist the political effect of the concentration of great wealth in the hands of a few?"

The answer would be no. By the end of the century the railroad would have changed California, and the United States, into something wholly unrecognizable to the Henry George of 1868.

One spur to that transformation was the flow of people into the American continental heartland, at a rate of three or four hundred thousand every year. The historian Frederick Jackson Turner declared the end of the American frontier in 1893, but what may be less appreciated is the role of rail in its disappearance. Wagon roads and canals eradicated the frontier between the East and the Mississippi in the 1840s and 1850s, but the truly revolutionary development was the penetration of the railroads into what had been judged the "great American desert," stretching from Missouri, Arkansas, and Iowa west to the Pacific. Turner described this territory as "surveyed into rectangles, guarded by the United States Army, and recruited by the daily immigrant ship, [moving] forward at a swifter pace and in a different way than the frontier reached by the birch canoe or the pack horse." As the empires of yore colonized their conquered territories around the globe, the railroad empires conquered and then colonized the American heartland.

AS CHARLES FRANCIS ADAMS had predicted, the railroads' influence soon did touch every facet of American life: politics, business management, finance, labor, farming. All these were essentially local before the Civil

War; all took on a national character afterwards, due to the ability of the railroads to transport goods and produce, wealth, and knowledge over vast distances with unprecedented speed, and to their insatiable demands for capital, manpower, technology, raw materials, and traffic.

One outcome was a disruption in social relations, especially between men and women. In the first part of the nineteenth century, the cultural assumptions of the middle class associated "respectable" womanhood with "domestic values and social deference," observes social historian Amy Richter.

Such constraints could not survive the age of rail travel. Women were now seen aboard on honeymoon trips, or joining their husbands in business travel, opening private domesticity to public view. Soon women were traveling unescorted by males, whether individually or in groups. This reflected their increasing participation in business and politics, including the women's suffrage movement, launched in 1848 by Elizabeth Cady Stanton and Susan B. Anthony. Articles and books by female train passengers began appearing soon after the Civil War, instructing women readers about what to expect of rail travel, how to dress, and how to conduct themselves safely and in comfort among male travelers, while warning of certain privations. Caroline Healey Dall, a feminist and reformer who embarked on a long train trip on the advice of her doctors in 1880, reported that "thirty-three women and children and two men used our dressing room . . . the latter entirely without right." She warned that decent meals and comfortable dining arrangements would be hard to come by, that luggage porters were ever grasping for tips and needed to be watched like hawks. "Do not travel alone if it can be helped," she advised. "If you *must*, associate yourself on the way with another traveller to whom your service will be as valuable as that she renders you."

Railroad managers and the male traveling public were unsure at first what to make of these customers. A stereotype of the female traveler permeated the popular press, which depicted her as perplexed about such simple matters as purchasing a ticket or reading a timetable, loaded down with excess baggage that burdened fellow passengers, and vulnerable to the attentions of dishonorable men.

Yet railroads, responding to the demands of the marketplace, were soon offering accommodations that female patrons might find more suitable—increasingly luxurious Pullman sleeping cars, for example—though the rail companies' all-male managements remained hidebound in their view of women travelers' habits. George Pullman, asked why he failed to equip the women's dressing rooms on his Palace Cars with locks or bolts, replied that if he did, "but two or three ladies in a sleeping car would be able to avail themselves of the conveniences, for these would lock themselves in and perform their toiletts at their leisure."

To one category of social interaction the railroads were impervious: racial integration. In the Deep South, the lines complied with the Jim Crow laws in states of the former Confederacy mandating segregation in public accommodations, including trains. It was common for conductors to evict black travelers from first-class compartments even when they held first-class tickets, and to order them into cars designated for "colored passengers."

Black leaders continually protested the conditions in the segregated cars and other indignities visited on black passengers. These "cattle cars" were always hopelessly overcrowded; one black pastor spoke of having seen "a squealing pig occupying a seat with two human beings, one of whom was a nicely dressed colored woman," the New York Times reported. In Georgia, a conductor ordered the Right Reverend D. A. Payne, seventy-one, senior bishop of the African Methodist Episcopal Church, into the second-class car designated for colored passengers despite his holding a first-class ticket. When he refused to move, the train was stopped and he was forced to walk five miles, carrying his own baggage, to the nearest depot.

Black women similarly were denied the deference afforded white women on the rails. The black journalist and activist Ida B. Wells recalled a conductor trying to eject her from her usual seat in the women's coach during a ten-mile trip on the Chesapeake & Ohio in Tennessee and sending her to the smoking car, where black and white passengers could mix. As she wrote in her autobiography, Crusade for Justice:

He tried to drag me out of the seat, but the moment he caught hold of my arm I fastened my teeth in the back of his hand. . . . He went forward and got the baggage-man and another man to help him and of course they succeeded in dragging me out. They were encouraged to do this by the attitude of the white ladies and gentlemen in the car; some of them even stood on the seats so that they could get a good view and continued applauding the conductor for his brave stand.

Wells disembarked at the next station, but held on to her ticket and sued the railroad. She won a $500 judgment, memorialized by the *Memphis Daily Appeal* under the headline "A Darky Damsel Obtains a Verdict for Damages Against the Chesapeake & Ohio Railroad." Four years later the verdict was overturned by the Tennessee Supreme Court, which ruled that the second-class smoking car and first-class nonsmoking car were "alike in every respect," and slandered Wells as having insisted on keeping her seat merely "to harass with a view to this lawsuit, and . . . not in good faith to obtain a comfortable seat for the short ride."

THE TITANS WHOSE careers and conflicts are described in these pages shared many characteristics—vision, stubbornness, and unshakable self-confidence among them. But their differences were as important as their similarities. J. Pierpont Morgan was the only one who had been born and raised in an environment of patrician wealth, an upbringing that bequeathed him a distaste for financial disorder that would prompt him to assume an almost dictatorial role in eradicating it from America's growing industries. Jay Gould was born to a tenant farmer in rural Massachusetts; from his father he inherited his obstinacy, and from the experience of losing his mother and stepmother at a young age he developed a preternatural self-possession and the conviction that whatever he could earn by the exercise of mental agility he deserved to keep for himself, never mind the claims of business partners or employees. Cornelius Vanderbilt, who died as reputedly the richest man in America, was the descendant of several generations of small farmers in the still largely wilderness precincts of Staten Island, New York, "a rustic of humble origin" in the words of his first biographer, W. A. Croffut. Harriman's origins fell somewhat between these two poles. He was the offspring of a destitute clergyman whose forebears were people of distinction and wealth; all his life he seemed to carry within him a determination to restore the family's stature. By the exercise of his own intellect he would succeed brilliantly.

All were very much products of their environment. That environment was transforming rapidly as they reached their maturity as business leaders. The railroads were not solely responsible for this transformation, but it could not have happened without them.

Still, in the first decade after the meeting at Promontory Summit, the railroad reigned as a potent symbol of America's emergence on the world stage. Walt Whitman offered a paean to the industry in his poem "Passage to India," which is thought to date from 1871 and appeared for the first time in the 1872 edition of his ever-changing *Leaves of Grass*.

> *I see over my own continent the Pacific railroad surmounting every barrier,*
> *I see continual trains of cars winding along the Platte carrying freight and*
> *passengers,*
> *I hear the locomotives rushing and roaring, and the shrill steam-whistle,*
> *I hear the echoes reverberate through the grandest scenery in the world,*
> *I cross the Laramie plains, I note the rocks in grotesque shapes, the buttes,*
> *I see the plentiful larkspur and wild onions, the barren, colorless, sage-deserts,*
> *I see in glimpses afar or towering immediately above me the great mountains,*
> *I see the Wind river and the Wahsatch mountains,*
> *I see the Monument mountain and the Eagle's Nest, I pass the Promontory,*
> *I ascend the Nevadas,*
> *I scan the noble Elk mountain and wind around its base,*
> *I see the Humboldt range, I thread the valley and cross the river,*
> *I see the clear waters of lake Tahoe, I see forests of majestic pines,*
> *Or crossing the great desert, the alkaline plains, I behold enchanting mirages*
> *of waters and meadows,*

Marking through these and after all, in duplicate slender lines,
Bridging the three or four thousand miles of land travel,
Tying the Eastern to the Western sea,
The road between Europe and Asia.

Even before the poem was published, Whitman would be compelled to confront the dark side of this great human achievement. For the enterprise of which he sang so soulfully was in the hands of scoundrels.

PART I

---~~~---

THE AGE OF SCOUNDRELS

UNCLE DANIEL AND THE COMMODORE

O N THE MORNING of November 8, 1833, a train of the Camden &
Amboy Railroad on a route connecting New York and Philadelphia
broke an axle and derailed, dragging many of its twenty-four passengers
down a wooded embankment, killing two and grievously injuring almost
all the others. Up to that moment, those riding in its three cars had
thrilled at the novel sensation of careening across the landscape at twenty-five miles per hour. Then, in the blink of an eye, disaster.

This was the Hightstown rail accident, the first in the United States
to result in the deaths of train passengers. Among the survivors was the
sixty-six-year-old former president John Quincy Adams, who recorded
for his diary "the most dreadful catastrophe that ever my eyes beheld."
Bodies were strewn all about the hillside, he wrote. "One man, John C.
Stedman of Raleigh, North Carolina, was so dreadfully mangled, that he
died within ten minutes. . . . The scene of sufferance was excruciating.
Men, women, and a child, scattered along the road, bleeding, mangled,
groaning, writhing in torture and dying, was a trial of feeling to which I
had never before been called."

Among the passengers on that train (albeit unmentioned by Adams)
was Cornelius Vanderbilt. The steamboat owner had crossed the Hudson to Perth Amboy, New Jersey, where the pioneering rail line had its
northern terminus, to judge the wisdom of making an investment. Now
he was lying prostrate at the bottom of a hillside, covered in blood, his

clothes torn to shreds, suffering from a broken leg, several broken ribs, and a punctured lung. Somehow he managed to command bystanders to carry him to a nearby farmhouse and have his family doctor summoned from New York; he was then transported in agony to his Manhattan town home, where he lay bedridden for a month.

Vanderbilt swore he would never again ride the rails. He had already expressed skepticism about this newfangled form of transport: In 1832 he had turned down an invitation to invest in the proposed New York & Harlem Railroad, which was to run from the Bowery at the southern tip of Manhattan to Harlem, then a suburb at the island's distant north. "I'm a steamboat man, a competitor of these steam contrivances that you tell us will run on dry land," he told the promoter. "I wish you well; but I shall never have anything to do with them."

Eventually, however, he would succumb to the siren call of opportunity.

AT THE TIME of the Hightstown accident, Captain Vanderbilt was in the process of assembling his first fortune, as a steamship entrepreneur. Robert Fulton and Robert Livingston had demonstrated the commercial possibilities of steam transport with the *Clermont* in 1807, but old-line rivermen persisted in their conviction that steam was "a mere plaything," ill-suited to carrying freight. Among other drawbacks, it was said that the engines took up needed onboard cargo space. Few rivermen objected when the New York legislature awarded Fulton and Livingston a monopoly on Hudson River steam transport.

One who did contest the monopoly was Thomas Gibbons, a wealthy Georgia plantation owner who began running rival steamboats in defiance of the New York monopoly by basing himself in New Jersey, where local authorities protected him from the threat of arrest for violating New York law—as long as he evaded New York authorities while afloat on the river. Gibbons admired Vanderbilt's pugnacious competitiveness in ferrying passengers and cargo across the Hudson by sail on his modest fleet of schooners. (Decades later, when he reigned as one of the richest men in

New York, Vanderbilt would say that nothing in his career had given him as much satisfaction as "when I stepped into my own periauger [or perogue, a shallow-draft vessel], hoisted my own sail, and put my hand on my own tiller." Vanderbilt had bought what became his flagship craft, which carried twenty passengers, at the age of sixteen.)

Gibbons hired Vanderbilt to captain his steamboats. The choice proved wise. During the twelve years of their partnership, Vanderbilt would harry Livingston's heirs, who inherited the monopoly, under the very eyes of New York constables, at one point evading arrest for sixty consecutive days. The conflict between New York and New Jersey was finally decided by the US Supreme Court in 1824. In a landmark decision following a legendary oration by Gibbons's attorney, Daniel Webster, Chief Justice John Marshall extended the commerce clause of the Constitution, which reserved to Congress the sole right to regulate interstate commerce, to navigation.

Marshall's decision surely came as a relief to Hudson River entrepreneurs, for the superiority of steam over sail had made itself known quickly. Hostage to the wind and weather, a sloop under canvas could take as long as nine days to reach Albany from New York City; on its first commercial voyage, the *Clermont* had made the trip in thirty-two hours. Soon, larger, faster, and more luxurious steamships were plying the river. "No one who has not seen these magnificent vessels can form a just idea of their vastness, their elegance of finish and furnishing, and the completeness of their equipment," marveled a writer in 1859. The grandest steamboats on the river were those belonging to Vanderbilt—who had bought out his former patron, Gibbons, along the way earning the unofficial honorific "Commodore"—and one Daniel Drew, perhaps the only ship owner on the Hudson who could match Vanderbilt in sheer cussed competitiveness.

The careers of Drew and Vanderbilt would remain intertwined virtually to the end of their days. As steamboat rivals, Vanderbilt and Drew engaged in ruthless mutual fare-cutting that eventually reduced the price of a passage across the Hudson to twelve and a half cents. The rate war almost broke them both, but Drew, whose fundamental commitment was to his personal financial condition rather than public service, flinched first.

From owning an unassuming sailboat ferrying passengers across New York Harbor, Cornelius Vanderbilt went on to build the grandest personal fortune of the Gilded Age.

Having accumulated a debt of $10,000 by operating his vessel, the *Water Witch*, at rock-bottom fares, Drew quietly sold it to Vanderbilt one winter. When the river reopened to traffic following the spring thaw, the *Witch* was still on the water, but now under Vanderbilt's ownership.

Although Vanderbilt vastly outstripped Drew in terms of fortune and preeminence, he would always harbor a curious affection for his rival. "About the only soft spot that the Commodore had in his nature," W. A. Croffut wrote, "was a sentimental willingness to help Mr. Drew out of scrapes." The two were close contemporaries — Vanderbilt was nearly three years older than Drew, but both were in their sixties when they moved into railroads, and they died two years apart. Vanderbilt saw in Drew, who had begun his career as a cattle drover, a man who had risen like himself from modest circumstances and a crude upbringing to command a fortune. Perhaps he was amused by Drew's relentless pursuit of profit, whatever the underlying treachery and disregard for the public welfare.

Vanderbilt may also have respected Drew as an adversary he had underestimated, as he would underestimate his eldest son, William H. Vanderbilt, known as Billy, before recognizing his talents. In his first en-counters with Drew on the Hudson River piers, the Commodore openly scorned him as out of his depth: "You have no business in this trade," he would tell Drew; "you don't understand it, and you can't succeed." But then Drew fought him to a draw, and Vanderbilt felt compelled to give the drover his due. In time they would become friends of a sort, meeting on occasion to "relax in each other's company, talk boats and money, and manhandle the language with impunity."

Although he was then known as an entrepreneur of Hudson River transport, Daniel Drew would ultimately earn a reputation as one of the great manipulators on Wall Street, in a period when an almost complete lack of regulation gave full scope to the most piratical speculators. Charles Francis Adams Jr. and his brother Henry would describe Drew as "shrewd, unscrupulous, and very illiterate," and "a curious combination of supersti-tion and faithlessness, of boldness and cowardice, of daring and timidity." In general, Wall Street's opinion of Drew was similarly dualistic — for ev-ery broker who regarded him as the embodiment of vigorous capitalism, another damned him as "a believer in the doctrine of total depravity."

Drew was expert at cloaking his swindler's instincts in a conspicuous display of spiritual piety; an ardent Methodist, he rarely missed a Sunday in church or allowed himself to be seen in public without a well-thumbed prayer book in hand. On Wall Street that sanctimoniousness garnered him the nickname "Uncle Daniel." Those who mistook him for "a coun-try deacon," however, did so to their misfortune, the veteran investor Henry Clews reported. Not a few of his business acolytes would discover

at one time or another that Drew, at the same moment he was urging
them to buy into a stock because it was destined to soar, was selling the
same shares short and driving their price to the cellar.

The most enduring yarn about Drew dated back to his early career as
a cattle drover. The legend was that before bringing his herds to market,
Drew fed them on salt; the thirsty animals would drink almost to bursting
just before being weighed and sold by the pound. The story might have a
twice-told flavor, but some on Wall Street detected in it the origin of the
term "watered stock," applied to shares issued at a price far beyond their

Outwardly pious but possessed of a brigand's soul, Daniel Drew, here seen
in an etching based on a photograph by Mathew Brady, served his fellow
railroad financiers alternately as ally and adversary.

actual value—a common element of railroad "financiering" in the age of manipulation.

Like Drew, the Commodore projected an outward appearance very much at odds with his true personality. Vanderbilt looked the part of a patrician, tall of stature with a condescending squint always playing in his eyes, whether they were trained on his partners at whist, his corporate adversaries, or his beleaguered son William, whom he had banished to a farm on remote Staten Island until he could be deemed worthy of succeeding to his father's business. (Cornelius, who initially dismissed his son as "dull and commonplace" and was known to call him a fool to his face, eventually came to rely on him as a full partner and adviser—with good reason, for as wealthy as Cornelius was when he died, William would multiply the family fortune many times over and make "Vanderbilt" the most glittering name of the Gilded Age.)

Even as a youth, Croffut reported, the future Commodore "was not blessed with popular manners. He was not conciliatory, and never seemed to care what people thought or said of him. . . . He was not choice of his language. He was sometimes harsh, abrupt, unceremonious, and even uncivil." Or as a later historian of Wall Street put it, Vanderbilt displayed "the upbringing of a wharf rat." For all that, Croffut allowed: "He was honest. He charged fair prices. He allowed nobody to underbid him."

Vanderbilt's competitive spirit was a watchword. In 1849, when the California gold rush inspired the greatest western migration yet known to the young United States, he had sent a steamer south to Central America to transport forty-niners across Lake Nicaragua as an alternative to the customary passage across Panama. When his engineers reported that the upstream route to get his steamer from sea level to the lake was not navigable, he assumed personal command, breasting rapids and other obstructions from the vessel's bridge "to the great terror of the whole party," as one of his engineers would recount. Vanderbilt's route shortened the journey by six hundred miles, its price sliced in half to $300. He sold the Nicaragua service a few years later to a group of investors who unwisely tried to abrogate the sales contract by refusing to pay him. Vanderbilt decided against taking them to court. "Gentlemen," he wrote them: "You have undertaken to cheat me. I won't sue you, for law is too slow. I will ruin you." And so he did, by launching a competing steamer fleet and driving them into bankruptcy.

By the time Vanderbilt had turned forty, in 1834, he was worth a half-million dollars and owned a fleet of twenty vessels. An admiring correspondent for Harper's Weekly would look back a quarter century later, in 1859, at the Commodore's challenge to the steamboat monopolists whose "wealth and obvious soullessness" had previously held commerce and passenger traffic hostage. "In every case . . . the establishment of opposition lines by Vanderbilt," the correspondent wrote, resulted in "the permanent reduction of fares. . . . The monopolies were sometimes ruined, but the public traveled at half the old rates. One may be sorry for the former, but, after all, the latter is entitled to some sympathy too." Now Vanderbilt was about to transfer his instinct for cutthroat competition onto dry land.

IN THE THREE DECADES since Vanderbilt had rejected the invitation to invest in the New York & Harlem in 1832, railroad transportation had made its power known. Even before the Civil War, Americans had understood that long-range freight transportation would be crucial for developing the nation's vast territory, but they assumed that the dominant mode of transport would be by water—that is, by riverboat and canal. A proposal by John Stevens of Hoboken in 1812 for a railroad traversing New York from the Hudson River to Lake Erie elicited mostly ridicule; the completion of the Erie Canal in 1825 seemed to have delivered the ultimate rebuke to the visionary concept.

Yet rail transport's superiority over the inland waterway was too obvious to ignore for long. One advantage was its speed: A trip on the Erie Canal's 363 miles between Albany and Buffalo took up to four days; a locomotive would soon be able to cover the distance in less than five hours. Also, a canal had more or less to follow the hydraulic path of least resistance, but a railroad could begin and end almost anywhere.

This would prove to be as much a drawback as a boon, for in the

early years of the rail era, wherever the lines could go, they went. Builders laid out their routes incoherently, without regard for commercial demand or potential. "There was a road from Hartford to New Haven," the
financial analyst John Moody recounted in 1919, "but there was none
from New Haven to New York." By 1842, he noted, New York State possessed several disconnected stretches of railroad between Albany and
Buffalo, even though the route between the state capital and the thriving grain depot on Lake Erie—the Queen City of the Lakes, as Buffalo
was nicknamed—was a key to New York State's prosperity. "It was not
until 1836 that a plan was adopted for a single line reaching several hundred miles from an obvious point, such as New York, to an obvious destination, such as Lake Erie," Moody wrote. That enterprise was the Erie
Railroad, which would become famous not so much for the resourceful-
ness of its designers but for the creativity with which it was plundered by
its buccaneering owners—Vanderbilt, Drew, and the disreputable duo
Jim Fisk and Jay Gould.

The America of that era was a youthful land—nearly two-thirds of
its population was age twenty-five or younger. The country was poised to
break out across a continent that for the most part was lightly populated
by those of European descent, for some 96 percent of that population
was nestled between the Mississippi River and the Atlantic Ocean, with
about a quarter residing in cities.

America was also an agrarian land, but its agriculture was overwhelm-
ingly focused on a single crop: cotton.

To say that cotton was king in mid-nineteenth-century America is no
exaggeration. Sven Beckert, an expert on antebellum history, calculates
that the crop accounted for more than half the nation's exports through
1860. It was the source of considerable wealth not only among Southern
plantation owners, but in the Northeast, where it fueled the business of
textile mill owners, bankers, and traders (including the Brown brothers of
Rhode Island, whose descendants would go into partnership in the 1930s
with E. H. Harriman's sons Averell and Roland to create Brown Brothers
Harriman, still one of the nation's largest privately owned banks). It is a

discomfiting fact that the primacy of cotton in the American economy in the early nineteenth century made Northerners and Southerners alike complicit in the crime of slavery.

Some historians treat cotton plantations, not the railroads, as "in fact America's first 'big business,'" Beckert has written, observing that the plantations were among the first businesses in America to become industrialized, with the installation of steam-powered spinning machines and looms.

In the years before the war, moreover, the South had become increasingly dependent on railroad transport. The railroad brought boom times to an economy that had depended on the unruly Mississippi River as its circulatory system for goods. The South was relatively underserved by rail, having only about 9,800 miles of track in 1860, compared with 20,800 in the North. But even that meager infrastructure allowed plantation owners to reach eastern markets faster and more reliably than they ever could via river steamboats, molested as the water craft were by the Mississippi's seasonal floods and droughts. The change made the South a net exporter of goods, chiefly cotton. "Railroads are the greatest revolutionists of the age," wrote a Cincinnati newspaper editorialist in 1854. "They do not respect rivers; and locomotives outstrip steamboats."

While the railroads facilitated the export of cotton from the South, they also served as an escape route for slaves. One was Frederick Douglass, who described how he boarded a busy train in Baltimore with borrowed seamen's papers one day in 1838 en route to Philadelphia and freedom. In choosing his plan, he recounted, "I considered the jostle of the train, and the natural haste of the conductor, in a train crowded with passengers." The conductor's entry into the Negro car to collect tickets was "a critical moment in the drama," Douglass wrote, for in Maryland he could still be arrested as an escaped slave, but his successful impersonation of a sailor on his way to join his crew carried the day. The freedom of movement of people and ideas across a newly developing continent was among the "influences, social, moral and political" that Charles Francis Adams predicted would upend his native land.

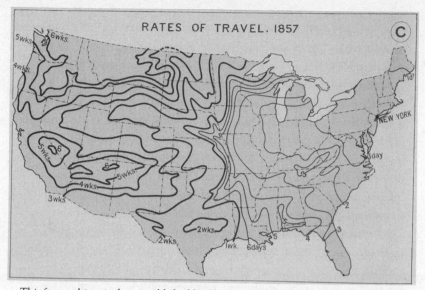

RATES OF TRAVEL. 1857

This famous historical map published by Charles O. Paullin in 1932 shows the benefits—and the limits—of rail transport in the mid-1800s: It took two days to get from
New York to Chicago by rail, but weeks to travel from the Midwest to the West Coast,
then still beyond the railroads' reach.

By the start of the Civil War in April 1861, most of the eastern half
of the country had been crosshatched with rails from Maine to Georgia,
across to Chicago, and from there due south to New Orleans; but the
railroads penetrated no farther west than Kansas City. In 1857, according
to a famous map published by the historian Charles O. Paullin, one could
reach Cleveland from New York in a day and Chicago in two by rail. But
then the tracks ran out and the burdens of overland travel took over:
Traveling to San Francisco from Chicago required four weeks and Seattle
nearly six.

This imperfection disturbed a New York merchant named Asa Whit-
ney. In 1844 Whitney was freshly home from a tedious trading trip to
China. The outbound and return voyages, routed past the Cape of Good
Hope, had each taken more than five months. The journey was protracted

even for that era of intercontinental sail, and rendered almost intolerable in Whitney's view by the afflictions of a cabin filled with the captain's impenetrable clouds of cigar smoke and excessive heat inside and out.

Shortly after this voyage, Whitney experienced his first trip by rail, a brief journey in upstate New York at the unimaginable speed of twenty-five miles per hour. "Time & space are annihilated," Whitney confided to his diary. "We pass through a City a town yea a country, like an arrow from Jupiter's bow." He converted the experience into a proposal he called his "Memorial relative to the construction of a railroad from Lake Michigan to the Pacific Ocean," which an obliging New York politician introduced in Congress on January 28, 1845.

Whitney assured the lawmakers that his three-thousand-mile railroad would be practicable and profitable. "To the interior of our vast and widely-spread country, it would be as the heart to the human body; . . . It would enable us, in the short space of eight days, and perhaps less, to concentrate all the forces of our vast country at any point from Maine to Oregon, in the interior, or on the coast." The plan also offered salubrious spiritual aspects, for the railroad "would bring all our immensely widespread population together as one vast city the moral and social effects of which must harmonise all together as one family, with but one interest —the general good of all."

He asked Congress to cede him a permanent right of way sixty miles in width along the entire route. Sales of that acreage, he estimated, would provide him with an estimated $50 million to build the railway, and another $15 million to run the road until it could pay its own way. His audacious plan elicited nationwide comment, much of it derisive. The project was condemned as "silly and chimerical" and the brainstorm of a "visionary"—at a time when that word denoted a person tormented by hallucinations. But Whitney barnstormed the country to drum up support, and gradually the ranks of railroad supporters swelled, especially after the Treaty of Guadalupe Hidalgo ended the Mexican War in 1848 and brought the United States most of what would become six western states. Suddenly a southern transcontinental rail route from New Orleans to the Pacific seemed plausible, notwithstanding Whitney's proposal for a northern route.

Still, the forces of skepticism were ascendant. Following government rebuffs and an unsuccessful fund-raising trip to Britain—and possibly demoralized by constant ridicule in the press—Whitney withdrew from the fight in 1852, marrying a wealthy widow and retiring to the life of a gentleman dairy farmer in Maryland. He died in 1872, having lived long enough to see his old dream realized with the pounding of a golden spike into a Utah hilltop.

For the spark Whitney lit had not gone out. With the outbreak of the Civil War, the necessity of moving troops and equipment cross-country endowed his idea with renewed urgency in Congress and inspired a surge of investment interest. A quartet of California business leaders founded the Central Pacific Railroad Company, and another group of eastern investors created the Union Pacific. The former were to run their line eastward from Sacramento, and the latter westward from the Missouri River, both to meet somewhere in the heartland. The government would grant them large swaths of territory on either side of the tracks as they laid the rails, as well as capital from bond financings of $16,000 to $48,000 per mile of completed track (depending on the demands of the topography). Many observers deemed the subsidy lavish; others derided the venture as foolhardy. To some, the entire enterprise looked like an irresistible opportunity for profiteering at public expense. On July 1, 1862, after the Pacific Railroad Act was signed by President Abraham Lincoln, the California group's principal lobbyist in Washington, Theodore Judah, dispatched a telegram home, reading, "We have drawn the elephant. Now let us see if we can harness it."

MEANWHILE, IN THE Northeast, Vanderbilt was wrangling with a different elephant. The builders of the New York & Harlem had tried to take advantage of the potential of rail travel by extending the road north into Westchester County. Then the line fell victim to the common ailments of American railroads of the era—looting by dishonest and incompetent executives, a lack of operating credit, physical decrepitude. Vanderbilt had been providing financial support to the Harlem Railroad—sometimes its only financial support—since about 1857. But starting in 1862 he took a more serious interest in the line, with the goal of becoming its sole proprietor. At that time the stock was trading at three cents a share and finding no takers. To Vanderbilt, however, the shares seemed alluringly priced, the intrinsic value of the line's right of way down the center of Manhattan unappreciated by the investor community. The burgeoning national interest in railroads spurred by the fledgling transcontinental project may also have sharpened his appetite.

As Vanderbilt's initial target in the railroad industry, the Harlem would provide him with the opportunity to put into practice a set of precepts for railroad management that his biographer Croffut summarized as follows: "1, buy your railroad; 2, stop the stealing that went on under the other man; 3, improve it in every practicable way within a reasonable expenditure; 4, consolidate it with any other road that can be run with it economically; 5, water its stock; 6, make it pay a large dividend."

Most of these rules were familiar enough to railroad operators of that early era. The second and third, however, were new. Cornelius Vanderbilt perceived that if one was determined to squeeze every dollar out of a railroad, it would prove more lucrative in the end to first turn it into a going concern. What made this concept revolutionary was that up to then almost no one had conceived the railroad business as anything other than a means to an end—the end being plunder.

There were two chief paths to extracting maximum value from the business with a minimum of the hard work of laying iron rails and operating locomotives and freight cars. The more direct option was to act as both capitalist and contractor—collect investment capital from individuals or the government for the purpose of building a road, and pay the money out to a construction firm in which one was a silent partner. The opportunities to inflate construction costs were almost limitless, the goal being to pocket whatever was not actually needed to lay rail across the territory. (The corollary to Vanderbilt's sixth rule was that the "large dividend" should be paid chiefly to the promoters themselves.)

The other path to plunder ran through the securities markets. At the time Vanderbilt set his eyes on the Harlem, the actual construction of railroad lines, much less their improvement, seemed to take a backseat to the manipulation of railroad paper. This was natural, in its way. The explosion of railroad building across the West could seldom be justified by existing passenger or freight traffic, for the lines traversed a wasteland. But given the fifth precept of railroad management, as outlined above, a towering edifice of waterlogged stocks and bonds could be easily erected upon a modest pedestal of capital expenditure.

The promoters exploited a popular craze for railroad shares that far outstripped rationality or practicality, but was based instead on the new technology's supposed potential to transform barren territories into bustling Edens. Wrote historian George Rogers Taylor: "People who had never seen a track, to say nothing of a steam locomotive, invested their savings and gave support to promoters who, even before many of the major technical problems of railroad building had been solved, planned ambitious lines crossing unsettled territory, spanning rivers, and tunneling mountains."

The issuance of watered railroad stock was so common a practice on Wall Street that it was often forgotten that the putative goal was to improve the transportation network to move people and goods farther and faster. In the early stages of Vanderbilt's campaign to acquire the Harlem, the manipulators mustered against him in full cry. "The stock was the favorite one of the whole catalogue, and was operated in, boldly, both on the long and short side, in amounts so large that the whole capital stock sometimes changed hands in a single day," recalled William Worthington Fowler, a veteran broker. "The idea that [Vanderbilt] was buying it for *investment* seemed intensely funny to the brokers. They sold it right and left, in the most dashing style, amid the laughter of their associates."

But Vanderbilt was deadly serious. "The Commodore did not believe in buying or selling invisible things," Croffut reported. "He bought opportunities, and sold achievements. . . . So now he went into Harlem stock, in the winter of '62–'63, in the honest conviction that it was a good thing to buy and own."

Bringing in as vice president his son William, who by then had proved his mettle by turning a decrepit Staten Island rail line into a profitable business, Vanderbilt repaired the deteriorating Harlem and upgraded its rolling stock of locomotives and carriages. The shares began to gain value, chiefly on rumors that the Harlem was about to be awarded a new franchise from the Common Council of New York, a rumor seemingly confirmed by vigorous buying of its shares by city aldermen. Sure enough, the council in April 1863 awarded Vanderbilt the authority to build a second Manhattan line along Broadway between Fourteenth Street and the Battery.

But the brokers and the politicians were not finished with him. Scarcely a month later, even as Vanderbilt's crews were ripping up Broadway's cobblestoned pavement to lay rail, a wave of short selling struck the Harlem—investors selling shares they had borrowed in the expectation that they would fall in price, which would allow them to buy them back more cheaply, return them to their original owners, and pocket the difference. "Something was in the wind," recalled Fowler. The "something" was a plot to rescind the franchise, evidenced this time by the appearance of numerous aldermen among the short sellers.

Vanderbilt was learning the hard lesson that politicians and their compatriots on Wall Street regarded railroads less as public utilities than as entities to manipulate for their own gain. He had profited from the first phase, when the council approved his franchise, and now he was going to pay. Legislators in New York City, in Albany, and in almost every other statehouse and city hall along the Eastern Seaboard would play this game for years, until the advent of a new generation of tycoons, men with a determination to professionalize the railroad industry, put an end to it.

When the council canceled Vanderbilt's franchise at the end of June 1863, the short sellers, including the politicians, prepared to reap their reward. Yet the Harlem's shares stubbornly refused to fall; mysteriously, they rose sharply, eroding the fortunes of the shorts with every surge skyward. The operators had failed to reckon with the obstinacy of Cornelius Vanderbilt, who had taken his adversaries' manipulation of his railroad shares personally. Vanderbilt dipped deep into his own fortune to buy every share offered by the shorts. Under normal conditions, the short sellers would be saddled with massive losses, for they had to pay much more for stock to deliver than they had collected by selling it. But these circumstances were even worse, for Vanderbilt was intent on cornering the stock—owning such a commanding stake (preferably, *all* the shares) that short sellers could not buy shares to cover their positions, leaving them exposed to Vanderbilt's pitiless vengeance. In the end the short-selling brokers were driven to the verge of bankruptcy or beyond. Vanderbilt let the aldermen off with a deal on his own terms: restoration of his Broadway franchise.

The Harlem corner was Vanderbilt's first corner. It would not be his last, or the last on the rails. The carnage led to a catchphrase: "When any one desired to say that an operator was irretrievably ruined," reported Fowler, it was merely said: "He went short of Harlem."

But not every participant in the short-selling scheme went bust. Among those who narrowly escaped was a man whom Vanderbilt had personally brought into the Harlem as a fellow director, but who had promptly become the leader of the short sellers and played their tribulations for his own gain: Daniel Drew.

The aging pirate had helped facilitate the short sales by selling call options on Harlem stock. Put simply, he sold others the right to buy Harlem shares from him at a set price over a period of thirty or sixty days. If the shares fell below that price, the options would expire unexercised, for no one would bother buying shares from Drew if they could be had for less on the open market. If the shares rose above the strike price, the shorts had insurance against their losses to the extent they owned the calls (and Drew had the resources to cover them). In the event, Drew's potential losses were magnified by the calls he had sold into a rising market; his exposure was estimated to be as much as $1.7 million.

Staring ruin in the face, Drew threw himself on Vanderbilt's mercies. Vanderbilt, however, disinclined to cut a break for a purported partner who had traded against him, refused to offer terms. Drew then declared that he had been conspired against, and flatly refused to make good on his calls: "These contracts merely say you may *call* upon me for so much stock; they say nothing about my *delivering* the stock." The prospect of prolonged litigation with Drew brought Vanderbilt and his brokers reluctantly to the table. According to Fowler, they eventually agreed to settle with him for $1 million.

Vanderbilt prevailed in his campaign to win control of the Harlem, and soon would add to his growing network the Hudson River Railroad, which paralleled and competed with the Harlem line, and subsequently the greater prize, the New York Central. Together these made him the first great organizer of the railroad industry—"The first tycoon," as he was dubbed by the biographer T. J. Stiles in 2009.

Vanderbilt's public esteem would endure until he replicated the monopolistic tactics of his adversaries on the river to create his own monopoly on land. That would happen during his 1867 campaign for control of the New York Central, which ran between Albany and Buffalo. The Central's owners made a deal with Drew, who had reemerged in the steamboat business. From spring through the fall, as long as the Hudson remained navigable, the Central carried passengers and freight from Buffalo to Albany, then transferred them to Drew's river craft for the southbound leg to New York City—thus denying the connecting business to Vanderbilt's Hudson River rail line.

Vanderbilt endured the slight for a single winter. The following year, as soon as the river froze solid, he retaliated by cutting the Central off. The next train he sent north along the river stopped a half mile from the railroad bridge into Albany, stranding cargo and passengers—some of them members of the state legislature—for the night, under a frigid sky.

"No more through freight came over the Central," reported Croffut. "Its stock went down fifteen per cent at a blow." The Commodore was summoned before a legislative commission. Asked why he did not respond to the pleas of passengers and shippers shivering in the cold, he explained, "I was at home, gentlemen, playing a rubber at whist, and I never allow *anything* to interfere with me when I am playing that game. It requires, as you know, undivided attention." The Central's owners yielded, and within two years would merge the Central with Vanderbilt's Hudson River line, giving him monopoly control of traffic from Lake Erie all the way to New York City.

Vanderbilt had won, but he and his old compatriot Drew would find themselves on opposite sides of one more encounter. This time, it was Vanderbilt who would suffer.

2

CHAPTERS OF ERIE

THE ERIE RAILROAD was a beleaguered upstate New York road that had been expected to be a paragon of advanced engineering and high commercial potential when it was first conceived in 1833. Its founders made innovative technological choices in designing the road, but almost always the wrong ones. They decreed a gauge (that is, the span between the rails) six feet wide, even though other railroads were standardizing at four feet eight and a half inches. Their reasoning was that this would allow the Erie's engines to negotiate the route's steep grades while the company held off competitors by preventing them from interconnecting with its tracks. The inability to link up with neighboring roads, however, turned out to harm the Erie's competitiveness for forty years, until the tracks were finally realigned at enormous cost. The founders also opted to build their tracks on pilings rather than a graded roadbed; before recognizing the folly of their decision they drove more than a hundred miles of these oaken stilts on which no track would ever be laid.

In financial terms, the Erie's history would be marked by a series of defaults followed by hairbreadth rescues staged by the New York legislature, by municipalities located along the expected route, and by private investors, including not a few with hopes of profiting by selling goods and equipment to the revived road. But these efforts failed to save the Erie from foreclosure in 1845. At that point, what originally had been mapped out as an 800-mile line traversing New York's southern tier and skirting the south shore of Lake Erie between the Hudson River and Chicago instead amounted to nothing but a "jerkwater affair of 40 miles" running from the Hudson barely to the Catskill foothills. When at long last the railroad became fully operational with 773 miles of track in 1868, the cost of construction had soared to $50 million from its original estimate of $3 million. By then the Erie had fallen into receivership twice more and been so repeatedly and unchastely bought and sold by profiteers of one variety or another, it was known as "the Scarlet Woman of Wall Street."

The period of its most wanton manhandling was still ahead of it. That chapter would be written by Drew and Vanderbilt, along with two equally unprincipled figures, operating out of Boston: Jay Gould and Jim Fisk.

These four would come to symbolize for the public the emergence of capital as a driver of American power in the world. Their crass unscrupulousness became part of the mystique of the new phenomenon of Wall Street. The enterprise of building the first American big business would not be completed in their lifetimes, nor would it finish in the style with which they began it. But it would originate in an epic contest over the ill-starred, spectacularly lootable Erie.

IN 1866 CORNELIUS VANDERBILT—newly in command of the Harlem Railroad and Hudson River Railroad, and beginning to plot his seizure of the New York Central—launched a greater plan for a railway network even more ambitious than his existing regional system. He aimed to cobble together a single railroad connecting Chicago with the Atlantic seaboard.

At seventy-three, Vanderbilt was still in the empire-building business. He had already employed his railroad strategy—stop the stealing and improve the line—to make going concerns of the Harlem and the Hudson, the latter of which he had acquired to shut down the rate war it had waged against the former. "I tell Billy," the Commodore said, referring to his son William, now a trusted lieutenant, "that if these railroads can be weeded out, cleaned up and made shipshape, they'll both pay dividends."

Vanderbilt's acquisition of the New York Central would extend his rail empire from Albany west to Buffalo. By November 1867, partially through his strangulation of cross-river freight and passenger traffic during the winter, he had forced the Central's shareholders—among them Edward Cunard and John Jacob Astor III—to place its management in his hands.

Then it was the Erie's turn. The railroad had been playing the same role in the fortunes of the Central that the Hudson had played in the Harlem's: as a competitive, rate-cutting spoiler. It had not always been so. Despite her difficult history, in earlier days the Erie had reigned as queen of the New York railroads, running along the state's southern tier "between the ocean and the lakes"—that is, from the Atlantic seaboard to Lake Erie. The underlying reality, however, was that the route was badly chosen, for it traversed sparsely settled, mountainous land less suited to agricultural development than that along the Central's more northern route, which roughly paralleled the Erie Canal through New York's midsection.

The consequences of the Erie's routing would be historic, as the road's first chronicler observed in 1900, for its creators' misjudgment opened the path to Vanderbilt's success. "The great Vanderbilt system of to-day is centered where the Erie might have been and should have been," wrote Edward Harold Mott. "If shortsightedness, incompetence, or what you will, had not reigned in Erie management two generations ago . . . there would have been no Vanderbilt kingdom today. . . . Who might now be the king of Erie it is impossible to know; but he would be the greatest railroad monarch of the age."

Instead, over the course of the decades, the Erie had been "milked dry by parasites and hangers-on . . . And it must be remembered that the leeches which have always fed on the Erie Railway have insisted on their meal in hard as in flush times," the *Nation* observed in 1866.

The Erie in 1867 was still being pillaged from the inside, for the treacherous Daniel Drew was one of its directors and its treasurer. Nevertheless, the road presented a competitive challenge to the Central—and a peculiarly unpredictable one, at that. "The road was acting as a guerilla cutting rates very sharply and without system or reason," wrote W. A. Croffut. "It made rates and broke rates, not in the interest of the public,

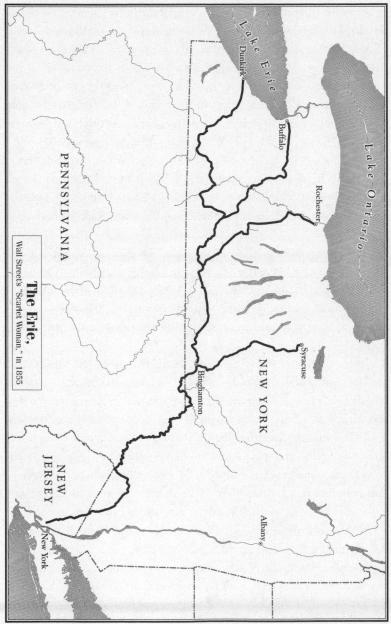

Lake Erie

Lake Ontario

Dunkirk

Buffalo

Rochester

Syracuse

Binghamton

Albany

New York

PENNSYLVANIA

NEW YORK

NEW JERSEY

The Erie,
Wall Street's "Scarlet Woman," in 1855

or of the road, but only of the speculators of the hour." Vanderbilt was determined to end this behavior by absorbing the Erie into his family circle. He may have assumed that since his old ally Drew was on the Erie's board, the takeover would be easy. He was wrong.

As treasurer and director of the Erie, Drew played the company stock as a "one-stringed Chinese lyre," in the words of William Worthington Fowler. On this lyre he "played two tunes; when its price was high, he sung 'who'll buy my Erye? . . . When it was low, he sung 'who'll sell me Erye, who'll sell me worthless Erye?'" Drew's relentless manipulation of Erie shares had earned him the title of "Speculative Director," though who bestowed it on him was never clear. To Charles Francis Adams, he was "at once a good friend of the road and the worst enemy it had as yet known."

Therefore, when it came to the Erie, the goals of Vanderbilt and Drew, those old allies and rivals, were hopelessly discordant. Vanderbilt was intent on "conducting his roads in the best possible manner," judged London-based *Fraser's Magazine,* while Drew's aim, as always, "was to put money into his own pocket by the skillful ensnaring of the speculating public."

In the first act of what would become a seriocomic saga, three parties vied for control of the railroad—Vanderbilt, Drew, and the team of Gould and Fisk, who were associated with a spavined enterprise called the Boston, Hartford & Erie. That railroad had been conceived as an extension to the Erie running from the Hudson east to Boston. On paper, this would allow the Erie to transport coal from Pennsylvania all the way into the New England markets. In reality, the Boston was "more fiction than fact." Yet its owners had contrived an elaborate transaction in which the Erie would guarantee its bonds, yoking the two crippled enterprises together.

None of the three cliques owned enough of Erie to control the line, but an alliance of any two could outvote the third. At the moment, Drew was in cahoots with the Boston group—or so he believed. But Drew had not reckoned with Vanderbilt's determination to obtain sole control of the Erie, which required shouldering him out of the way.

Quiet and retiring in his private life, Jay Gould won a reputation on Wall Street, and untold millions in profits, as a master of financial chicanery and manipulator of railroad securities.

Vanderbilt had secretly reached his own agreement with the Boston group to oust Drew from the Erie board at its annual meeting on October 8, 1867; afterwards, the Vanderbilt-controlled Erie was to absorb the Boston line and deliver a profit to its owners. Vanderbilt viewed the Boston group as a collection of easily manipulated provincial bumpkins, for Fisk was notable chiefly for his clownishness and Gould, as far as Vanderbilt knew, was an insignificant stock speculator.

Gould and Fisk were a quintessential odd couple in appearance and manner. Gould, according to a description in *Harper's Monthly*, was "small, cadaverous, bearded, with sunken, glittering eyes. He hardly ever speaks. While you speak he listens, and looks at you with eyes which freeze and fascinate." He seemed to accomplish his goals through hints and winks, leaving no written or eyewitness evidence that could be used against him. Not long after the Erie affair, when an unsuccessful effort by

Gould and Fisk to corner the gold market would come under government scrutiny, "out of twenty witnesses hardly three [could] testify that he ever spoke with them."

The gregarious Fisk, by contrast, went by the nickname "Jubilee Jim." He was "a large burly man, with a bull-dog face and heavy mustache," the owner of an opera house staffed with "a bevy of ballet dancers" and of "the showiest [carriage] team in New York."

Gould was the personally unassuming but brilliant strategist behind their joint schemes, Fisk the ostentatious front man who was not above

Never one to shun the limelight, Jim Fisk enjoyed parading about in fantastical military regalia and styled himself "Admiral" Fisk during what became known as the siege of Fort Taylor in 1868.

resorting to physical force on those occasions when possession—whether of stock certificates or corporate ledgers—was nine-tenths of the law. Gould was an abstemious paterfamilias known to break off business meetings to return home to his wife and children for the evening; Fisk an enthusiastic reveler who spoke his mind to the press in the most colorful (and quotable) terms. Through all their joint escapades in corporate theft, bribery, and the mulcting of innocent shareholders, Gould, it was said, at least had the good taste to keep out of the public eye. Not Fisk: He reveled in noisy vulgarity, draped his stout figure in "fancy suits and low-cut vests that allowed the cherry-sized diamond in his short bosom to blind the onlooker," and kept his mistress, the raven-haired, improbably buxom Josie Mansfield, permanently near at hand.

Vanderbilt underestimated them both. Together, Gould and Fisk would put their enduring stamp on an era.

THE ERIE ANNUAL meeting went as Vanderbilt planned, electing his nominees to the board, including Gould and Fisk. Drew was evicted from his positions as director and treasurer. Yet only two days later came a stunning about-face: One of Vanderbilt's nominees resigned and his place was taken by—Daniel Drew.

What happened? On the Sunday two days before the election, Drew had visited the Commodore at his Manhattan home on Washington Place. There he staged a fit of weeping and sniveling about the "beggary staring him in the face" if he were forced out of the Erie. It was perhaps the greatest performance of his life, with the most at stake. He promised to behave himself ever after and to execute all his conniving solely in Vanderbilt's interest. The Commodore gave in, his feelings softened again for the reprobate groveling before him—and quite possibly reckoning that it was safer to have Drew on the inside of the tent than outside it. Vanderbilt summoned Gould and Fisk to the house that night to inform them of the change in plans, and though they were shocked, they gave their assent. They were now on the Erie board, and that was the important thing.

It would not be long before Vanderbilt realized that Daniel Drew was even more dangerous inside than outside the Erie tent. As the Commodore launched the next phase of his plan to acquire total control of the Erie and absorb it into his empire, he discovered that some mysterious force was working against him. Rather than rubber-stamping his proposal for consolidating the Erie with the New York Central, Hudson, and Harlem, the full Erie board now demanded further negotiation. Meanwhile, his brokers, instructed to corner Erie by purchasing every share on the market, were confronted with a seemingly inexhaustible supply.

The culprit was Drew, who had made a separate peace with Gould and Fisk. In 1866, during one of the Erie's recurrent financial crises, Drew had loaned the road $3.5 million, secured by twenty-eight thousand shares of unissued stock and $3 million in bonds convertible at his whim into another thirty thousand shares. This hoard enabled Drew to expand or contract the float of Erie shares with the ease of a child inflating and deflating a toy balloon. He was currently in the inflating vein.

The Commodore, who formerly had bypassed the legal system because of its snail's pace, now called upon a pet judge on the New York state court

The battles among railroad barons such as Vanderbilt and the flamboyant Jim Fisk were irresistible grist for nineteenth-century illustrators such as Currier & Ives, who issued this commentary on the Erie Railroad war in 1870.

to enjoin the registration of any new shares, thus cutting off Drew's spigot, while commanding his brokers to keep buying. But Drew, Gould, and Fisk also owned judges, and theirs ordered the Erie to register every share. On a single day in early March 1868, the Erie directors were served with seven injunctions issued by four judges "all enjoining or commanding things wholly inconsistent," Charles Francis Adams reported. If the board rejected Drew's shares, it was in violation of one court order; if it accepted them, it was in violation of another. There were so many pending motions and appeals lodged in courthouses across the state that a lawyer for one of the parties, cornered by the press, pleaded that it was "impossible to keep track of the proceedings."

Vanderbilt kept buying. His fortune was now dependent on the market's continued confidence in his implacable determination. To falter even for a moment could bring his entire business edifice down in a fatal crash. But his resources were growing thin in the face of the torrent of new shares. The voluble Fisk was said to have confided to friends, "If this printing press don't break down, I'll be damned if I don't give the old hog all he wants of Erie."

A climax loomed. On March 11, Vanderbilt persuaded his judge to order Drew, Gould, Fisk, and their affiliated board members arrested for contempt of court. The very next morning, "a police officer patrolling his beat in West Street was startled to see a group of well-dressed, respectable-looking men, accompanied by a platoon of clerks, issue from the Erie building in a wild stampede and rush headlong toward the docks. With them they carried bundles of documents tied with red tape, account books, records and bales of money." Two directors who had not moved quickly enough were swept up by pursuing deputies like wildebeest calves snatched by lions, and clapped in jail. Drew, Gould, Fisk, and their remaining confederates crossed the river and fetched up at Taylor's Hotel in Jersey City. Guarded by a platoon of Jersey City police officers, the place would become known as Fort Taylor.

Over the next few weeks, skirmishes between Vanderbilt-employed toughs and the Jersey City defenders vied for the public's attention with the impeachment trial of Andrew Johnson, unfolding simultaneously in the Senate chamber in Washington. The siege of Fort Taylor was the more colorful event. Fisk swanked about in a gilded uniform as commander of the defense force, fashioning himself "Admiral" Jim Fisk and installing three twelve-pound cannons on the Jersey piers to repel invaders. He endowed Fort Taylor with the utmost in creature comforts, including Josie Mansfield, transported across the Hudson in grand style, surrounded by a swarm of avid newspapermen. From the hideaway Gould continued to conduct the Erie's business inconspicuously. The weak link in their line of defense, he and Fisk knew, was Drew. The old buccaneer fretted in exile, kept prisoner in his hotel room, spending all day and night in seemingly endless prayer. A bodyguard of a half-dozen men was stationed inside the room to forestall any contact from Vanderbilt.

Eventually a Vanderbilt spy masquerading as a traveling salesman managed to penetrate Fort Taylor and bribe a waiter to slip Drew a note:

> Drew: I'm sick of the whole damned business. Come and see me.
> *Van Derbilt.*

In truth, everyone in Fort Taylor was sick of the whole damned business. Gould missed his family and Fisk preferred to do his carousing in his familiar Manhattan haunts rather than the ratty confines of a Jersey City hotel. Exploiting a New York law that held them immune to arrest on the Sabbath, Fisk and Gould crossed the river every Sunday, Fisk to debauch, Gould to bask in family warmth, both taking care to be back at Fort Taylor by sundown. On one occasion Fisk flouted the law by partying on a weeknight at the Manhattan Club, a haunt of the Vanderbilt clique, but he scurried to a waiting tugboat the moment he spotted a Vanderbilt crony signaling for the police.

So it was that, early one Sunday in March, a sepulchral figure skulked its solitary way toward the Jersey City ferry boat landing. It was Daniel Drew, and his destination on this foggy morning was Vanderbilt's baronial redbrick town house at Washington Place, Manhattan. Normally Drew would have relied confidently on his Sabbath immunity from arrest. But he was afraid of being snared by his partners once they discovered that he had slipped out of Fort Taylor. So he kept to the shadows.

Drew's intention was to once again throw himself on the Commodore's mercy with an abject outburst of weeping and contrition. He hoped to plead as a free man, not a prisoner under lock and key. So he made his way carefully, finally ending up at Vanderbilt's mansion in full groveling mode. By Drew's own account, Vanderbilt received him magnanimously, showing his soft spot for the former drover. "Vanderbilt tole me that I acted very foolish in goin' to Jersey City," he testified later during one of the marathon investigations of the Erie war, according to Croffut's dialect-ridden version. "I tole him I didn't know but what I wus circumstanced in an ockerd [perhaps "unjust"] light."

Still holed up at Fort Taylor, Fisk and Gould prepared for what they expected to be the decisive battle of the Erie war—waged not in the streets of Jersey City, but in the state capitol in Albany, where they had arranged to introduce a bill that would stymie Vanderbilt by legalizing their Erie securities. They were counting on popular hostility to Vanderbilt as a transport monopolist to win them votes, but they also knew that in the state capitol, money talked loudest. At almost the same moment that Drew was sneaking toward Manhattan, Gould quietly decamped for Albany with a suitcase bulging with cash—as much as a half-million dollars, by Charles Adams's reckoning. Under the impression that his lawyer had won a temporary reprieve for him from a writ issued by a Vanderbilt judge, he checked in at the capital's Delavan House hotel on March 30, only to be arrested for contempt and transported to New York. He promptly bailed himself out and returned to Albany, where he began disbursing greenbacks from his valise in exchange for votes.

Or so it can be assumed. "The full and true history of this legislative campaign will never be known," Adams reported. "If the official reports of investigating committees are to be believed, Mr. Gould at about this time underwent a curious psychological metamorphosis, and suddenly became the veriest simpleton in money matters that ever fell into the hands of happy sharpers."

Erie company records give only the barest hint of the scale of the bribery, with more than $1 million having been spent from its treasury in 1868 for "extra and legal services," which a state assembly committee interpreted as sums "to control elections and to influence legislation." Gould, brought before the committee on April 12, 1873, attributed the spending vaguely to an "India Rubber Account," but could not recall a single specific transaction.

"I have no details now to refresh my mind," Gould testified. "When I went over a transaction, and completed it, that was the end of it; and I went at something else; you might as well go back and ask me how many cars of freight were moved on a particular day, and whether the trains were on time or late."

Vanderbilt, of course, had his own resources and his own agents in Albany. His and Gould's treasure chests fought each other to a draw, until finally Vanderbilt decided that he would spend not another dollar to purchase a legislator. Gould's Erie bill passed. But that was not the end of the affair. Gould and Fisk, knowing they could face years of litigation with the Commodore, in late June made their own pilgrimage to 10 Washington Place to negotiate an armistice. Fisk left the most vivid description of the meeting:

> Gould wanted to wait until the Commodore should have time to get out of bed, but I rang the bell and when the door was opened I rushed up to his room. The Commodore was sitting on the side of the bed with one shoe off and one shoe on. I remember that shoe from its peculiarity. It had four buckles on it. I had never seen shoes with buckles in that manner before, and I thought, if these sort of men always wear that sort of shoe, I might want a pair.

Vanderbilt crisply informed his visitors that he would keep his "bloodhounds" on their track until they reached a final settlement to his satisfaction. "I told him that he was a robber," Fisk related. "I said that it was an almighty robbery; that we had sold ourselves to the Devil, and that Gould felt just the same as I did." But they did settle, repaying Vanderbilt $2.5 million in cash and $1.25 million in bonds for his purchases of the inexhaustible Erie shares, and advancing another $1 million for an option on Vanderbilt's remaining fifty thousand Erie shares.

Gould and Fisk ended up with undisputed control of the Erie. Drew sniveled at the outcome but got no sympathy from his confederates, who now were intent on visiting upon him bankruptcy and final destruction. As Fisk sneered at Drew: "You should be the last man that should whine over any position in which you may be placed in Erie."

Gould and Fisk, who had landed the railroad by using the same methods Drew had pioneered, were not yet convinced their prize was of certain value, especially at the high price they had been forced to pay. The condition of the Erie showed the consequences of the speculators' relentless manipulation of the line's bonds and shares. The road owed more than $3.9 million in floating debt borrowed from Gould's cronies, but had no money in its coffers to pay it back—or to perform the stupendous amount of maintenance that had been left undone. Physically and financially, the railroad was "an empty shell." In March 1868 the line's superintendent warned the Erie board of its decrepitude. "The iron rails have broken, laminated and worn out beyond all precedent, until there is scarce a mile of your road . . . where it is safe to run a train at the ordinary passenger train speed. . . . Broken wheels, axles, engines, and trains run off the track have been of daily, almost hourly, occurrence." Of the company's 371 locomotives, 30 were "entirely useless, and some forty more are of but little value, owing to their long service and general infirmity being considered unsafe to carry even moderate steam pressure and sure to break down if run long distances."

This was the enterprise that Gould and Fisk now commanded, a tarnished prize, especially for Gould. For the Erie's subsequent chapter would involve a confrontation with the one man who could outlast, outflank, and outmaneuver him: J. Pierpont Morgan.

VANDERBILT, WHO EMERGED from the Erie war with about $1.5 million in uncompensated losses, never shed his resentment at his adversaries. He resolved to "never have anything more to do with them blowers," and

kept his pledge. A few years later, irked at having been linked in the press
with Gould's efforts to corner the Chicago & Northwestern Railroad, the
Commodore summoned a reporter from the *New York Sun* to 10 Washington Place. Showing "great irascibility at every reference to the name
of Jay Gould," the newsman wrote, Vanderbilt flatly denied having done
any business with Gould since 1868. Then why so distrust him now? the
reporter asked.

"His face, sir," Vanderbilt replied; "no man could have such a countenance as his, and still be honest. . . . I read Mr. Gould like an open
book the first time I saw him. . . . You have my authority for stating that
I consider Mr. Jay Gould a damned villain. You can't put it too strongly."
Not only would he have nothing to do with Gould, but he advised all his
friends to follow his policy. "He'll be sure to cheat you," he told them. As
the reporter headed off into a torrential rainstorm, the last words he heard
from the doorway were: "He is undoubtedly a damned villain, and you can
say I said so."

It was a remarkable outburst, even for those indecorous times. The
very next day Gould, who ordinarily did not care for "newspaper noto-
riety," uncharacteristically responded in kind by summoning the *Sun* reporter to his own home.

"With his deep-set, coal-black eyes, and one leg thrown across the
other," the reporter wrote, Gould reviewed the entire history of the Erie
war, and then gave his judgment. "The poor old Commodore is in his
dotage," he said, contrasting Vanderbilt with a younger generation with
whom he identified personally and expected to lead.

He can no longer go around as he used to and attend to business,
and he is feebly envious of those who can. There is a class of rising financiers whom the old man hates. They are young, full of
energy, and possessed of modern knowledge and appliances to aid
them in their business. . . . While he in his second childhood is up
town amusing himself with his horses, and listening to the flatteries
of sporting men, these young business men are rising into financial

The iconic "champagne toast" photo memorialized the driving of the golden spike binding the Union Pacific and Central Pacific into the nation's first transcontinental railroad at Promontory, Utah, on May 10, 1869.

power which will far exceed the old Commodore's even in his palmiest days. . . . He blows his little pellets of envy at them whenever he can.

As for Vanderbilt's aspersions about Gould's personal appearance, "he ought in his piety to attribute any defects in that respect to the same Wisdom that has bestowed on him his good looks."

Gould was right that the new generation of financiers would outdo the Commodore's exploits. But he was perhaps overly optimistic that he would be their leader. For his own history would militate against his assuming a position of trusted authority.

In the meantime, as these two tycoons sniped at each other, the industry that had once been their plaything had taken on a life of its own with the completion, three years earlier, of the first transcontinental railroad.

Promontory Summit, Utah Territory, was as graceless a site for national mythmaking as one could imagine. "It is sun that scorches, and alkali dust that blinds," the traveler and memoirist Albert Richardson wrote. "It is vile whiskey, vile cigars, petty gambling. . . . It would drive a morbid mind to suicide. It is thirty tents upon the Great Sahara, sans trees, sans water, sans comfort, sans everything." Chance had chosen it, however, as the place the Union Pacific and Central Pacific railroads would join together in the nation's interior, a few hundred miles west of the Continental Divide.

About an hour before noon on May 10, 1869, a last ceremonial rail was laid and bolted down. A tie of laurel timber, polished to an almost glasslike sheen, was slid in under the last joint. Holes had already been drilled to accept the final ceremonial spikes, several of iron, two of gold etched with triumphal messages, one of silver, and another of amalgamated iron, silver, and gold. (These have been condensed by historical shorthand into a single "golden spike.") There was a two-minute prayer by a Christian minister, followed by platitudinous speeches by the appointed spokesmen for the lines, Leland Stanford of the Central Pacific and Thomas Durant of the Union Pacific. They took up heavy mauls to drive the last spikes; legend has it that both men missed their targets on the first blow, sending titters through the crowd. But at 12:47 p.m. local time, a Union Pacific telegrapher signaled to the nation that the driving of the last spike was complete by tapping on his telegraph key the word "Done."

Celebrations broke out from coast to coast. In San Francisco every fire bell in the city was struck, to mark "a victory over space, the elements, and the stupendous mountain barriers separating the East from the West," the *San Francisco Bulletin* declared. One hundred cannons boomed in New York's City Hall Park.

But the adventure was just beginning.

3

PIERPONT MORGAN'S GRAND TOUR

A T 5 P.M. ON July 5, 1869—two months almost to the day since the Union Pacific and Central Pacific railroads had met at Promontory —a luxurious westbound train carrying John Pierpont Morgan and his traveling party pulled out of the Pennsylvania Railroad station in Jersey City, just across the Hudson River from Manhattan. Joining Morgan on board were his wife, Frances Louisa ("Fanny") Tracy Morgan; her sister, Mary Tracy; and Morgan's neurasthenic cousin, Mary Goodwin, who came along for her health but whose recurrent headaches and fainting spells the long trip would fail to relieve. Over the next eight weeks the party would travel six thousand miles, riding the iron rails stretching across the continent to behold parts of the United States known to only a very few Americans of their class. It would not be all pleasure; they would also experience all the inconveniences and privation of rail travel of that era, from which not even the wealthy were exempt.

At thirty-two, Pierpont, as he was known, was the crown prince of the merchant bank cofounded by his father, Junius Spencer Morgan. The family had grown rich managing investment capital from clients in London and steering it toward profitable opportunities in America. Among the most sought-after investments were bonds of American railroads, whose demand for funds had exploded when the end of the Civil War revived the nation's image as a land of unexampled economic potential. The firm then known as J. S. Morgan & Co. played an important role in

J. Pierpont Morgan, captured near the height of his wealth and influence by the photographer Edward Steichen in 1903.

allocating this river of capital to targets in the East and the agricultural South, but the firm had little familiarity with the railroads then reaching across the prairie toward the West Coast. Pierpont was to fill in the map during his two-month grand tour.

Pierpont Morgan was tall and broad-shouldered, just beginning to show the stoutness of middle age, his hooded eyes not yet locked into the unforgiving glare that haunts Edward Steichen's famous photo of him in his aristocratic maturity. He still labored under the oppressive thumb of his father, though as the head of the bank's New York office he was cordoned off by the wide Atlantic from Junius, who presided over the House of Morgan from his London headquarters. (They came together twice each year, Junius sailing west in the fall for a three-month visit and Pierpont heading to Europe in the spring.) Junius would maintain the dominant role in this relationship up until his death in 1890.

Born in Hartford, Connecticut, Pierpont had traveled widely, but chiefly in Europe. He had been educated in Switzerland and at the University of Göttingen, Germany; the farthest west he had journeyed in his homeland was New Orleans, where in 1859 he had launched an audacious —but unauthorized—gamble on an unclaimed shipment of Brazilian coffee. He sold the coffee in small lots at a profit, but the escapade cost him a partnership in Duncan, Sherman & Co., the bank that had brought him on as an apprentice banker as a favor to his father.

Pierpont had married Fanny, the daughter of a prominent New York lawyer, four years earlier. Their wedding came three years after the death of his consumptive first wife, Memie, whose memory he would revere for the rest of his days. With his second wife he had a daughter, Louisa, and a son, John Pierpont Jr., who were left home in New York with a troupe of governesses during the western trip. Fanny Morgan had bright, soulful eyes and was already acquiring the bearing of an aristocratic grande dame. (The incompatibilities of husband and wife that would shadow the marriage were yet to surface.) At twenty-seven, Fanny was game for the adversities of cross-country train travel. She boarded with an ample supply of palm-sized journals whose blank pages she would fill with pencil in a florid hand, categorizing every breakfast, lunch, tea, and dinner along the way as "fine," "poor," or "wretched," and recording the vistas of prairie, mountain range, and wildflower field with genuine appreciation, if not in the most evocative prose.

In touring the American West for the first time, Pierpont was expected to absorb every facet of the region's potential for growth in agricultural production and manufacturing and to assess the demand for rail transport to bring products to market. But there was an even greater point to his journey: He was to take the measure of the railroad industry itself, for this vast, unruly enterprise was destined to become central to the House of Morgan's fortunes.

THE RAILROADS HAD begun to exercise their influence over the banking industry and the capital markets as early as the 1840s, when the first construction boom had occurred in the eastern part of the country and spread rapidly west of the Allegheny Mountains. As the business historian Alfred Chandler would observe, the railroads' appetite for capital could no longer be raised "from farmers, merchants, and manufacturers living along the line of the road." Soon, not even the money markets in the East could fill the demand; "only the largest financial communities of Europe could provide the vast amount of capital required." That demand was considerable indeed. By 1865 the dominant corporation in America was the Pennsylvania Railroad, with fifty thousand employees and invested capital of $61 million.

The opportunity for American banking concerns such as the House of Morgan and Kuhn, Loeb, which had carved out the franchise of placing European capital in American enterprises, was inescapable. But delivering sage advice to their clients required the acquisition of hands-on knowledge. Pierpont already had dabbled in the field, helping to manage a $500,000 third mortgage in May 1869 for the Albany & Susquehanna, a modest upstate New York road, shortly before leaving for his grand tour across the continent. For him it had been a forgettable, routine financial transaction, completed hastily so as not to interfere with his embarkation on that long journey. The deal would ultimately present him with an introduction to the more squalid aspects of railroad finance.

Morgan's party traversed the first leg of the trip in civilized comfort, reaching Chicago in a day and a half. There they remained for almost two weeks under the solicitous eyes of Morgan's midwestern business contacts, among them George Pullman and his investment partner John Chippewa Crerar, a pious Presbyterian elder with a gleaming bald pate and enormous sideburns. At the end of their visit the travelers were escorted to the depot by Crerar, who by his constant attentions had all but made himself a member of the family, and who deposited them in a sleeping car christened the *Minnesota*. This was one of Pullman's early "Pioneer" cars, a vast improvement in ease and luxury over the customary passenger accommodations on rail. ("Such comfortable rooms surely never were on a rail road before!" Fanny exclaimed to her journal.) Pullman's cars were revolutionizing train travel in the United States. For sleeping, the seatbacks folded down to form the lower berths, and a hinged platform opened from the ceiling for the uppers. The compartments were separated by thin curtains, and washrooms were situated at either end. There were as yet no facilities on board for preparing food, however, so passengers took their meals at scattered restaurant sidings or browsed for themselves from supplies brought on board, such as the enormous hampers that Crerar arranged to be packed for the Morgans.

They left Chicago at 9:45 a.m. on Monday, July 19, heading due west and reaching Dixon, Illinois, in time for lunch, then crossed the Mississippi at Fulton in a raging downpour and via what Fanny described as a "fearful looking bridge, resting on one or two islands. . . . There were rafts coming down the river, and wild looking swamps on each shore." After a stop for tea in Cedar Rapids, Iowa, they were halted for hours at Marshalltown, near the dead center of the state, while crews mended a broken rail.

The Morgan party would soon experience more of the challenges facing travelers on the transcontinental railroad. As they would discover, the Union Pacific's rails had been laid at breakneck speed to claim a federal subsidy comprising long-term loans and grants of land along the right of way, an arrangement that encouraged the building of miles of excess track and discouraged the careful planning that would produce dependable infrastructure. Indeed, many of the western railroads funded with government grants were patchwork affairs. Entrepreneurs laid down their tracks with little regard for sound construction principles and at varying gauges, making efficient inter-line transfers of rolling stock, freight, and passengers impossible, and gave little thought to coordination of their routes or schedules. Breakdowns were recurrent and river crossings frequently washed out. It was not uncommon for passengers and freight to be stranded at a depot for hours, even days, until a connecting line's train showed up to carry them on their way. William Lawrence Humason, an adventurous cutlery manufacturer from Connecticut who traveled over the transcontinental route two months ahead of the Morgans, wrote of being decanted by the Union Pacific at a desert stop "into the hot sun, with no shade, no hotel, no house—surrounded by no comforts but sand, alkali, and sagebrush" because a quarrel between the superintendents of the Union Pacific and the Central Pacific prevented the latter's train from arriving until dawn.

On Tuesday, July 20, the Morgans awoke at what Fanny described as "a funny dusty little place that did not seem to have any special name." While the girls were "innocently dressing" before an open window, "the train drew slowly up before a platform covered like all Western platforms with men. The first the girls saw of it they heard a prolonged oh! And of course, there they dropped the curtains." After a delay of several hours, they "went slowly off through an almost interminable swamp, till we came to the point where they backed us down to the river and on the ferry boat" to cross the muddy Missouri.* On the far side they found themselves in a beautiful aspen forest, "which we would enjoy much more if we had only had breakfast." A railroad bridge would not span the Missouri until 1872.

Pierpont and his companions found sustenance at a roadhouse in Fremont, Nebraska, where they had to wait three hours to be picked up by the westbound Union Pacific train from Omaha. They spent the time gathering flowers and weighing themselves on the depot scale—Mary Goodwin 112.5 pounds, Fanny 140, her sister Mary 139, and Pierpont 200. Fanny complained of the dismal monotony of the fare, a feature of dining accommodations along the transcontinental railroad mentioned by other travelers almost without exception. "It was necessary to look at one's watch to tell whether it was breakfast, dinner, or supper that we were eating, these meals presenting invariably the same salient features of beefsteak, fried eggs, fried potato," reported the popular children's author Sarah Chauncey Woolsey, who rode from New Haven to San Francisco

---

* In her journal Fanny named the river they crossed as the Mississippi, but plainly she was mistaken.

over nearly the same route as the Morgans. "Sometimes the steak was a little tougher and was called antelope."

After Fremont, the group's next stop was Columbus, Nebraska, which had been conjured out of the prairie earth by the maverick financier George Francis Train. Famous for his world travels, Train would become the model for Phileas Fogg, the hero of Jules Verne's 1873 novel *Around the World in 80 Days*; he had helped found the Union Pacific and would run for president as an independent against Ulysses S. Grant in 1872, and then, rather more eccentrically, for "Dictator of the United States" in 1876.

In Columbus the Morgans encountered "a party of wild Pawnees just in from a fight with other Indians, riding the horses they had captured," Fanny reported. "Horrid looking wild creatures, with no clothes to speak of—blankets and skins and spears and a few such trifles. One came up and spoke to Pierpont, who, not understanding him, retired to the train immediately." As fearsome as the Pawnees appeared, Pierpont might have felt more at ease had he known that the tribe had been pacified by the government through the expedient of placing its members on the public payroll. In fact they were gainfully employed defending the railroad against less malleable tribes such as the Sioux. If the Pawnees truly had come fresh from fighting with other tribes, as Fanny reported, then they had done so as agents of the US Army.

The train continued across the plains: herds of antelopes, scampering away from the tracks over the dreary alkaline landscape dotted with skeletons of oxen and bison; magnificent sunsets "like scarlet and golden fire," Fanny wrote, the distant Rockies "like a glimpse of the Alps, all whitened with snow."

Then they were in Utah Territory, where they eyed the Mormon settlements they passed with all the curiosity they had earlier devoted to the bands of Indians. Fanny noted with evident surprise that the Mormons all looked "well and neat and prosperous." She described the scenery of the eastern part of the territory as beautiful "almost beyond description," but spared her diary the recollection of traversing Weber Canyon, where the Union Pacific bridge had originally been so ramshackle that passengers were required to disembark and walk across the structure, tie by tie, so the locomotives could pull empty cars across without risking its collapse. The Mormon leader Brigham Young had made deals with both the Union Pacific and Central Pacific to provide labor for track construction; among the crews' first tasks had been to shore up the bridge after its foundations had been eaten away by the ferocious snowmelt-fed Weber River. By the time of the Morgans' arrival the repair work had been completed and the passengers could remain aboard, but the height of the bridge and the rocking of the cars as they crossed still made for a harrowing traversal.

Pierpont, Fanny, and the two Marys transferred at Uintah to a horse-drawn coach for a side trip to the territory's capital, Salt Lake City, thirty-four miles to the south. It was a rough ride over rutted paths, "bumpety bump over rocks and stones and dashing down into the gullies and tearing up again without the least regard for our four poor horses," Fanny wrote. "All the valley is a barren wilderness without a tree," though the Mormon settlers "have turned it into a garden of plenty with their system of irrigation." The travelers arrived in Salt Lake coated in grime, the stench of the sulphur springs they had passed still stinging their nostrils, to find what Fanny referred to as "only a sort of second class (or third even) hotel" bare of "any luxuries at all, not overclean at that," and with bedding "apparently stuffed with chips of granite."

The prejudice against Mormons common at the time—Mary Tracy's reflexive term for the men was "Mormon swine"—clashed with the evidence before the Morgans' eyes of a thriving, industrious community. They visited the work site of the Salt Lake Temple, then in its sixteenth year of construction (it would not be dedicated for another twenty-four), where Fanny stepped into a pothole, wrenching her foot. While she was laid up that evening, she reported later, Pierpont and the two Marys paid a call on "the old sinner Brigham," who "seemed to take quite a fancy" to Fanny's sister, provoking giggles. At age sixty-nine, the polygamous Mormon leader had already been married fifty-three times (by some reckonings), most recently only a few weeks earlier. The next day, a Sunday, Pierpont and the girls attended a little Episcopal church for services while

Fanny stayed in the hotel. There she found solace by dipping into a popular devotional volume dedicated to Louise of France, the pious daughter of Louis XV who had taken vows as a Carmelite nun and was known as Madame Louise. Returning to Uintah on Monday after another bone-rattling coach ride, they discovered that their train would be seven hours late.

Two days later they reached California. The Central Pacific brought them over the Sierra Nevadas — "the scenery the finest I have ever seen," Fanny judged — and terminated in Sacramento; the last ninety miles to San Francisco had to be crossed by boat over the channels and bays of the Sacramento River delta. They were promptly taken under the wings of the city's business elite, especially Milton Slocum Latham, a businessman and politician who had served as California's governor in 1860 (for five days, or until he could appoint himself successor to US senator David Broderick, who had been killed in a duel). Latham settled the Morgan party in his palatial mansion and made sure the women were kept entertained by excursions to the theater and waterfront. Meanwhile he escorted Pierpont to the financial district so the young banker could cement business contacts for the future.

After a week they were on the road again, this time for an overland trip to the spectacular unspoiled country around Yosemite, including tours on horseback to Yosemite Falls and Mission Lake. They doubled back to San Francisco and then returned to Sacramento by way of Napa and Sonoma, the future winemaking regions then blanketed with fruit orchards — "we literally stuffed ourselves with peaches, figs etc.," Fanny wrote. Finally they reboarded the train to retrace their outbound journey. Fanny's journals exude ever-growing relief with every mile that brought them nearer to civilized Chicago, which they reached on Saturday, August 28. That evening they viewed a gallery exhibition of oils by Albert Bierstadt, who specialized in brooding, dramatic landscapes of mountain ranges, waterfalls, and rushing rivers. Among the paintings on display were views of Yosemite, bathed in purple light and orange sunsets. Fanny, having recently viewed the real thing, pronounced the artwork "not very satisfactory."

———

PIERPONT ARRIVED HOME in September armed with firsthand impressions of the transcontinental railroad and its territory west of the Mississippi. More to his purposes, he returned with a greater sense of the importance of the rail links between the Eastern Seaboard and Chicago, the growing city already shouldering its way toward its destiny as the paramount railroad center of the Midwest.

The journey left him with a long-lasting disdain for the Union Pacific, borne of weeks of uncomfortable travel over incompetent track laid through a vacant wasteland devoid of productive capacity or commercial demand. He had seen nothing on his journey to contradict an expert's description of the UP as "two rusty streaks of iron on an old road-bed." But this was an unduly pessimistic impression of the Union Pacific's potential, and arguably the costliest misjudgment J. Pierpont Morgan would make in his life. His error would not come back to hurt him until the emergence, many years hence, of the only man on earth who would challenge him for power and influence over the economic life of the United States.

That man was Edward H. Harriman, who at this moment of Pierpont Morgan's ascendance was an unknown broker just embarking on his own career on Wall Street, eleven years Morgan's junior and untold steps below him on the social ladder. Harriman would erect his own railroad empire on a scale that matched Morgan's in size and surpassed it in geographic reach—starting with the railroad from which Pierpont had just disembarked, the Union Pacific. When the two met for their climactic showdown at the very dawn of the twentieth century, the entire financial world would feel the tremors.

But that great test lay far in the misty future. For now, Morgan had a more immediate concern that involved the buccaneering Jay Gould and Jim Fisk. Having won command of the debt-laden, undermaintained Erie Railroad, they were aiming to solve their own problems by—how else? —creating new difficulties for their rivals.

The Erie was in decrepit condition, but Jay Gould's solution was based less on Vanderbilt's principle of improving the road than on the Commodore's habit of suppressing competition, as he had done by merging the Harlem and the Hudson roads. Hoping to outmaneuver the New York Central in the business of carrying coal from Pennsylvania to New England, Gould and Fisk turned their eyes to the Albany & Susquehanna Railroad.

This road ran 142 miles through "a difficult and sequestered region, neither wealthy nor of varied industries, opening to a new trade neither great markets nor a particularly active people," in the words of Charles F. Adams Jr. It had been conceived in 1853 to link Albany with Binghamton, New York, skirting the Catskill foothills. At the time it was mapped out as just another small upstate New York road. Construction began in 1863 but moved at a glacial pace; its constant financial tribulation made it a "very contractors' Golgotha," Adams wrote, adding that the work finally was brought to a conclusion in 1868 largely through the determination of its "originator, president, financial agent, legal advisor, and guiding spirit," a New York politician named Joseph H. Ramsey. By the time it was finished, the business landscape had changed. The once unprepossessing Albany & Susquehanna was now seen as a strategically important lever between two contesting trunk lines, the Erie and the New York Central —"an element of strength or a source of danger" to each, depending on which one ended up with control.

While Pierpont had been out West, Gould and Fisk had launched a campaign for control of the Albany & Susquehanna. Morgan remained unaware of their machinations until he arrived home in New York in September. His banking partners had been paying close attention, however, since on behalf of the firm Pierpont had helped the road with its mortgage financing just before leaving for his journey. Gould and Fisk are "carrying things with a high hand but they have found their match in Ramsey," James Goodwin, Pierpont's cousin and partner (and brother of Mary Goodwin, Pierpont's traveling companion) had informed Junius Morgan in August. He thought public opinion was rising against Gould and Fisk after years of watching them carry on in the railroad business —they are "losing their power somewhat, & if vigorous steps were taken there is a fair chance of getting rid of them," he wrote, adding, "they are a shame and disgrace to the country."

Now that Pierpont was home, the Albany & Susquehanna clamored for his attention. More precisely, Joseph Ramsey was determined to drag him into the fray. Pierpont, after consulting with his father-in-law, Charles Tracy, a high-minded lawyer who had had his own run-ins with Gould, agreed to help Ramsey fend off the attackers, provided that the matter was placed "entirely and absolutely in his charge." The ordeal would leave the young financier with the vivid impression of an industry so burdened by the manipulations of unscrupulous privateers that it would surely collapse unless it could be brought under adult supervision.

Gould and Fisk had been buying up the road's shares all summer, finally accumulating enough to challenge Ramsey's control. Once Ramsey noticed the action in his railroad, however, he launched a counterattack, quietly issuing himself ninety-five hundred new shares and concealing the maneuver by burying the stock subscription books in an Albany cemetery. There followed a crossfire of judicial writs similar to what had sent Drew, Gould, and Fisk fleeing to Jersey City a few years before. Fisk and Gould called upon a bought New York judge named George Barnard, who barred Ramsey from voting his shares, issuing the order from his temporary quarters in the apartment of Josie Mansfield, "where he was not averse to the charms of cards, champagne and vivacious female company." Barnard's writ was not the last word, however, for a countervailing order was promptly handed down by a judge in Albany friendly to Ramsey.

Brawn, not legalism, decided the next phase of the fight. Fisk assembled a squadron of tough maintenance workers from the Erie shops in Binghamton to board a train running north toward Albany on August 9, commandeering engines, cars, and depots along the way. Simultaneously, Ramsey dispatched a train carrying 150 burly personnel from Albany with corresponding instructions to seize all the railroad property they encountered on their way south.

The two tatterdemalion armies headed toward a violent confrontation, which took place at a long tunnel about fifteen miles from Bing-hamton. The Albany train, arriving first, halted just shy of the tunnel entrance. On the far side, the Erie's general superintendent, following Fisk's orders, tried to arrange his motley troops into some semblance of martial order. "A more unwieldy body could not well have been got to-gether," reported Adams. "The men were wholly unarmed, except, per-haps, with sticks. . . . They had been hastily summoned from the [Erie] shops, and were ignorant as children of the crazy errand they were about, nor had they the slightest enmity toward those opposite to whom they stood in ludicrous array." Their adversaries, however, were long-term Albany employees loyal to Ramsey, "thoroughly stirred up and ready for anything."

By 7 p.m. the Erie ranks swelled into "an unwieldy mob of some eight hundred men." Their fully loaded train moved through the tunnel and emerged at the other end, there to find the Albany train advancing upon it from around a blind curve. The Erie conductor leaped off his train and ordered the engineer to reverse, but in vain, for the grade back into the tunnel was too steep. The two locomotives came together in a crash. Men poured from both trains and the violence became general. Despite their inferior numbers, the Albany crews routed Fisk's men, who retreated in confusion back through the tunnel. There were a few further skirmishes before night fell, at which time the conflict degenerated into "loud shouts and excessive profanity," punctuated by the occasional pistol report. Eventually the state militia arrived, called out by Governor John T. Hoff-man to quell the riot.

Hoffman was forced to operate the Albany & Susquehanna under gu-bernatorial authority, with militiamen keeping order on the tracks, un-til the railroad's annual meeting a month later. By then he had become "heartily sick of running a railroad *a la militaire*," as the *New York Times* put it. With the conflict interfering with the governor's plan for a presi-dential run in 1872, he became "satisfied that in taking military possession of the road he 'put his foot in it,' and he is anxious to get it out again as easily and speedily as possible."

Morgan and Ramsey, backed by a contingent of Albany police, were in possession of the railroad's headquarters when Fisk and his troops arrived for the annual meeting. A melee ensued as the newcomers tried to move up the stairs to the office, resulting in Fisk's being "knocked off his feet and . . . back on the men who were coming up behind him." According to Morgan family legend, Pierpont personally delivered the blow, but his biographers tend to consider the story implausible.

The meeting finally convened in a stifling room filled to overflowing with members of the two camps and their raucous supporters. Fisk was "arrayed in his usual fancy style, and with his speckled straw hat and blue ribbon, looked as gay and frisky, and almost as Fisky, as when he hops about in his regimentals on the wheel-house of a Bristol steamer." (The *Times* again.) It would be said later that the insurgents waded into battle at a disadvantage. Jay Gould, their key strategist, had become preoccupied with his (ultimately unsuccessful) scheme to corner the gold market and had left the Albany affair in the hands of the bumbling Fisk.

In Pierpont Morgan, Fisk was dealing with a man who was learning to wield true financial power, not the bluster that was Fisk's stock in trade. Morgan had put his plan to control the Albany into action by acquiring six hundred shares of its stock, enough to restore Ramsey's majority and enabling him to elect a board of his own choosing. Once the election was certified, Morgan promptly leased the Albany & Susquehanna to the Delaware & Hudson Railroad for ninety-nine years. The tactic froze Gould and Fisk out of the Albany for good and placed the railroad permanently out of their reach.

IN STRICTLY FINANCIAL terms, Morgan's coup would have been a footnote in railroad history, except for what it presaged about his role in the industry going forward. As part of the deal, Morgan took a board seat, his first in a railroad company. This represented not merely a financial interest but management power, which was to become much more important.

It heralded a sea change in the administration of a rapidly expanding industry and hinted at its transition away from "the slippery and fraudulent" freebooters who saw the railroads merely as enterprises to be plundered by speculators out for the main chance, and toward control by builders with the vision to create America's first big business out of a patchwork of small concerns. Morgan was the new man, and the rescue of the Albany & Susquehanna a turning point in his career. He had demonstrated by force of personality and full control of strategy and tactics that he could stand up to pirates such as Gould and Fisk.

The Albany raid would permanently mark Gould in Morgan's eyes as a financial villain—"a ruthless destroyer of values when there was an opportunity to enhance his own fortunes," as Pierpont's son-in-law Herbert Satterlee would recollect. Over the coming years Pierpont, in his self-image as a man who earned his wealth by contributing his skills to the building of America, would become increasingly offended by those who followed Gould's approach to finance: "Other men built railroads," Satterlee reflected, channeling his father-in-law. "Jay Gould wrecked them.... He cared not at all for the upbuilding of the country; his end was the advancement of his personal position and the enlargement of his own bank account."

Gould's low morals irritated Morgan not merely on a spiritual or ethical plane, but in practical terms as well. For all that the House of Morgan viewed the railroads' insatiable thirst for European capital as opportunity writ large, Gould's machinations undermined the railroads' claim to be the sort of sturdy, stable investments the firm's clients valued most. The opportunity beckoning the Morgans would fade if the industry's two main problems were not solved. One was its habit of internecine strife and wasteful competition among duplicative roads—such as the Erie and the New York Central. The other was its record of speculative debauchery, exemplified by the activities of Gould and Fisk and their guru, Daniel Drew. It was already evident that the railroads wanted a disciplining hand. Pierpont Morgan, as the purveyor of stupendous amounts of capital, was well positioned to be that steadying influence. His purpose would be

to develop the railroads into functioning pieces of a rationalized, spectacularly profitable industry. Before he could do so, more scandals would
break, including one that threatened to tar the entire industry as a magnet
for fraud and to annihilate Pierpont's grand vision—and the promise of
American railroads.

4

THE KING OF FRAUDS

IT WAS THE late summer of 1872. The presidential race pitting the New York newspaper magnate Horace Greeley against Ulysses S. Grant in the latter's bid for a second term was just getting underway. Greeley, the owner of the *New-York Tribune,* had secured the Democratic nomination with a convention victory over Charles Francis Adams Sr., the grandson of the nation's second president, John Adams, the son of its sixth president, John Quincy Adams, and father of Charles F. Adams Jr., the railroad gadfly.

Several eminent Republicans had abandoned Grant to support Greeley, whose anticorruption platform targeted the shady characters clustered around the president and his family. Revelations from newspaper investigations of New York's William Marcy "Boss" Tweed and his Tammany Hall cronies hung in the air like an acrid miasma. The voters of Maine were due to hold their congressional election on Monday, September 9, in their tradition of casting their votes early to preempt the state's frigid Novembers, when the rest of the country went to the polls. As in every presidential election year, the Maine balloting would be closely watched: The state's record of forecasting the national vote through its choice of governors and members of Congress would later produce (following the 1888 presidential election) the political adage "As Maine goes, so goes the nation."

This year, however, the voting in Maine would be overshadowed by an event that would cast a long shadow over national politics—the publication on September 4 of an explosive disclosure about the Union Pacific Railroad by the *New York Sun*, which led with the following headline:

THE KING OF FRAUDS.

*How the Credit Mobilier Bought
its Way Through Congress.*

COLOSSAL BRIBERY.

*Congressmen who Have Robbed the
People, and who now Support the National Robber.*

HOW SOME MEN GET FORTUNES.

*Princely Gifts to the Chairmen of
Committees in Congress.*

The Union Pacific was not the most decrepit major railroad in the nation (myriad lines vied for that dubious honor) nor the most assiduously plundered (the Erie had retired that trophy for all time). But on that Wednesday morning the Union Pacific took pride of place as a national symbol of graft and corruption.

The firm Crédit Mobilier of America had been operated by the Union Pacific's own officers to front as the road's construction contractor. It was essentially a fiction, allowing the UP bosses to steer contracts to themselves, circumventing the law that prohibited such self-dealing on government-funded projects. The Crédit Mobilier was also a convenient tool for ensnaring politicians in the Union Pacific's web by plying them with shares, often at healthy discounts and paid for with loans from the railroad itself. The fuse of scandal had been burning ever since.

THE CRÉDIT MOBILIER scandal stands as one of the most intricate financial schemes in American history, but it had been hiding in plain sight.
Charles Francis Adams Jr. had pointed the finger of suspicion at the enterprise in one of his earliest efforts at muckraking, published in 1869 in the
North American Review, where his brother Henry was an editor. "A new
piece of machinery, called the Credit Mobilier, has come into play" in the
building of the Union Pacific, wrote Charles, who acknowledged that the
exact nature of this machinery was yet "shrouded in mystery." What was
known was that the Crédit Mobilier had been born as the Pennsylvania
Fiscal Agency, which was a useless shell corporation until the irrepressible
George Francis Train bought its charter, renamed it to create a Continental aura, and invited the directors of the Union Pacific to sign on. Adams
observed that the Crédit Mobilier was reported to be "the real constructor
of the Union Pacific, and now to have got into its hands all the unissued
stock, the proceeds of the bonds sold, the government bonds, and the
earnings of the road—in fact, all the available assets. Its profits are reported to have been enormous—reported only, for . . . there is nothing
but hearsay and street rumor to rely upon." In truth, Adams reported, the
firm was "but another name for the Pacific Railroad ring." He continued:

> The members of it are in Congress; they are trustees for the bond-hold-
> ers, they are directors, they are stockholders, they are contractors; in
> Washington they vote the subsidies, in New York they receive them,
> upon the Plains they expend them, and in the Credit Mobilier they
> divide them. . . . Here is every vicious element of railroad construc-
> tion and management; here is costly construction, entailing future
> taxation on trade; here are tens of millions of fictitious capital; . . .
> here is every element of cost recklessly exaggerated, and the whole
> at some future day is to . . . constitute a source of corruption in the
> politics of the land, and a resistless power in its legislature.

The goal of the arrangement was crystal clear. According to the later
testimony of J. M. S. Williams, an investor who held shares in both the
railroad and the Crédit Mobilier, the two enterprises were one and the

same, the scheme designed simply to siphon off money when cash moved from one to the other.

"Did this road cost the Union Pacific Railroad Company more than it cost the Credit Mobilier?" Williams was asked by a congressional committee.

"It depends upon how you look at it," he replied. "If your right-hand pocket had more money than your left, and you took some from your right and put it in your left, you would be neither richer nor poorer." Still, he agreed, the inflated cost of the construction — that is, the amount of the federal subsidy in excess of what the Union Pacific spent to build the road — ended up in the hands of Crédit Mobilier shareholders.

In his writings, Adams returned again and again to the suspicious doings of the "Pacific Railroad ring." The spark of public outrage did not ignite, however, until the resolutely Democratic *Sun* unearthed testimony by a Crédit Mobilier trustee and stockholder named Henry McComb, who had profited handsomely from the company but was nevertheless convinced that he had been swindled by his own partners. McComb's accusations had been delivered fifteen months earlier in a Pennsylvania courthouse, but to the outside world they were fresh, and damning.

The factual elements of the *Sun*'s exposé consisted almost entirely of McComb's direct testimony at the Pennsylvania trial, spread over six columns of its front page, another six on page 2, and a further half-column on page 3. To his version of events, delivered under oath but obviously one-sided, the newspaper added its own breathless gloss, labeling the revelations "the most damaging exhibition of official and private villainy and corruption ever laid bare to the gaze of the world." McComb testified that Crédit Mobilier of America was "the inside Ring of the [Union] Pacific Railroad, that outside of that the Pacific Railroad was not anything." His testimony bristled with exaggerations, but the gist would stand the test of time.

The *Sun* identified as recipients of Crédit Mobilier bribes the Republican vice president Schuyler Colfax and Speaker of the House James G. Blaine, along with "the chairman of almost every important committee in the House of Representatives." This was a defensible claim in Colfax's case, though ultimately refuted in Blaine's; as for the others, their venality eventually was documented even if their guilt in the eyes of the law, strictly speaking, was judged by their colleagues to be nonexistent.

The *Sun*'s most stunning revelation—the crux of the scandal, in fact —was that a handwritten list existed of thirteen members of Congress said to have received shares in the Crédit Mobilier from Oakes Ames, a Massachusetts congressman from a wealthy family who had joined the Crédit Mobilier enterprise with his brother, Oliver, sometime after its creation. The list, which included Colfax, Blaine, and Representative James Garfield of Ohio, a future president, had been attached to an 1868 letter from Ames to McComb. This seemed conclusive enough at first glance, for in the letter Ames discussed the placement of shares with selected members of Congress at discounted prices and "in trust," partially to keep the recipients' names confidential and partially to allow them to profit from any run-up in the shares without actually risking their personal capital. Ames further confided to McComb his intention to distribute his largess "where it will do the most good for us I think"—that is, to guarantee favorable votes for the Union Pacific on a host of matters due shortly to come before Congress. The list of alleged recipients, however, was in McComb's handwriting, not Ames's. It would turn out that the names referred to individuals Ames had considered approaching, not necessarily those who accepted shares from him.

In the political tumult of the moment this seemed an insignificant detail. The Republican Grant administration was already enveloped in scandal. There was the scheme in which Jay Gould and Jim Fisk had tried (and almost succeeded) to manipulate the guileless president into pumping up the value of their gold holdings. Graft by Grant's appointees at the New York Custom House, where the bulk of European imports were managed, and among appointees of Postmaster General John Creswell had been the topic of previous newspaper exposés.

The *Sun* further exploited the general public's habitual mistrust of politicians. "Mr. Blaine was a poor man when he became a member of Congress in 1864," the newspaper stated simply. "He is now a millionaire."

President Grant's supporters, for their part, pointed to the suspect

timing of the disclosures by the Democratic-aligned newspaper. Among
the *Sun's* critics was the staunchly Republican *New York Times*, which
described Charles A. Dana, the *Sun's* editor and part owner, as "the most
malignant and prolific libeler ever connected with the American Press."
According to the Republican defenders, Ames was an obvious liar and
merely a front for the Democrats. The fury of the pushback would seem
familiar to anyone steeped in today's reduction of official investigations
to "fake news" and "witch hunts": the *Times* charged that the *Sun* was
"quite capable of inventing the whole story, the suit, court, parties and all,
to serve its malice and mendacity. . . . A newspaper has no more right to
publish every foul slander upon public men that it can find, than any man
has to spend his time retailing scandal about his neighbors."

AT FIRST THE accusations appeared to leave their targets unscathed. In
the November election, Grant was returned to office with an overwhelming majority of 286 electoral votes to Greeley's 66; Greeley, exhausted
by the rigors of electioneering, despondent over the death of his wife on
October 29, and mortified by the scale of his electoral defeat, died before
the electoral votes were even counted. Blaine, Colfax, Garfield, and the
other alleged culprits all won reelection.

But the scandal could not be laid to rest so easily, given the direct accusations against sitting members of Congress. A few weeks after the election, the House empaneled two separate investigations. One, under the
chairmanship of Representative Luke Poland of Vermont, was assigned
to investigate the bribery charges against its members. The second, under
Jeremiah Wilson of Indiana, was to investigate whether the Union Pacific
and Crédit Mobilier had defrauded the federal government. The Poland
Committee convened first, but behind closed doors; a public outcry eventually forced it to hold its proceedings in the open, providing irresistible material for the popular press. That was especially so on February 11,
1873, when Oakes Ames appeared in the committee room and, before an
overflow crowd giddy with anticipation, produced a red Morocco-leath-
er-covered notebook in which he had recorded all the payouts of shares

and dividends to his fellow members of Congress. The session that day was "the most dramatic incident I ever witnessed," one veteran of the press corps would recall years later. Of Ames, he wrote, "sorrow and determination were written in every line of his strong face. He looked broken." For Ames had realized that the only way to defend himself against the accusations he faced was to sully the reputations of colleagues he had once counted among his closest friends, "to some extent declaring his own infamy. . . . Cost what it might, he was determined to vindicate himself."

The Poland Committee issued its report on February 18. Its very first pages made clear that Ames would be the fall guy in the affair, which was not to say he was blameless. The Crédit Mobilier had provided him with 343 shares to distribute at his discretion, the committee recounted.

In his testimony, Ames had displayed an insensitivity, not to say disingenuousness, about self-dealing that would be indefensible today, and that challenged standards of rectitude even at the time. Asked by the committee if he thought it was "entirely proper" for a member of Congress to hold stock in a railroad over which Congress had jurisdiction, he replied levelly, "There is no law and no reason, legal or moral, why a member of Congress should not own stock in a road any more than why he should not own a sheep when the price of wool is to be affected by the tariff." He said he had been unaware that anyone could have held a different view until that question was put to him.

Ames maintained that his efforts on behalf of the railroad deserved gratitude, not obloquy: "Those of us who were willing to aid this great enterprise were under the impression our acts were praiseworthy and patriotic." Yes, he said, "we wanted capital and influence. Influence not on legislation alone, but on credit, good, wide, and a general favorable feeling." With a childlike guilelessness, he acknowledged: "I did agree to sell to several, and did actually deliver to some members of Congress, without as much as a thought then or now of any corrupt purpose on my part or theirs, a small amount of stock." He offered some members a guarantee against loss; to others he offered shares without requiring a payment in advance, although as the stock began to return dividends he paid them over as if they had bought the shares legitimately. When some, including

Colfax, got spooked by the disclosures in the *Sun* and proposed to return their shares as though their transactions had never happened, he took them back with no questions asked. Garfield asked Ames to get him ten shares of stock "and hold it until he could pay for it. He never did pay for it." Blaine, he acknowledged, declined any shares.

The Poland Report amounted to a lesson in how to tailor an investigatory conclusion to exonerate the guilty, punish one's adversaries, and identify a scapegoat. The panel found that Representative William D. Kelley of Pennsylvania had acquired ten shares of the Crédit Mobilier from Ames without putting up any cash; Ames applied subsequent dividends on the shares to the purchase price of $1,047, and delivered to Kelley the balance of $329. Garfield not only received his ten shares gratis, but also pocketed a $329 balance. The committee found these transactions to be formally blameless, however, since the Crédit Mobilier was a state-chartered corporation "not subject to Congressional legislation." The fact that all its profits were ultimately derived from the Union Pacific, which did hold a federal charter, was of no moment, for that in itself "did not create such an interest . . . as to disqualify the holder of Credit Mobilier stock from participating in any legislation affecting the railroad company." The committee could not discern that any of the Republican members had been corrupted in their official duties by their interest in the Crédit Mobilier.

James Brooks of New York, the sole Democrat in the dock, was another story. He had badgered Ames and officers of the Union Pacific for two hundred shares of Crédit Mobilier; they eventually agreed to give him one hundred, plus $5,000 in Union Pacific bonds and $20,000 in stock. Brooks was a board member of the Union Pacific, representing the government, and thus barred by law from owning any interest in the railroad. Holding Crédit Mobilier shares may not have been "forbidden by the letter of the law," the committee acknowledged, "yet it was a violation of its spirit and essence." Brooks demonstrated his guilty knowledge by instructing Ames to place the securities in his son-in-law's name to conceal his ownership.

The committee directed its heaviest fire at Ames. He had brought the House of Representatives into "contempt and disgrace"; he had sold to several members of Congress stock in the Crédit Mobilier at par (that is, for $100 per share) "when it was worth double that amount or more, with the purpose and intent thereby to influence their votes and decisions."

The committee recommended that Brooks and Ames be expelled from the House. It was hard not to notice that Ames was to be punished for bribing members, even though none (except Brooks) had been deemed guilty of *accepting* a bribe. (The *Sun* editorialized on the "manifest injustice of punishing two men for the very crime of which others equally guilty are acquitted.")

On February 25, as the House prepared for the expulsion vote, the clerk of the House read a lengthy defense written by Ames and his lawyers. During the reading, it was reported, Ames sat by and "shed tears copiously. . . . At one time he became so wrought up he bowed his head on the desk before him, and blubbered like a child." Ames's statement recounted virtually the entire history of the Union Pacific and Crédit Mobilier, painting the firms as paragons of national advancement and himself as their instrument. "I have risked reputation, fortune, everything, in an enterprise of incalculable benefit for the Government. . . . Who will say that I alone am to be offered up as sacrifice to appease a public clamor or expiate the sin of others?" He said that if the House so chose, he would accept its condemnation, awaiting in "unfaltering confidence" for history to provide him with vindication. A few days earlier, he had unburdened himself to a reporter from the *New York World*: "It's like the man in Massachusetts who committed adultery," he said. "The jury brought in the verdict that he was guilty as the devil, but that the woman was as innocent as an angel. These fellows are like that woman."

In the event, the House quailed at the prospect of ejecting a member as an offender without documenting an offense. Knowing that the necessary two-thirds votes could not be mustered for removal, the House voted merely to censure Ames and Brooks. The two returned to their homes having avoided outright conviction but carrying the burden of vilification. Brooks, already in poor health at sixty-two, died two months later, on April 30. Five days later Ames suffered a stroke, and expired on May 8 at the age of sixty-nine.

As much as the nation's political leadership desired to put the Crédit Mobilier affair behind it, the scandal further darkened the reputation of Grant and his administration and dismayed his supporters. One of Grant's crestfallen followers was Walt Whitman, who added to his poem "Respondez!," which had first appeared in the 1867 edition of *Leaves of Grass*, a bitter parenthetical stanza:

> (Stifled, O days! O lands! in every public and private corruption!
> Smother'd in thievery, impotence, shamelessness, mountain-high;
> Brazen effrontery, scheming, rolling like ocean's waves around and upon you,
>   O my days! my lands!
> For not even those thunderstorms, nor fiercest lightnings of the war, have
>   purified the atmosphere;)

Whitman's journey from exaltation of America's industrial might to skepticism and ultimately denunciation was just beginning.

THE POLAND AND Wilson investigations have been faulted for depicting the Crédit Mobilier arrangement as unique in the railroad industry at the time. In truth, as the historian Nelson Smith Trottman observed a few years later, the creation of a construction company to funnel profits into the hands of a railroad's management had "become an established institution"; the Union Pacific's version was merely one of countless examples of "uncontrolled railroad finance."

Yet there was more to it than that. The scandal translated the railroad builders' intricate methods of profiteering at the expense of investors into a straightforward narrative easily grasped by the ordinary newspaper reader. In this case, moreover, the cheated investors included the public itself. That brought the matter home to Americans who might have regarded earlier depredations by the builders as dramas they could enjoy at a remove, like members of a theater audience.

The corruption of lawmakers by the Union Pacific was hard to overlook, despite the Poland Committee's effort to exonerate the graft takers. The committee was fully alive to the threat the scandal posed to Congress's reputation:

> This country is fast becoming filled with gigantic corporations, wielding and controlling immense aggregations of money, and thereby commanding great influence and power. It is notorious in many State legislatures that these influences are often controlling, so that in effect they become the ruling power of the State. Within a few years Congress has, to some extent, been brought within similar influences, and the knowledge of the public on that subject has brought great discredit on the body.

"In a free government like ours," it warned in its report, "we cannot expect the people will long respect the laws, if they lose respect for the law-makers."

The scandal was a painful setback for Wall Street financiers hoping that the railroad industry would finally acquire at least a veneer of respectability. Disclosures of the Crédit Mobilier's unsavory relationships with politicians reinforced the conviction of the bankers that Washington, DC, unlike their own community, was a hive of fraud and corruption, albeit one on which they were dependent to build their fortunes. Pierpont Morgan, among others, fretted that the scandal would unsettle the financial markets to his disadvantage—a fear that would prove warranted in 1873, only a year after the *Sun's* bombshell. The scandal also magnified public mistrust of the railroad industry itself, which was already becoming manifest in restiveness among shippers and employees.

Still, the scandal's principal impact was on the Union Pacific. Because the railroad's managers had profited from inflated construction contracts they awarded themselves via the Crédit Mobilier, they had felt no incentive to economize on construction or to make sure they got their money's worth. "Instead of gaining by cheap construction, they profited by dear," wrote the railroad management expert Stuart Daggett in 1908. "Instead of aiming to reduce the cost in every possible way, they schemed at making the contracts as lucrative as possible."

The legacy of the Crédit Mobilier would be seen in the Union Pacific's financial accounts for years. Its moral burden, moreover, would persist even longer. "The 'Credit Mobilier' investigation has tinged everything," lamented the Union Pacific's government directors in their report for 1874; the road would labor under the shame of scandal for decades. By some estimates the thievery related to the Crédit Mobilier put more than $20 million into the pockets of the insiders. The result was a capital structure that loaded the railroad with a punishing weight of debt. On the day the golden spike was struck, marking completion of the transcontinental railroad, the entire capitalization of the road was estimated at $111 million, or more than $106,000 per mile, of which 50 percent was water—capital that had never been spent on construction and had been pocketed by the promoters, but would still have to be repaid to investors.

Through the early 1870s the Union Pacific enjoyed a traffic surge. Smelting of iron ores had taken off in the mining territory around Salt Lake City, where the UP held a monopoly, and the tourist and trade boom in the West fattened its top line; had the road been capitalized at a responsible level it almost certainly would have thrived. Instead, it struggled perpetually to raise enough revenue to pay its annual interest, not to speak of funds needed for operations and maintenance. In 1873, for instance, the Union Pacific took in more than $4 million but owed $3.4 million in interest—and it earned that much only because it held a monopoly, for the moment, on transcontinental shipping in a booming economy. Upon the appearance of the first competing transcontinental line, or the first economic downturn—which was already lurking on the horizon—the road would be exposed to financial disaster.

That reality could not be kept from anyone who had a chance to examine the books. Horace F. Clark, a railroad executive from Chicago who was the son-in-law of Cornelius Vanderbilt, had bought into the UP in

1872 and become its president. His goal was to combine the road with other Vanderbilt holdings and create a semi-transcontinental line from the East Coast to Utah. But upon taking office he had discovered that the UP was, financially speaking, hanging by a thread. If not for loans backed by the credit of its directors, Clark told the Wilson Committee, the railroad would be bankrupt.

In this desperate state the Union Pacific was defenseless against financial manipulation by speculators operating in the guise of rescuers. The road, the Wilson Committee found, "is now helpless and dependent," so "weakened" as to make it an easy mark for "capitalists and powerful railroad corporations."

The committee was prescient. Within months of its report, the leading speculator in the United States surfaced with a controlling interest in the UP that had been acquired in secret.

But before Jay Gould could make something of the "helpless" Union Pacific, he would have to steer it through a crisis it shared with all the other railroads in the United States. This was the Panic of 1873, which would trigger a five-year depression — the worst the country had suffered in its short history. Even worse, the panic was the product of a heedlessly expanding railroad industry, including a headstrong gamble by a man who had staked his fortune and his stature as the leading financier in the country on the building of a second transcontinental railroad. The road was the Northern Pacific. The man was Jay Cooke.

5

THE NORTHERN PACIFIC PANIC

O F ALL THE transcontinental railroads built after the Civil War, the Northern Pacific had the oldest pedigree. Its route, which roughly followed the path of the Lewis and Clark expedition of 1804 to 1806, had been favored by Asa Whitney, the leading proselytizer of transcontinental rail as an expression of America's destiny, in the 1850s. Of the five alternatives surveyed by order of Congress in 1853, that northern route, reaching from Lake Michigan to the Columbia River and terminating on the Oregon coast or at Puget Sound, traversed the territory richest in economic potential—a treasure trove of timberlands, mineral deposits, and arable acreage.

As Whitney acknowledged, the route also crossed the homelands of bellicose Indian tribes, especially the "numerous, powerful, and entirely savage" Sioux, who "occupy and claim nearly all the lands from above latitude about 43 degrees on the Mississippi to the Rocky mountains." This he held to be a virtue in disguise, for building the railroad offered white America the best means of taming the tribe. Efforts to "civilize" smaller tribes in the region, he explained, had been stymied by the tribes' ability to take refuge in Sioux territory, but the incursion of the railroad and the settlers coming in its wake would close off this stratagem. "This road would put them asunder so that they cannot meet," he wrote; "and we can then succeed in bringing the removed and small tribes to habits of industry and civilization. . . . Their race may be preserved until mixed and

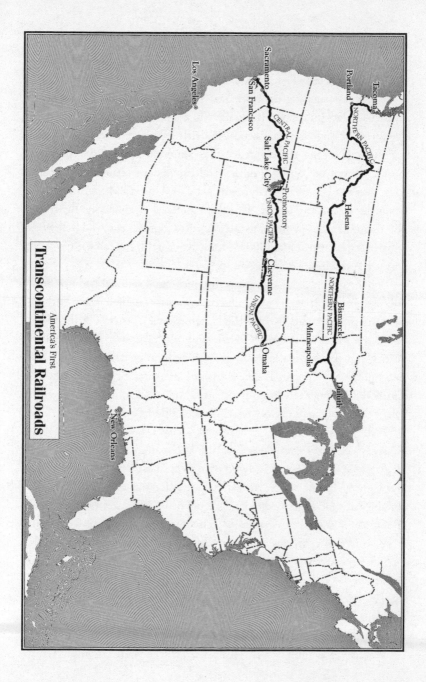

America's First

Transcontinental Railroads

Los Angeles

Sacramento
San Francisco

CENTRAL PACIFIC

Salt Lake City
Promontory

UNION PACIFIC

Cheyenne

UNION PACIFIC

Omaha

Portland
Tacoma

NORTHERN PACIFIC

Helena

NORTHERN PACIFIC

Bismarck

Minneapolis

Duluth

New Orleans

blended with ours, and the Sioux must soon follow them." Thus would the whites' sacred duty to bring "the savage, the barbarian, and the heathen" to Christianity be fulfilled.

The four other transcontinental routes mapped by the surveyors crossed desolate wastes offering little to lure homesteaders. By 1862, moreover, when Congress began seriously debating whether to fund a transcontinental railroad, the Confederate rebellion had placed the southernmost route out of bounds. Politics and expedience argued for a middle path, the prairie route ultimately traced by the Union and Central Pacific. Congress was anxious to bind far-flung California to the Union with iron rails to quell a movement there favoring the Confederacy. And the prairie route had the virtue of familiarity, for it had carried the forty-niners west during the California gold rush.

But the dream of a northern transcontinental railroad was not dead, only slumbering. It was reawakened by a promoter named Josiah Perham, who had originally applied for the congressional charters that had been awarded instead to the Union Pacific and Central Pacific. Perham subsequently transferred his application to a route running between Maine and Oregon. For his "People's Pacific Railway Company," he proposed to raise a hundred dollars each from up to a million small individual investors, with a down payment of only ten dollars required.

Perham was considered a "visionary" like Asa Whitney—and as in Whitney's case, the term described him as a man in the grip of delirium. He forswore the government bond financing that propped up the Union and Central Pacific roads, instead securing for the People's Railroad a commitment for government land grants of 12,600 acres for every mile of completed track in the states of Wisconsin and Minnesota and twice as much in the territories of Dakota, Montana, Idaho, and Washington. Despite his conviction that the small investments of a million Americans and the resale of land to settlers would be sufficient to finance the road, the absence of a direct government subsidy would become an albatross for Perham's enterprise. So too would the congressional mandate that the railroad begin construction within two years, complete at least fifty miles per year after that, and be entirely finished by the Fourth of July, 1876.

Within a year of obtaining his charter, Perham's vision was in a shambles. The stock subscription campaign having failed miserably, he was unable to begin surveys of the right of way, much less start construction, so no land grants were forthcoming and there were no land sales to generate income. Perham was pushed out of the company by a clique of New Englanders hoping to revive its fortunes by appealing to Congress for a direct government loan. Perham would die destitute in 1868, another railroad pioneer broken and embittered by dashed dreams.

The new owners soon discovered that congressional taste for advancing millions of dollars to speculative railroad ventures had soured after the handouts to the Union Pacific and Central Pacific. The northern road's land grants were deemed useless as collateral by would-be investors, who recognized that forty-seven million additional acres of northern prairie could only overfill a homesteading market struggling to absorb the millions of arable acres in Missouri, Iowa, Nebraska, and Kansas already granted to railroad builders.

Casting about desperately for a financial lifeline, the Northern's promoters soon turned, inevitably, to Jay Cooke. The most eminent financier in the country, widely regarded as the savior of the government during its gravest financial crisis, Cooke would put their dream on a realistic footing over the next five years—and then ride it to his ruin, taking the national economy with him.

WHEN THE CIVIL War began, Jay Cooke was an obscure banker who had just opened his firm's doors in Philadelphia. He was born in Sandusky, Ohio, on August 10, 1821, the son of a prominent lawyer and state legislator. The region was still mostly wilderness; Eleutheros Cooke, Jay's father, had erected the first stone house in town, choosing a site on the shore of Lake Erie where Ogontz, the burly local Wyandot chief, had built his wigwam before the tribe was removed to a reservation forty miles inland. The tribe still remained part of the community, regularly returning to the lakeside to pick fruit from the trees they had planted in years past and to collect their federal stipend. "Old Ogontz did himself and us the

Jay Cooke, the nation's preeminent financier at the end of the Civil War, was ruined in the Panic of 1873 by his investment in the Northern Pacific Railroad.

honor of occasionally sojourning for a few days on the spot where he had once dwelt in his wigwam," Cooke would recall in the memoirs he scribbled by hand in the last years of his life. "He was allowed to camp in our barn. . . . I was his favorite and occasionally was mounted on his shoulders for a ride."

While still in his teens, Cooke was invited by a brother-in-law to join his shipping company in Philadelphia. The business failed in the Panic of 1837, but young Cooke's diligence had been noticed by a local banker,

Enoch Clark, who brought him into his firm as a clerk. Cooke was a quick study with a native talent for business and finance. Upon Clark's death in 1856 he was appointed executor of the estate, and managed to bring the firm through another financial crisis, the Panic of 1857, "with an absolutely unruffled temper" while more established banking houses failed around him. This disposition would serve him well through some of the more challenging times to come.

The US government's finances were at a low ebb as the country careened toward war. On July 1, 1860, John Sherman of Ohio, chairman of the House Ways and Means Committee, informed his colleagues that the government carried $64.8 million in debt but had only $3.6 million in its coffers. The dire situation did not come as a surprise to the lawmakers. "Most of the members are aware," Sherman said, "that the Government has not been able to pay, for the last week or two, our own salaries." He recommended borrowing $10 million. But that would be a pittance compared with the Union's war needs over the next five years.

Cooke's entrée into the Union financing market came via his brother Henry, who back in Ohio had been a friend and business partner of Salmon P. Chase, Abraham Lincoln's first treasury secretary. Having a strong sense of patriotism and an abolitionist streak, Jay Cooke was determined to help the Union cause. In May 1861 Pennsylvania was struggling to place $3 million in bonds to finance its participation in the war. Cooke stepped in and by the end of June had sold out the entire issue.

"It is regarded as an achievement as great or greater than Napoleon's crossing the Alps," Jay boasted to Henry, who made sure it came to Chase's attention. The treasury secretary named Cooke the exclusive agent in Philadelphia and New Jersey for a $150 million federal bond sale in 1861. Cooke perfected a sales technique based on three pillars: patriotic ballyhoo, an appeal to legions of small investors being introduced for the first time to the concept of building their nest eggs with government securities, and a relentless publicity campaign. Newspaper editors were made to understand that if they desired advertising from Cooke and his partners, they would integrate his tub-thumping sales pitches for the bonds into their news columns, no questions asked. In Washington, meanwhile,

Henry Cooke lavishly entertained news reporters, inviting them to his Georgetown home to be "filled full to the brim not only with edibles and bibibles, but with the glorious financial prospects of the future."

Cooke would ultimately be credited with placing more than $1.5 billion in government debt during the war, roughly one-quarter of the total issued. His methods sometimes excited negative remark, as when he attempted to place an article in national newspapers with a headline describing the government debt as "a national blessing." The slogan was deplored by sober investment advisers for tempting small investors into imprudence, especially since the government's fiscal management had already come under fire. The title was eventually toned down to read "How Our National Debt May Be a National Blessing," and the article widely distributed.

The article and its headline were the handiwork of Sam Wilkeson, a reporter on the staff of the *New York Tribune* with a peerless talent for spinning seductive fancies from the barest facts, or no facts at all. Cooke had hired Wilkeson at Henry's urging to assist with publicity for a $600 million Union bond issue. "His specialty should be the manufacture of editorials, letters, notices and so forth," Henry told Jay, with an implicit emphasis on the word "manufacture." This marked the start of a long association between banker and publicity man, even if Wilkeson's rhetoric sometimes went too far, as in the case of the "national blessing" article. (It would not be the last time.)

The pace of bond sales slowed considerably as the war drew to an end, amid a general contraction in the market ascribed to expectations that the vigorous inflation of the war years would yield to deflation as the government tried to get its books back in shape. The greater threat to financial stability came with Abraham Lincoln's assassination on April 14, 1865. Cooke ordered his agents to support the market the next day, a Saturday, through unlimited purchases of "all United States bonds thrown on the market," pledging to cover any losses personally. The effort worked. As Cooke related in his memoirs, "it required the purchase of less than twenty millions in the space of seven or eight days to end the panic. . . . The spectacle was presented to the world of a nation with its credit unimpaired and its securities advancing in price while suffering from a terrible calamity."

By the time the war ended Cooke was the most famous financier in the country. His services to the Union had earned him as much as $10 million. No one was ever sure of the total, but Cooke's profits were sufficient to allow him to build a grand mansion of fifty-two rooms in the countryside just outside Philadelphia, which he christened Ogontz after the Wyandot chief who had carried him on his back so many years before, and to acquire Gibraltar Island in Lake Erie, just offshore from Sandusky, as a summer retreat. The firm of Jay Cooke & Co. won esteem as a paragon of financial stability, its founder reigning over the financial sector as an intimate of leading figures in business and government, including, after the election of 1868, President Ulysses S. Grant.

The promoters of the northern transcontinental road hankered after not only Jay Cooke's money but his reputation. "The manner in which [the railroad's securities] had been 'hawked about' in New York and elsewhere . . . had combined to give a taint to the whole concern," one promoter observed. "It could only be made reputable by being taken up by new parties." Cooke at first regarded the railroad men skeptically, once even reprimanding Henry for making commitments to them behind his back.

By fits and starts, however, the Northern Pacific wriggled into Cooke's favor. The railroad men were looking for a savior, and in Jay Cooke they happened upon a man with a messianic self-image. "Like Moses and Washington and Lincoln and Grant," he would write in his memoirs, "I have been—I firmly believe—God's chosen instrument, especially in the financial work of saving the Union . . . and this condition of things was of God's arrangement."

Cooke had also become enthralled with the economic potential of the upper Midwest. In 1868 he visited the western end of Lake Superior. The land he saw was rich, though the physical settlements were decrepit. The old town of Superior, nestled against the Wisconsin state line, had declined to a population of three hundred after peaking at about eight hundred before the Civil War. The town had been founded by wealthy

Southerners looking for "a watering place where they could be free to take their slaves with them," having been excluded from Saratoga, New York; Newport, Rhode Island; and other resorts where slaves were not admitted. Duluth, its sister township on the Minnesota side, comprised six or seven dilapidated wooden shacks. "The appearance of the towns is ludicrous, zigzag, rude, etc., and half filled with Indians," Jay Cooke wrote his brother Henry. But he compared their prospects favorably to those of his native town, Sandusky. To thrive, all they needed was a railroad.

The challenge beckoned irresistibly to both Cooke brothers. "If successful," Henry wrote back, "it would be the grandest achievement of our lives." Cooke & Co. signed on as the Northern's financial agent, with an undertaking to interest "the capitalists of Europe" in its securities. But Jay was planning to plunge deeper. He was about to irrevocably tie his and his firm's future to the Northern Pacific Railroad.

TO SELL THE Northern's bonds Cooke reached out again to Sam Wilkeson, who was marinating in the boredom of a New York publishing house, selling subscription works such as the Reverend Henry Ward Beecher's *Life of Christ* to rubes. Receiving a letter from Cooke asking if he would like to "increase his income," Wilkeson promptly replied, "You bet." He snapped into action, writing articles describing in great detail the amenities of Duluth and the riches ready to be drawn from the fecund soil of Minnesota and the western territories, despite never having visited the region. The first issue of bonds sold out so quickly, Henry Cooke complained to his brother, that none remained for him to scatter to members of Congress as bribes.

Contemplating deeper involvement with the Northern Pacific, Cooke sought a firsthand report of the railroad's prospects. In June 1869 he assembled an expedition to traverse the territory. Its members included Wilkeson; William Milnor Roberts, an engineer who had done work for Cooke in the past; Thomas Hawley Canfield, who had been an employee of the Northern dating back to the time of Josiah Perham; and R. Bethell Claxton, an Episcopalian minister whose Philadelphia church enjoyed

Cooke's lavish patronage and whose task was to assess the spiritual character of the peoples of the Far West.

Cooke assumed the travelers would return with a positive report. Among their other duties, they were instructed to gin up enthusiasm for the project among the residents of the distant region while they were in the field. Reaching Walla Walla, Washington Territory, they hired the largest hall in town to address the residents. Canfield took the podium first, to "a perfect storm of applause," according to an account in the local newspaper. He attacked Congress "for the niggardliness of its grants, as compared with the great and valuable favors bestowed upon the central road [that is, the Union Pacific and Central Pacific], and assured the people that the line would be built in spite of opposition." Claxton followed with a charming speech in which he declared that he had come West "expecting to see icebergs and polar bears in a land of perpetual snow," but now felt bound to report back that he had come upon "a tropical paradise."

Writing to Cooke, Wilkeson spared no hyperbole. From Puget Sound he reported that "salmon are not caught here, they are pitchforked out of the streams." He added, "Jay, we have got the biggest thing on earth. Our enterprise is an inexhaustible gold mine."

Wilkeson dispatched breathless accounts of the expedition's findings to eastern newspapers, typically under pseudonyms. One article, published under the name "Carleton," described for readers of the *Boston Journal* "a region . . . which comes nearer the Garden of Eden than any other portion of the earth. . . . gentle swells, parks, groves, lawns, lakes, ponds, pellucid streams—a rare combination of beauty and fertility. . . . Think of it, young men; you who are measuring off tape for young ladies, shut up in a store through the long and wearisome hours, barely earning your living. Throw down the yardstick and come out here if you would be men."

Few voices were raised against the torrent of marketing bombast. One naysayer was General W. B. Hazen, a Union Army veteran stationed in the Dakota Territory. Hazen warned would-be settlers about depictions of the region as "one uninterrupted field of fruitfulness," since "the interests of the railroad companies that it should be considered valuable land, are measured exactly by the number of millions of dollars for which it can be hypothecated." Hazen described the land beyond the Hundredth Meridian, which bisected the Dakota Territory and the states of Nebraska and Kansas, as "altogether sterile . . . a dry, broken, and barren country, with very little timber and, from lack of moisture, unfit for agriculture."

Skepticism was heard inside the Northern Pacific company, too. John Russell Young, a journalist who had worked on the government bond campaign with Wilkeson and had also come back onto the Cooke payroll, knew his colleague well enough to be wary of his claims. He told Cooke: "I hear that Sam has found orange groves and monkeys in his route." Cooke would have been wise to heed Young's implicit warning about Wilkeson's flights of descriptive fancy, for thanks to the implausible publicity, the Northwest region soon became known as "Jay Cooke's banana belt."

While beating the bushes for homegrown American capital, Cooke dispatched his partner William G. Moorhead to Europe to sound out the Rothschild banking family about investing in the Northern Pacific. Moorhead reported back that he received a chilly reception from the Rothschild bank, which was still run by risk-averse elders. Cooke tried to strengthen his resolve by telling him, deceitfully, that the clamor for the bonds in America was thunderous — "I have hundreds of applications . . . I can get thousands to take hold at once. . . . I tell you I am busy night and day about this great matter."

But Europe had had its fill of American railroad bonds, thanks to a surfeit of issues and to what Cooke's partner Harris C. Fahnestock cautioned was "the bad odor" attached to other overpromised and underperforming Pacific railroads, including the Union Pacific.

Cooke dispatched a second mission under George B. Sargent, a former New York broker, who arrived in Europe in the spring of 1870 with letters of introduction from Baron von Gerolt, the Prussian ambassador to the United States, whom Cooke had wined and dined at Ogontz. By July 16, Sargent was on the verge of signing a deal with a British syndicate to sell $50 million of Northern Pacific bonds in the European market. The syndicate was to deposit the sum in gold to Cooke & Co.'s account three days hence. On July 19, however, France declared war on Prussia. With the start of the Franco-Prussian War, the European exchanges collapsed into panic and Sargent's syndicate disappeared in a puff of smoke.

"I was stunned by the blow," Cooke wrote later. French and Prussian investors "could no longer unite. . . . If rumors of war had kept off a week longer the papers would all have been signed."

Cooke still found grounds for optimism. He sequestered Milnor Roberts at Ogontz to finish the report of the surveying expedition. As expected Roberts declared the railroad feasible, estimating that three years of construction would cost about $85 million. The project, he asserted, would benefit greatly from "emigration across the continent—the overflow of the redundant population of the Atlantic states and of Europe."

Armed with Roberts's say-so, Cooke announced the formation of a pool to raise the funds to launch construction of the Northern Pacific. Wilkeson wrote Cooke that upon hearing the announcement "I flung my hat to the ceiling." The road "will plant civilization in the place of savagery," he assured his patron, echoing Asa Whitney. "It will augment the national wealth beyond the dreams of the wildest economist."

Cooke tried to guarantee himself a profit from the railroad by striking a hard bargain with the Northern Pacific's Boston investors. The $100 million in loans he floated for the company carried a stiff interest rate of 7.3 percent, but of every $100 in face value, he kept a commission of $12 and advanced the railroad only $88. Experts who examined the deal with the hindsight of its ultimately dismal outcome detected the seeds of the Northern's eventual downfall in its terms: "No extraordinary foresight was needed to see that a railroad could not be built through two thousand miles of absolute wilderness, and settle and develop the vacant country along its line fast enough to provide from its net earnings $7.30 interest per annum on $100 for every $88 expended upon it," wrote the historian Eugene Smalley in 1883. "Bankruptcy was inevitable."

Yet at first the railroad sailed atop a surging confidence in America's manifest destiny. Cooke exploited this optimism for his sales campaign, along with a generous helping of graft. He distributed bonds among leading financiers, journalists, brokers, and politicians, including Vice President Schuyler Colfax. Wilkeson placed bonds in the hands of Horace

Greeley and Henry Ward Beecher, the prominent abolitionist preacher whose works he had previously sold on subscription, "with some pleasing concessions to them as to the time and manner of paying their installments." It was as if the Crédit Mobilier, in which Colfax had also invested, was again at large.

THE RAILROAD PROJECT did appear to deserve the hullabaloo, at first. Ground was broken on February 15, 1870. But this was mostly for public show, the ceremony being attended by more journalists than laborers. Anyone inspecting the photographs of the event had to notice that the dignitaries stood on a landscape encrusted in snow and that not a foot of the frozen earth had been broken by spades or pickaxes. The frigid weather meant that real construction could not begin for months; once it did, the crews immediately ran into marshy, boggy land and mosquitoes that attacked them in huge black clouds. From the start, embezzlement often left laborers without pay, food, or supplies.

Then there were the Indians. Asa Whitney's confidence that the railroad would civilize the tribes was not shared by military men in Indian country. General Winfield Scott Hancock, a hero of Gettysburg now stationed in the Yellowstone valley of Montana, cautioned that pacifying the tribes would be difficult and expensive. "It is not seen that the construction of a railway into their country . . . will in any way tend immediately to diminish them," he wrote Cooke, "but will most probably provoke their hostility . . . unless large subsidies be paid them to purchase peace. Our experience heretofore has not been favorable."

Army soldiers escorted Cooke's surveying teams as they made their way west toward the Yellowstone River. Through 1871 and the spring of 1872 the surveyors and their armed escorts worked largely unmolested, but they were jolted out of their complacency on August 14, 1872, when a surveying expedition on the Yellowstone was attacked by three hundred Indians under Sitting Bull and Crazy Horse, whose forces would prevail against US soldiers four years later at the Battle of the Little Bighorn.

At the so-called Battle of Poker Flat the Indians were driven back at the cost of only a modest toll among the US soldiers, but the encounter sent an unnerving message back East, thanks to highly embellished accounts witnesses dispatched home to family members, which inevitably turned up in local newspapers. "Our force was wholly inadequate to pass down the Yellowstone Valley," one surveyor wrote in a message published in the *New York Times*. "One morning the red rascals put four bullets into my tent, and four into my mess chest. . . . We held a council of war about two weeks later, and concluded to abandon the expedition."

Cooke was learning, meanwhile, that American bankers had no more taste for Northern Pacific bonds than their European cousins. So much railroad capital was sloshing around Washington as graft that when Henry Cooke offered Northern Pacific securities to House Speaker James G. Blaine, who had emerged from the Crédit Mobilier scandal unscathed, Blaine responded by trying to foist bonds in a southern railroad scheme on *him*. ("Mr. Cooke resisted this pressing invitation," reported Cooke's official biographer, Ellis Oberholtzer.)

The Northern Pacific took heavy fire from newspapers hostile to Cooke, led by the *Philadelphia Ledger*, which was part-owned by Anthony Drexel, Cooke's chief rival in Philadelphia's financial community. The *Ledger* had been editorializing against congressional assistance to the Northern Pacific since 1869, at one point provoking an infuriated Cooke to write Drexel: "Do you think if I should start a newspaper, or rather own one, I would permit its editors and conductors to persistently and constantly misrepresent and injure the position of a neighbor and life-long friend?"

When a bill to provide the Northern with government financing was introduced in Congress in 1870, the *Ledger* intensified the attack. There had not been a time "since the celebrated South Sea Bubble when so much money was running into wild hazard," the newspaper thundered. Cooke soon would have reason to suspect that Drexel was acting in concert with a new partner from New York: J. Pierpont Morgan.

Following the armistice ending the Franco-Prussian War in January 1871, Cooke made a third overture to European investors. In April he welcomed to Ogontz five Austrian and Dutch bankers intending to examine the route. After feting them at his estate he provided them with passage to Duluth by steamer under the leadership of Milnor Roberts. The delegates proved a sour bunch, most of their overheard remarks being "rather sneering," Roberts advised Cooke. "They seem to have a notion that anyone they meet who praises anything has been hired to do it," which may not have been far off the mark. Some of their reports upon returning home were so negative that Cooke suspected their authors' purpose was to extort money from him to suppress them.

Meanwhile, construction progress was anything but auspicious. Cooke was not a corrupt operator like Gould, Fisk, or the architects of the Crédit Mobilier, but he was managing the Northern Pacific at long range and his representatives in the field were every bit as venal and incompetent as their counterparts on other roads. They tolerated millions of dollars in cost overruns, in part because much of the excess went into their own pockets. The Northern's president, J. Gregory Smith, a former governor of Vermont who had been installed by the Boston group, handed out management posts to cronies—when he devoted any attention to the railroad at all. Incompetently built tracks were sinking into bogs and laborers were going unpaid. As early as 1870, William L. Banning, a shareholder from Minnesota who observed the progress of the Northern at close hand, had sounded the alarm: "I tell you, Mr. Cooke, what you want is so far as is possible to strip the Northern Pacific enterprise of all this slime." But it was not until the summer of 1872 that Cooke forced Smith's resignation.

By then, Cooke's partners had become frankly dismayed. "The present actual condition of the Northern Pacific, if it were understood by the public, would be fatal to the negotiation of its securities," Fahnestock told him in June. He warned that the railroad's problems were sullying the reputation of the entire firm. "Radical and immediate changes are necessary to save the company from ingloriously breaking down within the next year and involving us in discredit, if not in ruin."

TO MOST OUTSIDERS, Cooke & Co. seemed to be at high tide in 1872. As America's preeminent financier, Cooke was sought after for charitable subscriptions of every kind. As a capstone, he was appointed chairman of Philadelphia's Centennial Exposition, which in 1876 would mark the nation's one hundredth anniversary of the signing of the Declaration of Independence. An invitation to Ogontz was treasured as validation of a guest's position in the highest echelon of politics or business. The reelection of President Grant, with whom the Cooke family's relations were strong, seemed assured.

Behind the scenes, however, the Northern Pacific crisis was worsening. The railroad had borrowed more than $1.5 million from Cooke & Co. yet had virtually no prospect of raising the money to repay the loan—other than by borrowing more from Cooke. And Cooke's chances of unloading Northern securities on investors at home or abroad were shrinking fast. Through the first half of 1873 money got tighter. That August the *Ledger* quoted, with evident glee, a correspondent's report from Frankfurt that an American railroad bond would not sell in Europe "even if signed by an angel of Heaven."

Cooke also came under attack from a new quarter. The battleground was the government's plan to refinance $300 million in Civil War bonds at an interest rate reduced to 5 percent, a savings of a full percentage point. Cooke regarded the refunding, like the original Civil War debt, as his personal franchise. Not this time: Pierpont Morgan, in partnership with the financier Levi P. Morton and Anthony Drexel, and with backing from the British firm Baring Brothers & Co., was determined to shatter Cooke's monopoly on the government business, a step on his campaign to take the Philadelphian's place at the summit of American banking.

In January, Morgan and Drexel persuaded Treasury Secretary George Boutwell to split the $300 million refunding between their syndicate and Cooke. In financial terms the deal was not a coup for either camp, as the total commission to be divided between them was a paltry $150,000. But the bonds would not have to be delivered to buyers until the last day of 1873, which meant that if the securities could be sold promptly, the firms would have the use of the proceeds for most of the year—a lifeline, especially, for Jay Cooke & Co.

The bond issue turned out to be a fizzle. Contemporaries conjectured that Morgan deliberately slowed sales of the bonds to place pressure on Cooke, but that is implausible—Junius Morgan was unhappy that his son had participated in the financing without his permission, so it was hardly in Pierpont's interest to make the venture look even more ill-advised. In any case, the bonds' failure could be ascribed to a slump in general business conditions without having to adduce an ulterior motive on Pierpont's part.

The developing economic weakness had several causes. One was the hangover of wartime production of crops and steel, which became overproduction as wartime demand evaporated—and intensified as farms and factories tried to preserve income in the face of falling prices. Farmers and railroad operators alike were heavily indebted, leaving them vulnerable to any tightening in interest rates. In the spring of 1873, financial panics swept through Berlin, Vienna, Paris, and London. The foundations of America's economic expansion began to seem shaky. And that meant a loss of confidence in the main drivers of the expansion, the railroads.

By early September, faltering railroad investments were undermining investment firms all over the financial district. On September 8, the New York Warehouse and Security Co., which traded in commercial loans, declared itself insolvent; its president blamed its loans to "railways and . . . individual railroad builders." Five days later, Kenyon, Cox & Co.—where Daniel Drew was a partner—shut down, having tried unsuccessfully to call in a $1.5 million loan to the Canada Southern Railroad. The contagion began to spread among other firms with outstanding loans to other crippled railroads, meaning almost all of them.

PANIC WAS EVIDENT in the New York markets on September 17. President Grant spent that night at Ogontz after dropping off his son Jesse at a nearby private academy. At breakfast the next morning, the president spied Cooke buried under a blizzard of telegrams from New York, though the sight gave him no hint of impending disaster. Grant left to board the train back to Washington and Cooke headed for his Philadelphia office.

The ax fell with sickening speed. In New York, Harris Fahnestock summoned bank presidents to his office and informed them that Jay Cooke & Co. was closing its doors. Cooke received a wire with the news before 11 a.m. and ordered the Philadelphia headquarters closed too. He turned his face away from his assistants as tears streamed from his eyes. No one in the office had ever seen him weep before.

But that was nothing compared with the reaction in the exchanges. The news hit Philadelphia "like a thunderclap in a clear sky," reported the *Philadelphia Press*. The New York Stock Exchange was in an "uproar," and a pall fell on every trader on the floor. On the sidewalks of Wall Street desperate depositors mixed with curious onlookers to gawk at staggering brokers like rubberneckers at an accident scene. Among the witnesses was George Templeton Strong, a lawyer whose daily entries in his personal journal would win him fame as a diarist. On September 18, the day after Cooke's failure, he observed "one or two gentlemen who looked like they came from the country and who probably had monies on deposit with these collapsed bankers . . . walking about in an aimless sort of way and talking loud to nobody in particular about 'd——d infernal swindlers and thieves.'" Two days later, Strong remarked that the stock exchange had closed its doors: "A wise measure, and would that they might never be reopened," he wrote tartly. "The failure of these great stock-gambling concerns would be a public benefit but for its probable damage to so many honest businessmen." (Trading would remain suspended for ten days.)

There was widespread consensus about where to place blame for the crisis: on the railroads, especially the Northern Pacific. Cornelius Vanderbilt leveled his judgment like a biblical prophet, lecturing the *New York Herald* as follows:

> I'll tell you what's the matter. People undertake to do about four times as much business as they can legitimately undertake. . . . There are many worthless railroads started in this country without any means to carry them through. . . . Building railroads from nowhere to nowhere

at public expense is not a legitimate undertaking. . . . Mistrust will be
engendered till we, as a nation, do our business on a more solid basis,
and pay as we go.

In the heat of the crisis, with institutions failing all around, many on
Wall Street hoped that the Commodore would step in and rescue the
market with his unlimited resources, even as he was about to enter his
eighth decade. But it was a forlorn hope; Vanderbilt himself was strapped.
The collapse had driven down shares of his three major holdings: the New
York Central; the Lake Shore & Michigan Southern, which ran between
Chicago and Buffalo; and the telegraph company Western Union, by
more than $50 million combined. The Union Trust Company, previously
a reliable banking partner of the Vanderbilt railroads, called in a $1.75
million loan to the Lake Shore, which the road could not pay—threatening bankruptcy for the entire Vanderbilt empire and the Union Trust
itself.

Pierpont Morgan surveyed the crash with relative equanimity from a
vantage point safely removed from heavy exposure to the railroads, thanks
largely to his foresight that a slump was coming and undercapitalized railroads would bring down their bankers. "The kinds of bonds which I want
to be connected with are those which can be recommended without a
shadow of doubt, and without the least subsequent anxiety, as to payment
of interest," he had written to his father as early as April 1873. He was
wise to seek out the safest possible investments, for the aftermath of what
came to be known as the Panic of 1873 would stretch far beyond that year.

UNTIL THE EVEN vaster economic calamity of the 1930s, the Panic of
1873 and its six-year aftermath would be what Americans meant when
they referred to the "Great Depression." It was a classic bubble, born of
frenzied growth in the railroad industry that had long-term financial obligations but funded them with short-term debt and the issuance of grossly
overvalued securities. The downturn, like its later cousin, would leave a
lasting imprint on American industry, society, and politics.

The most immediate damage could be traced in the national accounts of profits, losses, and unemployment. The economy shrank by nearly a third from 1873 through 1879; bankruptcies doubled from fifty-one hundred in 1873 to more than ten thousand five years later. Virtually every sector of the economy was stricken. Wheat prices fell from $1.78 a bushel to $1.25. Bank failures rose from 3 in 1870 to 140 in 1878. Railroad construction ground almost to a halt. The industry had added a record 7,436 miles in 1872; three years later the construction boom was scraping bottom with only 1,606 new miles. It would not exceed the previous high-water mark until 1881.

The crisis exposed the incapacity of the government to manage the economic cycle. A few days after the stock exchange suspended trading, Grant made a pilgrimage to Wall Street with Treasury Secretary William A. Richardson, who had succeeded George Boutwell. They came to the Street as supplicants to bankers for a solution to the crisis, but the bankers themselves had no good ideas, beyond urging the government to buy in government bonds to pump inflationary funds into the economy.

The bankers' fear was palpable: At the Fifth Avenue Hotel, where the president and secretary were staying, *Harper's Weekly* reported, "the corridors and parlors swarmed with a multitude of frenzied people, who supposed that incalculable disaster impended and that the President had the power of staying it by a word, and of saving the country from financial, as he had saved it from political, ruin." The mob included "speculators and gamblers in railroad stocks, . . . all passionately desiring that the President would use the public money for their relief."

But Grant did not believe he could "establish a precedent of such momentous consequences" under the law. He ended up taking the half measure of allowing the release of $26 million in retired greenbacks — currency treated as legal tender but not backed by gold or silver, which had been issued during the Civil War and now was being bought in. This was a comparatively minuscule priming of the pump, for it amounted to less than a tenth of the greenbacks then in circulation; it was enough to help Wall Street past its immediate crisis, but did nothing to alleviate the pall enveloping the rest of the country. Unlike Franklin Roosevelt sixty years later, Grant would continue to resist inflationary measures, vetoing an "inflation bill" that would have drastically increased the money supply.

As the depression ground into its second year, Grant acknowledged in his annual message to Congress the "prostration in business and industries such as has not been witnessed with us for many years." He recognized that "the greater part of the burden . . . falls upon the working man." But he reiterated his uncompromising policy of "a return to specie payments, the first great requisite in a return to prosperity." In other words, contracting the money supply to correspond to the supply of gold and silver. Grant's policy was similar to that followed in 1932 by Herbert Hoover, who insisted on keeping America yoked to the gold standard in the face of economic disaster. It would have a similar result politically—in Grant's case, a drubbing suffered by his Republican Party at the midterm election in 1874.

The Panic of 1873 sharpened the divide in America between the working class and its increasingly corporatized employers. The depression that followed also dramatically changed the internal dynamics of the railroad industry and the relationship between the roads and their workers. Prior to 1873 the roads existed in a sort of paradise of serene mutual cooperation, with "official" rates based on the value of freight and adhered to generally, despite secret or even overt rebates here or there. Railroad employment was strong, and an entire cadre of workers entered the industry with the expectation of long-term employment. During the depression, these informal harmonies came to an end. "With the increasingly desperate search for traffic, rate agreement collapsed," observed the business historian Alfred Chandler. Competition among large, sprawling, powerful enterprises—especially those with high fixed costs to cover—was a new phenomenon in American business. By 1876, cutthroat competition for diminishing traffic would send more than half of America's railroads into bankruptcy, their workers cast into the cold.

Before then, the wealthy Americans who had contributed to the crash had launched themselves upon an era of unprecedented conspicuous consumption. The action driving *The Gilded Age*, the acerbic 1873 novel by Mark Twain and Charles Dudley Warner, was its characters' efforts to seek their fortunes in railroad speculation. But the title soon came to signify more generally the ostentation and amorality of the "robber barons," to use the label first applied in the United States to Cornelius Vanderbilt by the German-born political reformer Carl Schurz. In popular usage, that label itself broadened to signify all the railroad, steel, and banking magnates who were thought to control the nation's wealth, with the "insinuation that pernicious conduct was typical of all big businessmen."

These new aristocrats increasingly settled in New York. By the end of the 1870s, reckoned the stock trader and social observer Henry Clews, the city had "more wealth than thirteen of the States and Territories combined. . . . The great metropolis attracts by its restless activity, its feverish enterprise, . . . its imperial wealth, its Parisian, indeed almost Sybaritic luxury, and its social splendor. It is really the great social center of the Republic, and its position as such is becoming more and more assured."

In New York, the frenzy of conspicuous spending fed on itself, slowed only temporarily by financial panics such as that of 1873. The colonization of a few blocks of Manhattan facilitated the trading of suspect railroad paper; the financiers were all neighbors who could pop into each others' homes of an evening to execute their deals or accomplish their mutual betrayals out of the eyesight of the public and their small investors. Proximity also facilitated the contest of ostentation. The robber barons competed to build the biggest mansions and throw the most lavish parties. According to the gossipy boulevardier Ward McAllister, who assiduously chronicled the era's excesses (and had coined the term "the Four Hundred" for the crème de la crème of nouveau riche society, supposedly to denote the largest crowd that could be accommodated in Caroline Astor's ballroom), the premier venue for these events was Delmonico's on Fourteenth Street, which was "admirably adapted" for balls of seven or eight hundred guests. "Certainly one could not have found better rooms for such a purpose" in this "era of great extravagance and expenditure," McAllister reported in his book *Society As I Have Found It* (issued in a deluxe edition limited, somewhat mischievously, to four hundred copies).

The new tycoons had not only established New York as the social and financial center of the nation, but established the railroads as the focus of banking and finance. Railroad "financiering," which was not at first considered a salubrious practice, became a profession—indeed, for many investment houses the principal source of income.

Few contemporaries judged the industrial princes of the era to be paragons of cultural sophistication. Charles Francis Adams left an especially acerbic assessment. "Money-getting," he wrote in his autobiography,

> comes from a rather low instinct. Certainly, so far as my observation goes, it is rarely met with in combination with the finer or more interesting traits of character. I have known, and known tolerably well, a good many "successful" men—"big" financially . . . and a less interesting crowd I do not care to encounter. Not one that I have ever known . . . is associated in my mind with the idea of humor, thought or refinement. A set of mere money-getters and traders, they were essentially unattractive and uninteresting.

Writing just two years before the end of his life, he counted himself lucky to have survived his encounters with this stratum of society free of contamination.

THE HAVOC WREAKED throughout the American economy by the Panic of 1873 would not fully dissipate until the end of the decade. The pace of bankruptcies did not peak until 1878, when businesses worth more than a quarter-billion dollars went under. Farm debt was driven ever higher by a collapse in crop prices, giving rise to a movement for the inflationary coinage of silver that would roil American politics virtually to the end of the century.

The panic also profoundly affected the fortunes of some of America's leading tycoons. Vanderbilt survived the carnage, but in a temporarily humbled state. His near failure inspired him to reorganize his empire into a more integrated and manageable system, which would continue past his death in 1877 as one of the major railroad networks in the country.

Jay Cooke was virtually wiped out, never to regain his position at the summit of financial affairs during the final three decades of his life. Cooke's departure from the scene left the future open for Pierpont Morgan. Having detected signs of economic weakness in advance, Morgan had strengthened his firm's financial position sufficiently to ride out the storm, though he was shaken by the collapses around him. Not yet having reached a position where he could take direct part in resolving the panic, he drew from it the lesson that when the government's ability to address serious downturns came into question, it would be up to responsible individuals to step in. Come the next major panic, in 1893, he would take on that role.

The one notable survivor of the panic was Jay Gould, who was able to pick over the wreckage for bargains during the long aftermath. In the next few years he would accumulate railroad lines across the Midwest, the Western Union Telegraph Company, and what may have been the grandest prize of all: the Union Pacific.

6

JAY GOULD RETURNS

Jay gould customarily kept his business maneuvers opaque. His takeover of the Union Pacific, that original component of the first transcontinental railroad which Congress's Wilson Committee said had been rendered so "helpless" by the predatory activities of the Crédit Mobilier, was no exception. To the Pacific Railway Commission, which was established years later to examine the condition of the UP and other roads financed with government bonds, he described the takeover in almost the same terms the historian J. R. Seeley used to recount Britain's acquisition of empire — as the result of "a fit of absent-mindedness." Gould explained that in Chicago one day in the spring of 1873 he had run by chance into Horace Clark, then the UP's president. He became so intrigued by Clark's description of the road's possibilities that he "sent an order down, I think, to begin at 35 and buy the stock on a scale down."

Clark up and died that June, and his brokers dumped his stock. While Gould was on a retreat "off up in the woods," he claimed, his standing order sucked up more than he expected. Suddenly, he discovered himself to be the owner of one hundred thousand shares, or nearly one-third of the total. At that point, he said, he sent for Sidney Dillon, who had succeeded Clark as president, and they set about to rescue the Union Pacific from its multiple financial crises.

Historians tend not to take Gould's story seriously. His biographer Julius Grodinsky labeled the yarn "factually correct," but "not . . . strictly truthful." A rather different narrative soon emerged. According to this version, Gould had actually hired a banker named David B. Sickels to buy up all the Union Pacific stock he could find, on the sly. Sickels later revealed that he acquired 132,000 shares for Gould, and that Gould then instructed him to bring Dillon to Gould's home, where they struck a deal in which Dillon would remain president and Gould would serve as a member of the executive committee — a silent partner.

The idea that Jay Gould could now control the storied, if troubled, Union Pacific appalled many in the railroad world and the financial community. Ranked high among their misgivings was Gould's record as a speculator looking out only for himself. On Wall Street, "various have been the surmises as to what Mr. Gould's intentions might be . . . , whether he had any idea of applying his shrewd executive capacity to the improving of the road, or whether he had some little game of his own to play which would redound to his personal pecuniary advantage," the *New York Times* reported.

There was a further moral component to their doubts: The better class of financial merchants felt that "the elevation of Mr. Gould to a social and commercial recognition, following upon the heels of an infamous career, is far from a good example to the rising generation," the *Times* continued. There was no confidence in him as "a man of honor," but rather a conviction that he was "a very shaky individual with no fixed policy of action beyond self-advantage."

DOUBTS ABOUT GOULD'S morality stemmed chiefly from his most spectacular escapade, his attempt to corner the gold market in 1869.

The gold corner had been an outgrowth of Gould's investment in the Erie Railroad. Like many of his schemes, this one had been born of a combination of necessity and opportunity. The necessity arose from the Erie's position as a link between midwestern grain farmers and East Coast ports. The higher gold rose in price, the easier it was for American farmers to sell their wheat overseas, and therefore the more robust the traffic on the Erie. The Erie's stock price rose with those shipments, which was crucial for

Gould because he had pledged his stock as collateral for loans financing his efforts to acquire a network of connecting railroads.

The opportunity originated in the federal government's plans for reversing its wartime inflation. This had been spurred by the Lincoln administration's issuance of greenbacks, which were dollars whose value was based purely on the government's credit, rather than their convertibility to specie, or gold. Under Lincoln's successor, Andrew Johnson, the government began to drain this ocean of excess currency with the goal of returning the dollar to full convertibility to specie. The resulting contraction in the money supply caused a mild recession, felt most severely in the rural agricultural belt of the Midwest. The government's program also created an opportunity to speculate on the price of gold, which bobbed up and down on waves of rumors about government policy.

Rumormongering thrives on uncertainty, and the prime uncertainty in 1869, when Ulysses S. Grant took office as president, was whether he would continue Johnson's policy. Desperate to know the president's mind, Gould befriended one Abel Rathbone Corbin, the hapless husband of Grant's younger sister, Virginia (known as Jennie).

Corbin was given to bold talk about his influence with his brother-in-law. To onlookers, he indeed appeared to be well settled within the Grant family circle. In mid-June, when Grant was visiting the Corbins at their town house, Corbin even managed to secure an invitation for Gould to a face-to-face meeting with the president. Throughout the summer Gould urged Corbin to impress upon the president that a higher gold price would benefit farmers by strengthening their overseas sales. He paid Corbin generously for his ostensible entrée into the Grant administration, opening an account for him with $1.5 million in gold on September 2. Corbin specified that the account was to be opened in his wife's name, and the written notification of the account opening to be addressed to "Mr. — —," creating what Henry Adams called "a transaction worthy of the French stage."

That very day Grant, visiting the Corbins at home, showed Corbin a letter he had addressed to Treasury Secretary George S. Boutwell advising him to cease all government sales of gold, thereby supporting the price.

Corbin tipped off Gould, who, privy to this nugget of information even before most government officials, ordered his brokers to plunge into the market the next morning. Meanwhile, his partner Jim Fisk browbeat his cronies into buying by informing them that whatever they failed to buy on one day would only be more expensive on the next. Gold moved inexorably higher.

But then Gould overplayed his hand. In mid-September he prevailed on Corbin to write once more to Grant, reiterating the wisdom of keeping the gold price high. This was one message too many, for it finally awakened the president to the intrigue that had been going on in the bosom of his own family. Finding his wife at her writing desk with an unfinished letter to his sister Jennie, he dictated a postscript advising his sister to tell Corbin "to have nothing whatever to do with—— [presumably Gould]. If he does, he will be ruined, for come what may, he (your brother) will do his duty to the country and the trusts in his keeping." The letter went out by the first mail and was in Jennie Corbin's hands, and therefore her husband's, before nightfall on September 22. In a full-scale panic, Corbin sent for Gould.

Reading the letter over Corbin's shoulder, Gould "saw the whole extent of the danger," congressional investigators later reported. "New victims were prepared and a new scheme devised to save himself." This scheme required Fisk to keep buying while Gould himself quietly sold as much gold as he could without raising suspicions in the Gold Room, a sumptuous chamber in the financial district where gold trades were reached and finalized around an indoor fountain featuring a gilded statue of Cupid cavorting with a dolphin.

The machinations of Gould and Fisk culminated on September 24, 1869, a day that would become known as Black Friday. Gould and Fisk traveled downtown together and stationed a line of burly guards in front of their office door. But the pair was working at cross purposes, almost certainly unbeknownst to Fisk—Gould selling, Fisk buying. Gold opened strong at $145 and ran up to $150, then $155.

The night before, however, Grant and Boutwell had decided to sell $4 million in government gold. Exactly as expected, word of the sale fell

upon the Gold Room like a thunderbolt. The floor was gripped in pandemonium, shrieks and wails and shouts drowning out the bids of brokers
trying to save their skins as the price almost instantaneously collapsed.

Fisk's candidate for a scapegoat in the disaster was Corbin. During
the panic selling, Fisk sped uptown to Corbin's town house and roundly
cursed him out as a "damned old scoundrel" for failing to deliver Grant as
he had promised; the truth was that Corbin's influence over his brother-
in-law had largely been a figment of his own imagination. Corbin "was
weeping and wailing," Fisk later testified, "and I was gnashing my teeth."
Corbin agreed to make an overnight trip to the White House for one final
appeal to Grant, but returned to New York empty-handed.

"Of course matters took such a turn that it was no use," Fisk reflected.
"It was each man drag out his own corpse."

In the end, both Gould and Fisk managed to escape the crash with
their carcasses largely intact. Fisk simply repudiated his contracts for gold
purchases, claiming that they were made on behalf of his broker, William
Belden; it was a move reminiscent of Drew's repudiation of his Harlem
calls during Vanderbilt's campaign to corner that railroad. Fisk and Gould
were both protected from the consequences of their gold-market intrigue
by the intervention of their wholly owned judges, George Barnard and
Albert Cardozo (the father of future Supreme Court justice Benjamin
Cardozo, whose reputation for probity would outweigh Albert's corruption). Barnard and Cardozo issued no fewer than twelve injunctions the
week after the crash, preventing the Gold Exchange and its clearinghouse
from enforcing their rules to compel Gould and Fisk to settle their contracts with their counterparties. Gould was said to have profited by as
much as $11 million from his timely sales.

The real impact of the gold crash fell upon innocent bystanders, in
part because the recession it produced sowed considerable economic destruction. "Hundreds of firms engaged in legitimate business were wholly
ruined or seriously crippled," congressional investigators observed. "For
many weeks the business of the whole country was paralyzed—a vast volume of currency was drawn from the great channels of industry and held
in the grasp of the conspirators. Hundreds of active, ambitious men were

lured from the honest pursuit of wealth by the delusive vision of sudden fortune"—perhaps as concise a description of the temptations of easy, disreputable gain as any financial scandal has yet produced.

The scheme further "dealt a heavy blow to our credit abroad by shaking the faith of foreign capitalists in the stability of our trade and the honesty of our people," the investigators lamented. As banker George Opdyke had testified, the affair "produced an impression . . . not only in this country but all over the world, that we here are a set of gamblers, and it is not safe to enter into any contracts with us when it is possible for a small combination of speculators to monopolize one branch of our currency."

Henry Adams deplored the escape of Gould and Fisk from retribution. He expressed hopefulness that "Messrs. Gould and Fisk will at last be obliged to yield to the force of moral and economical laws," which was unduly optimistic. More pessimistically—and astutely—he observed that for the first time an enormous corporate entity had "proved itself able to override and trample on law, custom, decency, and every restraint known to society, and as yet without check." The belief already was common among the public, he added, that the "system of quiet but irresistible corruption" created by Vanderbilt, Fisk, and Gould "will ultimately succeed in directing government itself." The "clever" machinations underlying the gold scheme, he wrote, seemed to have had "the single fault of requiring that some one, somewhere, must be swindled." There would be more swindles, and more victims.

UNION PACIFIC INSIDERS had separate grounds for concern about Gould's takeover than the gold scheme, for his appearance on the scene revived memories of the "Fisk Raid," a notorious episode in the railroad's history. The event dated to 1867, when Thomas C. Durant, one of the organizers of the Union Pacific (and an architect of the Crédit Mobilier) became embroiled in a leadership challenge with the brothers Oakes and Oliver Ames. Durant enlisted Fisk to play the role of paper owner of twenty thousand shares, which were to be voted on Durant's behalf. The issue was eventually resolved without the need of Fisk's votes, and that's where matters rested until about a year and a half later, when Fisk resurfaced. Irked that Durant had reneged on paying a $3,200 bill for his expenses, he threatened to file a lawsuit to block the Union Pacific from transacting any business unless he was paid a bounty of $75,000.

To the railroad's management this smacked of blackmail, but it was no idle threat, since Fisk had New York judge George Barnard in his pocket. The Union Pacific was at a critical pass, as it was still racing frantically toward Promontory while struggling to cover a debt of almost $14 million. "Fisk had told us, 'I will break you up so that you cannot pay your obligations, and the first one you default on I will buy it up, until I get control of the road, the same as with Erie,'" UP shareholder Cornelius Bushnell later testified to a congressional committee. "He bragged that he would do that."

When his demand was refused, Fisk followed through on his threat. His lawsuit loomed over the Union Pacific for eight months, finally coming to a head in March 1869, when Judge Barnard issued the injunction Fisk sought and brazenly appointed William M. Tweed Jr., the son of Tammany's "Boss" Tweed, as the railroad's receiver. The uncompleted road's entire existence hung in the balance.

The railroad simply ignored Barnard's injunction, at which point the judge ordered the seizure of its Manhattan offices. Tipped off, the railroad's officers managed to gather up all its books and securities and decamp with them one step ahead of a sheriff's posse to New Jersey, safely out of Barnard's jurisdiction — replicating, perhaps unwittingly, the flight of Fisk, Gould, and Drew to "Fort Taylor" the year before. There followed a comic-opera denouement in which the sheriff's men battered in the doors of the corporate safe — "the most infamous thing I ever saw in my life," recalled John Pondir, who witnessed the event as the railroad's newly appointed fiscal agent — only to find it empty. In due course, the Union Pacific relocated its headquarters, and its papers, to the safe haven of Boston. But according to Bushnell the Fisk raid cost the company $7 million from the depreciation of its bonds during the event. Another $50,000 was quietly paid to Fisk, Oliver Ames later testified, to get him to slink away.

For Union Pacific officers and shareholders struggling to bring the

Union Pacific through the Panic of 1873 and its aftermath, the Fisk Raid reflected horribly on Gould—not merely because Gould and Fisk had been partners in so many financial misadventures, but because it was generally suspected that Gould was more than an innocent bystander in the episode. Pondir, for example, testified that Gould personally had been present during the attack on the safe. If Gould were so willing to connive in the blackmailing of the Union Pacific in the past, it was thought, what reason could there be to trust him now?

NOTWITHSTANDING THE INSIDERS' suspicions of Gould's faithlessness, his tenure as the power behind the throne at the Union Pacific got off to an auspicious start. His own expectations, as he described them later, were not great. The railroad "was in rather a blue condition," he told a Senate committee in 1883. The road was on the verge of receivership, with a large floating debt and $10 million in bonds due within a month. "I made up my mind that I would carry it through," Gould said. "I immediately went to work to bring the road up. I went out over it, started coal mines, and to the surprise of everybody it soon began to pay dividends."

This version, retailed by Gould's defenders to this day, portrays him as almost single-handedly saving the railroad from failure. It is too simple by half. On the plus side, he restructured the road's crushing debt, saving thousands of dollars in annual interest; on the other hand, he failed to address the UP's pending debt to the US government. That debt would become payable starting in 1895, when it would amount to some $70 million.

Placing the road on a dividend-paying basis had been Gould's explicit goal from the outset. This policy, of course, stood to benefit him greatly, for he was the owner of between one-third and one-half of its outstanding stock. Starting its own coal mines facilitated a spurt of profiteering that made the road's government directors exceedingly uneasy, for it produced gains for the road at the expense of its own customers. Under Gould, the road charged independent mines 10 to 35 percent more per ton to carry their coal than the price at which it sold its own mine production to customers, placing the independents at a hopeless disadvantage in the marketplace. The government directors labeled this an "odious" policy that was "without justification or excuse; injurious to the true interests of the company" and a detriment to "the development of the country through which the line passes, and on which it depends for traffic."

The strong increase in traffic and earnings the UP experienced after Gould's arrival was to a great extent the product of luck. The West, that barren territory across which its rails had been thrown, was filling up with settlers. The territory traversed by the Union Pacific had been condemned as a "perfect waste" by a government committee investigating Asa Whitney's brainstorm in the 1840s; by 1876, however, the same landscape was teeming "with farms and villages, and herds of cattle and flocks of sheep, and embraces mineral wealth . . . beyond computation and almost too great for human belief," in the words of the government directors' report to the interior secretary that year. The population of the four states and territories through which the railroad passed—Nebraska, Colorado, Wyoming, and Utah—more than tripled in the decade after its completion, from 270,430 in 1870 to 830,970 in 1880. Some of its most important cities evolved from mud holes in the years before the railroad's construction into metropolises after its completion—for example, Omaha grew from 1,883 souls in 1860 to 30,518 in 1880, Denver from 4,749 to 35,629 in the same time span.

Beef and mutton from the prairies, gold and silver from western mines, and tea and silk from the Far East were filling the railroad's cars to the rafters. In 1873 California farmers reaped a record grain harvest, further stoking the Union Pacific's freight traffic. The railroad's books reflected the bounty, with profits rising from about $2 million in 1869 to $6.5 million in 1875. And why not? In this region the Union Pacific held an unregulated monopoly in which it could set rates wherever it wished.

These circumstances allowed Gould to declare a 6 percent dividend in the spring of 1875, raised three months later to an annual rate of 8 percent. Was this wise? Later analysts would find the strategy dubious, and the railroad's fate after Gould's departure suggests they were right.

In the early 1880s it was possible to overlook headwinds gathering against the UP. The economy was booming, and where economic growth fell short, the climate of feverish speculation took up the slack. This was the boom that followed the long depression triggered by the Panic of 1873. In the euphoria of recovery, the role played in that earlier disaster by railroad overcapitalization and mismanagement was quickly forgotten. Land speculation spread across the West like a prairie fire, abetted by railroad advertisements depicting Kansas and Nebraska as Gardens of Eden in the making; a few years of abundant rainfall in that climatologically unstable region bolstered the impression that its agricultural potential was rich. Revenues and profits soared at the Union Pacific, as did its spending on new branch line construction, which doubled between 1880 and 1883 to $8 million. Over that period the railroad's shares gained 30 percent in value.

Gould's prominence among railroad tycoons during this period was partially an artifact of his having outlasted almost all his most important compatriots and rivals. Jim Fisk had been the first to go. On January 6, 1872, having crammed a full life into his thirty-six years, Fisk was shot in the gut by one Edward Stokes, a rich dandy who had become Josie Mansfield's lover and been publicly accused by Fisk of blackmail. Jubilee Jim expired the next morning, allowing his gambling cronies to settle their hundred-dollar wagers over how long he would survive the bullet.

Daniel Drew died penniless at the age of eighty-two in 1879, leaving behind a quarter-million dollars in unpaid commitments to the theological seminary that bore his name. His erstwhile partner and sometime foe Cornelius Vanderbilt had already passed on, also at eighty-two, on January 4, 1877. He died with his reputation intact as the richest man in America, his medical condition closely followed by newspapers chronicling every turn for the worse during his final days. ("Commodore Vanderbilt Very Low," the *New York Times* reported on New Year's Day, noting that Vanderbilt had suffered several fainting spells the day before and "his death may be expected at any hour.") The Commodore would leave most of his fortune, estimated at $100 million, to his son William.

But Gould also had the survivor's skill of knowing when to double down on his bets and when to turn in his chips. He was canny enough to detect the turn of the wheel from boom to bust with near perfect precision. And he was not above stabbing his erstwhile partners in the back, especially if it could confer him an advantage at such a critical moment.

AS IS TYPICALLY the case during boom times, economic naysayers were scarce in the early 1880s, though not nonexistent. One was the businessman and financier Cyrus Field. In June 1881, in a conversation with the *New York Evening Mail,* Field foresaw another depression.

> Can any sane person believe that this condition of things can continue when stocks are seen rising in the market several per cent daily? . . . I have hardly seen a sane person since my return from Europe. Speculation is making people crazy. Why, when I went to Delmonico's for lunch this afternoon, I saw a throng of pale and anxious men congregated about a stock indicator, watching it as if it had been the pulse of a dying friend. It was a melancholy sight . . . sheer madness.

Over the next few years, concerns like Field's would be heard more often, as the possible consequences of an economic slump for America's overcapitalized railroads began to give pause to the savviest investors. Gould was among them. With the Union Pacific facing what he believed to be its moment of truth, he quietly voted with his feet, unloading almost all his stock by 1883, though not before seizing one last opportunity for plunder. Indeed, few maneuvers demonstrated Gould's habit of enriching himself at the expense of his own partners as did his takeover of the Kansas Pacific Railroad and development of the unprofitable line into a weapon against the Union Pacific.

Gould had first interested himself in the Kansas Pacific in 1877. The 745-mile line ran from Kansas City west to Denver and thence north to Cheyenne, paralleling the Union Pacific much of the way. It was a paragon of overcapitalization and mismanagement; the German-born Henry Villard, who had not yet launched his career as a railroad and newspaper magnate but was serving as a receiver of the Kansas line on behalf of its

German creditors, deemed it to be "in wretched condition" and "utterly out of repair." Its books, reported the accountants of the Pacific Railway Commission, "reflect the chaotic character of the management," leaving it impossible to glean "an accurate and faithful statement of the actual condition of the corporation." The few facts that were known about its financial condition were dismal indeed: The Kansas Pacific turned a profit only twice from 1867 through 1879, while accumulating a deficit totaling more than $11 million. In that era, when shares of stock were issued at $100, or "par," Kansas Pacific was quoted as low as $9, or nine cents on the dollar.

Gould, however, viewed the Kansas Pacific as "an immensely valuable property intrinsically." He acknowledged that its "general condition was bad; it had been badly financed . . . [and] so badly managed that it got clear down in the rut." What he liked about it, however, was its potential to torment the Union Pacific. As Grodinsky would observe, "while the Kansas Pacific was not financially strong, as a threat to its competitor it had the strength of Samson."

The complacent UP board had long regarded the Kansas Pacific chiefly as a nuisance. As a parallel line running west past Denver, the railroad had been able to erode the UP's profits in Colorado through rate cutting. But the board assumed that as long as it was dependent on the UP for freight to and from the West, there were limits to how aggressive its owners could be. That subservience would disappear only if the Kansas line were extended from Cheyenne to Ogden, Utah, where it could bypass the UP. But since the Kansas was mired in poverty, its ability to build such an extension was dubious.

Then Gould suddenly remade the landscape. He had acquired control of the Kansas while quietly reducing his holdings in the Union Pacific from two hundred thousand shares to twenty-seven thousand (even as he retained his seat on the UP board). He was now prepared to reposition the Union Pacific from his ward to his victim. In November 1879 he summoned his fellow directors to New York to propose a merger of the Union Pacific, the Kansas, and another Gould holding, the Denver Pacific, all at par — that is, valuing each equally.

The meeting went badly, for "the Union Pacific had reported an annual surplus, the other two roads an annual deficit; the Union Pacific had not defaulted, the Kansas and Denver Pacific had done little else," the historian Stuart Daggett would observe. A reasonable arrangement would have valued the Kansas and Denver at no more than 30 percent of the Union Pacific, but Gould refused to accept such a valuation and the UP directors refused to offer any more. Gould responded truculently. "Gentlemen, you are making a great mistake," he snapped, stalking out of the room. Recalled F. Gordon Dexter, one of the board members on the scene: "He had his war paint on."

With the Kansas Pacific now in the hands of a speculator with ready access to capital and nothing resembling scruples, the UP directors realized their position had become desperate. After the meeting Oliver Ames, the son of Oakes Ames, encountered three UP directors—Sidney Dillon, Dexter, and his cousin Fred Ames—and described them "as gloomy and unhappy a set of men as I ever saw. . . . If you had seen them, as I did . . . you would have pitied them."

Gould soon fulfilled their fears, announcing a plan to extend the Kansas all the way to Ogden. Asked later for his own assessment of what would have happened to the Union Pacific if he had followed through, he answered bluntly: "It would have destroyed it." The UP directors knew he was right. They were ready to capitulate.

In January 1880 Gould resigned his directorship of the UP and summoned his former colleagues from Boston back to his office in New York, this time to demand their signatures on a consolidation that was essentially identical to the deal they had rejected as absurd only a few weeks earlier. Gould was no longer angry and irritated but amiable and "chipper," magnanimous in victory but still not willing to yield an inch. Dexter, remarking on the terms, observed that the only real change from November was that "every one of us felt at that time that we could not accept them, and every one of us felt at this time that we were very glad to get the offer."

Gould maintained to the last that the deal was a very good one for the UP, on the grounds that the road would have had to confront competition from a resurgent Kansas Pacific sooner or later. A railway commissioner astonished at his intriguing against a firm that he served as a board member put it to him directly: "According to the ethics of Wall Street," he asked, "do you consider that it is absolutely within the limits of your duty as a director in a great corporation to purchase, while such director, another property which . . . would absolutely ruin the property in which you were a director?"

No, Gould replied indulgently; that was why he followed through with the merger of the railroads instead of building the extension. In any case, he observed, he was no longer a UP director on January 14, when the deal was signed. The other directors maintained that they had entered into the consolidation of their own free will and not at all under pressure from Jay Gould, but this was a show of independence transparently designed for public consumption.

Villard would estimate Gould's profit from the episode at more than $10 million. Later analysis suggests this may be an exaggeration by about twofold. But there is no question that it reestablished Gould as an important force in the railroad industry—and crippled the Union Pacific for years to come.

THE BLOATED AND unsteady entity that emerged from the merger of the Denver, Kansas, and Union Pacific lines—rechristened the Union Pacific Railway Company—began life in immeasurably worse condition than its predecessor. The Union Pacific Railway inherited all the problems facing the original UP, including years of underinvestment in physical plant, the looming deadline for repayment of its government loan, and an overall capitalization overflowing with water. Now it assumed the added burden of the extravagantly overpriced and insolvent branch lines purchased from Gould and financed by more watered stock.

The UP directors could congratulate themselves on having eliminated the Kansas Pacific and the other Gould holdings as sources of competition. But the cost was crippling, as was soon shown by the railroad's inability to shoulder a new economic downturn looming on the horizon.

Until 1883 the company had actually been expanding, thanks to a nation-wide economic boom and, especially, a mining boom in Colorado, which prompted it to expand its network of branch lines. But it would eventually be discovered that the boom rested upon a foundation of quicksand, as most do. In 1883 Gould severed his connection with the Union Pacific, having sold all his stock and decided, as Daggett would write, that he "had obtained from the Union Pacific all that he thought possible"—for the moment.

After Gould's departure, management of the road was left in the hands of the sixty-nine-year-old Sidney Dillon, who had once been Gould's vig-orous front man but was now "old, and had lost his nerve," in the judgment of Charles Francis Adams. Dillon resigned soon after his patron exited the railroad. In his place, the board named as president Adams himself. Ad-ams thereby inherited not only the legacy of the Crédit Mobilier, but of Jay Gould, which was almost as weighty a burden. The Union Pacific was about to enter its most desperate period.

It would be a cleansing crisis that set the stage for a brighter chap-ter, and the railroad's revival under a new owner, Edward H. Harriman. Gould, meanwhile, was left to work his dark magic on the remaining rail-roads in his empire. It would not be a peaceful experience—neither for his rivals, nor for Gould himself.

7

YEAR OF UPHEAVAL

Master mechanic leroy Bartlett, head of the St. Louis shops of the Missouri Pacific, walked onto the shop floor at the 10 a.m. bell on March 6, 1886, only to be confronted by an extraordinary sight. The men were all shedding their work clothes and lining up in street clothes in double file. Then they marched out of the shop, three hundred strong. "In the space of half an hour," he would recall, "they were all gone."

The Great Southwest Railroad Strike of 1886 had begun.

The walkout spread rapidly across Jay Gould's rail network that day —indeed, almost instantaneously: 700 men in Sedalia, 340 in De Soto, 300 in Little Rock. "The organization of the strikers was perfect," the historian Frank Taussig would observe. "At every important point, the roads were bared in an instant of men indispensable for the movement of trains." Within two days local newspapers were running headlines such as this one in the *St. Louis Post-Dispatch:* "Traffic Throttled: The Gould System at the Mercy of the Knights of Labor."

The year 1886 would become known as "the great upheaval" in American labor history, especially for the railroads; some 610,000 workers joined in an estimated fourteen hundred strikes, more than twice the number of the previous year. The Great Southwest strike would be a special case, "extreme in its magnitude, extreme in the methods and the temper of the strikers," in Taussig's words. The strike would trigger a lasting change in the perception of the railroads among its workers and the communities they served; it would lead to the end of the Gould era and usher in the era of J. Pierpont Morgan and of "Morganization," aimed at stabilizing the industry by rigorous management of individual railroads and the competition among them. The strike was at least partially prompted by the recognition that the roads were no longer mere businesses. Instead they had become economic forces capable of total domination of their environments, their owners bent on using their wealth to beget more wealth.

The railroad strike's immediate trigger was the firing of a union official named Charles Hall from his job as a carpenter on the Texas & Pacific line, ostensibly for having left work to attend a meeting of his union, the Knights of Labor. (Hall maintained that his foreman had given him permission to attend, then fired him for absenteeism.) But the strike was a long time coming. Behind it was a year of unkept promises by Jay Gould, progressively steeper pay cuts, and rising workplace discrimination. And behind that lay an even longer record of labor mistreatment. The expansion of the railroads from the Eastern Seaboard across the Mississippi and into the Far West had opened vast new opportunities for skilled workers to ply their trades and for unskilled workers to earn decent pay in the rapidly industrializing economy. But during downturns, when railroad managers looked for a way to reduce expenses, they would see eliminating jobs and cutting wages as their only options. Tensions between labor and management were bound to come to a head.

THE NOBLE AND Holy Order of the Knights of Labor was founded in 1869, amid convulsive changes being wrought across the United States' industrializing economy. The order was destined to become "the most imposing labor organization this country has ever known" up to that time, but the description was short-lived, for the organization would reach its apogee in 1885 and become almost extinct after 1886. In the process, however, it would leave a historic mark as the nation's first truly national industrial union.

The Knights' founder, Uriah Stephens, was a Philadelphia garment cutter with intellectual pretensions. His years of membership in the Masons and the Odd Fellows may have inspired the order's ritualistic habits, which in its earliest phase included secrecy oaths—members were not permitted to divulge its name or even acknowledge its existence—and titles for officers such as "venerable sage" and "grand master workman."

The Knights did not resemble the worker organizations that preceded it or the labor unions of later decades. In the 1860s the only national labor organizations had been fraternal mutual-aid societies serving trades such as printers, stone cutters, and hat finishers, without any idea of engaging in the sort of collective bargaining that would become the hallmark of the labor movement generations later. Indeed, the Knights sprang from a garment-cutters union of which Stephens had been a member.

But Stephens's ambitions were greater. He aimed to reform the relationship between capital and labor by educating workers in the virtues of solidarity and urging them to reach their goals by means of legislation, rather than through direct confrontation with management. The order was broadly inclusive, welcoming men and women, blacks and whites, unskilled laborers and skilled workers alike. Its credo held that to "defend [labor] from degradation; to divest it of the evils to body, mind, and estate which ignorance and greed have imposed; to rescue the toiler from the grasp of the selfish—is a work worthy of the noblest and best of our race."

Stephens's successor as grand master workman was Terence V. Powderly, a former mayor of Scranton who took over in 1879. Less complaisant than Stephens in outlook, though not by much, Powderly was described by a reporter for the *New York Sun* as "short and slight, with soft blue eyes half concealed by gold-rimmed spectacles." The writer added that when Powderly spoke, "he seemed like an invalid sitting up when he should have been in bed, but he talked like a level-headed, clear-minded man." Powderly consistently opposed direct job actions such as strikes. Under his leadership, the Knights' main goal was the institution of an eight-hour day for all workers.

Powderly also chipped away at the Knights' "rigmarole" of secrecy—

under Stephens, the name of the organization could not even be written, but was printed as five stars. Once the organization shed those commitments, its membership began to rise—growing to one hundred thousand in 1885 from twenty-eight thousand just five years before.

It was a key moment for labor activism. Laborers, especially railroad workers, were the Americans squeezed most by the depression of the 1870s. From their vantage point, the promise of an egalitarian America had receded as the country prepared to celebrate its 1876 centennial. "Capital has now the same control over us that the aristocracy of England had at the time of the Revolution," wrote the editors of the *National Labor Tribune*, a Pittsburgh weekly, in December 1874.

Until the Panic of 1873, plentiful work and rising wages had kept the peace among those who labored on the railroads. But the widening gulf between the comfort of the railroad owners and the despair of the rank and file could not go unaddressed for long. As the railroads worked their way toward a pinnacle of economic influence, the working class became increasingly, and unhappily, aware that this trend was developing at its expense.

For the aftermath of the 1873 panic included stringent wage cuts. The reasons that workers bore the brunt of the economic retrenchment of the era are not hard to discern. Railroad managements faced a pitiless choice between defaulting on their debt payments and reducing expenses, of which the bulk was in wages. But creditors had the power to assume control of a railroad by foreclosure, while workers were insufficiently organized to defend themselves effectively against "long hours, low wages, and arbitrary dismissal." This was especially true for unskilled workers, given the teeming population of job seekers who could be slotted interchangeably into laborers' jobs.

A class war loomed. On one side would be workers belonging to some of the earliest labor unions in American history; on the other an ever more powerful cadre of railroad magnates, exemplified for the newly militant laborers by the secretive and manipulative Gould. The relentless economic pressure placed on railroad workers would soon manifest itself in a wave of strikes.

American workers had benefited over the previous decade from an economic surge, but now they were experiencing the anguish of having their gains snatched away. "The power of money has become supreme over everything," thundered the labor reformist John Swinton during a rally in 1874. "This power must be kept in check; it must be broken, or it will utterly crush the people."

Worker fury was naturally focused on the capitalists who stood at the apex of the economic pyramid, the leaders of the industry that had most represented the surge in American prosperity, and now would take the blame for its sudden collapse: the railroads.

Although in 1870 nearly half of the male population still consisted of farmers or farm laborers, outside the farm many workers were craftsmen who valued their independence and felt strongly about the principle of "free labor," which meant the right to negotiate the sale of their skills to employers as equals. The notion of "at-will" employment, which would become a legal millstone around the necks of the laboring class in the 1920s and 1930s, was seen at the time to be a boon to craft workers, for it signified personal ownership of their skills. During the Civil War, advocates of at-will employment and free labor, especially in the North, could point to slavery as a stark counterexample. In fact, the principle of free labor had been an essential part of the Knights' platform. "The aim of the Knights of Labor—properly understood—is to make each man his own employer," Powderly had declared.

Yet even before the war, some workers had felt the pressure of an industrial system that made their skills increasingly dispensable. The technological revolution that had begun in textile mills was spreading, bringing with it regimentation on the factory floor and downward pressure on wages.

Then the railroads took this trend to a new level.

The railroads' expansion showed the necessity of a new model of large-scale industrialization. American railroad workers were the first to be employed by "the big impersonal corporation," as the business historian Alfred Chandler put it. They were also among the first to be stratified into skilled and unskilled workers, which enabled the railroad bosses to

foment internal dissension among the rank and file, and thus limit the
appeal of organizing movements. Skilled workers included locomotive
engineers, firemen, brakemen, and switchmen, who were relatively difficult to replace. They stood at the crest of the labor structure, at the base
of which were easily replaceable maintenance workers and laborers, who
faced a greater threat of wage cuts and layoffs and therefore had greater
incentive to agitate.

In the first decades after the Civil War, engineers and other skilled
workers moved from boomtown to boomtown along with the railroads'
western expansion. The work of these "boomers" was arduous, not in-
frequently crippling or even lethal, but the pay was good—better than
that of most other laborers, and even better than their brethren on the
older rail lines of the Northeast. Railroad work was romanticized, bound
up with the era's conception of prideful masculinity. As a veteran boomer
named Charles B. George wrote in 1887, "Knowing that amid the dark-
ness of night, the storms of winter, and the war of the elements, hundreds
of human beings are to be kept in safety carries with it a peculiar dignity
and sense of responsibility that is felt all along the line, from the man at
the switch, the man on the locomotive, . . . even to the highest." The
butchery they experienced on the job was also romanticized, notably in
ballads such as "The Wreck on the C&O," which lamented the fate of an
engineer who crashed his train while trying to meet a timetable: "Mur-
dered on a railroad line and laid in a lonesome grave."

It was perhaps natural that the boomers would expect their standing in
the railroad communities and their high pay to be permanent. But these
conditions would not last. In regions where the railroads commanded
monopolies, companies might be able to continue charging rates high
enough to maintain good wages for large workforces. Once competing
lines appeared and rates fell, however, the old wage scales seemed just a
waste of money. When the first waves of layoffs and pay cuts came, the
workers' pain was proportionately sharper.

These changes in railroad employment took place against a greater
social convulsion, also a product of railroad expansion. As the missionary
and social commentator Josiah Strong observed in 1885, the previously

uninhabited prairie crossed by the railroads in the West developed very
differently from the territory that comprised the original colonies and
their adjacent lands. In those older regions, he wrote, "the farms were first
taken, then the town sprung up to supply their wants, and at length the
railway connected it with the world, but in the West the order is reversed
—first the railroad, then the town, then the farms. Settlement is, consequently, much more rapid, and the city stamps the country, instead of the
country's stamping the city." America was becoming an urbanized nation,
its rural institutions and economics overtaken by people who aquired land
and property not for their own sustenance, but for the sake of accumulation, ultimately to use it for the domination of society and their fellow
Americans.

Walt Whitman tried to find grounds for optimism in the changing
America, but could not keep discouragement from coloring his words.
"The final culmination of this vast and varied Republic," he predicted,
"will be the production and perennial establishment of millions of comfortable city homesteads and moderate-sized farms, . . . life in them complete but cheap, within reach of all." For the moment, however, "excep-
tional wealth, splendor, countless manufactures, immense capital and
capitalists, the five-dollar-a-day hotels well fill'd . . . form, more or less, a
sort of anti-democratic disease and monstrosity."

The political clout of the railroads was demonstrated by the role the
Pennsylvania Railroad played in the Compromise of 1877. This was the
deal that settled the disputed 1876 presidential election by designating
Republican Rutherford B. Hayes as the victor over Democrat Samuel Til-
den, who had won a majority of the popular vote but fell short in the
electoral college by a single vote. The compromise gave the Republicans
the White House in return for their commitment to withdraw Union
troops from the South, thus ending Reconstruction. But as the historian
C. Vann Woodward later argued, the path to compromise was greased by
Tom Scott, head of the Pennsylvania, who was anxious to draw the South
back into national politics to fulfill his dream of a transcontinental line
anchored by his railroad and traversing the defeated region. Scott saw
to it that Pennsylvania's congressional delegation supported the compro-

mise. He kept a close eye on the process, even to the extent of providing Hayes with a private train car to bring him to Washington for his inauguration on March 4. The Pennsylvania's $22 million in annual profits made it the most powerful corporation in the country. To many labor activists, the deal cemented big business in place as the keystone of the national power structure.

Almost as soon as Hayes took office it seemed as if the ultimate confrontation might be at hand. The era of organized revolt may be said to have started on July 16, 1877, when workers at the shops of the Baltimore & Ohio Railroad in Martinsburg, West Virginia downed tools to protest the company's second wage cut in a year, reducing them to a level of income they said would force them to "steal or starve." Within a week, the strike spread spontaneously to a million railroad workers, in the first labor walkout to unfold on a national scale and the first to provoke government intervention.

The Pennsylvania's Scott demanded that Governor John Hartranft call out the state militia, with the memorable exhortation to feed the strikers "a rifle diet for a few days and see how they like that kind of bread." On July 21 a militia fusillade and bayonet attack killed twenty strikers in Pittsburgh; the surviving workers were provoked to burn thirty-nine buildings and destroy more than thirteen hundred locomotives and railcars. Further attacks occurred in Reading, with twelve deaths, and then spread beyond the state line to Chicago, where the toll was another twenty, and Baltimore, twelve.

To local political leaders, the 1877 strikes presaged more disorder. Some viewed the situation in frankly apocalyptic terms. "It is wrong to call this a strike; it is labor revolution," declared alarmed editorialists at the *Missouri Republican* of St. Louis, where a general strike brought the city to a halt on July 22. The *New York Herald* detected parallels with the Civil War, still sharp in Americans' memory: "Not since the dark and threatening hours of 1861," the newspaper fretted, "has the nation been called upon to confront such a grave condition."

Some detected the dark influence of communism. (Marx and Engels had published their *Communist Manifesto* in 1848, but it was the establishment of the radical but short-lived Paris Commune in 1871 in the wake of the Franco-Prussian War that had put the word "communism" on the lips of the defenders of capital.) "This enemy of all civilized society touches the railway system, and, as if by magic, twenty thousand miles of rails cease to bear the commerce of a continent, . . . two thousand millions of property are deprived of present value, half a million of workmen spend a week in voluntary or enforced idleness," wrote William Mason Grosvenor, an editor for the *New York Tribune*, in a September 1877 article titled "The Communist and the Railway." "A Republic is government by the many. That form of government will wither and die if the thousands who pay taxes get no protection from the millions who govern."

Newspapers depicted strikers as disaffected denizens of society's fringes. According to a compilation by labor historian Samuel Yellen, on July 26 alone the *New York Times* described participants in various strikes across the country as roughs, hoodlums, rioters, bad characters, thieves, blacklegs, looters, communists, rabble, labor-reform agitators, gangs, tramps, law breakers, ruffians, rapscallions, brigands, robbers, riffraff, felons, and idiots — among other labels.

In the *Times*'s view, however, the chief villains were not the strikers themselves, but state and local authorities who allowed them to disturb the peace without pushing back, preferably with military-like violence. The newspaper cursed city officials in Pittsburgh and Buffalo who had placed their cities "in the hands of roaming bands of worthless fellows who should not have been permitted for an hour to go unchecked." In an observation that would be echoed often over the following decades, the newspaper attributed the timidity of the officials to their dependence on votes from "people who own no property and pay no taxes."

Goaded by such editorial pressure, the governors of nine states called on President Hayes to send them troops, but after discovering that the two hundred soldiers he had dispatched to Martinsburg at the start of the disorders were reluctant to move into action against workers, Hayes took a more measured stance, relying on punctilious legalism to delay sending more soldiers. He required that the governors provide him with written assertions of striker violence or that federal judges issue suitable orders, and he instructed those troops he did send to restrict themselves to the protection of public buildings, the better to avoid direct physical engagement with any strikers. As it happened, most of the strikes were already playing out by the time the troops appeared, or their arrival alone was sufficient to quell whatever disorders had occurred, without the need for further action.

The 1877 strikes were short and yielded little in the way of concrete improvement in the workers' lot, but they hinted at labor's desire to challenge the increasing power of the railroad magnates. Hayes's demands for written grounds for intervention may have limited the interposing of federal authority, but they had a downside, for they created legal precedents for federal action in future labor disputes. As Gould and the other railroad barons would soon discover, the discontent of railroad labor was a ticking time bomb.

THE RAIL MILEAGE under Gould's control expanded from 1,960 in 1884 to more than 8,400 just three years later, mostly through the acquisition of competitors and feeder lines. But Gould's empire was weaker than it looked; in the words of his biographer Maury Klein, he had made the Missouri Pacific, now the hub of his system, "prosperous and powerful but not secure."

By 1884, several Gould lines had already been placed in receivership. As usual, the consequences were chiefly borne by the workers. Wage cuts swept through the Gould workforce in 1884 and 1885, but that was not the extent of the imposition. Workers who graduated to journeyman status continued to receive apprentice wages—if they got paid at all, for the time between paydays lengthened from a week to two weeks or a month, and sometimes ceased indefinitely. Work crews were cut to the bone and working conditions became more dangerous as low-paid novices were given assignments that required more experienced men.

"Was it not because there was not work enough to keep you employed the full time?" a trackman named James Barrett was asked during a congressional investigation of the 1886 strike.

"Work enough? Yes, sir," Barrett replied. "There was work enough for a hundred right along, let alone the six men that was on. They could work twice as many men and have just as much as they could do."

The shrinking wages and hours reduced families that only recently had enjoyed solid working-class incomes nearly to poverty. A report in 1884 by the Illinois Bureau of Labor Statistics found that wives in a fourth of railroad workers' households had been forced to supplement household income "by laundering clothes; selling eggs, chickens, and home-grown vegetables; or taking in boarders."

In February 1885 workers on the Wabash line, a feeder for Gould's Missouri Pacific that was among those operating in receivership, were hammered with a 20 percent pay cut. The Wabash workers walked out, and at the sound of the whistle on March 7, some four hundred employees of Missouri Pacific shops in Sedalia, Missouri, downed tools in sympathy. Hundreds more left work at other system shops across Missouri and another thousand in Texas. By the second week of March, forty-five hundred employees of the Gould system had walked off the job.

The strikers reasoned that notwithstanding the Wabash's receivership, responsibility for its condition belonged to Jay Gould. "Who put the Wabash in the hands of a receiver?" one striker asked. "Was it them who worked for it, or the man who owned it?" The same sentiment may have contributed to another feature of the strike: the support of the public and the press in an agricultural region that had seen plenty of evidence that Gould and his fellow tycoons had been profiteering at the farmers' expense. The strikers policed themselves to avoid violence or intimidation, established guard units to protect railroad property, and limited their blockades of traffic to freight, allowing passenger trains to proceed unmolested.

The Knights of Labor played no direct role in organizing and launching the 1885 strike. But many of the shop workers who were most active behind the scenes were Knights. And once the walkout began, the union assumed de facto leadership, dispatching veteran organizer Joseph Buchanan to Missouri with $30,000 to succor the workers and lend them the growing weight of its name. Buchanan would describe the speech he delivered to a gathering of Gould employees in Kansas City, Missouri, as "one of the most eloquent ever made to a band of unorganized strikers — it had $30,000 behind it."

At the start of the walkout, Gould appeared to be overmatched. His Missouri Pacific sought intervention from Missouri governor John S. Marmaduke, a former Confederate general, but Marmaduke refused — possibly in retaliation for the railroads' support of his opponent for the Democratic nomination for governor in a previous election. Once it became evident that the state government would remain neutral, Gould withdrew the wage cuts and the men returned to work. Following protracted negotiations during which he met personally with Powderly, Gould consented to a comprehensive settlement in which the Missouri Pacific agreed not to discriminate against members of the Knights and to reinstate workers who had been fired simply for their membership in the order. In return, Powderly agreed not to call any future strike against the railroad until first conferring with the road's officials. This would turn out to be an unwise concession, for Powderly presumed he could exert more control over the organization's assemblies — their local divisions — than was possible within the Knights' loose organizational structure.

The settlement was initially viewed as a massive victory for the Knights of Labor and a crushing defeat for the formerly indomitable Jay Gould. "No such victory has ever before been secured in this or any other country," declared the St. Louis Chronicle.

The settlement coincided with a remarkable surge in Knights of Labor membership, which grew to seven hundred thousand from one hundred thousand in a single year. The timing of the surge has tempted historians to attribute it to the Knights' victory over Gould, but that is to give the settlement far more credit than the Knights themselves gave it at the time. In fact, Powderly was deeply concerned that membership among railroad workers generally and Gould system employees in particular was too meager. Although an estimated forty-eight thousand Gould workers were eligible to become members of the Knights of Labor, only three thousand had actually joined. Powderly judged this to be an "alarming fact" not merely because of the sparseness of recruits, but because the new members were mostly "raw recruits who were unacquainted with the aims and objects of the Knights of Labor." Powderly's fear was that the newcomers, having been led to believe that the order was bent on direct confrontation with the railroads, would be easily manipulated into voting to strike at an inopportune moment. He was soon proven right.

Powderly attributed the membership surge to two alternative factors. One was an increased interest among all working people in the eight-hour workday, the Knights' keystone goal. The second was the "sensational" popular press. Powderly pointed specifically to an article in the *New York Sun* in the fall of 1885 that identified the Knights' leaders as "five men in this country [who] control the chief interests of five hundred thousand workingmen. . . . They can array labor against capital, putting labor on the offensive or the defensive, for quiet and stubborn self-protection, or for angry, organized assault, as they will."

The article did "incalculable mischief," Powderly complained. "The organization began to boom, but those who sought its shelter were led to believe that they could secure the cooperation of the '500,000 workingmen' in the shutting off of the railroads."

As time passed, the 1885 settlement showed itself to be not quite the victory for the Knights that it had seemed at first. The Knights had obtained from Gould merely an expression of nondiscrimination and the promised reinstatement of fired members, without a firm deadline or any mechanism for enforcement. They had failed to obtain formal recognition of the union or the right to collective bargaining. On the other side of the ledger, Gould, who had been unprepared to sustain a long strike, managed to avert one via the settlement without giving away anything of value in return. He would be better prepared for the next strike. As things would turn out, the Knights' dubious victory of 1885 would set the stage for its profound defeat only a year later, followed in short order by its utter destruction.

THE FIRING OF Charles Hall upon his return from a Knights of Labor meeting put the capstone on nearly a year of indignities Gould had inflicted on his workers since the 1885 Wabash settlement. From the workers' standpoint, Gould had reneged on every provision of the deal. Despite promising to treat members of the Knights without discrimination, the railroad had rehired only about one-fifth of the Knights-affiliated strikers. Wages had not been restored to pre-strike levels and every excuse had been offered for denying the men overtime pay. The Gould railroads never gave an inch: A brakeman named D. H. Hartley told the congressional panel that overtime had been promised on shifts of twelve hours, but it was refused if the shift ended at even "eleven hours and fifty minutes."

Complaints poured in to Powderly's office. Knights official E. G. Pagette recalled that the railroad spurned every attempt to negotiate grievances. "We saw very plainly that inside of another six months they would have the employees of the system back exactly where they were at the time that agreement was entered into," which was to say as targets of "one of the most notorious starvation cuts that ever wages in the West received." Members from the shops in Moberly, Missouri, objected that "the settlement so far is no settlement at all." A member of another Missouri local wrote of the shame he felt walking among his neighbors: "They all give us the Horse Laugh and say we were all dam fools for ever coming out and getting Left that way."

It was not only the workers who felt the sting of deceit. Father C. F. O'Leary, a thirty-six-year-old Catholic priest in the Missouri railroad town of De Soto, told the congressional investigators that, based on what he heard from the workers, the behavior of the railroads was entirely responsible for the strike. "The whole system of railroad corporations," he testified, "is begotten in fraud; it is carried on by trickery; and the whole thing is a grievance." He cited "the rottenness, injustice, and spirit of tyranny that exists on the whole system from Gould down to the lowest officer."

The rising discontent posed an elemental problem for Grand Master Workman Powderly, given his personal aversion to strikes. He understood the appeal of walkouts, even their romance — in the abstract. He was familiar with the idea embodied in the adage that "the blood of the martyr is the seed of the church" — that "if men and women suffered and starved for sake of a cause in the here and now their sacrifice would rebound to the benefit of posterity." But he reflected that it never seemed to be the martyrs themselves who spoke so glowingly of the virtues of sacrifice. In the heat of the moment, the strikers overlooked the practical consequences of walking off the job, Powderly observed: "Precious lives were lost in strikes; homes were wrecked and children deprived of education . . . , millions of dollars were lost to labor, and in the main this great waste and loss could have been avoided."

Powderly wore his own blinders, however. Bookish as he was and diffident toward Gould, he failed to comprehend the true nature of the intensifying conflict between labor and capital, in which his members stood on the front lines. "There are people who say that this struggle is the beginning of the war between capital and labor," he would write Gould in April 1886, after the great strike had ended with the Knights' defeat. "That statement is false. This certainly means war; but it is a war between legitimate capital, honest enterprise and honest labor on the one hand, and illegitimate wealth on the other hand." His attempt to draw a line between "legitimate" and "illegitimate" capital, as if the former were the workers' ally and only the latter their adversary, would prove hopelessly naive.

As the mood of Gould's employees darkened, Powderly became especially concerned about the hunger for a walkout evinced by the Knights' District Assembly 101, which incorporated thirty locals representing Missouri Pacific employees. District Assembly 101, he knew, was utterly unprepared to conduct an extended job action. It was $800 in debt, filled with hotheaded novices, and infiltrated by paid spies who "reported every move to the company." Among them were not a few agents provocateurs who "were loudest in denunciation of the practices of the railroad officials." Their activities were among the many indications that Gould was intent on goading the workers to a strike. He almost certainly understood that the Knights were weaker than they seemed, and in any event he had boxed them in by writing into the 1885 settlement the guarantee against sudden strikes.

One Knight took the bait—or at least is blamed for it: Martin Irons. The head of District Assembly 101, Irons would emerge as one of the most enigmatic figures of that year of great upheaval—the one genuine martyr of the conflict, blamed for fomenting the strike in disobedience of Powderly, and worse, for losing the battle. Whether this was truly Martin Irons's fault has been the subject of historical debate ever since.

What is known is that DA 101 treated Hall's firing as a direct breach of its employment rights. The assembly collected pledges of support from other regional Knights assemblies, then demanded Hall's reinstatement. When the railroad refused, the strike was on—called so suddenly that Powderly himself only learned of the walkout the next day, when he was alerted by a telegram from A. L. Hopkins, an officer of the Missouri Pacific. Hopkins complained that the Knights were violating Powderly's 1885 agreement "that no strike should be ordered without consultation" with the railroad. Sheepishly, Powderly wired Irons from Philadelphia, where he was presiding over a Knights executive board meeting, with a request for "full particulars" of what had caused the strike. The terse reply came back: "Violation of contract by company."

The job action by DA 101 placed Powderly in a difficult position. He may have erred in promising the Gould organization that the Knights would consult with it before calling a strike, but promise he did. It was now clear that he had no authority, much less ability, to control his own members. Powderly was correct that the strike was ill-timed, unorganized, and doomed to catastrophic failure—so much so that it could plausibly be said that the canny Gould had deliberately provoked the walkout. The strikers' gravest miscalculation may have been to presume the support of the skilled locomotive engineers, brakemen, and firemen. These workers, however, typically owed allegiance to their own brotherhoods, not the Knights. This stratification was the product of the railroads' divergent treatment of skilled and unskilled labor, the former a scarce commodity and the latter—trackmen, cleaners, baggage loaders, and shop engineers —easily replaced. Because the brotherhoods refused to join the strike, the Knights' ability to bring the lines to a halt was limited—they could stop traffic for a time, but once their members were replaced with strikebreakers, the cars could roll again under the hands of the skilled trainmen.

Increasingly desperate, the strikers resorted to force. They avoided attacks on personnel, but not on equipment. The preferred technique to immobilize freight trains was to "kill" the locomotive, generally by drenching the engine's furnace with water and removing its steam pipes. The railroads eventually would report that of the 598 engines in service, 434 were disabled this way during the strike.

Through the first several weeks of the walkout, the Missouri Pacific's general manager, H. M. Hoxie, maintained a strategy of what Taussig labeled "masterly inactivity." Hoxie knew that, given the Gould system's low reputation in the Southwest, any steps he took to break the strike would produce a negative public reaction. Beyond a few pro forma attempts to ram trains through the strikers' blockades, Hoxie allowed traffic to come to a standstill. He calculated that losses from the shutdown would soon be felt by nonstriking workers and the communities the system served, which would turn sentiment against the Knights. He was right.

IT WAS NOT long before the strike began inflicting real economic pain. With freight trains becalmed, the railroads laid off engineers, conductors, and station agents, turning them into unwilling martyrs to the strikers' cause. In St. Louis, merchants' shelves lay bare and brickworks and flour mills were shut down for lack of raw materials and fuel. Pressure to end the strike emerged from meetings on March 24 of merchants' organizations in St. Louis, which fretted over the prospect that the shutdown of freight service "will force merchants and manufacturers, who have prepared for the spring trade, into bankruptcy and enforce the discharge of large numbers of laborers" and "ruin such farmers as are dependent on prompt transportation of perishable products." The groups issued a "demand of the strikers to resume work or to keep out of the way and cease intimidating others who may be willing to work."

Plainly sentiment had shifted against the Knights. The day after the merchants' meetings, the Missouri Pacific again moved a freight train out of St. Louis. It carried fifty police officers, with an equal number stationed along the tracks. Within days, freight was moving again systemwide.

The strikers chose to view Hoxie, the Missouri's general manager, as their prime enemy, but the truth was that the person in charge all along was Gould. Early on he had given Hoxie explicit orders by cable: "You shall be fully supported in dealing with the strike. If shop-men at Sedalia, Denison and other places stop work, why not close the shops; and if trains are interfered with . . . suspend the whole pay-roll during the continuance of the strike."

Gould and Hoxie led the trusting Terence Powderly on a ruthless run-around. On March 27, Powderly sought a personal meeting with Gould, perhaps under the impression that Hoxie, who had refused to meet with the Knights, was exceeding his brief. The conversation lasted several hours, during which Powderly expressed frustration with the intransigence of the local Knights. A sympathetic Gould agreed to wire Hoxie with authorization to reemploy all striking workers, except those who had damaged railroad property. The wire included the line "We see no objection to arbitrating any differences between the employees and the company, past or future."

To Powderly this was a major concession on arbitration, a goal the Knights had sought from the first. Immediately he wired Irons, "Jay Gould has consented to our proposition for arbitration. . . . Order men to resume work at once."

But Powderly had been led astray by Gould's habit of speaking with the vagueness of an oracle, thereby reserving for himself perfect deniability. As soon as Powderly's cable to Irons was published in the newspapers, Gould pulled the rug out from under his feet. The railroad's position on arbitration was "unchanged," he told Powderly. All he had meant was that Hoxie could arbitrate if he wished; but he knew full well that Hoxie would not so wish. In another exchange of cables with Powderly, Gould refused to clarify his position any further.

In the meantime, thanks to Gould's bait and switch, traffic resumed throughout the Gould system. Irons issued one last broadside against Gould in a fruitless effort to rally the citizenry to the strikers' cause. Published in the newspapers of April 1, it asserted that Hoxie had broken his word by refusing to meet with the Knights of Labor or recognize any of its members as employees. "In short, after himself and Mr. Gould have conveyed the impression to the world that they are willing to settle, they refuse to settle. . . . How much is long-suffering labor to bear?" The statement cursed Gould for "his policy of duplicity and oppression. . . . If we can not be allowed to return to work the strike must go on."

But the strike was over, its participants reduced to abject demoralization. Hoxie simply ignored Gould's purported directive to reemploy strikers regardless of their affiliation with the Knights, presumably with Gould's assent. The only strikers accepted back to work were those who were unaffiliated with the Knights or agreed to abandon their membership.

Several weeks after the strike's end, Terence Powderly received an invitation from Jay Gould. One Sunday night the overawed grand master workman sat down with Gould in the same room where they had met before — when Gould had issued the wire that Powderly had innocently misinterpreted as a commitment to arbitration.

Powderly again showed himself to be unsuited to the role of muscular union leader so needed by the labor movement. Instead he was a throwback to the pre–Civil War era of mutual aid and educational brotherhoods. He was "essentially a pedagogue," the labor historian Norman Ware would conclude damningly, with "no interest in, nor equipment for, the major trade union job of negotiation."

According to Powderly's description of the encounter on that April Sunday, Gould caught him off-guard by complaining that the Knights of Labor had described him as a liar and a cheat. "You did me a grave injustice in charging me with these offenses, Mr. Powderly," Gould said. "I have learned to regard you as an honest man. I don't mind what Wall

Street men say of me, but when you make charges against me it hurts."
He told Powderly that his only ambition was to "build up a railroad system such as the world never saw before" and "to leave it as a heritage to
the American people." He denied that he ever treated his workers in bad
faith. "Make inquiries of workingmen, businessmen, and professional men
as to our treatment of our workmen," he said. "See if you don't find they
are as well treated as the employees of any other system."

Powderly knew he had no reason to trust Gould; after all, he had heard
directly from his own members of mistreatment and unfulfilled promises
from Gould's railroads and had experienced Gould's duplicity firsthand.
Nevertheless he marked Gould's "earnest, . . . pleasant, exceedingly out-
spoken" manner on this occasion. He turned away Gould's offer to provide him with rail transport and stenographers to conduct the inquiry,
telling Gould that were it to result in a positive report, "your enemies and
mine would say you had bought me up."

Powderly did conduct his own inquiry, but it was a wan affair. He
wrote later that he was "never able to make a thorough investigation,"
but did not specify why. He came away convinced, however, that the mistreatment of workers was chiefly the work of division foremen and local
bosses engaging in "petty schemes to oppress and humiliate the workers."
He sent a report on his findings to Gould via Sidney Dillon, Gould's right-
hand man, but never received even an acknowledgment in return.

Powderly was solicitous of Jay Gould to the last. He wrote that "watering of stocks, sharp practice in dealing in stocks, and oppression of workingmen and women employed by corporations are wrong," but "how far
Jay Gould entered into such transactions I do not know." Such practices,
after all, were rife among business leaders on Wall Street, and "except in
degree, he was no more to blame than they."

The truth, of course, is that Jay Gould was a master of all the practices
Powderly decried, and had invented quite a few of them himself. It is unlikely that any of his managers or their underlings treated their workers
in any manner of which Gould did not approve—perhaps tacitly in some
cases, but explicitly in others. That Gould managed his far-flung railroad

empire via intermediaries was certainly the case, but it could hardly excuse him of the behavior undertaken in his name. Only someone as preternaturally indulgent as Terence Powderly could fail to see that.

THE YEAR 1886 was both the high point of the Knights of Labor and the beginning of its mortal decline. The collapse of the strike, a severe blow in itself, was accompanied by two other disasters. One was a job action by Chicago meatpacking workers affiliated with the Knights. The packers had launched a successful strike on May 1 for an eight-hour day with no reduction in pay from the previous ten-hour schedule. But Powderly, as was his habit, refused to allow the strike to spread to noncompliant companies in the stockyards. The industry exploited his indulgence, and returned to a ten-hour day by the fall. It was as though Powderly had snatched defeat from the jaws of victory.

Public respect for the Knights was shaken further by the Haymarket affair, in which a dynamite bomb was exploded at a rally for the eight-hour day in Chicago's Haymarket Square on May 4. In the ensuing melee, seven police officers and four civilians were killed, some by police bullets fired in confusion. Eight purported anarchists were eventually tried and convicted in the affair, although the identity of the bomb thrower was never conclusively established. Among the accused, however, were two members of the Knights.

Time was passing the order by. In 1887 alone the Knights lost three hundred thousand members. Its representation among railroad workers had fallen away almost entirely, and Powderly and the other leaders tried to make up the loss by reconfiguring the order into a farmers' union, without notable success. Powderly's aversion to strikes made the organization seem increasingly irrelevant in a period of intensifying labor agitation. In 1893 he was voted out of office, but by then he was acknowledging to his associates that the order was "in the throes of dissolution."

Powderly had been correct in recognizing that he and his members had been engaged in a historic struggle during the strike of 1886, but he was wrong in denying that it was "the beginning of the war between capital and labor." The Great Southwest Railroad Strike was indeed the beginning of that war, as it applied to the railroads. The railroad tycoons read it as a sign of their firm grasp of power over labor. But the end of the strike was not the end of the war. The ultimate battle would be staged just a short time later. In the meantime, however, a new figure joined the pageant of railroad monarchs.

PART II

MORGAN AND HARRIMAN

8

THE RISE OF NED HARRIMAN

Edward harriman's life would have provided suitable grist for a novel by Horatio Alger, whose rags-to-riches tales reached the peak of their popularity during Harriman's lifetime. Like a stereotypical Alger hero, Harriman rose from raw (if genteel) poverty to the economic and social heights, reigning as one of the two most important railroad magnates in the nation, his only equal in influence over the economic life of the United States being J. Pierpont Morgan. For the last decade of the nineteenth century and the first of the twentieth, Harriman and Morgan would dominate American business like twin colossi.

As reckoned by the eminent railroad economist William Z. Ripley, Harriman at the peak of his power

> controlled fifty thousand miles of railway—more than there were in existence in the entire country at the close of the Civil War. He was a dominant factor in the inner circles of the greatest banking institutions.... Ramifications of his political power, Federal and State, extended to every quarter of the land. State and even national conventions took his orders. Members of Congress did his bidding. Laws were enacted at his will.

At the outset of his career he would be consistently underestimated by his rivals, invariably to their disadvantage; by the time of his death he would be reviled, perhaps unfairly, as a quintessential robber baron, labeled by his onetime friend Theodore Roosevelt as among the "malefactors of great wealth." Roosevelt was one of only two men "who ever dared to block his path," Ripley observed. The other was Pierpont Morgan, who would not go unscathed in the effort.

By combining a brilliant financial mind with an instinctive eye for operational efficiency, Harriman emerged as a new kind of figure in the railroad industry. Upon his death, after two decades as a business leader, he would be hailed by the distinguished investment banker Otto Kahn as "the last figure of an epoch." Harriman's railroads by then spanned the continent, bringing goods and riches to farmers, industrialists, and rural and urban dwellers. One of his roads, the Southern Pacific, had come to symbolize the economic oppression of the Gilded Age even before he took it over, however, having become known as "the Octopus" after the title of an allegorical novel by Frank Norris describing the railroad's stranglehold on California wheat farmers.

Ned Harriman, as he was known to associates, gathered friends not merely from among bankers, brokers, and business partners, but scientists and naturalists, for whom he sponsored a notable expedition to Alaska, one of the most remote corners of the known world. Among the unlikeliest such colleagues was the environmentalist and preservationist John Muir, who formed a lifelong bond with the railroad man after being invited to join Harriman on that expedition in 1899, when Harriman was in the very thick of his climactic contest with Morgan. In a slender volume of posthumous reminiscences, Muir drew on imagery from the natural world, the object of his and Harriman's shared devotion, to describe Harriman as an almost elemental force.

"He fairly revelled in heavy dynamical work and went about it naturally and unweariedly like glaciers making landscapes," Muir related, "cutting canyons through ridges, carrying off hills, laying rails and bridges over lakes and rivers, mountains and plains. . . . A great maker and harvester of crops of wealth, . . . he used his income as seed for other crops of world-wealth in succession." Fortunes, Muir wrote, "grew along his railroads like natural fruit." While engaged in business, Harriman retreated behind his

Frequently underestimated by his competitors but never for long, Edward H. Harriman brought a single-minded focus to the management of his railroads that made his empire the most expansive in the nation.

cold, deep-set eyes; settled amid friends and family, he exuded "the loving-kindness that, like hidden radium of the deep buried fires of ice-clad volcanoes, was ever glowing in his heart."

Contrary to Theodore Roosevelt's words of vilification, Harriman left a legacy of good works—among them thousands of acres of parkland do-

nated to the public, and the first Boys' Club in the world, founded in a
Tompkins Square basement to induce youths of the Lower East Side to
come off the streets by offering them sing-alongs and indoor athletics.
Perhaps his proudest achievement was saving California's Imperial Valley,
an agricultural breadbasket exporting $2 billion of produce a year, from
a catastrophic flood caused in 1905 by an ineptly designed canal cut into
the banks of the Colorado River. At Roosevelt's insistence, Harriman applied the vast resources of the Southern Pacific to the task of returning the
raging Colorado to its proper course after three previous efforts by others
had failed. He had taken a moment to give the go-ahead to his engineers'
$3 million restoration plan while standing at a window in the Southern
Pacific's Oakland headquarters, contemplating the smoldering wreckage
of San Francisco and his own rail yards, which had been devastated by
earthquake and fire on April 18, 1906, three days earlier.

Roosevelt pledged to reimburse Harriman for the rescue of the Imperial Valley, but Congress never made good on the promise. Nevertheless,
Harriman described the project to a newspaper correspondent years later
as "the best single bit of work ever done on my authority and responsibility." Shortly before his death in 1909 he visited the valley one last time.
While he inspected the levees his crews had erected under punishing conditions while utter ruin lurked on the horizon, an interviewer from the *Los
Angeles Examiner* asked him whether, given the government's refusal to
repay the huge expenditure, he did not regret his company's involvement.

"This valley was worth saving, wasn't it?" Harriman asked.

"Yes," the reporter replied.

"Then we have the satisfaction of knowing that we saved it, haven't
we?"

EDWARD HENRY HARRIMAN was born on February 25, 1848, in the Episcopal rectory of Hempstead, New York, where his father served as pastor of an impecunious Long Island congregation. The first Harriman in
America, Edward's great-grandfather William, had come to New York
from London in 1795 to establish himself in the West Indian trade. Only

one of his eight sons, Orlando, survived to adulthood. Like his father, Orlando thrived in business—until the Great Fire of 1835, which destroyed more than six hundred buildings in New York City, including Orlando's warehouses and all his inventory. He "never fully recovered," the Harriman family chronicle acknowledged, though he eventually rebuilt his business sufficiently to retire at least in relative comfort.

Orlando's eldest son and Edward Harriman's father, also named Orlando, compiled a distinguished academic record at Columbia University, but joined the Episcopal ministry instead of following his father into business like his younger brothers. He was ordained in 1841 and that same year married Cornelia Neilsen, the daughter of a well-connected New Jersey physician. Orlando's marriage was fortunate, for Cornelia proved a steady, secure, and moralistic influence on her offspring throughout the difficult years to follow, in which Orlando Harriman's churchly career traced a slow trajectory into penniless mediocrity. "Cold and austere in manner, . . . he lacked the magnetic personal charm which might have given popularity and success to a clergyman of much less ability," reported Edward Harriman's first biographer, George Kennan.

Orlando flitted from congregation to congregation in the New York suburbs, from Sing Sing (later known as Ossining) to Tarrytown to Hempstead to Staten Island. It was a dismal existence, complicated by the tendencies of poverty-stricken vestries to skimp on their pastor's wages. A pay dispute in 1850 prompted Orlando to abandon the East entirely, leaving Cornelia and their four children behind until he could lay down roots in California, which was then in the thick of gold rush euphoria. Answering an invitation from a parish in the state's mountainous North, he departed in midsummer, crossing the continent by way of Panama. There, exhausted by weeks of travel across the humid isthmus on foot and by mule, he fell ill and was delayed by a month.

Continuing his journey by sea, Orlando would read the burial service over seven fellow passengers felled by fever before reaching San Francisco. Upon landing he learned that his congregation, having heard nothing of him for weeks, had filled his job with another candidate. He spent a year as an itinerant preacher in the mining camps of California before finally returning East, broken and humbled. It would fall to his son Ned to carry the family name back to California, in triumph, more than a half century later.

Orlando resumed his career in New Jersey as what was known as a "semi-attached curate." As before, he was generally underpaid, sometimes cheated of his stipend entirely. The records of a Hoboken church state that Orlando was hired as rector in 1859 at $200 per year; seven years later, when he resigned, the congregation still owed him $374 in back pay, on which he "compromised at $250, payable in six months, with interest."

Over this period of Ned Harriman's life "hangs a heavy cloud," the contemporary financial chronicler C. M. Keys reported. It was made worse by the distance the family had fallen from the prosperous upbringing that Orlando and Cornelia had both experienced in their youth. Ned Harriman would seldom speak of this phase of his childhood; indeed, he would take pains later in life to eradicate the evidence, spending his own money to convert the down-at-the-heels rectory where he was born into a whitewashed three-story homestead, and refurbishing its chapel as a house of worship fashionable enough to attract congregants from the high society of metropolitan New York.

The family's lot improved a bit in the late 1860s, when Cornelia inherited a bequest allowing Orlando to retire. Now there was money to send Ned, their youngest son, to the private Trinity School in Manhattan, which the child reached every day by ferry from Jersey City. He was small for his age but "scrappy," indifferent to studies but nimble at athletics. Family lore had it that after two years at Trinity, fourteen-year-old Ned marched up to his father, threw down his books, and announced, "I am going to work."

Ned found employment with the Wall Street firm of D. C. Hays, earning five dollars a week as a "pad shover." This lowly job involved carrying from office to office notebooks on which the latest prices of securities and their bids were scribbled. From his earliest years in the financial district, Ned Harriman displayed that bifurcated personality John Muir would notice many years later. When engaged in business, he showed a frigid, uncompromising determination: "Not one man in a thousand found him genial, not one in ten thousand congenial, . . . a cold-blooded little cuss," was the recollection offered by an early acquaintance. Yet he must have shown some capacity for ingratiation, for by age twenty-two he had been elected a director of the sociable Travelers' Club and was a welcome participant in its Saturday-evening smokers. He joined the Tenth Company of the New York militia's Seventh Regiment, the "society" company, which placed him in close proximity to the politician and financier August Belmont and other rich, influential contacts. Still an undersized runt of a man, he nevertheless became known for his prowess at boxing, riding, shooting, and billiards—all skills sure to endear him to this set of aristocratic young bloods.

One thing on which almost all the early witnesses agree is that Harriman displayed a preternatural affinity for the stock market, along with an ambition to make the most of his talents. No average pad shover, he could keep in his head the intricate figures that others had to write down. More important, he had an instinct for the underlying value of securities that were viewed in the prevailing trading mentality of the Street merely as scraps of paper swirling about in search of the greater fool. In that environment, the man with foresight had a subtle advantage over his fellows. Harriman's compatriots had a hard time comprehending the secret of his trading success, chalking it up vaguely to his "extraordinary 'nose for money'."

Harriman rose quickly at D. C. Hays, becoming a managing clerk at the age of twenty. Two years later he touched his uncle Oliver, a successful businessman, for $3,000 to buy a seat on the New York Stock Exchange, and opened a third-floor office at the corner of Broad Street and Exchange Place.

It was the start of a career that would bring him to the heights of the most dynamic industry in America.

THOSE WHOM HARRIMAN brought into his circle as business associates seldom forgot their first encounter with him. For Otto Kahn, it happened on a hot summer afternoon in 1894, when he found himself sitting across his desk from a bantam-sized middle-aged man with an intense stare.

The German-born Kahn had joined the firm of Kuhn, Loeb & Co. only the year before, after having been trained in high finance at the London office of Deutsche Bank and following his wedding to Addie Wolff, the daughter of a Kuhn, Loeb partner—fulfilling a tradition in that banking firm, where partnerships were based not only on financial acumen but ties of blood and marriage. At twenty-seven, Kahn was dignified, cultured, and impeccably groomed. With his pomaded hair and a mustache waxed to two needle-sharp points, he was a living counterpart of the stately appointments of his office suite.

The man occupying the chair facing him was his opposite in almost every particular. He looked weary, rumpled, and pale, with a mustache that drooped like a wet mop and a visage that seemed to have every one of its nearly fifty years written in its creases. Nor was the business proposal he submitted for the firm's approval much more prepossessing, at least as it seemed at first. Kahn listened politely before stepping away to present the details to his partners, and presently returned to deliver their judgment to his visitor: They would pass. The man shuffled to the door, turned, and said, "I am dead tired this afternoon and no good any more. I'll tackle you again tomorrow, when I am fresh. I'm bound to convince you and get you to come along."

He did return, the next day and the day after that. Eventually the partners yielded to his "sheer persistency and the lucidity of his arguments," Kahn recalled years later. Kahn was not specific about the details of the visitor's business proposition when he related the encounter for his memoirs; but he did recall that "by the way, his judgment was right; the business turned out very well."

Harriman already had done some small business with Kahn's firm, which by 1894 knew him as an executive of the Illinois Central, a respected midwestern railroad, but this was the first opportunity Kahn had had to size him up. As in many more transactions to come, Harriman "simply brought to bear the stupendous force of his will and personality," Kahn would reflect. "Smooth diplomacy, the art of leading men almost without their knowing that they are being led, skillful achievement by winning compromise were not his methods. . . . His dominion was based on rugged strength, iron will, irresistible determination, indomitable courage, tireless toil [and] amazing intellect." One time when Kahn counseled him that he might win over his adversaries more by gentle persuasiveness than stiff-necked obstinacy, Harriman replied crisply, "I can work only in my own way."

Harriman had arrived on Wall Street "at a moment that was ripe for the making of men," wrote C. M. Keys. He had carried his pads from firm to firm while Gould, Fisk, Drew, and Vanderbilt were waging war over the Erie. "It was a time when men played the game with aces up their sleeves," Keys observed. But the door was opening for a new stamp of player.

In the period between the end of the Civil War and the Panic of 1873, the stock market had undergone a historic transition. The market's leaders were determined to give it an image of professional respectability, despite the private immorality of syndicate operators squeezing profits out of public investors gripped by enthusiasms that followed one upon the other—for gold, for iron, for railroad stocks. After the end of the Civil War, a torrent of capital flowed into Wall Street from Europe. This created fortunes for families like the Morgans and firms like Kuhn, Loeb, but required that they project impeccable integrity to secure the trusting patronage of British and German investors.

Yet Wall Street did not relinquish its unsavory reputation so easily. Just before Ned Harriman opened his office as a member of the New York Stock Exchange in 1870, Jay Gould and Jim Fisk had staged their scheme to corner gold—an enterprise that, once thwarted, produced a recession. The downturn, albeit brief, might have been bad enough to suffocate Harriman's young firm in its cradle had not his natural conservatism kept a solid financial foundation under his feet. All around him, less prudent brokerages failed, taking their customers' nest eggs with them and prompting Walt Whitman to curse "the depravity of the business classes of our country," which he felt had infected all levels of American government with "corruption, bribery, falsehood, maladministration." Whitman's moralistic soul was repelled: "In business, the one sole object is, by any means, pecuniary gain. . . . The best class we show, is but a mob of fashionably dress'd speculators and vulgarians."

Whitman's jeremiad was a reminder that the activities of Gould, Fisk, Drew, and Vanderbilt were still the bedrock of much of Wall Street's wealth. To many people inside the markets or observing from outside, the "integrity" of the new breed was simply a veneer hiding the venery beneath. Drew, after all, had cloaked his unscrupulousness in the garb of prayer and piety. The success he gained from such duplicity taught his followers a lesson not easily forgotten.

Efforts to erase Wall Street's image as a casino in which only insiders could win had stumbled over its recurrent scandals: the gold scheme, followed three years later by the Crédit Mobilier exposé, which had redefined the first transcontinental railroad not as a great enterprise deserving of national pride but as a shameful epic of greed, graft, and fraud.

For many denizens of Wall Street at the time, the measure of a man was not his honor or the value of his word, or even his net worth; it was the audacity of his scheming, regardless of whether the securities he was trading were legitimate, fabricated, or even his to sell. Typical was the career résumé delivered to reporters by Alden Stockwell, a cheerily corrupt manager of a steamship pool who deployed generous bribes to obtain government contracts, only to be bested in the end by the even more unscrupulous Jay Gould:

> When I first came to Wall Street I had $10,000, and the brokers called me "Stockwell." I scooped some profits, and it was "Mr. Stockwell." I got to dealing in a thousand shares at a time, and they hailed me as "Captain Stockwell." I went heavily into Pacific Mail, and folks lifted their hats to "Commodore Stockwell." Then one day Jay Gould came along, smash went Pacific Mail, and I went with it. They did not call me "Commodore Stockwell" after that, but "that red-headed son of a bitch from Ohio."

Harriman knew he was launching his career without the advantages enjoyed by his wellborn and well-capitalized competitors. A friend recalled years later that at the very birth of his career as a stockbroker, Harriman had pulled a hundred-dollar bill from his pocket. "I can't lose much, anyhow," he remarked; "that's all I've got." But he proved adept at attracting influential customers, if not through personal charm then through his intellect and determination to serve them as a broker. Among his first major clients was a noted speculator and partner of Cornelius Vanderbilt's named Dick Schell, an obese man who hated to climb stairs. Schell offered to send Harriman enough business to cover his rent if he would only move his office to the ground floor. Harriman did so, earning the patronage of Schell as well as his three brothers, who were the presidents of two banks and the New York Central Railroad.

Ned Harriman also inherited his father's talent for marrying up. In 1879 his Wall Street friend George Clark had introduced him to his wife's cousin, who was visiting New York from her home in Ogdensburg, a city hard by the Saint Lawrence River in the farthest reaches of upstate New York. Mary Williamson Averell was three years Harriman's junior. She was not a notable beauty, with heavy-lidded eyes and a firm, even severe, mouth. But almost immediately she and Ned formed a deep bond that would last for life. Like her mother-in-law, she brought her family a stability and moral tone that her husband deeply cherished. "Any biography of Mr. Harriman which omits his family life misses the point and loses the light of the whole story," reported one of Harriman's business associates after Mary died in 1932. "It was not unusual for him, in the midst of transactions of such importance as to make men dizzy from concentration, to stop in order to speak a word on the telephone or send a message to Mrs. Harriman. . . . His attitude toward her was more than devotion. It was profound admiration, respect, and unfailing attention and courtesy."

The Averell family influenced the direction of Harriman's life in another way, by introducing him into the railroad business. The connection was first made at the couple's wedding on September 10, 1879. Arriving at the Ogdensburg station for their honeymoon trip, they came upon a special train ordered by the bride's father, with E. H. HARRIMAN painted on the engine's side. But that was just the beginning.

HARRIMAN'S FATHER-IN-LAW, William H. Averell, had been appointed a director and receiver of a decrepit 118-mile railroad hugging the New York side of the Canadian border. The Ogdensburg & Lake Champlain had been chartered in 1845 to carry coal and goods east to Boston in competition with railroads running from New York City. This was a hopeless dream. The line had declared bankruptcy three times by 1879 and was deeply in the red when Averell named Harriman to the board and asked him to scare up new financing.

Over the next year, Harriman and his Wall Street friend Stuyvesant Fish achieved a near-miraculous resuscitation by restructuring the debt to reduce its interest rate to 6 percent from 8 percent and folding the crushing arrears on the road's preferred share dividends into the 6 percent bond. An improvement in the upstate economy did the rest, and by 1880 the line had swung from a loss of about $150,000 to a profit of $61,000. It was Harriman's first experience of rescuing a railroad, but it would not be his last.

Fish was the most highborn of all Harriman's young friends, and his closest companion during these years. His grandfather Nicholas Fish had been a mainstay of the Federalist camp during the Revolutionary War and a close friend of Alexander Hamilton's; his grandmother a descendant of Peter Stuyvesant, the last Dutch governor of what was known as New Netherland before that colony was ceded to the British and its largest city, New Amsterdam, was rechristened as New York. Stuyvesant Fish's father, Hamilton, had been a governor of New York and United States senator, and had served in the Grant administration until 1877, when he handed in his portfolio with the inauguration of Rutherford B. Hayes.

Harriman and Fish made almost as unlikely a pair as Jay Gould and Jim Fisk; where Harriman was thin, short, and dark, sporting his unruly black mustache, Stuyvesant Fish was "tall, blond, leonine," with a luxuriant set of handlebar whiskers. Their family lifestyles could not have been more different: "Mrs. Harriman was busy having babies, Mrs. Fish busier grooming herself to succeed Mrs. William Waldorf Astor as social Empress of New York." A "big-hearted, hand-shaking chap whom nobody feared much but whom everybody loved," Fish provided the polish and charisma that Harriman lacked. The *New York Times,* stalking Fish as he strolled down Wall Street one day in 1906, reported, "It is a common thing to hear men say, 'See that tall man there with the broad shoulders? That's Stuyvesant Fish.' E. H. Harriman, too, is a frequent stroller afoot through the downtown crowds, but he goes unrecognized. He is too close to the average type to be marked."

The Ogdensburg refinancing cemented the early friendship of Harriman and Fish. Their next exploit concerned an even more decrepit specimen of railroad.

The Lake Ontario Southern was another artifact of the dashed ambitions of that overoptimistic railroad-building era. Conceived as a 155-mile connection linking the bituminous coal region of western Pennsylvania and Canadian grain growers on the northern shore of Lake Ontario, by 1881 the line extended only 34 miles south from Sodus Bay, a harbor on the south shore of the lake, to Stanley, in New York's Finger Lakes region. Its sole virtue was that it intersected both the Pennsylvania and New York Central railroads, which made it an appropriate target for acquisition by one or the other. But it was "badly managed and unprofitable," and so unprepossessing—with little more than "two crippled locomotives, two passenger cars, and seven freight cars" to its name—that it had been ignored by both.

The Lake Ontario Southern would teach Harriman, at the outset of his railroad career, two related lessons. One was that the greatest profits were to be made in promising yet undervalued properties; the Lake Ontario Southern, Harriman would recall later, "had great strategic value which nobody seemed to recognize." The other was that investments in the capacity and capabilities of a property would yield exponential returns.

Harriman and Fish bought into the line with Silvanus J. Macy, the scion of a family of New York oil traders who owned properties in the Sodus Bay region. What brought the obscure line to their attention is unknown, although Harriman's brother-in-law William Averell, who lived in nearby Rochester, was an investor. Harriman, Fish, and Macy promptly connived to buy out the handful of existing shareholders by naming a

Wellborn Stuyvesant Fish brought Harriman into the railroad business and gave their partnership the polished image that Harriman lacked, but eventually faded into his partner's shadow.

price at which they would either sell their own shares or buy up the others. After Macy delivered a discouraging report on the road's earnings and prospects at a board of directors meeting in October 1883, the shareholders duly bailed out. The new owners improved the line's physical condition, built a grain elevator at Sodus Bay to encourage more cross-lake shipping from Canadian farmers, and renamed the railroad the Sodus Bay & Southern. In truth, their aim was not so much to turn the railroad into a profitable concern—a goal they failed to accomplish in their nine months of full ownership—but to dress it up for sale to the Pennsylvania or New York Central.

Harriman ruthlessly played each of the potential buyers against the other, bringing them both to the table in 1884. To the Pennsylvania, he talked up the virtue of extending its Northern Central line to Sodus Bay, which he promoted as "the best harbor on the lake" and therefore a prime outlet for Pennsylvania coal headed for Canada. Meanwhile, he warned William Vanderbilt and his New York Central partners of the Pennsylvania's interest. "I knew that if I put it in good physical condition," Harriman recalled, "the Pennsylvania Railroad would jump at a chance to buy it, in order to get an outlet on the lake; and that the New York Central would be equally anxious to buy it, in order to keep its rival out."

Vanderbilt moved first, buying a one-month option expiring on July 1, with the right of renewal. The Pennsylvania bid higher for the road a few days later, but now had to wait for its rival's option to expire. Vanderbilt unwisely delayed until the last moment to signal his intention to renew the option, and when that day arrived, Harriman strategically arranged to be out of his office. This enabled him to let the Vanderbilt option lapse so he could close the deal with the Pennsylvania, at a large profit.

Harriman had established himself as a resourceful railroad financier and a nimble negotiator with an instinctive understanding that investing in a railroad infrastructure was necessary for turning a profit. The "importance of proper physical condition in a transportation property," he would recall, "was a lesson . . . I have never forgotten."

But he was still a small player in a burgeoning industry. Thanks to his friendship with Stuyvesant Fish, that was about to change.

9

THE FIRST SKIRMISH

THE ILLINOIS CENTRAL had been a storied railroad for nearly three decades before Stuyvesant Fish brought Ned Harriman into the company.

The IC owed its existence to Stephen A. Douglas. The so-called Little Giant of Illinois politics would secure for himself a permanent place in the history books years later as Abraham Lincoln's adversary in a landmark series of debates during a contest for the US Senate. But as a congressman in the early 1840s and a senator after 1847, he was better known as the proponent of a plan to fund the construction of railroads in Illinois and other prairie states through grants of federal lands along the rights of way. The Illinois Central was the first railroad financed by a method that would reach its culmination, financially and geographically, with the meeting of the Union Pacific and Central Pacific at Promontory in 1869.

Construction of the IC began in 1851 and proceeded at a breakneck pace. The road was an unusual venture in many ways. For one thing, it covered a part of the country that was as yet largely untracked: When the first rails of the Illinois were being laid, nearly two-thirds of the nation's nine thousand miles of track were still located in the nine New England and mid-Atlantic states. Also, instead of following the expansion trajectory of American commerce from east to west, like most other trunk lines, the IC ran north-south. Its route bisected Illinois like a spine of iron reaching from Chicago all the way south to Cairo, at the confluence of the Mississippi and Ohio Rivers. A second trunk line split off at Centralia and ran like the left arm of a Y to the northwestern corner of the state, terminating at a point just across the Mississippi from Dubuque, Iowa.

From its inception, the IC was a source of statewide pride and anticipation. Newspaper editorials expected the road to liberate Illinois from the troublesome uncertainties of riverborne commerce: "The road will be a commercial avenue which will never freeze over or dry up . . . There will be no shoals, sand bars, or snags," stated the *Tri-Weekly Advance* of Shawneetown, on the Ohio River about a hundred miles upstream from Cairo, in an article reflecting the seasonal complaints of local barge operators.

Drumming up public support was important for the project, but its promoters' main challenges were scarcities of capital and labor. The first was especially acute at the start of construction, when American securities were facing one of their periodic bear markets in Europe and skepticism about the new road's management was rife among European investors.

Then there was the shortage of manpower. As the railroad industry extended its reach beyond the Mississippi, the bidding for experienced construction hands became increasingly ferocious. Fewer than one-fourth of the necessary crews for the IC could be found in Illinois, so recruiters were dispatched to eastern ports with promises of as much as a dollar in commission for every worker they could grab fresh off the boats, luring brawny Scandinavian, German, Polish, and Irish immigrants into the Midwest. Advertisements placed in East Coast newspapers offered wages of $1.25 per twelve-hour day to willing workers, supplemented by a one-way fare into the hinterland by rail and steamboat, a passage valued at $475. Two years of steady work were guaranteed in "a healthy climate," a promise that glossed over the cholera epidemics that periodically swept across the prairie.

The IC's advertisements offered laborers a new life after the railroad work was completed, in a region "where land can be bought cheap, and for fertility is not surpassed in any part of the Union." They declared a preference for "men with families"—for two reasons. First, the road was fearful of the brawling that regularly erupted in all-male construction camps, interfering with the smooth progress of the work. Second, the Illinois

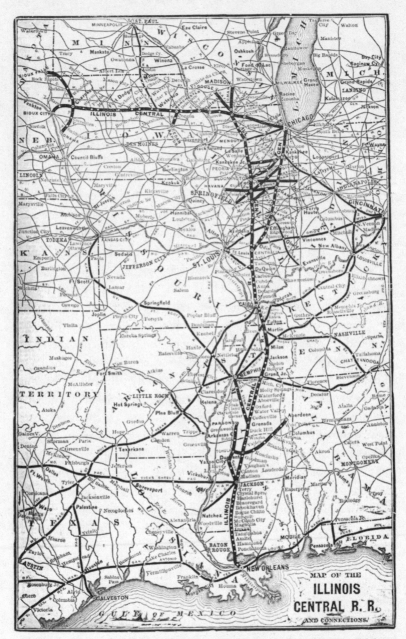

Under Edward Harriman and Stuyvesant Fish, the Illinois Central expanded from its home state across Iowa and upgraded its southern link to New Orleans.

Central, like the transcontinental lines reaching across the prairie, knew that to grow the crops and generate the trading demand that produced profits for the railroad, the region's vacant parcels of arable land had to be tilled by productive settlers—and spouses and children all represented sources of free labor.

And so the Illinois Central became another employer of the growing army of boomers, those itinerant professional track-layers and engineers who built the midwestern railroads with their brawn and brains. Its initial wage offer of $1.25 a day proved insufficient to keep its employees from jumping to better-paying roads. By 1853 the going rate was more than $1.37, and by 1855 ordinary laborers were earning $1.50, skilled hands even more.

Despite these obstacles, the main line of the IC was completed in only five years. In 1856, when its original charter was fulfilled, the system extended 705 miles, making it the longest railroad in the world—far longer than the 483-mile Erie, which upon its completion had been dubbed "the work of the age" and hailed by none other than Charles Francis Adams, its harshest critic, as "a monument . . . of engineering skill."

The Illinois Central met all the expectations of the citizens it was built to serve. William K. Ackerman, who had joined the line as a clerk shortly after its charter was issued, recalled riding in November 1854 on the first train to pass through southern Illinois (a region known even now as "Little Egypt"). He wrote of the throngs in which "the 'Egyptians' turned out to witness the novel sight, to them, of a locomotive engine and train of cars."

They lined the track on both sides at every station, the men dressed in their snuff-colored jeans, and the women with gaudy-colored calicoes, check-aprons, and big sun-bonnets. They stood dumb with amazement. Many of them looked as though they had come out 'between the shakes' of fever and ague.

The IC became the state's biggest industrial enterprise. Among its employees in the mid-1850s was a lanky lawyer transplanted from Kentucky named Abraham Lincoln, who possessed an annual pass for travel over its route; scarcely a decade later, the Illinois Central would carry his body part of the way from Chicago to Springfield, on the final leg of the slain president's funeral journey.

European money flowed into the railroad's shares and bonds. By 1854, half of the IC's shares were held by English investors, more than a fourth by the Dutch. Over time, trade in IC paper would enrich not only those overseas investors but their American agents—including Pierpont Morgan and Edward Harriman.

IN 1883, THE year before he sold the refurbished Sodus Bay & Southern Railway to the Pennsylvania Railroad, Harriman had joined the Illinois Central as a director. While he had dabbled in railroads before, this was his introduction to the industry on a major scale and his first experience as an operating executive. And he owed this lucky break to his old friend Stuyvesant Fish.

Fish's history with the Illinois had begun in 1871, when through family connections he secured a job as secretary to the line's president in Chicago. He left the railroad a year later to take a Wall Street job, but returned as a director in 1877. From that perch he was well positioned to throw business Harriman's way.

The first big deal landed in 1881, with a large issue of IC bonds to finance its extension south to New Orleans. At the urging of Fish, whose job included overseeing the railroad's securities, Harriman bought a $2.5 million block of the bonds. The transaction turned into a riskier venture than Harriman anticipated, for on July 2, just after the sale closed, President James A. Garfield was shot by a mentally unbalanced drifter named Charles Guiteau. The assassination attempt threw the American capital markets into a swoon that lasted until Garfield's death on September 19, eighty days later, and the inauguration of his vice president, Chester A. Arthur. Harriman had no choice but to hold on to the bonds in a weak market—his firm kept afloat, it was said, by "the assistance of rich friends"—until eventually he was able to unload the securities at a profit.

The Illinois Central was an ideal training ground for Harriman, and Fish the ideal partner, for Fish was pushing the line's cautious management toward more energetic expansion south and west. Needing an ally on the board, Fish orchestrated Harriman's election as a director in 1883, knowing that his friend—if not many others on Wall Street—endorsed his goal. With IC shares in a slump thanks to investors' misgivings about Fish's plans, Harriman became an aggressive buyer. "It's the best line in the country," Harriman assured his Wall Street contacts. "It won't cost us a cent to carry; the 'shorts' will carry it for us." He was right; when the investors who had bet on the continued decline in the stock's price threw in the towel, the shares coasted higher.

Fish understood that the key to the IC's success prior to the Civil War had been its breakout beyond the Illinois state line. Before the war, the IC had begun racing its Chicago-based rivals into Iowa and soon reached clear across that state to the Missouri River. After the war, the South beckoned even more urgently. Dixie's entire transport system lay in ruins —"twisted rails, burned ties, gutted depots, destroyed bridges, and lost or dilapidated rolling stock scattered from Louisiana to Virginia." The journalist Whitelaw Reid, who accompanied Chief Justice Salmon P. Chase on a reconnaissance mission across the blasted landscape in May 1865, reported landing in the harbor of Beaufort, North Carolina, and searching in vain for transport off the waterfront. Finally a commander of the Union occupation force provided the party with "a train composed of a wheezy little locomotive and an old mail agent's car, with all the windows smashed out and half the seats gone."

Bereft of resources by war and Reconstruction, the South was slow to rebuild its rail system. Ten years after the war's end, there was still no rail link between Cairo and New Orleans. The nearly six-hundred-mile gap tormented shippers and growers. As long as it remained unfilled, goods from Louisiana were "shipped by steamboats to St. Louis, trans-shipped up the Illinois River by smaller steamboats, trans-shipped again to canal-boats, and reached Chicago by the Michigan Canal," as William H. Osborn, a former president of the IC, informed his board after touring the region. This meant delays of a month or six weeks, he reported. Worse, the cost of packing and repacking the cargo was immense and "the waste and shrinkage [i.e., theft] was serious." In 1872 the IC decided to invest $5 million in an extension beyond Cairo, a move considered unimaginably risky at the time. Instead, Osborn would boast in 1882, the extension turned the Illinois Central into "the most important north and south trunk line in the world."

But Stuyvesant Fish was convinced there was more to do. With Harriman, he represented the new management style of a line that had been the "bluest of blue chips in a region where the ledgers of many roads bled a steady stream of red." Older investors cherished the road's traditionally conservative approach, which it maintained even in its expansion into Iowa, and the policies of these two easterners with even more ambitious expansion plans unnerved them. Samuel Sloan, an upstate New York railroad man who earlier had helped bring Pierpont Morgan into the Albany & Susquehanna fray against Gould and Fisk, had no more taste for the new man than he had had for those buccaneers. "I don't like that Harriman," he confided to a friend. "He and 'Stuyv' Fish are going to get Osborne in trouble with the Illinois Central, if he don't look out."

This uneasiness was widespread on Wall Street, where bankers and investors were accustomed to the IC's penny-pinching tradition of plowing surplus profits into healthy dividends for shareholders. They struggled to accept Harriman's aggressive borrowing to finance expansionary investments, and feared that profits might be harder to come by just as interest obligations rose. Harriman shrouded the IC balance sheet in mystery — its declared assets seemed to have nearly quintupled in his first year as a director, without explanation. Examining an entry labeled "cash and other assets," the *Commercial and Financial Chronicle*, then the weekly bible of Wall Street, asked, "How much of it is cash, and how much something else? . . . In all these facts, is there not evidence of some lack of the conservative spirit so long dominant in the company's affairs?"

From 1883 through 1889, Fish and Harriman increased the Illinois Central's mileage by about a thousand miles. Its physical condition was better than ever before in its history. While millions were spent on this expansion and improvement, the railroad's financial health actually improved. "Somehow or other," recounted Otto Kahn, "it never had bonds for sale except in times when bonds were in great demand; it never borrowed money except when money was cheap and abundant; periods of storm and stress ever found it amply prepared and fortified; its credit was of the highest." This was evidence of Harriman's instinctive handle on the financial markets.

As part of their expansion program, Fish and Harriman brought the venerable Wabash, St. Louis & Pacific into the Illinois Central after the Wabash failed in 1884, and then added the Mississippi & Tennessee, which fed traffic into the IC from Memphis. They founded the Chicago, Madison & Northern Railroad to give the Illinois its first wholly owned connection into Chicago, relieving it of the $200,000 a year it had been paying to lease a right-of-way into the city. Harriman emerged as a master strategist, exploiting the collapse of Jay Gould's rail empire to claim the Champaign, Havana & Western from the wreckage of receivership in 1886.

The crowning achievement of the IC's new management came on October 29, 1889. To the citizens of Illinois, it was the moment that cemented the state's position as the keystone of the national railroad grid. The place was a crossing over the Ohio River near Cairo, at the very southern tip of the state.

Presidents of the Illinois Central had dreamed of building a fixed span across the Ohio for two decades. Rival lines had managed to bridge the river at Louisville and Cincinnati as early as 1870, but the IC's passengers were still required to disembark from their trains and shippers to offload their freight before crossing between Illinois and Kentucky; all then transferred to ferries for the trip to the opposite shore. This placed the Illinois Central in a hopelessly uncompetitive position for traffic with the South. Economic slumps, political disagreements, and internal squabbling had stood in the bridge project's path, but finally Stuyvesant Fish and Edward Harriman had cleared the obstacles away. Now the project was ready for service. Twelve boxlike steel trusses resting on ten stone piers stretched more than ten thousand feet across the river, forming the longest steel bridge in the world.

A gala atmosphere reigned that Tuesday morning in Cairo, where the hotels had filled up with railroad officials, journalists, engineers, and spectators. The Illinois Central tracks were jammed with the Pullman cars and carriages that had brought dignitaries to the celebration. At 9 a.m., nine connected Mogul locomotives, each weighing seventy-five tons, began inching their way across the span. Harriman and Fish stood shoulder to shoulder with the crew in the cab of the lead engine, as the throngs watched expectantly to see if the span would hold fast under more than seven hundred tons of rolling iron. It did so with ease. A cacophony of steam whistles greeted the engines when they reached the Kentucky shore, and pandemonium erupted in town.

Fish, as the senior executive on hand, received most of the credit for the railroad's achievement. But Harriman, then the road's vice president, was its mastermind. His achievement was made even more notable by the low expectations onlookers had for him. "When Harriman had first joined the official family of the Illinois Central many had considered him little more than a rather ruthless junior-sized copy of Jay Gould, the notorious wrecker of railroads," observed the IC's historian, John F. Stover. "But soon he was showing a remarkable grasp of the problems involved in the operation and fiscal management of a major midwestern line." What Harriman learned at the Illinois Central he would use to great effect when faced with the more daunting challenges ahead.

THE OPENING OF the Ohio River bridge in 1889 was Harriman's most notable accomplishment as a member of the road's management in the 1880s. But in terms of his early career as a railroad tycoon, his greatest triumph had been notched two years earlier, five hundred miles from Cairo, when he outmaneuvered Pierpont Morgan in what became known in Illinois Central lore as the battle of Dubuque.

The conflict originated in a deal that looked good at the time it was made, but had long since outlived its usefulness. During the Illinois Central's expansion into Iowa, it had leased the 143-mile Dubuque & Sioux City Railroad in 1867 for a rent equal to 36 percent of the Dubuque's annual gross revenues. The lease remained profitable for more than a decade. Immigrants were pouring into Iowa and points west, Sioux City was the main transfer point for supplies crossing the Missouri River, and no other railways existed in the northern half of the state. Freight and passenger rates were gratifyingly high and seemed to be on a permanent trajectory higher.

By 1885, however, traffic had stagnated. Railroad mileage in Iowa had more than quintupled to 7,509 miles, most of it belonging to sixteen railroads competing with the Illinois Central. Many of these rivals offered shorter routes to Chicago and the East, and rates were plummeting. The IC was losing about $200,000 a year on the Dubuque lease, not including the thousands more it was obligated to spend on upkeep. The IC felt that the Dubuque could be made vastly more efficient and profitable if it expanded its branch network. But the Dubuque's shareholders were disinclined to spend the money themselves on new branches and the IC was unwilling to make the expenditure, given that its investment would yield a handsome return chiefly for the Dubuque's owners. A decision point loomed just over the horizon in 1887, when the original twenty-year lease expired and the Illinois would have to decide whether to abandon the lease or renew it for another two decades.

To Harriman the solution was clear: The IC must buy the Dubuque outright. It took him two years to bring his fellow directors around to the notion, but once they did so, placing the negotiations in Harriman's hands, he faced another obstacle: The Dubuque's shareholders had sensed a windfall in the offing. Their agent was J. Pierpont Morgan, who offered the Illinois Central the straightforward choice between renewing the lease at a sharply higher rent or buying out the Dubuque shares at par, or $100. That was a huge premium for shares that then hovered in the low $60s.

Morgan may have thought he had cornered the Illinois Central into capitulating to the lease renewal on his terms, but in Harriman he suddenly found himself confronting a Wall Street type he was unaccustomed to meeting as an equal. Morgan looked down on Harriman as someone not of his milieu, or indeed of his class, as his son-in-law Herbert L. Satterlee recalled years later. Pierpont knew Harriman only as someone "who

had previously been a broker in New York City and now was in the investment business executing orders for the Illinois Central people and
others." This judgment amply conveyed the condescension of the elite
financier, who made decisions in the name of his rich clientele, for the
menials who shuffled paper on orders from their betters. Morgan at this
stage of his career already commanded an army of bankers poised to do his
bidding; Harriman, sniffed Satterlee, "did everything himself . . . He was
not a 'clubman' and had very few friends."

Morgan and Harriman both embarked on buying sprees in the
Dubuque. Morgan's firm, Drexel, Morgan & Co., ended up with proxies
for 32,680 shares, a clear majority. Harriman directly owned about 15,000.
As 1886 drew to a close, no more shares could be acquired by either side,
for with aggressive buying having pushed the Dubuque's price all the way
to $100, the remaining shareholders were hanging on to their stock in
anticipation of a lush payday. By mid-December the trading was so meager that the Dubuque's shares were no longer even quoted on the stock
exchange.

This was the situation as the date of the Dubuque's annual meeting,
February 14, approached. But a few days in advance, Harriman unveiled
the fruits of his painstaking work ethic: He had discovered a provision in
Iowa law that prohibited voting shares by proxy. The rule would invali-
date all Morgan's votes at a stroke. When Harriman appeared in person
at the annual meeting, his shares were the only ones that could legally be
voted. The meeting accordingly elected a slate of directors composed of
Harriman and three confederates. Morgan's agents marched out in high
dudgeon and elected their own slate, comprising Morgan himself, James
A. Roosevelt (an uncle of the future president Theodore Roosevelt), and
three other associates. The fate of the Dubuque seemed to be up in the
air. "There is no doubt," observed the *Commercial and Financial Chronicle*,
"but that the final adjudication of the matter will be made by the courts."

That was true, up to a point. The litigation dragged on for two
months, but it was obvious from the outset that in legal terms Harriman
held much the stronger hand. The pressure to settle became inexorable in
late March, after the Illinois Central announced it would terminate the

Dubuque lease, thus leaving that railroad bereft of any source of traffic to its east. The truth was that the IC and the Dubuque needed each other, but the Dubuque's need was the greater. Harriman's offer to buy the Morgan shares at $80, delivered as an ultimatum on April 2, looked almost magnanimous; it was below the $100 that Morgan had demanded, but well above the $60 that seemed to be the natural value of the shares. The Dubuque accepted the deal on April 7, and the railroad passed into the hands of the Illinois Central.

Morgan's acolytes would depict the battle of Dubuque as an assault by the giant Illinois Central on the defenseless shareholders of a small railroad, with Pierpont himself serving merely as the agent of those abused investors. But the ramifications were more personal than philosophical or financial, for Harriman's spectacular victory was one of the very few counted against Morgan even at that early point in his financial career. As such it left Morgan with a bitter taste that would not be easily cleansed.

To Morgan, Harriman's maneuverings were not the acts of a Wall Street gentleman. The incident "made Pierpont very angry," Satterlee recalled. "His own way of doing business and the method to which he was accustomed in others had been for competitors to bid against each other," as though on a level playing field in which price was the only metric. Instead, the battle of Dubuque struck Pierpont as "a recurrence of the Jay Gould method of resorting to lawyers and to technicalities." The ground was shifting beneath his feet. The episode, Satterlee judged, gave Morgan "a prejudice against Harriman that kept him in later years from cooperating with him when it might have been better had he done so."

This was a wise judgment by Satterlee, and it would be proven true again and again. Pierpont's next encounter with Harriman would be even more irksome than the first, for it would strike at the heart of his ambition to be the "Bismarck" of the railroads. Just as the ironfisted Prussian minister had completed his plan to create a unified Germany out of a patchwork of duchies in 1871, Morgan envisioned himself as the only man in America with the stature and trustworthiness to turn a collection of squabbling companies permanently on the edge of insolvency into a cohesive and thriving industry. That ambition gave rise to Morgan's creation of a concept known as the "community of interests" and the tactics that became known as Morganization.

Industrialists and economists would debate whether these innovations stabilized American industry or sapped its energy. What was clear, however, was that they would revolutionize the structure of American business and, eventually, draw to Morgan the unwelcome attention of a new breed of Washington reformer.

10

A COMMUNITY OF INTERESTS

Two months after Morgan's defeat in the battle of Dubuque, a congressional commission began examining the same problems he had detected in the railroad industry's structure and behavior.

On the surface, the United States Pacific Railway Commission had a narrow charge — to determine the financial condition of the railroads built with government loans and their ability to repay that money. More precisely, the commission's target was the Union Pacific. That road was not only the best known and most expensive of the land-grant railroads, but the one in the most parlous economic straits. In the course of its inquiry, however, the commission would lay bare everything that had gone wrong with the industry in the years since the meeting at Promontory.

The UP's chief problems were excessive competition and plunder by insiders, which left the road physically decrepit, financially crippled, and under the control of a hostile Congress disinclined to give it a break. Had the railroad's senior bonds been held by private individuals, the commission reported, they would have been "almost valueless." The government had powers of foreclosure not available to individuals, the commission observed, but this step would merely give the taxpayers ownership of a wasting asset, "a result which can not be desired by any intelligent legislator." As was observed in 1885 by the railroad's government directors (put in place ostensibly to safeguard the federal investment in the road), the Union Pacific had been endowed with a "perfect and absolute monopoly" and "princely" profits, yet its finances were a shambles. The fact that the company had collected enough revenue to float $40 million in securities and pay out more than $26.6 million in dividends on its shares, yet still had not the means to redeem its government debt, pointed inescapably to the conclusion that "the past history of the company appears now like a travesty upon corporation management."

The government directors and the commission together expressed the hope that conditions henceforth would be different under Charles Francis Adams Jr., who had been appointed president of the Union Pacific three years earlier, in 1884.

Seen through one lens, Adams seemed miscast to take over the railroad's management. The UP was a huge enterprise in a complicated industry, but Adams had no operational experience as a business manager at any level (though he had served on the UP board since 1882.) The co-author of the muckraking classic *Chapters of Erie* (parts of which were written by his brother Henry), it was Adams who years earlier had predicted that the UP would end up as "two rusty streaks of iron on an old road-bed" if speculators continued to manipulate the road's finances under the nose of Congress. (This description was commonly paraphrased as "two streaks of rust.")

Critical challenges faced the Union Pacific in 1884. The speculative piracy of which Adams warned had come to pass, and worse was in store. Jay Gould was gone, which was a good thing; but he had left the road desperately ill-equipped to meet the looming maturity of the government loans that had financed construction through to the driving of the golden spike. The initial installment of debt, calculated at more than $50 million in principal and interest, was scheduled to come due on November 1, 1895. Whatever sentiment might have existed in Congress to forgive the loans or take repayment at a discount had evaporated with the Crédit Mobilier disclosures, for a failure by the government to demand payment of principal and interest in full would look like an endorsement of flagrant criminality. In 1878 Congress had attempted to anticipate the maturity deadline by passing the Thurman Act, which created a fund to sequester all payments the government made for official use of the railroad, along

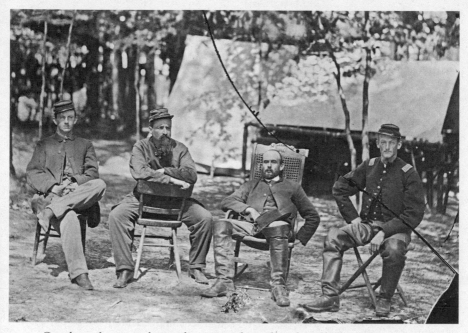

Grandson of one president and great-grandson of another, Charles Francis Adams, second from right in this photo taken with fellow officers during the Civil War, was the railroad industry's first muckraker. But he failed miserably when he tried to apply what he had learned about railroad management as president of the Union Pacific in the 1880s.

with a portion of the UP's annual profits. The expectation was that the fund would grow enough by 1895 to cover the debt repayment, but it was a forlorn hope. By that point, it now seemed clear, the fund would hold only about $17.6 million.

Unless the government debt could be renegotiated and the resulting freed-up capital applied to refurbish its physical condition, the Union Pacific would be unable to meet the competitive challenges of the coming decades.

Seen through that lens, Adams could be considered almost the perfect man for the job. He was Gould's polar opposite, unsullied by a record of speculation and looting. Not only was his personal character unassailable, but he had devoted much of his career to exposing the very piracy that had brought the railroad industry to bankruptcy and disrepute. He seemed to be the new broom the UP needed at that moment.

No one felt more strongly about his suitability than Adams himself. "With a good deal of natural confidence in myself, I looked upon assuming the management of a great railway system . . . as the legitimate outcome of what had, in my case, gone before," he would recall years later. "I was simply playing my game to a finish. I was not yet fifty, and I did not want to break off and go into retirement in mid-career."

He was not unaware of the pitfalls ahead. The Union Pacific "was in bad repute, heavily loaded with obligations, odious in the territory it served; . . . A day of general reckoning was at hand." Shortly before taking office as president, Adams made a reconnaissance trip along the line with his fellow director Fred Ames, the son of Oliver Ames. They found conditions to be "in a shocking bad way," he would recall. The line's "service was demoralized, it had just backed down before its employees in face of a threatened strike, and it was on the verge of bankruptcy."

Despite these challenges, Adams remained convinced to the end of his days that his scheme for renewal via renegotiating the government debt had been "well-conceived [and] entirely practicable." The only real flaw, he acknowledged, was his own weakness of character. "Unfortunately for myself, I lacked the clean-cut firmness to adhere to it. Had I only done so, I should have achieved a great success, and been reputed among the ablest men of my time." Adams had overestimated himself, but also underestimated the challenges he faced. He accepted the presidency of the Union Pacific filled with good intentions and ambition; but the six and a half years he spent in that post would be the most miserable of his life.

CALLING THE UP's reputation with its prairie customers "odious" was a charitable way of looking at things. Railroads across the nation were anything but popular among their customers, but the Union Pacific was especially detested, for not only was it a monopoly along much of its length, but an especially pitiless monopoly. According to the government directors' 1885 report, its rates were set "upon the principle that corporate extortion is a performance in which a railroad management may indefinitely indulge with impunity." Compounding the evil of extortionate rates were the freight rebates and free passenger passes the UP bestowed upon politically well-connected shippers and their cronies, which invested the whole enterprise with the acrid stink of corruption. Rank dishonesty seemed to be baked into its bones.

As for the Gould legacy, the looming economic downturn would expose the folly of his management style just as a receding tide exposes derelict vessels to the open air. One appalling example uncovered by Adams involved the Denver & South Park Railroad, a branch line Gould purchased in 1882 from John Evans, the governor of Colorado Territory. "Everything in Colorado was in that very inflated condition which usually precedes a great collapse," Adams testified to the Pacific Railway Commission. "The chief source of revenue was in carrying men and material into Colorado to dig holes in the ground called mines, and until it was discovered that there was nothing in those mines the business was immense. . . . Everyone was crazy. When [the craze] broke down and these mines and villages were deserted—and they stand there deserted to-day —of course the business left the road." But the branch line stayed in the UP portfolio, draining resources at a rate of $60,000 a year.

Adams took office armed with the best wishes of the Union Pacific's customers and government patrons. At the outset he seemed to fulfill their hopes. Adams and his managers "have done away with a great deal of obnoxious abuses" and done much "to smooth down the differences of difficulties between the people of this state and their road," an Omaha newspaper editor told Congress in 1886. The Pacific Railway Commission praised the Adams administration for having "devoted itself honestly and intelligently to the herculean task of rescuing the Union Pacific Railway from the insolvency which seriously threatened it at the inception of its work."

Yet Adams's efforts were doomed to founder on hidden shoals. Raised in a family devoted to government service and as experienced in the ways of Washington as any clan in the country, he was deeply shocked at the moral climate of the capital in the 1880s. He wrote that his initial visit to

Capitol Hill, where he hoped to fend off legislation consigning the Union Pacific to receivership, became "my first experience in the most hopeless and repulsive work in which I ever was engaged—transacting business with the United States government, and trying to accomplish something through Congressional action."

On Capitol Hill he had run smack into "the most covertly and dangerously corrupt man I ever had opportunity and occasion carefully to observe in public life." Adams had the patrician grace not to identify his adversary by name in retailing this history in his autobiography, but he was undoubtedly referring to Senator George F. Edmunds of Vermont. Adams wrote that his experience with Edmunds contradicted the Vermonter's reputation for "ability and . . . rugged honesty" in every respect: "I can only say that I found him an ill-mannered bully." Assessing Edmunds's integrity, Adams judged that the senator's antipathy toward the UP derived entirely from his pique over the railroad's refusal to put him on its payroll.

Edmunds blocked Adams's every effort to reach a financial agreement with the government. In the end, Adams slinked away in defeat: "I was —there is no use denying it, or attempting to explain it away—wholly demoralized," he wrote of his final eighteen months as UP president. "I hated my position and my duties, and yearned to be free. . . . Railroads, and the railroad connection, occupied over twenty years of my life; and when at last, in December 1890, I got rid of them, it was with a consciousness of failure, but a deep breath of relief." He would never engage with the railroad industry again.

But Edmunds's corruption had been only one obstacle Adams faced. There was also the behavior of his fellow railroad bosses. The building of new competitive lines had fallen off after the Panic of 1873, but resumed with the return of prosperity. Every surviving railroad faced new rivals; staggered by the crushing fixed costs bequeathed them by the watered financing of the post–Civil War era, they had no choice but to attract freight contracts by any means at hand—most often by cutting rates to the level of fixed costs or, in the most desperate situations, even lower, just to have some revenue flowing in.

Through the 1880s the railroad bosses tried to fight against rate cutting with every form of collusion they could contrive, chiefly through pools. These were agreements in which competing railroads apportioned traffic among themselves or shared the income from secretly fixed rates. Instead of undercutting one another, in other words, the railroads strived to keep rates high, jointly pocketing the excess profits.

The pools all failed, for two main reasons. First, customers' perception that the roads were colluding against them gave rise to official investigations and legislative action to outlaw the arrangements. Second, the railroad bosses simply were unable to work in concert, even for mutual gain. As the *Commercial and Financial Chronicle* observed, every railroad leader "has been wholly selfish, bristling all over with hostile purpose towards every other. No right of territory, no settlement of rates, no adjustment of business, stood for a moment as a hindrance to the insatiable craving of getting business."

As president of the Union Pacific, Adams had joined in a pool to end a rate war among eastern railroads; the pool's collapse in 1884 taught him the inevitability of failure. The final meeting of the presidents "struck me as a somewhat funereal gathering," he recounted. "Those composing it were manifestly at their wits' ends. They evidently felt, one and all, that something had got to be done; yet no one knew what to do. Everything had been tried and everything had failed. . . . They reminded me of men in a boat in the swift water above the rapids of Niagara. They were looking one at another in blank dismay, and asking 'What next?' and no one could tell what next."

Initiatives by several states to outlaw pools were overruled in 1886 by the US Supreme Court on grounds that they had no authority under the Constitution to regulate interstate commerce. That dumped the matter into the lap of Congress, which responded in 1887 with the Interstate Commerce Act, the first major effort at industrial regulation in American history. At first the railroads fought the act as ferociously as they had been fighting each other. Eventually, they settled for keeping the Interstate Commerce Commission, which was to administer the act, securely under their thumbs.

By the time of the act's passage, the railroad industry was in a state of anarchy, desperate for someone to impose order—a Bismarck. The hour produced the man, in the person of Pierpont Morgan. The challenge confronting Morgan was daunting indeed, but he was fully aware of its magnitude. "For forty years," observed John Moody, "American railroad promoters, reckless optimists, gigantic thieves, huge confidence men— magnified a hundred times by the size of their transactions—had juggled and manipulated and exploited this great business for their own profit and the general loss of every one else concerned. Morgan had been watching."

PIERPONT MORGAN HAD exploited the knowledge he gained during his 1869 grand tour to dabble in railroad securities throughout the 1870s. Then, near the end of the decade, came the deal that brought him into railroading in a major way. It involved the vast holdings in the New York Central of William H. "Billy" Vanderbilt, who had inherited the stake in 1877 upon the death of his father, the Commodore. Billy decided in 1879 to shed a large portion of the unwieldy investment, in part because he had wearied of the constant warfare it provoked with his family's old adversary, Jay Gould. Moreover, the investment was threatened by a movement in the New York legislature to ban single-family ownership of major railroads. Vanderbilt hired Morgan to unload the shares through an international syndicate, converting the New York Central from a private family holding into a public company. The sheer scale of the transaction was breathtaking: The sale of Vanderbilt's 250,000 shares was "the largest ever made by a single owner of railroad stock," reported the *New York Tribune*, which added that the result would affect "the entire railroad interests of this country." That was because the deal effectively united the interests of Vanderbilt and Gould, whose "Wabash syndicate" became the largest holder of the New York Central by acquiring 60,000 shares.

What was perhaps most significant was that in consummating the deal, Pierpont took a seat on the New York Central board as well as the authority to fill two other seats, which he gave to Gould associates Cyrus Field and Solon Humphreys. Although Vanderbilt remained the president of the New York Central—and would continue in that role until

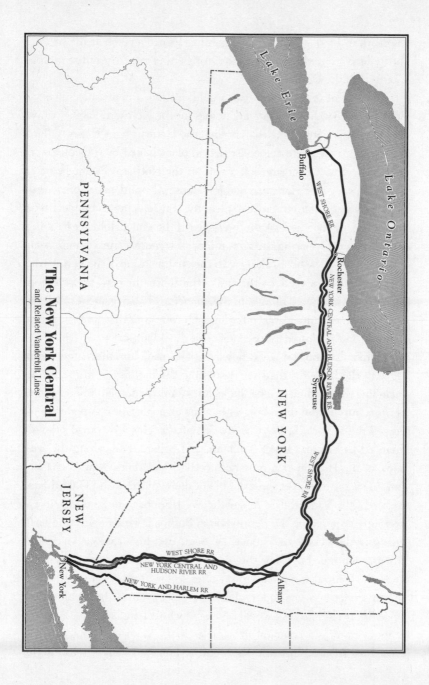

his death in 1885—Pierpont Morgan had gained a perch at the heart of the industry from which to start exercising power over "the entire railroad interests" of the United States.

Over the next decade Morgan would continue to build his influence. Starting in 1880 he managed financings for the Northern Pacific, whose mercurial new controlling shareholder, the German-born Henry Villard, was trying to complete the construction plans halted by the collapse of Jay Cooke & Co. Morgan took a seat on the Northern Pacific board in 1883, the same year Harriman had joined the IC board, and subsequently helped to oust Villard in order to clear the way for a more complete reorganization. In 1885 he took on the rescue of the Philadelphia & Reading, a declining road serving the coal mines of western Pennsylvania, again taking a seat on the board along with the chairmanship of the voting trust that controlled the road. By the end of the 1880s, the news that Pierpont Morgan had interested himself in the financing or management of an otherwise hobbled railroad was often enough to restore that line's access to investors in the United States and across the Atlantic.

Pierpont's hands-on work, however, also made him intimately familiar with the behavior that was destroying the industry from the inside, including the building of superfluous lines for no reason but to harry competitors into buying them out. The prime example in his experience involved the New York, West Shore & Buffalo. This was a road partially financed by Gould, George Pullman, and Villard, built along the west bank of the Hudson as a nuisance to the Vanderbilts' New York Central line across the river (an example of the conflicts with Gould that so wearied Billy Vanderbilt). When the West Shore went bankrupt it was promptly acquired by the Pennsylvania Railroad, which under the leadership of the imperious Thomas A. Scott and his successor George B. Roberts continued to harry the New York Central with rate cutting. By 1885 the Central was forced to set rates so low it was operating its passenger service at a loss and its shares were being crushed. "I look on the West Shore road just as I would on a man whose hand I had found in my money drawer—a common, miserable thief," Vanderbilt fumed to the *New York Tribune*. In truth, the Pennsylvania was merely returning to

Vanderbilt the same treatment it had received at his hands, for he earlier had built the South Pennsylvania Railroad, an unnecessary line from
Harrisburg to Pittsburgh, to compete directly with the Pennsylvania's own
route to the coal fields. The two camps could have settled their conflicts
in a draw, but Vanderbilt's refusal to take the West Shore off the Pennsylvania's hands at anything above pennies on the dollar prolonged the
conflict.

Morgan assumed the task of bringing the hostilities to an end. Planning his voyage home to New York from his annual excursion to London
in May 1885, he contrived to book the same steamer as Vanderbilt, then
used their week in close quarters to hector Vanderbilt into reaching a
deal. After they landed in New York, the final settlement was cemented
on Morgan's yacht, Corsair, as it steamed up and down the Hudson. It
was not a relaxing cruise. The July weather was sweltering even into the
night. George Roberts, the Pennsylvania's president, was determined to
punish the New York Central for its earlier incursion into his territory.
("Mr. Roberts was not an easy man to deal with," recalled Satterlee, who
found him to be, like Vanderbilt, "a product of the times [who] lived in a
world of railroad strife and was accustomed to giving and receiving hard
blows.") Morgan, who by then filled out his six-foot frame with two hundred pounds of flesh, watched over the negotiations as a lowering presence, fingering a big black cigar, inserting an occasional sharp interjection
when the unruly discussion needed to be put back on course.

Eventually Roberts capitulated not merely to Morgan's authority as
one of the Pennsylvania's bankers but to the inescapable logic of striking a
compromise. Vanderbilt agreed to acquire the West Shore at a reasonable
price, and the Pennsylvania to buy the South Pennsylvania from Vanderbilt. Because the Pennsylvania state constitution forbade the Pennsylvania Railroad to acquire a competing line, the nominal purchaser of the
South Pennsylvania was J. Pierpont Morgan. The complex transaction
gave rise to one of the legendary verbal exchanges of Pierpont's career,
starting with his instruction to Vanderbilt's legal adviser, one Ashbel
Green, to reduce the provisions into legal form. Green presently reported
back that he thought the plan could not be executed legally.

"That is not what I asked you," Morgan barked. "I asked you to tell me how it *could* be done legally. Come back tomorrow and tell me."

Green presently proposed an intricate sequence of securities trades in which a Morgan syndicate bought the West Shore and leased it in perpetuity to the New York Central, while Morgan himself bought a 60 percent stake in the South Pennsylvania and traded it to the Pennsylvania for the bonds of another railroad. The multifaceted deal was widely regarded as a signal achievement for Morgan, who used it as a model for ending several other competitive wars vitiating the railroad industry. His formula was reduced to the term "community of interests"—a recognition that competing magnates would secure mutual benefits by rationalizing rates, ending wasteful construction, and exploiting what were, after all, natural monopolies by crafting mutual alliances. Morgan communicated to the road presidents that until they learned to work together, none of them would be able to turn a reliable profit. Consequently, none could hope to raise capital in the European markets, which would invest only in a rationalized industry. Failure to come to terms meant stagnation and eventually extinction.

Morgan was playing with fire, for the public's growing disenchantment with the concentration of economic power represented by the development of railroad combines would soon produce the Sherman Antitrust Act of 1890, the first US law to declare monopolies illegal (even if it was only patchily enforced in its first decade).

Pierpont himself embodied the very concept of a community of interests. In time he became not only a director of the New York Central, but of the New York, Providence & Boston, which carried passengers from Grand Central Station to South Station in Boston; he was in constant demand for service on railroad boards along the Eastern Seaboard, not seldom because he also was those lines' banker; and his partnership Drexel, Morgan & Co. was financier to the Pennsylvania.

Pierpont's goal was to supplant the old pooling arrangements, which were so brittle in their terms and toothless in their enforcement, with "gentlemen's agreements." On the surface these seemed even looser than the old pools, for they exchanged the superficial formality of the pools for what Herbert Satterlee described as undertakings resting "solely on the spoken word between executives. . . . The only punishment for disregarding the object of these associations was to place the offending management in a very unfavorable light before other railroad men." But it would be a mistake to assume that the informality alone worked where formality had failed. The element that was expected to make the gentlemen's agreements function was a central authority, and that authority was Morgan.

Not everyone was willing to concede him that power. Railroad presidents as a species were accustomed to getting their own way and distinctly unaccustomed to taking orders from others. Jay Gould, for his part, remained under the impression that he was still the most powerful figure in the industry and therefore the man to dictate the terms of peace. In early December he presented Morgan with a roster of proposals to squelch competition, including a five-year ban on construction of parallel lines, all to be binding upon railroad presidents on pain of their being blacklisted for refusal. Gould's record, however, had won him Morgan's enduring disdain. According to Satterlee, Morgan was convinced that Gould and his cronies had "made it easy for the self-appointed champions of the people's rights to build up a public opinion unfriendly to the railroads. . . . [They] had wrecked railroads and disrupted lines that might have grown into systems. . . . Their methods had often made legislatures and courts of law bywords of contempt." (By contrast, Satterlee judged indulgently, his father-in-law "had the best interests of the public and the railroad employees at heart.")

Numerous railroad presidents had stated publicly that they would not attend any meeting at which Gould would be present or "join in any arrangement Mr. Gould may propose," the New York Tribune reported. But Morgan knew he could not avoid including Gould in the railroad confederation he envisioned, since it would be better to have Gould's roads inside the arrangement than taking shots at it from the outside, so he tendered the buccaneer an invitation to participate. The proposal Morgan eventually put forth would share some features with Gould's, but it would be made clear that the ideas were Morgan's, not Gould's, and that Morgan was driving the train, with Gould merely one passenger among many.

———

MORGAN SUMMONED A dozen railroad presidents and their bankers to his sumptuous art-filled mansion at 219 Madison Avenue on December 20, 1888, for the opening stage of his campaign to end the railroad civil wars. The underlying purpose of the meeting was for "the representatives of capital . . . to show the railroad men the whip," one of Morgan's confidants later explained. "They intended to convey a very definite impression that further misbehavior would be punished by cutting off the supplies" of capital.

Charles Francis Adams arrived at 9 a.m. to find the railroad men seated grumpily around Morgan's dining room table, joined by representatives of the banking firms Drexel, Morgan & Co.; Kidder, Peabody; and Brown Brothers. Adams marked Gould as looking "dreadfully sick and worn," as he recorded in his daily journal. (Gould was, in fact, suffering from the tuberculosis that would kill him three years later.)

From the head of the table, Morgan brusquely informed the railroad men that he had called the meeting "to cause the members of this association to no longer take the law into their own hands when they suspect they have been wronged. . . . This is not elsewhere customary in civilized communities, and no good reason exists why such a practice should continue among railroads."

The railroad presidents bristled at Morgan's tone. "I object to this very strong language, which indicates that we, the railroad people, are a set of anarchists," groused Roberts of the Pennsylvania. He was right to be irked, for none of the overbuilding that provoked the rate cutting could have taken place had not the bankers in the room connived to finance the excess construction.

The railroad leaders were not yet ready to yield a dictatorial role to Morgan, though they had nothing novel to offer. Ransom Reed Cable, the truculent head of the expansion-minded Rock Island line, offered a scheme to fix rates that Adams mentally judged to be "the old story once more — proposing to bind the railroads together with a rope of sand." Cable's plan, which carried no provision for enforcement, was greeted with "expressions of contempt," Adams noted. After the meeting adjourned for the day, Adams trudged up Madison Avenue with his old rival Jay Gould. "I told him that it seemed to me to be the merest child's play for us to be going round and round in this old circle," he recalled. "We might as well go home and leave events to take their course," unless the joint arrangement they mapped out would be subject to some "compulsory force which would establish obedience." Casually, Adams suggested using the very entity that the railroads had worked so hard to render toothless — the Interstate Commerce Commission. To his surprise Gould jumped at the suggestion and even offered to present it personally to the gathering the next day.

The more Adams turned the idea around in his mind, the sounder it seemed. "The railroad situation today is one of simple anarchy," he reflected. "We need law and order. We resemble nothing so much as a body of Highland clans—each a law unto itself—each jealous of its petty independence, each suspicious of any outside power which could compel obedience. Such a state of affairs . . . cannot—and will not—last. The thing is to back it up. In other words, a railroad Bismarck is needed," he concluded, using the increasingly common term for a dictatorial authority. Would Morgan be able to exercise the authority needed to bring the rest of the presidents to the same conclusion? "It remains to be seen," Adams mused.

The next day's meeting did not start auspiciously. Gould presented the idea of bringing in the ICC, "but in so weak and vague a way that it made no impression," Adams recalled. Adams took over, and according to his own recollection, finally made the idea take—though not before he delivered some home truths to his colleagues. The industry's troubles, he told them, "lie in the covetousness, want of good faith, and low moral tone of railroad managers, in the complete absence of any high standard of commercial honor." The question was whether the railroad bosses were prepared to publicly state that they would violate the precepts of the Interstate Commerce Act "rather than submit to arbitration" by the government regulators. The meeting ended with an agreement to meet again on January 8, and for Morgan in the meantime to interest the ICC commissioners in the plan.

The January 8 session convened in an atmosphere of mutual resentment, for another round of rate cutting had occurred in the interim. Yet improbably—and surely to the amazement of all concerned—the meeting resulted in what appeared to be an enforceable agreement, signed by twenty-two railroads. The ICC agreed to assume the role of arbiter of interline disagreements by convening a board to take testimony when necessary. One ICC member, Aldace Walker, the commission's only experienced railroad man, resigned to become chairman of what was dubbed the Interstate Commerce Railway Association, an example of the revolving door between government and private service that is generally frowned upon today but was interpreted then as a sign of confidence in the arrangement.

Morgan won universal praise for his role and the agreement itself was hailed as the harbinger of a new age of harmonious cooperation in a major industry. "When the party that furnishes all new money needed, and the party that owns the old money invested, and the party managing the corporation meet, the result means revolution," gushed the *Commercial and Financial Chronicle*. The *Chronicle* was certain that the ICC's arbitration board would act effectively: "Kickers"—that is, railroad presidents who violated the terms—"will be brought into line or suppressed. . . . With, then, the stockholders of American roads and with the world's capital as its reserve backing this new institution, there need be no fear of a lack of strength to enforce its decisions."

Yet Morgan's compact was doomed to failure as inevitably as the pooling arrangements it supplanted. Within two months of its signing —"barely enough time for the railroad presidents to get back from Morgan's," historian Gabriel Kolko reflected—a new rate war erupted in the West. Adams's own Union Pacific was at its center, in a contest for coastal traffic with Henry Villard's Northern Pacific. By June, Kolko noted, "the chaotic status quo was restored."

For more than a year, Morgan struggled to reimpose order. In December 1890 he summoned another clutch of railroad presidents to his town house, emerging with another compact among fifteen railroads and another proclamation that peace was at hand. "Think of it," Morgan told the press—"all the competitive traffic of the roads west of Chicago and St. Louis placed in the control of about thirty men." To later generations, power concentrated to this degree would seem scandalous; to Morgan, it made the agreement "as strong as could be desired." But his optimistic words could scarcely conceal the enmity that had afflicted the presidents' dealings with one another. It soon transpired that at one point during the negotiations A. B. Stickney, formerly the president and now chairman of the Chicago, St. Louis & Kansas City road, had blurted, "I have the utmost respect for you gentlemen individually, but as railroad presidents I wouldn't trust you with my watch out of my sight." Thomas Oakes, the head of the Northern Pacific, snapped in response: "Have you reached that opinion recently, Mr. Stickney, or did you entertain it when *you* were a president?"

That attempt to conjure up a "community of interest" would fail like all those that came before it and followed afterwards. The chaos among the railroads only grew wilder in the first years of the 1890s, and left the industry utterly unprepared to face what would be the worst crisis in its existence: the Panic of 1893.

UNLIKE ITS PRECURSOR in 1873, the Panic of 1893 was not primarily triggered by the railroads, though they would be among the most deeply injured enterprises. The immediate cause, instead, was the failure of the most admired of the industrial trusts that had sprung up over the previous decade, the National Cordage Association. The "cordage trust," which controlled some 90 percent of the rope market in the United States, had been riding high in investors' esteem as recently as January 1893, when it issued a 100 percent stock dividend, shaving its share price to $70 from $140 to enhance its appeal to Wall Street speculators. (The stock dividend did not change the capitalization of the trust, for it merely doubled the number of shares, which traded at half the previous price—a share-holder who previously owned one share valued at $140 now owned two valued at $70 each.) The collapse of the trust was another example of the ills of monopolization that had prompted Congress to enact the Sherman Antitrust Act in 1890.

The real problem, as was true of many other overgrown trusts of the era, was that the financial condition of the cordage trust was opaque to its investors and even its bankers. Of its directors, only the president and treasurer knew all the facts—specifically, that the trust was hobbled by overproduction, a lack of credit, and the evaporation of its working capital. On May 2, the trust had assured the public that it had $4 million in ready funds. In fact, the cash box held but $100,000.

Businesses dependent on public confidence are the most vulnerable to sudden collapse when the first crack appears in the wall of trust. The end came for Cordage on May 5, when it abruptly announced that it had placed itself in the hands of bankruptcy receivers. "Cordage has collapsed like a bursted meteor," reported the Commercial and Financial Chronicle the next day, "and the other industrials have all of them shared to a considerable extent in the decline." Belatedly, the Chronicle rued the lack of transparency of the nation's biggest industrial concerns. "We know little about 'Cordage,'" the journal observed. "We know but little also about most of the other industrials; indeed it is because so little is generally known of these properties and prices are consequently so largely speculative that confidence in them has been so grievously disturbed."

To be sure, the Cordage collapse did not occur in a vacuum. Disquieting currents had been swirling within the American economy for years. One was a persistent conflict over the monetary system. Laborers, farmers, miners, and other producers of commodities, all of whom would benefit from inflation, favored an expansion of the money supply through the free coinage of silver to supplement gold as the specie backing the US currency. Manufacturers and bankers were on the other side. They demanded adherence to the gold standard, which governed international trade and promoted stable currency values. These were important to bondholders and other investors expecting periodic returns over long periods of time;

devaluation of the dollar through an expansion of the money supply could only sap their investments of their worth.

This conflict played out in the presidential election of 1892, particularly in the contrast between Grover Cleveland, seeking his nonconsecutive second term as a gold-standard Democrat, and James Weaver, the candidate of the new Populist Party, which advocated silver coinage. At the time, the silver lobby appeared to be in the ascendance, due to passage of the Sherman Silver Purchase Act of 1890, which mandated limited government purchases of silver. Cleveland balanced his ticket with Adlai Stevenson, a silver-coinage advocate, as his vice presidential running mate, and won a plurality of the popular vote and a decisive electoral-vote majority when the Populists and Republicans split the pro-silver vote. (In a political turnabout, the Populists later would merge with the Democratic Party, which would nominate silver advocate William Jennings Bryan as its presidential candidate in 1896, 1900, and 1908.)

The consequence of silver coinage for the United States proved Gresham's law, the economic principle that "bad money drives good money out of circulation"—that is, people will hoard good money (in this instance, gold) and use debased currency to settle accounts wherever possible. Because only gold, not silver, was accepted by foreign creditors in settlement of international trade, gold began to flow out of the United States at ever-increasing volumes. Silver became the preferred settlement currency only for domestic transactions. A loss of confidence abroad in the stability of the US economy and a slowdown in economic activity were the harvest.

Benjamin Harrison, the Republican who occupied the White House between Cleveland's two terms, tried to put the best face on a faltering economy. "There never has been a time in our history when work was so abundant or when wages were as high, whether measured by the currency in which they are paid or by their power to supply the necessaries and comforts of life," Harrison said in his final annual message to Congress on December 6, 1892. "If any are discontented with their state here, if any believe that wages or prices, the returns for honest toil, are inadequate, they should not fail to remember that there is no other country in the world where the conditions that seem to them hard would not be accepted as highly prosperous."

Harrison put in a plug for the tariffs he had imposed: "I believe that the protective system . . . has been a mighty instrument for the development of our national wealth and a most powerful agency in protecting the homes of our workingmen from the invasion of want."

But matters worsened after Cleveland began his second term. In the panic year of 1893, more than 640 banks failed—5 percent of all the banks in the United States—and fifteen thousand businesses went bankrupt. Of the nation's nearly 178,000 miles of railroad track, roughly one-fifth were owned by railroads in receivership.

JUST AS THE panic struck that summer, Morgan allowed himself to be dragged into another railroad rescue. This time the object was that perennial damsel in distress, the Erie, still wearing the scarlet letter pinned on its finances by Drew, Vanderbilt, Gould, and Fisk. The inevitable bankruptcy occurred in mid-1893. Morgan was tasked with the reorganization. The work would be notable not merely as a step in the evolution of Morganization—but as the occasion for a second clash of wills between Morgan and Edward Harriman.

Morgan's plan laid most of the burden of the restructuring on holders of the Erie's second-mortgage bonds, while protecting its shareholders from any sacrifice. This struck many observers as unjust on its face, since shareholders normally were last in line among a bankrupt enterprise's investors. Among the holders of second-mortgage bonds was Harriman, who commuted on the Erie to New York City from his estate at Arden, New York. He obligingly stepped up as a spokesman for the objecting bondholders. In a series of open letters, the publication of which Harriman orchestrated, the creditors attacked Morgan's plan as "unjust" and, more to the point, financially imprudent, since it would do nothing to reduce the Erie's fixed charges—the real cause of the bankruptcy.

Morgan bulled through his reorganization plan at the Erie shareholders' meeting that March. But he did not reckon with Harriman, who formed his own committee and filed a lawsuit to block the plan. (This episode gave rise to one of the more persistent, if fanciful, anecdotes about Harriman. It was said that he had visited Morgan's offices to present his objections to the reorganization plan in person. When asked by Morgan whom he represented, he snapped, "Myself!" The journalist who appears to be the first to retail this story, Edwin Lefèvre, acknowledged in his article that "it may not be true," but that as "characteristic of Harriman" it was plausible enough to be published.) When the dispute came to court, Harriman was dealt a defeat by the financial establishment: A New York judge ruled that, since holders of $31 million of the $38 million in second-mortgage bonds had assented to the plan and Harriman owned a bare $40,000, "the court should not interfere."

Harriman's last-ditch effort accomplished little beyond intensifying Morgan's animosity. "Harriman always wanted to get terms which were a little better than other people's," remarked Satterlee (though Morgan himself was hardly above extracting the best terms possible in his own transactions). What truly irked Morgan was that Harriman "followed his usual tactics of retaining counsel and fighting in court," Satterlee continued. "But he was unsuccessful in the end."

That might have been true tactically, but subsequent events showed that Harriman had been absolutely correct in his assessment of the plan's risks. Within a year, the Erie defaulted on the interest payments due on the reorganization securities, just as Harriman had forecast. Morgan was forced to put through a second reorganization plan that finally reduced the Erie's fixed-charge burden so it could profit from the economic recovery of the final few years of the nineteenth century.

Morgan may have communicated his distaste for Harriman to the managers of the Erie. Soon after this second skirmish, Harriman sought a routine courtesy from the Erie typically offered by railroads to executives of other lines, such as the Illinois Central. One day Harriman missed the Erie local he had planned to take from New York to the trotting races at Goshen, about twenty miles away. He phoned the Erie to ask if its Chicago Express would make an unscheduled stop in Goshen to let him off.

This time he was flatly refused. Still, since he knew that the westbound Chicago Express could be flagged to pick up any passenger for boarding along the way, he wired a friend in Goshen to buy a ticket to Chicago. When the train stopped in Goshen to pick up the phantom passenger, Harriman hopped off.

But the Erie contretemps, like the earlier confrontation over the Dubuque & Sioux City, was only a prelude to the struggles to come.

Harriman was as yet little known to the public as a railroad leader and little respected in Morgan's elite circle. That was about to change. What would finally bring Harriman to prominence was the railroad that Morgan and his fellows still dismissed as "two streaks of rust"—the Union Pacific. Jay Gould, in one final act of destructiveness, had provided Harriman with the opening.

11

SAVIOR OF THE UNION PACIFIC

FOR CHARLES FRANCIS ADAMS, the reemergence of Jay Gould as a suitor for the Union Pacific was the last straw. The aging buccaneer had shrouded his resurgent financial interest in the railroad in misdirection; to some newspapers he disavowed any interest in regaining control of the road while orchestrating attacks on Adams's management through others. Adams detected undercurrents swirling against him, but not until the very end did he realize they had been set in motion by Gould.

Starting in early 1890, Adams would recall,

> I was receiving assaults from all quarters of the West, from a hand which I could not see, and could not understand. There would be something published in Chicago, and then copied in the East, attacking our credit, and then there would be an attack upon us in some Salt Lake City paper, or at Portland, Oregon, and the ball would move around the country to hit us in the back. I thought it was some attack from our rivals in the railroad business. I even suspected the Vanderbilts.

As late as November 11 Adams assured the *Boston Herald* that rumors of Gould's interest in the UP were nothing but "a revival of the old story that was put in circulation some five or six years ago." He said he did not "know anything about it," and that acquiring control "would be a task of enormous proportions even for Gould."

That very day, however, Gould had already secured control and begun to inform the world of his intention to sack Adams. "Under his direction," Gould was quoted in the *New York Times*, "the Union Pacific, more than any other railroad in the West, has disturbed and upset harmony, knocked down rates, and forced the handling of business without profit." He revealed that his backers included the Rockefeller family and other long-term shareholders, who "invited us to assume the control, direction, and management of the property. We accepted." His comments to one reporter explaining his reemergence dripped with faux sentimentality: "There is nothing strange or mysterious about it. I knew [the railroad] very intimately when it was a child, and I have merely returned to my first love."

Just days after scoffing at the very idea that Gould could be reestablishing his control of the Union Pacific, Adams showed up at Gould's downtown office to capitulate. In his autobiography he described the episode as his having been "ejected by Jay Gould from the presidency of the Union Pacific," but he acknowledged his relief. "In the course of my railroad experience," he would recount bitterly, "I made no friends . . . ; nor among those I met was there any man whose acquaintance I valued. They were a coarse, realistic, bargaining crowd."

It was barely two years since Adams and Gould had sat down with a dozen other railroad presidents and bankers at J. Pierpont Morgan's town house to craft an industrywide peace plan. Clearly, peace was more distant than ever. But that was not Gould's fault—not solely, at least.

Gould was not entirely wrong about Adams. The sad truth was that despite the ambitions Adams had brought to his service as Union Pacific president, the railroad was in worse shape after six years of his stewardship than when he took office. The decline was not all his fault: Freight fees dropped sharply in the last years of the 1880s because of falling commodity prices—a harbinger of the dreadful crash to come. Meanwhile, competition for transcontinental business had steadily increased.

The lack of progress on settling the road's looming government debt was the fault of a recalcitrant Congress more than Adams. But Adams had also spent some $42 million to acquire some three thousand miles of branch lines. He defended the acquisitions by pointing out that they produced $5 million a year in revenues needed to cover the UP's fixed charges, while glossing over the fact that the roads all operated at a loss. He shored up the railroad's increasingly dire financial condition with loans from European banks, notably Baring Brothers; but on November 15, 1890, just a few days after Adams's dismissive comments about Gould to the *Boston Herald*, the Barings firm failed. With it went the UP's once-rock-solid source of credit—and any confidence Adams might have had about holding Gould at bay.

GOULD'S DISCONTENT WITH Adams had been brewing for months. Adams had been making deals for the Union Pacific with western and southwestern roads in a bid to quell rate wars. But these arrangements typically left Gould's railroads on the outside looking in, while promoting the interests of Gould's business enemies. Among them was Collis Huntington, whose Central and Southern Pacific had been competitors of Pacific Mail, a steamship line serving the Far East out of San Francisco, which Gould earlier had acquired by outsmarting its owner, the stock manipulator Alden Stockwell. In May 1890 Huntington wrested control of Pacific Mail from Gould and his son George, a deal that left Gould's railroads especially vulnerable to an alliance between Huntington's roads and Adams's Union Pacific.

Particularly irksome to Gould was an arrangement Adams reached giving the Rock Island, the Chicago & Northwestern, and the Chicago, Milwaukee & St. Paul exclusive rights to use the Union Pacific's bridge over the Missouri River at Omaha. This allowed the Rock Island and the St. Paul to pick up freight at Denver and carry it across the river to Chicago, and allowed the Northwestern to carry traffic from Chicago to Omaha and offload it directly to the Union Pacific. The deal was a dagger aimed directly at Gould's Missouri Pacific, the odd road out.

But then opportunity beckoned, in the form of a collapse in the Union

Pacific's share price. The shares, which had been trading at $65, fell to the mid-$40s during the autumn of 1890, as a consequence of Adams's failure to resolve the road's financing problems, of the persistent rate wars, and conceivably of Gould's own machinations. Gould was flush with cash, holding a war chest estimated by contemporaries at $15 million to $20 million. Indeed, he seemed to be the only investor interested in saving the Union Pacific; Adams's quest for a white knight had failed utterly, as he realized when word reached him at the last moment that William H. Vanderbilt had refused to invest rescue capital into the UP. With all chance of resistance having faded away, Gould's takeover of the road became one of the simplest, if one of the last, transactions in his career.

The railroad Gould reacquired, however, soon took on the appearance of a poisoned chalice. Traffic on the road was improving, but the crush of interest due was unremitting. Gould's efforts to ease the Union Pacific's overhang of debt were no more fruitful than Adams's. In June 1891 Gould was forced to loan the railroad nearly $2 million out of his own pocket to meet its interest bill.

Meanwhile, Gould's relationship with the country's most important railroad financier, J. Pierpont Morgan, was fraying. Despite Gould's position as owner of the most storied franchise in the railroad world, Morgan disparaged him as an inconsequential participant in the "community of interest" negotiations he was leading at the time, ignoring the numerous proposals Gould had offered to address the industry's self-destructive habits of competition.

In their face-to-face dealings over the restructuring of Union Pacific debt, Morgan, who was managing the operation, treated Gould with unalloyed condescension, according to newspaper accounts plainly sourced in the Morgan camp. Morgan "had a talk with Mr. Gould yesterday," the New York Times reported on September 27, "and 'the wizard of Wall Street' was given to understand that he was no longer a 'wizard.'" According to the report, Morgan brusquely informed Gould that unless he "acted the part of a straightforward man he would not only be hustled out of the Union Pacific, but that his power in Wall Street would end summarily."

Morgan demanded that Gould put up millions of dollars in excess collateral to guarantee the rescue debt. By then Gould no longer had the energy to resist. In 1891 one blow followed another: The Missouri Pacific skipped a quarterly dividend, foreign shareholders began agitating to oust him from the Union Pacific, and competitive rate-cutting was again draining his railroads of revenue. His businesses were failing and economic storm clouds heralded a recession, or worse, just over the horizon.

When the storm broke in 1893, Jay Gould would be spared the spectacle. Hollowed out by the final ravages of tuberculosis, he died on December 2, 1892. It had been so long since he had commanded affairs on Wall Street that the markets barely rippled at the news. "After his death, there was no one to carry on his work," reflected his biographer Julius Grodinsky. "Although he left his cash, current assets, and stock holdings, he left no plans." The Gould empire would pass to his son George, who was intellectually and temperamentally ill-suited to manage it. Gould's passing would clear the way for Morgan and Harriman, who ultimately would solve the problems of rate stabilization and profitability that had long eluded their predecessors. But first, there was a major panic to deal with — and the indolent George Gould was having a devilish time holding his father's railway system together.

A sharp decline in income is never welcome in business, but the Panic of 1893 and the "industrial paralysis" that followed, in the words of the *Commercial and Financial Chronicle*, wreaked havoc on the Union Pacific's finances at precisely the wrong moment. Three-year notes issued in 1891 to retire the road's floating debt were due to mature on August 1, 1894. An even weightier obligation loomed, for between November 1, 1895, and January 1, 1899, some $52 million in principal and interest on the government's construction bonds would come due. A default would give the government the right to take over the Union Pacific, down to the gravel in its roadbeds. Yet while the railroad was manifestly unable to cover the debt, no one on Capitol Hill saw government operation of the Union Pacific as an attractive option. Some compromise would be necessary, but none that could win approval from Congress had yet emerged.

In October 1893 the Union Pacific acknowledged it was insolvent and went into receivership. Over the next two years, the UP's earnings fell by nearly $7 million, or about one-third. Not merely the general depression, but the collapse of silver mining in the West after the repeal of silver monetization in 1893 caused significant damage. Add the rate wars continuing among all the transcontinental roads, and the result was the transformation of the Union Pacific's $2 million surplus of 1892 into a $2.6 million deficit in 1893. "Not . . . nearly as bad a showing as might have been expected under the circumstances," the *Chronicle* judged upon examining the carcass, but still cause for alarm.

In these dire circumstances the railroad's security holders, under the leadership of US senator Calvin Brice of Ohio (representing the government's interests) appointed a reorganization committee to take the road out of the hands of its receivers. It was a sterling group, comprising General Grenville Dodge, the Union Pacific's original builder; A. H. Boissevain, an experienced Dutch railroad investor representing the Europeans who at that point owned about half the shares; and in a subsidiary role, Pierpont Morgan.

The committee had only three realistic options. The first was for the government to accept as much as the railroad could pay for its bonds and write off the balance as a loss. The only positive aspect of this plan was that it would relieve Washington of a costly and troublesome burden, for managing its interest in the UP cost the government thousands of dollars a year, ensnared it in seemingly endless litigation, and forced both houses of Congress to maintain standing committees overseeing the railroad amid ceaseless legislative wrangling.

The second option was to extend the loans deep into the future at a sharply lower interest rate. A fifty-year bond issue paying as little as 2 or 3 percent was the preferred formula, but congressional critics regarded this as a far too indulgent treatment of a railroad that had been born and built in an atmosphere of persistent criminal fraud.

The third option was for the government to foreclose and run the UP itself. The advantage of this option was that it would give the government a direct hand in curbing the general iniquity of the transcontinental railroads: "All, unfortunately, have had their Credit Mobiliers, and all have had their Jay Goulds," observed the business historian John

P. Davis during the reorganization discussion. It would be a lesson to the other roads, he reasoned, to "see the stale water boiled out of the Union Pacific." The government, he noted further, was hardly blameless in the UP's fraud, and might itself learn a few things from having "to suffer the consequences of being in bad company." But it was hardly to be expected that Congress would see things the same way.

The reorganization committee's ultimate proposal involved converting the government debt into a $300 million revolving credit line paying 3 percent. The plan was stillborn. It was published in December, and when June arrived without its even receiving a vote in Congress, the reorganization committee disbanded in frustration. It would be two years before failure could be turned into success. That transformation would bring a new figure onto the scene: a banker who would play a central role in the coming showdown between Harriman and Morgan.

IN THE LATE fall of 1895, Jacob Schiff, the senior partner of the investment bank Kuhn, Loeb & Co., was approached by Winslow S. Pierce, the personal lawyer of George Gould, with an invitation for Schiff to lead a fresh attempt to reorganize the Union Pacific. Gould was an indolent shadow of his father, devoted more to attending society fetes and raising racehorses than husbanding the family fortune. But he was not too dull to recognize that his extensive Union Pacific shareholdings, a legacy from his father, were at risk if another reorganization attempt failed.

Schiff was an inspired choice. As head of Kuhn, Loeb, the Frankfurt-born banker's authority on Wall Street was second only to Pierpont Morgan's. A man of medium physical stature and unshakable dignity, Schiff spoke impeccably grammatical English, albeit with a heavy German accent. Deeply religious, he maintained the ritual of blessing his children for the Sabbath every week at Friday-evening dinner and rarely allowed business to interfere with his attendance at synagogue; in one youthful letter soliciting a job in America, he had specified "a position which will leave me free on that day, because I am inclined by principle to devout religious observance." As it would happen, Schiff's insistence on keeping the Sabbath would cost his future client Edward Harriman dearly at a critical juncture.

Soon after his arrival at Kuhn, Loeb in 1873, Schiff was being regularly welcomed to the Solomon Loebs' Fifth Avenue home for Sunday dinners. It seemed almost preordained that he would marry their eldest daughter, Therese. This placed him within the firm's tradition of cementing its business bonds through marriage. The senior partner, Abraham Kuhn, was cofounder Solomon Loeb's brother-in-law; another young banker who joined the firm at the same time as Schiff, Sam Wolff, was the son of another partner, Abraham Wolff (whose daughter, Addie, would marry Kuhn, Loeb partner Otto Kahn). Many years later Jacob Schiff's own daughter, Frieda, would marry Felix Warburg, yet another Kuhn, Loeb partner.

Jacob and Therese were married on May 6, 1875. After honeymooning in Niagara Falls, they moved into a house at 57 East Fifty-Third Street, just off Park Avenue, a gift from Solomon Loeb.

Notwithstanding his stature as a banker and his leadership of Wall Street's Jewish community in 1895, Schiff's attitude toward his patrician rival Pierpont Morgan was deferential. "He was a hero-worshipper, although in a restricted and unusual sense," observed his colleague and biographer, Cyrus Adler: Schiff admired individuals not necessarily because they served in elevated positions, but in recognition of the talents that had gotten them there and kept them in place. Morgan fit the model, although his father's wealth and success had given him a leg up in making his way on Wall Street. He had, after all, brought the House of Morgan to heights that Junius Morgan could not have dreamed of.

Aware that Morgan had been a principal of the Union Pacific's first reorganization committee, Schiff was under the impression when he was approached by Winslow Pierce that Morgan had not given up the effort, only placed it on hold. "That's Morgan's affair," he told Pierce when he came to his office as George Gould's emissary. Pierce assured him that Morgan's committee had abandoned the reorganization as a hopeless task.

Still doubtful, Schiff visited Morgan a few days later. He got an earful. Congress's refusal to give the reorganization committee's plan even the

Kuhn, Loeb chairman Jacob Schiff, seen here in top hat promenading with his wife, Therese, the daughter of his firm's cofounder, became Harriman's banker and strategist of his campaign to win the Northern Pacific.

courtesy of a vote had soured Pierpont on the entire enterprise, reinforcing a view of the Union Pacific that hewed close to its enduring description as "two streaks of rust" and derived in no small part from his grand tour back in 1869. "He was so disgusted with the political intriguing and wire-pulling" surrounding the reorganization and so pessimistic about the prospects, Schiff reported to his partners, that he would not even allow his firm to invest money in the new effort.

The Union Pacific in 1895 was even more derelict than it had been a few years before. The failure by Congress to treat the railroad as an asset worth saving had left it at the mercy of a pack of lupine creditors, who had been permitted by the receivers to foreclose piecemeal on branch lines from one end of the system to the other. By May 1895, these amputations had reduced its total mileage by nearly half, to 4,469 miles. This occurred even though any experienced railroad operator could see that once the economy revived, the UP would need a larger, not smaller, network.

Notwithstanding Morgan's doubts, Schiff agreed to proceed with the reorganization effort at Pierce's urging. The railroad was in such low regard on Wall Street that Schiff had to bring in an entirely new set of business leaders to serve on the reorganization committee. Kuhn, Loeb, he told his partners, "would have to paint the whole thing over fresh." The new committee members included Marvin Hughitt of the Chicago & Northwestern Railroad and Chauncey Depew, president of the New York Central. Since both were known as "Vanderbilt men," rumors immediately spread in the financial press that the rescue of the Union Pacific was covertly a Vanderbilt affair, the ultimate goal of which must be the merger of the New York Central and Union Pacific to create another transcontinental trunk line. Schiff chose not to quash the rumors, reasoning that the Vanderbilt glow, however factitious, could only enhance the image of the hobbled Union Pacific on Wall Street when he brought its securities back to market.

By October, Schiff's reorganization committee was ready with a plan: The government would foreclose on the Union Pacific, after which the committee would buy it back for $45 million; that plus the $17 million in the sinking fund established by the Thurman Act of 1878 would make the government almost whole on its construction subsidy. The plan promptly garnered the approval of bankers, railroad executives, and the press. But late in 1896 obstacles unaccountably emerged. Objections to the deal were being aired in Congress, the press had turned hostile, holders of the old Union Pacific shares were launching legal challenges, and opinion among bankers on Wall Street and in Europe turned decidedly chilly. Rumors reached Schiff that the pushback was coming from none other than Morgan, who purportedly had become embarrassed by Schiff's success and jealously sought to regain control of the reorganization.

Schiff paid Morgan a second visit. Firmly denying the rumors, Pierpont offered to investigate their source. Presently he invited Schiff back to his office to reveal what he had heard. "It's that little fellow Harriman," he said, "and you want to look out for him."

If true, this was a genuinely new aspect of the matter. Schiff knew Harriman vaguely as the shrewd financial mind behind the success of the Illinois Central. But of Harriman's interest in the Union Pacific he had had no clue—though he could have reasoned it out, for the Illinois Central and the UP competed directly in several markets. It made sense that the Illinois would desire to secure some control over—or at least a partnership with—the UP. Additionally, the Vanderbilt cronies on Schiff's committee posed a threat to the Illinois Central: If the New York Central and the Chicago & Northwestern—Depew's and Hughitt's roads—gained control of the Union Pacific via the reorganization, the Illinois Central would be shunted aside, deprived of access to the East Coast, Chicago, and the Pacific Northwest at a single stroke.

Schiff made an appointment with Harriman to complain about the mysterious opposition that had emerged to the committee's reorganization scheme. "I understand this opposition is being directed by you," he said. "What have you to say about it?"

Harriman answered with characteristic directness. "I am the man," he acknowledged.

"But why?" Schiff asked.

"Because I intend to reorganize the Union Pacific myself."

The confession struck Schiff as baldly quixotic. "How do you propose to do that?" he asked. "Most of its securities are in our possession. What means do you have?"

Harriman fixed Schiff with his icy glare. "We have the best credit in the country," he said, explaining that he would finance the takeover by floating $100 million in bonds of the Illinois Central at 3 percent. He expected the securities to sell at full price. "You, at the best, can't get money for less than four-and-a-half percent. In that respect I am stronger than you are," he told Schiff. "The Illinois Central ought to have that road, and we are going to take charge of the reorganization."

Schiff asked Harriman to name his price to stand aside. "There is no price," Harriman replied. "I mean to get possession of the road." Harriman said he would join forces with the reorganization committee only if he were named chairman. Schiff refused; the position had been promised to Winslow Pierce, who after all had brought the opportunity to Kuhn, Loeb and represented powerful interests on his own.

Harriman waved a hand in dismissal. "Very well, Mr. Schiff," he said. "Go ahead and see what you can do. Good day."

HARRIMAN CONTINUED TO orchestrate opposition to the reorganization plan until Schiff finally offered him an olive branch. If Harriman would stand down, Schiff would promise him a seat on the reorganized company's executive committee. "If you prove to be the strongest man in that committee," Schiff said, "you'll probably get the chairmanship in the end."

Schiff may already have taken Harriman's measure and concluded that the offer would appeal to his self-assurance. He was right. Harriman accepted, joining Schiff's syndicate and putting in an investment of $900,000.

Harriman was elected to the Union Pacific board on December 6, 1897, and immediately found himself in hostile territory. "Mr. Harriman was a newcomer, and by several members of the Board his advent was not regarded with friendly eyes," related Otto Kahn, Schiff's partner and a member of the same executive committee Harriman now joined. "He was looked at askance, somewhat in the light of an intruder. His ways and manners jarred upon several of his new colleagues, and he was considered by some as not quite belonging in their class, from the point of view of business position, achievements or financial standing—a free lance, neither a railroad man nor a banker nor a merchant." Kahn boiled down the reaction of his contemporaries as: "Ned Harriman! Why, I knew him years ago as a little 'two dollar broker.' What should he know about practical railroading?"

Among the skeptics was the executive committee's most eminent banker, James Stillman, the forty-seven-year-old president of the National City Bank (the distant ancestor of today's Citigroup). As the Rockefeller family bank, National City was celebrated as "the greatest reservoir of cash in America," and was expected to provide a good deal of the capital needed to complete the reorganization. Stillman confessed in an interview years later that "a very prominent man had told me to 'look out' for Ed. Harriman. 'He is not so smart as some people think and he is not a safe man to do business with.'" Upon receiving that warning, Stillman said, he had deliberately "steered clear of him," until Harriman's appointment to the Union Pacific executive committee forcibly brought them together.

At that point Stillman, along with the other members of the board, discovered that Harriman was in fact much smarter than he had been given credit for. "I have been acquainted with all of the prominent men of this country during the last forty years," Stillman recollected, "and I can truly say that Harriman, in his conception of vast achievements and his skill, energy and daring in bringing them to realization, far surpassed any other man I have ever known. His brain was a thing to marvel at." For the next decade, until Harriman's untimely death in 1909, Stillman would remain his principal banker.

Harriman would make believers of the other board members too. The following May, less than six months after he was named to the Union Pacific board, he was elected chairman of its executive committee, effectively becoming the man in charge—just as Schiff had predicted.

Harriman's appointment to the board was little marked in the financial press, possibly because his prior railroad experience in the Midwest, out of earshot of the East Coast financial journals, had kept him in obscurity. But after his accession his transformative role could not be overlooked.

12

THE RECONSTRUCTION

THE SUCCESSFUL REORGANIZATION of the Union Pacific would stand as a milestone of the economic recovery following the Panic of 1893. In a meeting with President William McKinley, Grenville Dodge, observing that the deal included the final payment on the government loan, asked the president "if he didn't think a monument ought to be raised by the Government to the men who built that road and paid the Government debt, an unheard of occurrence at that time." McKinley, who was pleased to be relieved of the perennial Union Pacific controversy but determined to receive a share of the credit, replied, "Yes, General, but don't you think that a monument should also be raised to the President who made them do it?"

The man who actually deserved the credit was Edward Harriman. He assumed his duties as chairman of the railroad's executive committee in 1898 with a vigor that left his new colleagues, not to mention his employees, gasping for breath.

Shortly after taking office, Harriman set out on an inspection trip across the full length of the Union Pacific's route. He was replicating, perhaps unwittingly, Pierpont Morgan's grand tour of 1869 — but Harriman would come to a very different conclusion about the railroad.

Accompanied by his daughters Mary and Cornelia and five Union Pacific managers, Harriman departed from Kansas City on a train with an observation car placed at the front and the locomotive at the rear, affording him an unobstructed view of the countryside and right of way. They rolled across the prairie to Denver and thence northwest to Portland, traveling exclusively by daylight. They spent weeks to make a trip that could normally be completed in four or five days, stopping at every important station to give Harriman the chance to vacuum up information. Harriman closely examined "the physical condition of the road, estimated the value of its equipment, interviewed the shippers who made use of it, judged the characters of the officials in charge of it," and began to make plans to set right all the shortcomings he discovered.

An indefatigable tourist, Harriman also took time out for an overland trek up to Pike's Peak. He and his party continued by rail to Cheyenne and on to Utah, where they were able to travel on a rail spur to Salt Lake City that had not existed in Morgan's time. Reaching the Far West, Harriman examined the Oregon Short Line and Oregon Railway, which had been stripped from the Union Pacific during the foreclosure frenzy and which he was determined to reacquire. Then they headed south, reaching San Francisco on the Fourth of July. Finally they returned across the prairie, Harriman drinking in every detail of the territory, weighing its potential as a market for transport and judging what improvements were needed to restore the Union Pacific to its competitive prime.

While Harriman was taking the measure of his employees, they were acquainting themselves with their new patron. W. H. Bancroft, the general manager of the Oregon Short Line, knew almost nothing of Harriman "even by reputation," but had imagined a man "larger in stature" than the bantamweight who stepped down from the observation car in Portland.

"He impressed me as a man of unusual ability, with a wonderful grasp of affairs, full of energy, and apparently of physical strength," Bancroft recorded, but the qualities that struck him most of all "were his general knowledge of the properties with which he had become so recently associated, and his rapid observation of all matters of detail." Harriman insisted on learning pertinent facts as quickly as his officials could provide them: "His manner, at first, seemed to me brusque; but this was an erroneous impression, for I soon found that it was only his thorough way of transacting business."

The same incisive decision-making and gruff demand for information would be remarked on by others. "He saw every poor tie, blistered rail, and loose bolt on my division," recalled one superintendent. Julius Kruttschnitt, a Southern Pacific executive who would eventually serve as Harriman's right-hand man in the West, spoke of walking the line with his new boss shortly after Harriman acquired the Southern Pacific, inspecting the track virtually inch by inch. Harriman's sharp eyes picked out a track bolt that was protruding well beyond the nut. When he asked about the oversized fixture, Kruttschnitt replied, "It's the size which is generally used."

"But why should we use a bolt of such a length that a part of it is useless?"

"When you come right down to it," Kruttschnitt allowed, "there is no reason."

"Well," Harriman calculated, "in the Union Pacific and Southern Pacific we have about eighteen thousand miles of track and there must be some fifty million track bolts in our system. If you can cut an ounce off from every bolt, you will save fifty million ounces of iron, and that is something worthwhile. Change your standard."

Before his trip was finished, Harriman would have countless more such interactions—each helping, bit by bit, to bring the Union Pacific into the modern age.

RAILROAD HISTORIANS HAVE debated whether the Union Pacific was as decrepit as Harriman's advocates made it out to be, or whether they exaggerated the challenges to magnify his accomplishment. One can make the case that the post-1893 depression left the UP in no worse shape than some other western rail lines. But it is certainly true that at the time of Harriman's appearance on the scene, the railroad's own officials considered it ill-suited to serve the traffic that he expected to materialize. Much of the track and facilities still displayed the corner cutting and slipshod engineering of the race to Promontory three decades earlier. The rails were too light, the roadbed not properly ballasted, the grades too steep, and the route mapped out to circumvent topographical challenges rather than meet them head-on, resulting in hundreds of excess miles of rail.

"The depots were roughly constructed of boards nailed upright on the framing, the cracks battened, and without foundations other than posts," recalled William L. Park, who had joined the railroad as a brakeman in 1875 and rose to the position of general superintendent. "The stone work consisted of native stone, which very rapidly disintegrated." Drainage culverts were "primitive [and] very cheaply constructed. . . . The tools and appliances were crude. . . . There were no signals or railroad crossing protection. . . . The ties were small and of irregular size. . . . None of them were treated [with preservatives] at that time; they were in their native condition."

Years of neglect compounded these shortcomings. Jay Gould and other buccaneering owners had plundered the enterprise of millions of dollars of earnings while spending less than $180,000 a year on upkeep. Harriman reported to the board that of the company's 10,634 freight cars, more than half were too old to be serviceable and most were too small to carry freight profitably.

There was no denying, furthermore, that the Union Pacific had been grievously dismembered during its receivership. "All its feeders, as well as its through connection to the Pacific had been cut off," reported William Z. Ripley, the leading railroad expert of the period.

It was not only the neglected and shrunken condition of the road itself, but the destitution of the countryside that made the Union Pacific look like a lost cause to skeptics like Pierpont Morgan. The Panic of 1893 produced the deepest and most prolonged depression of the post–Civil War period. "Never before has there been such a sudden and striking cessation of industrial activity," fretted the *Commercial and Financial Chronicle* in mid-September of that year. "Mills, factories, furnaces, mines nearly everywhere shut down in large numbers. . . . The complete unsettlement of confidence and the derangement of our financial machinery . . . had the effect of stopping the wheels of industry and of contracting production

and consumption within the narrowest limits, so that our internal trade
was brought almost to a standstill—and hundreds of thousands of men
thrown out of employment."

The devastation was still evident two years later, during Harriman's
grand tour. The depression had exposed the nation's apparent prosperity
in the first years of the 1890s as an illusion. The pre-1893 boom had been
fed by a frenzy for agricultural land, luring thousands of migrants to the
prairie, many of them innocent of the barest fundamentals of agriculture.
Land values reached ridiculously inflated levels: "If it was called a 'farm,'
and if somebody stood ready to cultivate it, Eastern moneylenders were
willing to finance the development of it." Speculators bought up large
tracts, subdivided them into parcels too small even for subsistence farming, and sold them to homesteaders from the East, saddling the buyers
with mortgages far larger than the properties were worth.

The downturn brought a tidal wave of farm foreclosures, bank failures,
and the depopulation of the agricultural zone as ruined settlers returned
East. Harriman saw from his observation car that "the great tracts of land
bought by speculative syndicates were no longer salable and remained
uncultivated; town sites were abandoned, and municipalities which had
floated loans in the East ceased to exist," related his biographer George
Kennan.

Morgan had not been alone in thinking of this destitution as almost a
permanent condition, or at least one destined to last so long that investing in a recovery was imprudent. When Harriman returned from his tour
fairly vibrating with optimism about the economic potential of the railroad and the territory, Otto Kahn dismissed it as "pretty wild talk," even
after Harriman revealed that he had put his own resources into buying up
all the Union Pacific stock he could find at prices below $25 per share.

"Union Pacific common is intrinsically worth as much as St. Paul
stock," Harriman told Kahn, referring to the Chicago, Milwaukee &
St. Paul, one of the most financially robust roads in the country. "With
good management it will get there." To Kahn, the comparison between
the Union Pacific and the St. Paul seemed fanciful. "I did not take it
seriously," he wrote years later. "Union Pacific, just emerged from wreck

and ruin: St. Paul, an old seasoned dividend payer that had passed with ease through the panics and devastations of the preceding years, and was even then selling above par!" Before a decade passed, however, Harriman would indeed get the Union Pacific there, and beyond.

HARRIMAN'S PAINSTAKING SCRUTINY of the West as he traveled the Union Pacific line revealed to him signs of an economic turnaround that eluded bankers and investors who surveyed the American economy chiefly from behind their desks and at lunch with one another. His conversations with farmers and cattlemen and bankers in the heartland convinced him that the downturn was bottoming out and made him a believer in the untapped potential of the western United States. Upgrading the Union Pacific so it would be capable of handling the coming surge in traffic, therefore, was imperative. Even before returning from his journey, he telegraphed the railroad's board for permission to launch a renovation program valued at $25 million. The reasons he gave in a follow-up wire were that "he clearly discovered signs of returning prosperity after the period of long depression," recalled Kahn; "that he believed this prosperity would assume proportions corresponding to the depth and extent of the long-drawn-out and drastic reaction that preceded it; that labor and materials were then extremely cheap, but would begin to advance before very long, and that the Union Pacific should begin to put itself in shape."

Twenty-five million dollars: The sum made the Union Pacific's directors quail. Someone remarked within Kahn's hearing that if Harriman's recommendation were followed "the Union Pacific would find itself in receivers' hands again before two years had passed." Kahn agreed: "It seemed a pretty hazardous thing to venture upon this huge outlay simply on a guess of coming unprecedented prosperity." The board deferred taking action on Harriman's wire, waiting for his return. As it happened, he already had begun to let contracts for the work and equipment he deemed necessary. Once he returned to New York he browbeat his fellow directors into ratifying the decisions he had made without them.

Harriman concluded that the Union Pacific needed heavier locomotives than its fifty-ton engines, and longer freight cars; with such equipment a thousand tons of freight would cost scarcely more to carry than five hundred, but the profit would be exponentially larger. Running such equipment, however, required heavier rails laid on a well-ballasted roadbed; curves had to be straightened and grades sheared down. The western part of the road featured grades as steep as eighty-seven feet in height to the mile; Harriman decreed a maximum of forty-three feet. His engineers set about the work with equipment that had never been seen before on a railroad—grading machines, dump wagons, steam shovels—and that in some cases had to be invented on the spot. When Harriman was finished with the Union Pacific, the road would reflect in every detail "the chisel and the straightedge of the Harriman engineers," judged Frank Spearman, an authoritative chronicler of the railroads at the turn of the twentieth century.

Harriman's crews did battle not only with the judgments of the railroad's original designers, which had not been challenged in the intervening three decades, but with Mother Nature, whose quirks had dictated the original route. They assumed the task of cutting mountains down to size and filling whole valleys with gravel and earth. The Dale Creek crossing just west of Cheyenne required a fill 900 feet long and 130 feet deep. "In these granite wastes the engineering figures assumed at once unheard-of proportions," Spearman wrote. "Cubic yards went into the calculations in millions instead of thousands."

Harriman treated the original right-of-way unsentimentally. Between Omaha and Ogden, Utah, a distance of nearly a thousand miles as the crow flies, the crews abandoned 150 miles of the old line (the equivalent of the entire New York Central between New York City and Troy) and built a new, straighter roadbed that saved twenty-two complete circles of curvature and 40 miles in distance. They widened and ballasted 196 miles, installed one million new ties, laid forty-two thousand tons of new rails and strengthened four thousand feet of wooden bridges with steel superstructures. Two hundred light locomotives were sold for scrap and 4,760 new rail cars with twice the capacity of the old were added to the fleet. Scarcely any request for equipment went unanswered. "We heard that a couple of compound locomotives had been ordered," William Park recalled; "when they arrived there were sixty of them. Some freight cars were needed; five thousand were ordered." All this was accomplished in the first sixteen months that Harriman was in charge.

No money was spared, but neither was human capital, which was treated pitilessly. "The pace, of course, was terrific," Park recounted, "and men sometimes fell by the wayside—those without brains or brawn got out of the way—but the elimination was through the survival of the fittest. There was no favoritism; those who made good were remembered while those who did not were forgotten."

The reconstruction demanded not merely new equipment but innovative industrial techniques. The railroad's maintenance shops in Omaha bustled with pneumatic equipment for handling heavy materials, and a facility for burnettizing wood ties—bathing them in a solution of zinc chloride to fend off rot—was expanded and refurbished.

Not all the improvements required the most modern technology. The railroad solved the problem of unloading recalcitrant herds of sheep from livestock cars by employing trained goats. This drew the attention of a government lawyer twenty years later, in the course of a federal lawsuit.

Park was on the stand. "The mention of goats is interesting to me," the lawyer remarked. "What do you mean by the use of goats in that connection?"

"In the night it was a very difficult matter to get the sheep out of the cars, and we finally hit on this scheme, which I think is peculiar to the Union Pacific," Park explained. "A goat was taken up into the car and walked around through the sheep, and as he walked out they seemed impelled to follow him."

"You say you 'employ' these goats," the lawyer asked sarcastically. "What salary do you give them?"

"We give them chewing tobacco," Park replied. "That is about all they get out of it."

All told, rebuilding the road through the Rockies amounted to a spectacular feat of engineering and sheer human determination. But one project stands apart. J. B. Berry, the road's chief engineer, was ordered to shorten a twenty-one-mile stretch of track in the Wasatch range just west of Salt Lake City by ten miles and reduce the sixty-eight-foot grade to Harriman's forty-three-foot maximum. This meant drilling a tunnel fifty-nine hundred feet through a mountain. It would be known as the Aspen tunnel.

On the surface this was not necessarily a greater challenge than those the crews already had faced on their transit through Wyoming—"The contractors uncovered a little of everything in the Rockies, from oil pockets to underground rivers," recounted Spearman. But this time they were fighting their way through "a mountain that for startling developments broke the records in the annals of American engineering." The crews encountered deposits of shale, sandstone, oil, and coal underground, as they had in other locations. Here, however, the geology seemed to be diabolically alive. The tunnel's path refused to stay put for two days at a time. "It moved forcibly into the bore from the right side, and when remonstrated with stole quietly in from the left; it descended on the tunnel with crushing force from above and rose irresistibly up into it from below."

Iron plates, bolted to the tunnel walls at night, "looked in the morning as if giants had twisted them." Sixteen-foot steel beams were contorted into S-shapes as though they were as pliant as rubber. Twelve-by-twelve pine timbers snapped like toothpicks; one day an engineer standing on what he thought was solid pine got propelled three feet into the air by the surging floor. Workmen became superstitious about the unruly forces deep underground. Their fears were validated one day when a gas pocket ignited, "ejecting men, mules, and timber from the mouth of the tunnel like a cannon's shot," in Park's words. ("It took brave men to go back into the headings after the funerals," he added, without revealing just how many funerals there had been.)

The problem eventually was identified as a layer of shale that swelled and twisted when exposed to air. Only after a stretch of seven hundred feet was lined with a reinforcing floor of steel and concrete to tame the willful geology was the tunnel completed—in 1901, more than a year late. The men, Park reported, had "conquered, and one morning Mr. Harriman appeared on the scene," as though to celebrate personally the victory over "so many unexpected obstacles."

The transformation of the UP under Harriman's leadership became the stuff of legend—and the goals he set became the benchmark for railroads coast to coast. Harriman, having originally taken weeks to inspect the Union Pacific from end to end, put the road in such tiptop condition that in an emergency a few years later he was able to ride it and its tributaries from San Francisco to New York, a journey of 3,255 miles, in the record time of seventy-one hours and twenty-seven minutes. The trip lowered the previous record by nearly eleven hours, of which ten were saved on the rails of the Union Pacific alone. John W. Gates, the Gilded Age barbed-wire and oil tycoon known as Bet-a-Million Gates for his freewheeling gambling style, would remark that in his experience, which included travel over nearly every railroad line in the country, the Union Pacific ranked as "East or West . . . the most magnificent railroad property in the world."

One of Harriman's pioneering initiatives would be turned into legend by Hollywood. This was his effort to end train robberies on the Union Pacific. The railroad's route through Wyoming "had long been a Mecca for outlaws," Park related. That stretch of track was especially vulnerable to raids because the roadbed was hemmed in by mountains on both sides, affording robbers "opportunities for the 'get-away' which is essential in the highwayman's profession." Typically, the raiders would strike in early evening and be safely on their way to the canyon-etched foothills known as the Hole-in-the-Wall country before a posse could be assembled.

Two members of the protean community of outlaws, Robert Leroy Parker and Harry Longabaugh, aka Butch Cassidy and the Sundance Kid, have been credited with the longest successful string of bank robberies of the period. They would be immortalized in a 1969 film, *Butch Cassidy and the Sundance Kid*, starring Paul Newman and Robert Redford, as was Harriman's solution for the repeated robberies: the creation of a team of special agents to be shuttled along the Union Pacific tracks on their own train and supplied with horses that could travel a hundred miles in a day.

Seeking to quash train robberies on the Union Pacific, Harriman outfitted a special car with strong horses and expert lawmen. In an episode memorialized by Hollywood, the posse seen here assembled to track down perpetrators of a robbery outside Wilcox, Wyoming, on June 2, 1899, attributed to the gang headed by Butch Cassidy and the Sundance Kid. The bandits' participation was never conclusively determined.

The presence of a rapid-response brigade, superbly equipped and trained, discouraged raids on the Union Pacific and prompted robbers to concentrate their attentions on competing lines. Among the agents' leaders, Joe La Force (or Lefors) would become legendary in his own right as the hero of several fictional potboilers published around the turn of the twentieth century.

"The expense was infinitesimal," Park stated of this private defense force, "compared with fruitless expenditures to capture the outlaws after robberies had occurred, to say nothing of the bad advertising such incidents gave to a railroad."

For Harriman all this effort and expenditure was first and foremost a business proposition, a necessity for making the road "the best line through the Rocky Mountains . . . so that we could operate it to advantage and at the least cost, and permit more business to go over it," he would testify in 1909, a few months before his death, while fighting a federal lawsuit aimed at breaking up his transportation empire. But he left no doubt that he considered the heroic reconstruction of the Union Pacific a matter of personal pride. Asked in the witness box whether similar projects had not taken place "on all of the American railroads," he replied, "No, sir, not to that extent."

"Haven't every one of them spent millions in improvements?"

"They are now, but they have not done it as quick as we did."

"No other railroads have improved as the Union Pacific has?"

"No, sir," Harriman stated bluntly. "Not one in the country."

This was true. During Harriman's first three years at the helm of the UP, he spent $25.7 million on improvements and new equipment; the Atchison, Topeka & Santa Fe, which had 70 percent more mileage, spent a mere $11.3 million and the Northern Pacific, 10 percent longer, only $6.9 million.

Some contemporaries held that the unprecedented success of the Union Pacific under Harriman was the product of chance—the unforeseen nationwide boom that followed the depression of the mid-1890s. "Fortune favored the enterprise from the start," sniped Ripley, an indefatigable critic of Harriman's financial machinations. "An unusual rainfall in the semi-arid belt brought heavy crops and prosperity at a crucial time . . . The annexation of the Philippine Islands also largely stimulated transcontinental and Oriental business." But even Ripley had to acknowledge that Harriman's policy of investing earnings in permanent improvements had reduced operating costs to less than 53 percent of revenues in 1902 from 62 percent in 1896. Harriman, he conceded, placed the company "in prime financial condition, with strong credit and unsurpassed banking connections."

Not to be overlooked was Harriman's uncompromising ambition and vision. His goal, Ripley understood, "was really the creation of an absolute monopoly of all transcontinental business." At the turn of the twentieth century, the West Coast was served by five mostly competing transcontinental routes. The most important was the "Sunset Route," comprising steamship lines running from the Atlantic seaboard to New Orleans, where they connected with the Southern Pacific Railroad. Then came the Gould lines, which connected with the Central Pacific — the western end of the first transcontinental. Third came the Atchison, Topeka & Santa Fe, and fourth a partnership of steamship companies connecting with each other over the Isthmus of Panama. Finally, there was the Union Pacific, still dependent on the Central Pacific and Southern Pacific for its access to the sea.

Harriman aimed to eliminate the first four of these enterprises as competitors, either by acquisition or partnership. Before his death he would succeed. The great enterprise had begun with his acquisition of the Union Pacific, the initial step in creating "the most discussed and possibly the most efficient transportation system in the country" and the core of "a near-monopoly in transcontinentals [that] rivalled Morgan's pretensions to dictatorship in the American railway industry," the railroad expert E. G. Campbell observed. But the UP was just the beginning.

A NEW ERA in the history of American railroads had been launched, endowing those who brought the industry forth from disaster with unprecedented wealth. Their profit making — or profiteering — would in time be seen in a negative light. Looking back on this era from the vantage point of two decades later, the Pujo Committee of the House of Representatives, led by Democratic representative Arsène Pujo of Louisiana, judged the process by which the railroad industry had been reorganized to be "archaic, extravagant, and utterly indefensible." The reorganizations almost always involved connivance between the managements that had led the companies into the mire and the bankers brought in to drain the swamp. Bondholders and shareholders were almost always placed in the position of sheep led to the slaughter, Pujo concluded. If they objected to the terms they were presented, their only option was to form another reorganization committee, "if they can arrange to combine their scattered forces and find influential men who have the courage to oppose the banking house.

"It is not easy," he observed wryly, "to find such men."

Railroad reorganization became so lucrative for the reorganizers that some investment banking houses abandoned their other businesses in order to devote their efforts exclusively to the railroads. "They say it is the most profitable work they have been engaged in in recent years," *Railway World* reported in 1896. The fees for reorganization managers were concealed within the total bills of the procedure and amortized through the new issues of stock and bonds given to existing security holders in exchange for their paper and floated to new investors on the open market. The investors, old and new, paid the price often without knowing how much, so there was little pressure to keep the fees reasonable. The typical fee was 1 percent of the value of the securities, plus whatever commissions were collected when the bankers marketed the shares. The Metropolitan Life Insurance Company, which joined Kuhn, Loeb in several reorganization syndicates, earned a $131,594 profit from underwriting the Union Pacific reorganization alone. Morgan's typical fee was reported to be $1 million.

The process cemented Morgan's role as the preeminent figure in American finance and industry. John Moody, founder of the financial and credit analysis firm that bears his name, described the network of Morgan trusts in steel, shipping, electrical supply, rubber, and other industries as the only industrial enterprise in the world that could rival Rockefeller's Standard Oil Trust in economic power. But "it is in the railroad world that the Morgan influence makes its greatest claim for public attention." The federal government had made no real effort to quell the rate wars, whether by limiting the construction of superfluous parallel lines or restricting the issuance of the watered stock and bonds that financed them (and that made them especially vulnerable to the downturn of 1893). Morgan took on the task, largely to uphold the railroads' self-interest.

In 1890 the railroad industry had been made up of a great number of small, independent systems, almost every one facing competition from rivals in their service regions. Ten years later the independents had practically disappeared, for the industry had coalesced into six major trusts dominated by a single man or a small group working as one. Morgan's was the largest—Moody estimated that Morgan-connected railroads embraced more than forty-seven thousand miles of track, or nearly twice that

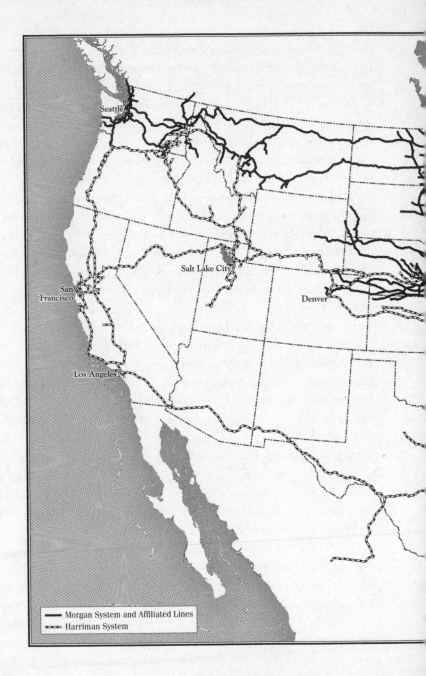

Seattle

Salt Lake City

San
Francisco

Denver

Los Angeles

▬▬ Morgan System and Affiliated Lines
✕✕✕ Harriman System

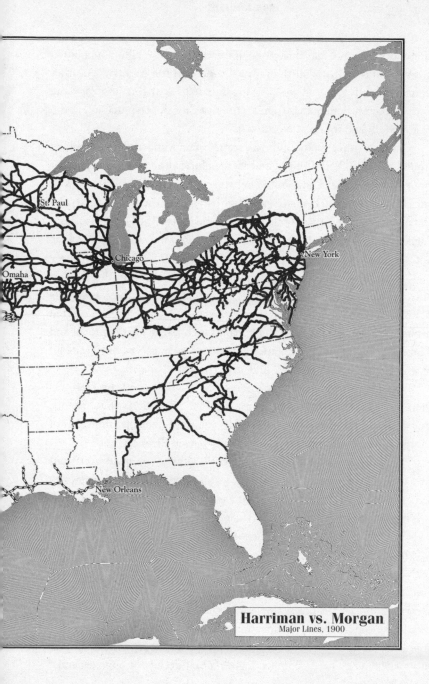

St. Paul

Chicago

Omaha

New York

New Orleans

Harriman vs. Morgan
Major Lines, 1900

of any other group, and that its capitalization of $2.3 billion amounted to nearly one-fourth of all the railroad capital in the country. "Another feature about the Morgan group," Moody added, "is that in most cases the lines absolutely dominate certain sections of the country; such as . . . the entire South and the great Northwest."

The five other major railroad trusts were Vanderbilt's, assembled around the New York Central and its tributaries; the Gould-Rockefeller group, the remnant of Jay Gould's network, now managed mostly by William Rockefeller; the Pennsylvania Railroad group; the Rock Island; and Harriman's, based on the Union Pacific and (after 1901) the Southern Pacific. But as Moody observed, the distinctions among these groups were not always clear-cut, for several had interconnections leading ultimately to Morgan: The Pennsylvania group had become allied with the Vanderbilts, thanks in part to Morgan's own peacemaking, and the Vanderbilts were allied with Morgan. Then there were the ways that Morgan exerted his influence indirectly, through big banks such as the First National and Chase National and life insurance companies such as New York Life, all of which were at least partially under his control.

This was the community of interests in the flesh, and the flesh was Pierpont Morgan's. Only Harriman, with an obstinate self-confidence that matched Morgan's, stood apart. His goals did not differ from that of Morgan and his compatriots, but he would pursue them on his own.

The Morgan system would permanently alter the railroads' relationship with their communities, passengers, and shippers. Under the new system, the quest for profits unfolded on a much greater scale than before. It was no longer possible for a lone buccaneer to plunder a single line in the style of Drew, Gould, and Fisk; henceforth, fortunes would be made and lost in battles waged by titans over ever-larger consolidated enterprises, with commensurately titanic consequences for the national economy and the financial markets.

The railroads' customers would soon discover that this change substituted a new evil for the old one, and was much more costly at that. As Interstate Commerce Commissioner Charles A. Prouty told an economists' conference in 1902, reflecting on a half decade of unprecedented upheaval: "Five years ago the crying evil in railway operations was . . . mainly discrimination between individual shippers. While many rates were too high, the general level was low." That was no longer the case. As a result of the consolidation of the 1890s and the railroads' recognition that "competition in rates is always suicidal," competition had been eradicated. Rate discrimination had disappeared, "but in its place comes that other danger which always attends monopoly, the exaction of an unreasonable charge." Put simply, the same shippers who earlier resented favoritism shown to their competitors, even if within an environment of lower rates for all, now discovered that the price of eliminating favoritism was the imposition of higher rates for everyone, with no opportunity for negotiation.

This stubbornness permeated the industry, not only in its relations with customers, but with its workers. As the century drew to a close, George Pullman, one of the most bullheaded men in American business, provoked a confrontation that would reverberate in US labor-management relations for decades to come. To passengers on long-distance train trips who passed the nights in his sleeping cars, Pullman's name had been identified with comfort and luxury on the rails. To his employees, it signified the relentless seeking of profit at their expense. Pullman's reckoning with his labor force, when it finally came, would raise anxiety among the public and on Capitol Hill about railroad tycoons' concentration of economic power and their ruthlessness in exercising it—anxiety that would cause political trouble especially for Morgan and Harriman.

13

"A PIG-HEADED AFFAIR"

IN THE SPRING of 1894 the nineteen-year-old seamstress Jennie Curtiss wrote to a Methodist Episcopal minister named William H. Carwardine about her life as an employee of the Pullman Palace Car Company and a resident of Pullman, Illinois, the company town.

Located on the South Side of Chicago hard by Lake Calumet, Pullman was an immaculately groomed community, its spotless streets lined with handsome brick cottages and laid out around a central commons featuring a schoolhouse and an indoor arcade. All this was designed to evoke in real estate terms the luxurious comfort George Pullman strived to provide passengers on his railroad sleeping cars, the source of his fortune. The general impression in town was of an "all-pervading air of thrift and providence," Johns Hopkins economist Richard T. Ely wrote in *Harper's Monthly*. Yet there was something else about what Ely labeled "the experiment called Pullman."

Jennie Curtiss knew what that something was: George Pullman's greed. She also knew that Carwardine would lend her a willing ear. The thirty-four-year-old minister was almost unique among local pastors in his willingness to preach from the pulpit on behalf of the workers and against Pullman. Steeped in the populist and pro-labor Social Gospel movement rising at the time, Carwardine had damned Pullman in a sermon on May 20 for paying meager wages, calling him "a pampered millionaire, entrenched behind his gold, . . . to heed not the tears of wives and children who have been simply existing upon the crumbs which fall from the rich man's table."

In her letter to Carwardine, Curtiss underscored much of what the minister had already observed in Pullman's company town. She wrote of her father, who had worked for the company for ten years:

> Last summer he was sick for three months, and in September he died. At the time of his death we owed the Pullman Company about sixty dollars for rent. They told me I would have to pay that rent, give what I could every pay-day, until it was paid . . . Many a time I have drawn nine and ten dollars for two weeks' work, paid seven dollars for my board and given the Company the remaining two or three dollars on the rent, and I still owe them fifteen dollars. Sometimes when I could not possibly give them anything, I would receive slurs and insults from the clerks in the bank, because Mr. Pullman would not give me enough in return for my hard labor to pay the rent for one of his houses and live.

Curtiss also depicted conditions on the Pullman factory floor, where "the tyrannical and abusive treatment we received from our forewoman made our daily cares so much harder to bear . . . No doubt she [the forewoman] will remain in the employ of the Pullman Company, as that is just the kind of people they want at the heads of their departments—one who will help grind down their laborers." Thus the inescapable dissonance of life as an employee of George M. Pullman: a spotless environment outside the factory, and endless, grinding torment inside.

The conditions Curtiss described grew worse throughout the crushing depression that followed the economic crash of 1893. They would lead to a strike and boycott that began on June 26, 1894, swept across the Midwest, disrupted rail operations across the nation, and finally brought the US government into the fray—on industry's side. The Pullman Strike was the largest job action in the United States up to that time, dwarfing by several times the Knights of Labor action against the Gould system eight years before. It still ranks as one of the most significant strikes in

American history. Neither the railroads nor organized labor would ever be the same.

GEORGE PULLMAN'S TIDY township was part of a movement during the Industrial Revolution to place working men and their families in salubrious surroundings, partially to provide spiritual uplift and partially to enhance productivity. The movement gave rise to two especially notable attempts at industrial utopias: Saltaire, which was founded in 1851 by the woolens manufacturer Titus Salt by the Aire River not far from Liverpool, England; and Familistère, or the Social Palace, which was launched in 1859 by the iron stove manufacturer Jean Baptiste André Godin at Guise, 125 miles from Paris.

The balance between the spiritual and practical elements varied from one to the other of these communities, although their builders always professed to place the contentment and moral improvement of the residents at the forefront of their worldviews. "The Social Palace is not only a better shelter than the isolated house of the workman, it is also an instrument for his well-being, his individual dignity and progress," Monsieur Godin explained to *Harper's*. "It is precisely because it affords him the right conditions for the full development of his *physical* life, that it opens to the world a new horizon for our *moral* life." (Emphasis in the original.)

In the promotional material about his own company town, George Pullman outlined the same general rationale of spiritual improvement, but put a bit more stress on the economic element. "The Pullman car solved the problem of long, continuous railway journeys, and the town of Pullman, along new lines, gives a hope of bettering the relations of capital and labor," he stated in a company brochure. "The Pullman enterprise . . . has illustrated the helpful combination of capital and labor, without strife or stultification, upon lines of mutual recognition." In practice, none of the towns' paternalistic philanthropists exploited their commercial potential as sedulously as George Pullman.

Almost without exception, visitors to Pullman, Illinois, were struck by its cleanliness and abundant amenities, at least at first. But these always

Pullman Palace Sleeping Car (Interior)

George Pullman's Palace Cars brought comfort to long-distance travel on the rails; their plush benches converted into beds and the angled hideaway compartments above folded down to form the upper berths.

looked most impressive from a distance. "As seen from the railway by a passing tourist, [the town] presents a beautiful picture," Rev. Carwardine reported in his book *The Pullman Strike,* published in 1894 while the crisis was still ongoing. "In fact, it appears to be a veritable paradise. Beautiful trees and flowers, pretty fountains, glimpses here and there of artistic sweeps of landscape, gardens, rows of pretty brick houses, church in the distance, public buildings of different description."

Yet closer inspection revealed these vistas to be those of a corporate Potemkin village, for "strife, mutual suspicion and discord" simmered behind the facade. Pullman's luxurious community library could fairly claim to be "one of the most complete of its kind in the United States," Carwardine wrote, as it was furnished with plush reading chairs and a carpeted floor, stocked with 20,900 volumes including 5,479 reference books, 2,245 scientific treatises, and 2,073 volumes of poetry. But the annual charge for membership was three dollars per adult and one dollar per child. That was a steep rate for Pullman employees struggling to make do on as little as fifteen cents an hour, or nine dollars for a sixty-hour work week, especially at a time when the communities surrounding Pullman were starting to build public libraries open to every resident for free. As a result, out of a population that reached twelve thousand or more, the Pullman library enrolled only about 250 subscribers a year.

The Arcade, in which the library was located, was a large building on the main square that also housed the offices of the *Pullman Journal*, the community's only newspaper, its sole bank (owned by the Pullman company, it was the issuer of the company paychecks), and the only retail shops permitted in town (also owned by the company). The *Journal* was edited by one Colonel Duane Doty, who served as the historian and statistician of the Pullman company and assured all visitors that the community was one "from which all that is ugly, discordant and demoralizing is eliminated."

Occupying a central location was what was known as the "greenstone church" for the color of the imported serpentine stone of its exterior, a unique material in the largely redbrick community. But the church and its attached parsonage were vacant, because no congregation could afford the rent. Carwardine's Methodist flock had tried to negotiate Pullman down from $300 a month but met with a firm refusal. "When that church was built," George Pullman explained to the pastor, "it was not intended so much for the moral and spiritual welfare of the people as it was for the completion of the artistic effect of the scene." In any case the building was

Centerpiece of the company town of Pullman, Illinois, the Arcade building housed
the community's library, bank, newspaper, and retail shops, all controlled by the Pullman company. To the left is the greenstone church: George Pullman intended it to
host all denominations, but local congregations judged it too expensive to lease and
useless for practical church purposes.

judged useless for sectarian purposes, since it consisted of a single large
auditorium but had no classrooms for Sunday school or offices for private
conferences. The Catholics and Lutherans built their own churches just
over the town line, while the Methodists contented themselves with a
meeting room in the Arcade, which they leased for $500 a year. "No pri-
vate individual owns to-day a square rod of ground or a single structure
in the entire town," observed Ely in *Harper's Monthly*. "No organization,
even a church, can occupy other than rented quarters."

What was especially oppressive about life behind the scenes in Pullman was that everything in town came with a price tag posted by the company, with the exception of the public school. (Schoolbooks, however,
had to be purchased by the parents.) The school board was an elected
body, but the candidates invariably were officers of the Pullman Palace
Car Company or other affiliates that bore his name. That was true also
of the town clerk and treasurer and officers of the community's water and
gas company.

The Pullman's Company's authority reached everywhere. Observed a visiting reporter from Pittsburgh, "the corporation trims your lawn and attends to your trees; the corporation sweeps your street, and sends a man around to pick up every cigar stump, every bit of paper, every straw or leaf; . . . the corporation does practically everything but sweep your room and make your bed, and the corporation expects you to enjoy it and hold your tongue." The company employed a physician to treat injured employees free of charge; but the doctor in place at the time of the strike, John McLean, was also expected to obtain a statement from every patient of the cause of the injury, which invariably shifted blame away from the company and on to the individual. It was McLean's habit to urge upon injured workers the wisdom of accepting any settlement offered by the company instead of placing their fate in the hands of lawyers. If a lawsuit followed, McLean was expected to testify for the company.

"This is a corporation made and a corporation governed town, and is utterly un-American in its tendencies," Carwardine wrote in his book. Pullman's dominance fostered not only corporate arrogance, but indifference. The company rotated its own executives through municipal offices, where "each new superior appears to have his own friends, whom he appoints to desirable positions," Ely reported. "Favoritism and nepotism, out of place as they are in an ideal society, are oft-repeated and apparently well-substantiated charges . . . The power of Bismarck in Germany is utterly insignificant when compared with the power of the ruling authority of the Pullman Palace Car Company in Pullman . . . Every man, woman, and child in the town is completely at its mercy, and it can be avoided only by emigration." That was more easily said than done, however, for it was widely understood that the town's residents gained preference for promotion or for reemployment after layoffs — indeed, during slack periods, workers living outside the town limits were required to move into Pullman if they wished to keep their jobs. (The exceptions were Pullman's sleeping car porters, who were all African Americans and often former slaves and were not welcome in his company town. The job of porter was the only employment open to black workers in the Pullman company.)

This situation might have been marginally tolerable, had the company not expected a minimum return of 6 percent a year on all its invest-ments in the community, including the houses it built and the utilities it provided. The company's position was that its residences were superior to those available in neighboring suburbs such as Kensington, and cheaper too. Hundreds of apartments were available for rent in Pullman for six to nine dollars per month, plus two dollars for cooking gas; the company claimed it was supplying water to its tenants at a loss, based on what it was paying to the local public waterworks. The company was earning only 3.82 percent on its investment in the residences—"a manifestly inade-quate return," George Pullman told a government commission empan-eled by President Grover Cleveland in July 1894 to investigate the strike's causes. Pullman spoke as though the accommodations he provided to his workers for a fee were tantamount to philanthropy.

But Pullman's figures were highly dubious. The commission deter-mined that rents in neighboring communities were typically 20 to 25 per-cent lower than equivalent lodgings in Pullman—and during the post-1893 depression, as much as 50 percent less. The company was reselling water to its residents not at a loss but at five times its cost, and gas at a threefold gain. Pullman's relentless rent-seeking from his own employees would soon prove to be the flashpoint for a historic conflagration.

GEORGE PULLMAN HAD had reason for concern about the effect of the Panic of 1893 and the ensuing depression on his business. Orders for new sleeping cars had evaporated, leaving only the Pullman repair shops busy. For efficiency's sake, the company closed its Detroit maintenance shops, idling about eight hundred workers, and shifted all remaining repair ac-tivity to Pullman.

But the company also instituted wage cuts that piled almost all the burden of lost business on the rank and file. By April 1894, Pullman em-ployees were earning 30 percent less per hour on average than they earned in May 1893. On May 7, 1894, a committee of forty-six workers from the Pullman plant met with Vice President Thomas H. Wickes to request that wages be restored to the levels of June 1893. Wickes was in the process of explaining the "absolute necessity" of the wage cuts when Pullman himself strode into the room. He informed the workers that restoring the old wage scale would be "a most unfortunate thing for the men," because no one would place an order for cars at prices based on the wages of mid-1893. Under those conditions "the works would necessarily close down and the great majority of the employees be put in idleness, a contingency I am using my best effort to avoid."

But wages were not the workers' only concern. There was also the matter of rents, which the company flatly refused to lower. Pullman maintained that the portion of the company that managed the residential properties was entirely independent from the car shops—"The renting of the dwellings and the employment of workmen at Pullman are in no way tied together," he told the disbelieving delegation—adding that in any case the company was losing money on rent.

Employees were under no illusion that there was any distinction between Pullman the employer and Pullman the landlord. On payday, anyone in a Pullman house or tenement received two checks—one for the rent (payable in advance), and one for anything left over. At the bank, they were required to sign the rent check over to the company on the spot.

Thomas Heathcote, a sleeping car builder who would become one of the labor leaders at Pullman, would later tell of having seen family men weeping at the pay window "because they only got 3 or 4 cents after paying their rent . . . I have seen them stand by the window and cry for money enough to enable them to keep their families; I have been insulted at that window time and time again by the clerks when I tried to get money enough to support my family, even after working every day and overtime."

The employees were painfully aware that no company executives, officers, or forepersons had suffered any reduction in pay, nor had the shareholders suffered a reduction in their annual dividend of 8 percent. From July 1893 through July 1894, wages had fallen from $7.2 million to $4.5 million, but the dividends paid had actually *risen*, to $2.9 million from $2.5 million.

The railroad industry's habit of imposing the costs of economic down-turns largely on its workforce had inspired a surge in labor activism dat-ing back to the mid-1880s. But it also exposed the vacuum of leadership among workers: The traditional railroad brotherhoods were not designed to directly challenge management prerogatives, and by 1890 the Knights of Labor were already in eclipse. The desire to counter the policies of the tycoons was hamstrung by the absence of instruments to do so.

The way was open for a new approach, and a new leader. He would appear in the person of Eugene Victor Debs. The Pullman Strike would catapult him into worldwide fame.

A native of Terre Haute, Indiana, the thirty-eight-year-old Debs had worked as a railroad painter and fireman—that is, a stoker of locomo-tive boilers—before moving into the public sphere and labor leadership, first as a Democratic state legislator in Indiana, and then as leader of the Brotherhood of Locomotive Firemen, one of the old-style mutual-aid organizations. Having witnessed the disaster of the Knights of Labor's strike against the Gould system at close hand, he drew from it some useful lessons about organization and strategy when he founded the American Railway Union in June 1893.

In personality and outlook, Debs was the polar opposite of Terence Powderly, the Knights' bookish grand master workman. He was a spell-binding orator and charismatic leader of working men; throughout his career he braved unstinting vituperation from railroad executives and conservative politicians while commanding the admiration of his mem-bers and such luminaries as Clarence Darrow, who would serve Debs as defense counsel during his trial on conspiracy charges arising from the Pullman Strike. "There may have lived some time, somewhere, a kindlier, gentler, more generous man than Eugene V. Debs," Darrow would write in his memoirs, "but I have never known him. Nor have I ever read or heard of another."

Debs was not opposed in principle to strikes or other job actions aimed at securing recognition for his organization and its members. But the Great Southwest strike had shown him the hazards of staging a walkout

before the workers and the union were ready. His ARU aimed to avoid
an error that had weakened the Knights from the start—the division of
railroad workers into individual brotherhoods that destroyed any sense
of cohesiveness, making the differences among the workers more important than their similarities, obscuring their common interests and handing
railroad managements a wedge with which to set worker against worker.
The ARU's goal was to unite the nation's 850,000 railroad workers into
a single great brotherhood so they could negotiate as one for wages, work
conditions, and hours. (The cause was unfortunately qualified, for unlike
the Knights, the ARU's membership was restricted to whites—a policy
enacted by ARU convention delegates ostensibly against the wishes of
Debs.) By the beginning of 1894 the ARU already had 150,000 members. That was enough to ignite genuine panic among railroad presidents
who perceived that, at last, a force may have emerged that could challenge their unassailable power over the workplace. The panic would soon
spread to their friends in politics.

To Debs, however, a large-scale strike seemed premature. That was so
even though in April 1894, less than a year after its founding, the ARU
had staged a strike on James J. Hill's Great Northern Railway over a wage
cut, managing to bring its freight service to a complete halt and—somewhat to its surprise—forcing the pugnacious Hill to agree to arbitration.
It was a clear union victory, but in Debs's reckoning the time was not yet
ripe for turning it into a broader campaign.

Debs sensed the same overconfidence that had forced the Knights into
their disastrous strike against Jay Gould. At a meeting of union officers in
late April, he recounted, "we concluded that many of our members might
possibly be flushed with the triumph of that strike [i.e., on the Great
Northern], and if we were not extremely careful we would be precipitated
into other disturbances." Debs was anxious "to avoid any strike if it was
possible to do so." So he was perturbed when, days later, on May 11, he received word that the Pullman workers, acting one step ahead of a rumored
lockout by Pullman, had walked off the job.

———

"THE GREAT TROUBLE with the Chicago strike," opined Carroll D. Wright, the chairman of the presidential commission, "was that it was a pig-headed affair all around."

Wright's judgment was unfair, in that the outstanding pigheadedness belonged to the railroad bosses. Their instrument was a body known as the General Managers' Association, which had been formed in 1886 to coordinate the operations of the twenty-four railroads serving Chicago. The GMA initially confined itself to organizing switching and loading schedules, and livestock weighing and transfers. But it presently assumed the role of establishing regionwide wage rates, the better to suppress pay demands by one railroad's workers that might force raises upon the others.

The railroads tried to conceal their collusion but it was no secret to the ARU, which could not help noticing that wage cuts were always applied in concert by railroads across the region. Since Chicago rates influenced those of all connecting lines, moreover, the cuts rapidly propagated nationwide. By late 1893, with labor discontent spreading, the GMA became the agency through which the railroads colluded on lockouts of workers and the recruitment of strikebreakers. "Today there is no more air-tight railroad organization on the face of the earth," the unabashedly pro-business *Chicago Herald* declared admiringly in May 1893, a year before the Pullman Strike was launched. "All the roads have bound themselves to act exactly as if the strike were on their own line."

The labor leaders saw other intolerable conditions clearly. A few days after the strike began, Debs arrived in Pullman for a personal inspection tour. Reluctant as he had been to countenance a job action, he determined that in this case, the employees were "fully justified . . . in the course they had taken." Their wages and expenses were "so adjusted that every dollar the employees earned found its way back into the Pullman coffers" and "they were daily getting deeper into the debt of the Pullman company. . . . I made up my mind, as president of the American Railway Union, of which these employees were members, to do everything in my power that was within law and within justice to right the wrongs of those employees."

For the first few weeks of the Pullman Strike, or until the beginning of June, it remained possible to reach a settlement and keep it from spreading. The strikers sought chiefly to arbitrate their grievances, which in addition to the pay cuts and the rent charges included the firing of three of their organizers on the eve of the walkout. George Pullman, however, seemed intent on exacerbating the situation. The moment the strike was declared, he shut his shops and laid off six hundred employees who were not themselves strikers, thus spreading pain across his company town and the larger community. He flatly refused to arbitrate; a delegation from the Civic Federation of Chicago, composed of eminent citizens from "all grades of respectable society," tried twice to bring Pullman to the table. Both times his reply was that there was "nothing to arbitrate." He scorned the ARU as illegitimate, refusing to meet with anyone representing the union or to consider appeals from anyone retaining membership. Debs, still hoping to keep the walkout from expanding, leaned over backwards to allow the company to arbitrate on its own terms, even waiving the right to name any member of the arbitration panel, "virtually permitting them to select three out of five representatives," he recounted later. (The other two would be selected by the other arbitrators.) Pullman rejected the overture.

Pullman's stubbornness—his pigheadedness, so to speak—pushed the situation toward a nationwide crisis. The tinderbox was the first national convention of the ARU, which opened in Chicago on June 9, barely a month before the strike began, with four hundred delegates in attendance. The sessions were open to the press and public. On June 15, the delegates heard from a procession of Pullman workers, including Jennie Curtiss, who repeated what she had told Carwardine and pleaded for the ARU's support. The convention appointed a committee to meet with Wickes, the Pullman vice president, but he refused to make any concessions. On June 21, the convention voted to give the company five days to agree to arbitrate. If not, ARU members nationwide would refuse to operate any locomotive hauling a Pullman sleeping car. There was not a single dissenting vote. With no response having arrived from the company, the boycott began on June 26.

The stage was now set for the entry of the US government into the conflict. But its intercession would be far from evenhanded.

No one could have been surprised that in his second term President Grover Cleveland would favor the railroads, for his cabinet could have passed for any railroad company's board of directors. Cleveland himself had made a fortune in the four-year interregnum between his terms by practicing law in partnership with Francis Lynde Stetson, who was Pierpont Morgan's attorney. Secretary of State Walter Q. Gresham, in his pre-cabinet post as a federal judge, had issued a string of pro-railroad rulings in labor disputes dating back to 1877. Secretary of War Daniel S. Lamont had been an active investor in urban railways on Wall Street. Postmaster General Wilson S. Bissell had been an executive, director, and counsel of at least three railroads operating out of Buffalo, ties that he refused to sever upon joining the cabinet.

The outstanding railroad man in the cabinet was Attorney General Richard Olney, who had spent a decade as a director and counsel of the Boston & Maine and almost as long with the Chicago, Burlington, and Quincy. The latter kept Olney on its payroll for $10,000 a year even after he assumed his duties as attorney general, which paid only $8,000.

As if this was not enough to stack the deck against the strikers, popular sentiment was starting to turn against labor. The public was growing weary of worker unrest, as the myriad strikes following the Panic of 1893 evolved from small, localized disputes into regional work stoppages and threatened to spread even further. In April 1894 an Ohio reformer named Jacob Coxey assembled a band of one hundred unemployed men to march on Washington. His call reverberated across the country, and soon platoons of jobless men, including many laid-off railway workers, were heading east. They demanded free transport on the rails and, when refused, commandeered trains and turned them toward the capital. At first they won considerable public support. But as demonstrations yielded to violence, the fellow feeling of unemployed onlookers began to dissipate. (The "army," which reached an estimated five hundred men, dissipated after Coxey was arrested and charged with trespassing for walking on the grass of the US Capitol.)

The march of "Coxey's Army" had coincided with the ARU's Great Northern strike. Together, these episodes prompted the government to step in with a declaration that interfering with trains carrying the mail would be prosecuted as a federal offense. In effect, this order placed under the protection of the US government every car of any train with a mail bag aboard—a "legal time bomb" ticking away, as historian Gerald G. Eggert would describe it, "to explode . . . with full force upon Eugene Debs and the American Railway Union."

Notwithstanding the threat, the ARU's boycott of Pullman trains spread rapidly. On June 27, the second day, 5,000 men had left their jobs and fifteen railroads were shut down. A day later, 40,000 workers were participating and traffic had been halted on all roads westbound out of Chicago. On day four, 125,000 had walked off. Some of the sympathetic strikers may have been motivated by their own mistreatment at the hands of railroad managements, including wage and hour cuts; others by news that the General Managers' Association had begun recruiting strikebreakers through bureaus in New York, Philadelphia, Cleveland, and other cities. Reports reaching Debs said that as many as 250 scabs were being hired every day.

Debs had his hands full trying to discourage violence and ensuring that the mails were unmolested, but sporadic fighting broke out along with the commandeering of mail trains. As had happened in the Great Southwest strike, major newspapers took up the cry against the strikers. The *Chicago Tribune* ran two alarmist headlines on June 30, one declaring, "Mob Is in Control" and the other, "Law Is Trampled On." Sporadic outbreaks of violence and the febrile press reaction would soon trigger concrete government action.

Olney and three Chicago-based government appointees—US attorney Thomas Milchrist, John W. Arnold of the US Marshals Service, and Edwin Walker—had spent the first days of the boycott pumping up each others' hysteria. Milchrist fired the first rhetorical shot with a wire to Olney on June 30, reporting the stopping of two mail trains outside Chicago. He expressed his determination to "aid in the repression of lawlessness" and asked Olney to allow Arnold to appoint deputies by the hundreds "to guard the various mail trains likely to be interfered with." After Olney obligingly issued the order, Arnold began to pin deputy badges on a ragtag group of armed men that eventually numbered in the thousands, many of them strikebreakers and security guards on the railroads' payrolls.

That very same day Olney named Walker as special counsel to the government, vesting him with the authority to obtain court injunctions against the strikers and arrest warrants against Debs and other ARU leaders. This placed Walker, a veteran attorney for railroad companies, in a massive conflict of interest, but that disturbed Olney not a whit; to the attorney general, the interests of the railroads and those of the government were indistinguishable.

"It has seemed to me," Olney told Walker upon his appointment, "that if the rights of the United States were vigorously asserted in Chicago, the origin and center of the demonstration, the result would be to make it a failure everywhere else." He advised Walker "not merely to rely on warrants against persons actually guilty of the offense of obstructing United States mails, but to . . . secure restraining orders which shall have the effect of preventing any attempt to commit the offense." This novel strategy of restraining activities before they occurred would have a lasting impact on labor relations.

Arnold was already in full panic mode. By July 1 the US marshal had sworn in more than four hundred deputies. "Many more will be needed to protect the mail trains," he wired Olney. "Shall I purchase 100 riot guns? I think it very essential that we should have them."

A day later, Debs and his fellow ARU officers were served with an injunction "sweeping in its terms," as Walker approvingly described it to Olney, forbidding them to interfere with the mails and interstate commerce by continuing the strike. But it had little effect on the strikers themselves. "Have read the order of court to rioters here," Arnold reported, "and they simply hoot at it, pay no attention to it, and have made their threats that they will not allow any Pullman car to pass through on the Rock Island road." He estimated two thousand "rioters" in his way, placing "mail trains in great danger."

Over the next few days, Arnold's estimate of the crowds grew even more feverish. He had exhausted the supply of dependable civilians to deputize and was now scraping men in off the street. Initially, the deputies were men known to Arnold or employees of the boycotted railroads. They were vouched for by railroad officials and dragooned by nonstriking railroad staff, although the vetting process for the new recruits was less than rigorous: "Probably every man that was at liberty . . . went out to find men," a Rock Island executive told the strike commission. "We might find them down town or we might find them elsewhere . . . Perhaps the appearance of a man would indicate whether he could be trusted; that was all that was required of any of them."

During the later rounds of recruitment, the street denizens press-ganged into service tended to lack even superficial signs of trustworthiness. "The deputies sworn in yesterday were of no possible value," Walker confided to Olney. "They were men taken from a crowd that applied for employment [i.e., strikebreakers], and in character were scarcely any improvement upon the strikers themselves. The marshal himself [Arnold] was assaulted yesterday, and one of his principal deputies severely injured."

On July 3, President Cleveland injected a new element into the conflict by sending troops to Chicago. He did so at Olney's urging but over the objection of Illinois governor John Peter Altgeld, who had expected the government to follow the traditional protocol governing federal deployments for law enforcement: First, rely on local civil authorities as the front line to keep order; then, if the police were overwhelmed, respond to a request by the governor for militia troops (not yet widely known as the National Guard); and, solely as a final measure, dispatch federal military units. Altgeld would blame Olney and Cleveland for conniving at the creation of a new policy in which the federal government became the strikebreaking force of first resort. "The trouble at Chicago," he reflected, "was so magnified to make it seem that we were bordering on anarchy and that consequently federal interference was necessary." The only thing holding up railroad traffic, in Altgeld's view, was the railroads' inability to hire workers to run the trains.

Olney and Walker shared the conviction that the key figure in the labor disturbances was Debs; they thought the best option for ending the strike was to put him on ice. On July 6, a day on which gunfire erupted between Arnold's deputies and the strikers, resulting in the deaths of two of the latter, Walker reported to Olney that "we have now sufficient evidence at hand for indictment of Debs and all the leaders of the association for conspiracy." He was confident that local judges would impose punitive bail, so that the defendants "will remain in jail until their cases are called in the Federal court for trial."

Olney was known to have expressed misgivings about Walker's tactics against the ARU only once, when federal agents seized Debs's private papers in the course of his arrest; Olney ordered the action "publicly disavowed and the papers at once returned," observing that "the Government, in enforcing the law, can not afford to be itself lawless." Walker complied begrudgingly, but it was a unique upbraiding by Olney and the storm quickly passed. The attorney general and his special counsel remained united in their obsessive quest to defeat the strikers at all costs.

ONE NIGHT A few weeks into the strike, the general counsel of the Chicago & North-Western Railway Company stood in a railroad yard, deeply conflicted as he watched several cars go up in flames. He was Clarence Darrow, who had entered into corporate law two years earlier after a long stint as a Chicago city attorney and despite a personal affinity for the progressive ideology of Henry George. Now thirty-seven, Darrow noticed that most of the crowd sharing the view with him were boys and young men; not a few were ruffians whom Arnold had hired to keep the peace. What was clear to Darrow, however, was that most of the onlookers were in sympathy with the strikers.

Once the strike loomed on the horizon, Darrow's heart had ceased to be with his employers. The railroads' stubborn refusal to grant their employees better pay and working conditions seemed destined to goad the rank and file into walking out. "I realized my anomalous position," Darrow would write years later. "I really wanted the men to win, and believed that they should." Unable to reconcile his conflicted loyalties, he resigned from his corporate job.

As a free agent, Darrow gained a clearer view of the legal inequities confronting the strikers. First there was the effort by the government and the railroads, acting in collusion, to obtain court injunctions against the strike. He considered this strategy a raw abuse of judicial authority—"Preserving peace is part of the police power of the state, and men should be left free to strike or not," he observed. "When violence occurs this is for the police department and not for a court of chancery."

Then there was the appointment of Edwin Walker as a lawyer for the government in the injunction cases while he remained counsel to the railroads' General Managers' Association. In fact, Walker was wearing three hats, not two, for he also served as attorney for the Chicago, Milwaukee & St. Paul Railroad. "I did not regard this as fair," Darrow remarked dryly. Finally, there were the conspiracy charges against Debs and the other ARU leaders—another distortion of the law, in Darrow's view, for they were framed in a way that allowed prosecutors to magnify any misdemeanor into a felony. "If there are still any citizens interested in protecting liberty, let them study the conspiracy laws of the United States," Darrow would write in his memoirs, published in 1932. "They have grown in the last forty years until to-day no one's liberty is safe."

Darrow came into court as defense counsel for Debs in his criminal case for conspiracy to violate the federal injunction. The conspiracy case would collapse after almost all the testimony was heard when a juror was taken ill, leaving only eleven to finish the case. After a mistrial was declared, the government chose to drop the charges, possibly because word had emerged that before it was sent home, the first jury had been leaning 11 to 1 for acquittal.

The outcome of the civil injunction case was less equivocal. Debs and his fellow ARU leaders consistently lost in federal court, beginning with a federal judge's holding them in contempt for violating the injunction in July 1894 and culminating in a unanimous Supreme Court decision on May 27, 1895, upholding the government's authority to enjoin any interference with interstate commerce, such as the rail boycott. Despite these unhappy results, Darrow's representation of Debs would launch his career into a new phase as a warrior against legal oppression.

By the time of the Supreme Court decision, the Pullman Strike was widely recognized as a failure. Its leadership had been disrupted through arrests and jailings, the railroads had been able to resume traffic without settling with the American Railway Union, which had failed to gain recognition as a representative of the rank and file. Years later, Darrow recapped the disaster in detail: "The A.R.U. was destroyed. For many years its members were boycotted; they changed their names and wandered over the land looking for a chance to work." Economic historian Alfred Chandler (among many other experts) judged that "the strike never had a chance." The ARU was still too unorganized and impoverished to carry on an extended walkout, while the railroads had prepared themselves with armies of strikebreakers and secured the promise of federal intervention well in advance.

Debs himself was not so sure. It was only his arrest by federal authorities that killed the strike, he told the strike commission. He recounted having answered a knock on his door at Chicago's Leland Hotel, finding Arnold on the threshold with a warrant issued that morning, after a federal grand jury had handed up an indictment for conspiracy to interfere with interstate commerce and other related crimes. "It was not the soldiers that ended the strike; it was not the old brotherhoods that ended the strike; it was simply the United States courts," Debs testified. ARU headquarters were "demoralized" by his arrest, he said. Had the ARU leaders remained in the field, "our men were in a position that never would have been shaken."

Olney regarded the deployment of federal troops in Chicago as a triumph for government policy, but it would prove to be a Pyrrhic victory for the administration he served. His own rhetoric would come under more concentrated scrutiny as the strike passed into memory. On the eve of the deployment, for example, Olney had told newsmen, "We have been brought to the ragged edge of anarchy." Such language seemed distinctly hyperbolic in retrospect, especially once it was learned that Debs and the ARU had offered to submit the boycott issues to arbitration if the railroads would only agree to rehire all the men, union members and others, without discrimination.

President Cleveland emerged from the episode looking like an ineffectual, detached leader all too willing to cede his authority to his attorney general, who had taken it and run wild. Populists in Congress joined with members of Cleveland's own Democratic Party to empanel an investigative committee to examine the strike. Democrats also considered a bill making it unlawful to enjoin workers from job actions if they offered to arbitrate and the employers refused.

Stung by this repudiation by his own party and looking ahead toward a reelection campaign in 1896, Cleveland signed a bill establishing Labor Day as a national holiday just days after the strike was crushed. The party was moving away from its old association with big business, and at the 1896 Democratic convention the nomination of William Jennings Bryan for president ended Cleveland's bid for a third term. In the eyes of history, the sole victor in the Pullman Strike may have been Eugene V. Debs, who spent six months in federal prison in Woodstock, Illinois, and emerged with worldwide fame as a defender of the rights of the working person.

But Debs's members and their fellow unionists were among the losers. The Pullman Strike signified to labor that industry was in command of working conditions, backed by the government and its newfound power of injunction. Discontent may have continued to simmer under the surface, but fears of unemployment in the still uncertain economy helped to keep labor unrest in check. After Cleveland, the Democratic Party tried to position itself as a populist bulwark against capitalist abuse of the working person by nominating Bryan for president, but it was the Republicans and their candidate, William McKinley, who secured the workers' support by promising an era of prosperity that would bring jobs and higher wages —"a full dinner pail," as McKinley's reelection slogan in 1900 put it.

Organized labor went into eclipse. Wages fell, and the eight-hour day seemed as remote as ever—the average workweek stuck at between fifty-four and sixty-three hours, and even longer in steel mills and the textile sweatshops where women and children toiled for pennies an hour. Nothing would be heard from America's political leadership about workers' rights to collective action and a living wage until the Progressive Era began with the accession of Theodore Roosevelt to the presidency, at the dawn of the next century. It was a short eclipse, to be sure. But in the meantime, the path was cleared for the creation of a system of imperial railroad companies — and a new and more fearsome phase in their struggle for supremacy.

The unwillingness of the federal government to contain the worst impulses of these new railroad emperors was nowhere clearer than in the proceedings of the strike commission itself. During their inquiry, the commissioners questioned Pullman closely about why he had not reduced the wages of officers, managers, and superintendents, rather than rolling back some of the pay cuts or reducing some of the rents borne by the workers. Here Pullman revealed, perhaps despite himself, that he regarded the line workers as essentially disposable — unlike supervisory staff, who were irreplaceable. "It would be impossible for me, as the president of a corporation, to reduce the salaries of my officers arbitrarily, because I would find myself possibly without them," he said.

"You might reduce your own, perhaps," Commissioner John D. Kernan remarked.

"I might, if I chose," Pullman retorted brusquely, "but the difference that it would make on the cost of a car would be so infinitesimal and fractional that it would not be worth considering."

The commission observed that reductions in the executive salaries "would have shown good faith, would have relieved the harshness of the situation, and would have evinced genuine sympathy with labor in the disasters of the times." But that was not on Pullman's agenda — not as long as government power weighed on the railroads' side. A change in the balance would not occur for more than thirty years.

14

THE EMPIRE BUILDER

D R. CLINTON HART MERRIAM was working in his cramped office at the US Department of Agriculture on the morning of March 25, 1899, when Edward H. Harriman arrived uninvited and introduced himself in what Merriam recalled as an "unassuming, matter-of-fact way." The visitor informed Merriam that he was planning to cruise the Alaskan coast in a private steamer and planned to bring along a party of scientific men. Could Merriam help him select the passengers?

Merriam scrutinized his visitor quizzically, his lips pursed behind his drooping bottlebrush mustache. Contemplating this proposal by a stranger to bring fifteen or twenty eminent naturalists along on a family vacation, he thought at first he must be the victim of a hoax. But in due course he would help launch one of the most unusual ventures undertaken by a business leader entering the prime of his career. At a moment when he had millions of dollars of crucial transactions pending on Wall Street, Harriman absented himself for a two-month expedition to the coastal wilderness of Alaska.

The moment provided a nearly perfect illustration of the differences between Harriman and Pierpont Morgan in their approaches to business and to their avocations outside business. At the same time when Harriman was making arrangements for his Alaska trip, Morgan was preparing for an expedition of his own—in his case a pleasure cruise to Europe. Morgan boarded the liner *Majestic*, bearing a shopping list of books, manuscripts, and artworks for acquisition, on April 5, only a few days after Harriman had materialized in Merriam's doorway. For the next ten weeks Morgan "had a grand time" in the marketplaces, Herbert Satterlee reported. He bought two entire libraries—of the private collector James Toovey and of the late third Earl of Gosford—and numerous other antiquarian rarities, including books printed on vellum and illuminated manuscripts from the fifteenth century. He spent his idle hours shopping and dining out, and before the end of the month he had reached Aix-le-Bains, his favorite watering hole in the South of France. Harriman was also on a collecting spree—but his quarries were scientists and scientific knowledge.

As for business matters, Morgan occupied himself in the final years of the millennium with extending the principles of industrial consolidation he had applied to the railroads to new industries, such as steel and electric lighting (efforts soon to culminate in the creation of United States Steel and General Electric). Harriman's work was devoted to consolidating his own railroad holdings rather than casting his net wider.

In so many ways, Harriman and Morgan seemed to be following divergent paths in this critical period. But their courses would soon converge —and dramatically.

THE PERIOD SPANNING the last half of 1898 and the first few months of 1899 had been the most productive of Edward Harriman's railroad career. His dominating concern at the time was the Herculean reconstruction of the Union Pacific—replacing equipment, realigning tracks, and shoring up its finances—following his election as its chairman in May 1898. But he also extended his influence deeper into the railroad industry through his involvement in three major reorganizations.

The first was the Chicago & Alton, a once-proud road connecting Chicago, St. Louis, and Kansas City that had fallen far behind its competitors in construction and maintenance. By 1898, when a group of discontented shareholders invited Harriman to take it over, the road was facing extinction. As an expert who examined its condition observed, the Chi-

cago & Alton "had not added one mile of road in seventeen years" and
had "little or no reserve capacity to conduct a larger business." With his
new partners—James Stillman of the City Bank and Jacob Schiff—Harriman set the line back on the path to profitability, albeit via a financial
restructuring that later would be condemned by his critics as more an act
of plunder than of improvement.

Around the same time, Schiff invited Harriman to join the board of
the Baltimore & Ohio, the nation's oldest trunk line, which ran from
Baltimore west to St. Louis, with spurs to Detroit and New York, and
which also was in a demoralized state. There Harriman first encountered
the northwestern railroad tycoon James J. Hill, who would become one of
his chief adversaries in the chapter to come. During their joint tenure on
the B&O board—which Schiff told Hill he had arranged so "you and Mr.
Harriman should . . . join hands" to ensure the success of the property going forward—their relations appeared to be cordial. The good fellowship,
however, was at best superficial.

Then there was the Kansas City Southern, which ran from Kansas
City south to the Gulf of Mexico and which a maladroit group headed by
the steel-wire tycoon John "Bet-a-Million" Gates had tried to reorganize.
Gates, a flamboyantly profligate gambler, quickly discovered that he had
no aptitude for the railroad business and turned the enterprise over to
Harriman, in the prelude to what became one of the most exasperating
deals of the latter's career.

All those transactions were overshadowed by a plan just over the horizon—Harriman's quest for the Southern Pacific, an immense California
railroad. This acquisition would be his biggest of all, with the capacity to
catapult him into the forefront of the railroad industry.

But first, Alaska beckoned. At the urging of then–secretary of state
William Seward, the government had purchased the vast territory from
Russia in 1867; its moniker of "Seward's Folly" only recently had begun
to fade with the discovery of gold in the neighboring Yukon Territory of
Canada and the raising of hopes that a similar discovery might be made
in Alaska. Still, at the moment, its main interest was still for naturalists

The steamship *George W. Elder* carried Harriman's 1899 expedition to Alaska; when it returned to Seattle after the two-month trip, laden with artifacts including a sixty-foot-tall totem pole and a variety of insect specimens, a reporter described it as "a floating curiosity shop."

intrigued by the prospect of new discoveries of flora and fauna in a land near the very limits of human exploration.

Harriman's impetus for the expedition was a bit murky. Harriman himself later described its original purpose as "a summer cruise for the pleasure and recreation of my family and a few friends." His youngest son, Roland (who was three years old when the *Elder* set sail with him aboard), reported years later that his father had been advised by his doctors to take a rest cure from overwork. The true motivating force, however, may have been Harriman's insatiable curiosity about the world around him—which is where Merriam came into the picture.

Despite his formal training as a medical doctor, Clinton Hart Merriam's fascination with ornithology as a child growing up in New York's Adirondack mountains had steered him into a career as one of the foremost naturalists in America. One of the thirty-three founders of the National Geographic Society in 1888, Merriam had been appointed chief of the United States Biological Survey (later the US Fish and Wildlife Service), a body that commanded nationwide scientific respect at the time even though it formally comprised only himself and two assistants.

Harriman's name was a blank to Merriam, but calls to a couple of industrialists of his acquaintance—for the visitor had mentioned that he was in the railroad business—filled it in. Within the industry, he learned, Harriman was known as "a man of means and a rising power in the railroad world." Merriam could not have known it at the time, but the trip that Harriman was planning would soon solidify his reputation outside the railroad industry to complement the respect he had gained within it.

That evening, Merriam invited Harriman and his personal physician, Lewis Morris, to dine at his Washington home, where he listened with growing interest to a proposal for a unique scientific venture. Harriman disclosed that he already was refitting the steamship *George W. Elder* for the Alaska voyage and collecting an onboard library of books, treatises, and maps relevant to the expedition. "He thought there should be two men of recognized ability in each department of natural science," Merriam recollected—"two zoologists, two botanists, two geologists, and so on," as though he were assembling a veritable Noah's Ark of scientific talent. When Merriam mentioned that few scientists could meet the expenses of such a trip, Harriman revealed that all the members would be traveling as his guests.

Despite Harriman's generosity, Merriam had some trouble filling out the passenger manifest. One holdout was the world-famous naturalist John Muir, who was also unfamiliar with the Harriman name. Muir would confess later that he was "unwilling to accept the hospitality of a person of whom I knew little," at least before learning what services would be demanded of him in exchange for free passage. Muir hesitated until the last moment, finally signing on when told that the voyage would take him to parts of the Alaskan coast he had missed on his two earlier expeditions to the region. He remained skeptical even after agreeing to go, writing to his fellow naturalist Charles Sprague Sargent, with whom he had explored the forests of northern New England during the previous summer: "Pray for me . . . I wish I were going to those leafy woods instead of icy Alaska."

The preparations for the two-month, nine-thousand-mile trip underscored Harriman's aversion to doing anything by half measures. The *Elder* was equipped with a steam launch, two "naphtha launches" fueled by a sort of kerosene, several small boats and canoes, and a full complement of canvas tents and sleeping bags. The library Harriman had mentioned to Merriam numbered five hundred items. The passenger list of 126 included Harriman, his wife, their three daughters and two sons, Mrs. Harriman's cousin William Averell and his wife and daughter, and three servants. A cow was brought on board to provide fresh milk for Roland, the baby of the Harriman household. The academic and professional passengers comprised twenty-five renowned scientists; three artists, two photographers, and two stenographers; a surgeon, his assistant, and a nurse; a chaplain; eleven hunters, packers, and camp hands; and sixty-five officers and crewmen. Reviewing a roster of scholars from three museums of natural history, six universities, and four government scientific bureaus — many of whom had national reputations in their fields and some of whom were known even to the lay public — Harriman's authorized biographer George Kennan judged that "no more distinguished body of American scientists was ever gathered together for an expedition of this kind."

Harriman transported the East Coast contingent from New York to Seattle, the disembarkation point, on a special train. On the first day of the transcontinental leg he called together the scientists traveling with him to inform them that he was placing the details of the expedition's itinerary entirely in their hands and to encourage them to form a committee to map out the route.

The *Elder* left port on May 31. As it made its way into the Alaskan spring, the zoologists were delighted with the abundance of birds and other wildlife, the botanists with a coastline "abloom with wild geranium, columbine, Jacob's-ladder, iris, cypripedium, shooting star, rhododendron, bluebells, primroses, and forget-me-nots." And all were enthralled by the sheer beauty of the land. "Day after day," recorded the naturalist John Burroughs, the expedition's official rapporteur, "a panorama unrolled before us with features that might have been gathered from the Highlands of the Hudson, from the Thousand Islands, the Saguenay, or the Rangeley Lakes in Maine, with the addition of towering snow-capped peaks thrown in for a background . . . It was along these inland ocean highways, through tortuous narrows, up smooth, placid inlets, across broad island-studded gulfs and bays that our course lay."

Early in the trip, Muir sounded a few discordant notes. The *Elder* stopped at Kodiak Island to afford Harriman an opportunity to achieve one of his personal goals, the shooting of a Kodiak bear. He managed to bring down a giant female along with her cub, to Muir's intense distaste. (The adult animal's pelt would be repurposed as a rug for Harriman's office.) A day or two later, a still grumpy Muir listened to his fellow scientists talking "of the blessed ministry of wealth, especially in Mr. Harriman's case, now that some of it was being devoted to science. When these wealth laudations were sounding loudest I teasingly interrupted them, saying, 'I don't think Mr. Harriman is very rich. He has not as much money as I have. I have all I want and Mr. Harriman has not.'"

Someone reported the remark to Harriman, who sat himself next to Muir at dinner that night. "I never cared for money except as power for work," he told Muir. "What I most enjoy is the power of creation, getting into partnership with Nature in doing good, helping to feed man and beast, and making everybody a little better and happier."

Muir was unaccustomed to rubbing shoulders with the wealthy, even less so with industrialists who could talk so candidly of aspirations beyond the getting and spending of money. From that point on the skeptical naturalist felt himself being won over by his host. "I soon saw that Mr. Harriman was uncommon," he would recall. "He was taking a trip for rest, and at the same time managing his exploring guests as if we were a grateful, soothing, essential part of his rest-cure, though scientific explorers are not easily managed, and in large mixed lots are rather inflammable and explosive, especially when compressed on a ship." But Harriman was as good as his word. The *Elder* followed the route the scientists dictated; periodically a group would be dropped ashore with provisions for land exploration, and picked up later on schedule.

On the way north they stopped at Muir Glacier, discovered by its namesake in 1879. Muir regaled the group with what Merriam suspected was a "fairy tale about the abundance of wolves in a little snowy valley" some eighteen miles deep into the glacier, which Muir called "Howling Valley." His curiosity stoked, Harriman organized a hunting foray for himself, Merriam, Dr. Morris, and two companions. (Muir himself begged off, on the grounds that he was "no hunter.") The men, each carrying a pack weighing twenty pounds, disappeared into the frosty mist, tramping over ice and snow into which they sank first to their ankles, and soon up to their knees. Harriman positioned himself "always either in the lead or near the front," Merriam recollected. On the first day they hiked until midnight, roped together for protection against hidden crevasses, then rested in their sleeping bags flat on the ice until the penetrating cold forced them back on their feet and on their way. Finally they reached the valley, finding it completely buried in snow and devoid of wolves. Having made it as far as Muir's valley, Harriman ordered an about-face. The party reappeared at main camp at nightfall on the second day, footsore, chilled to the bone, but unanimous in their admiration for Harriman, who at the age of fifty-one and without having had a day's training away from an office desk had led them on a thirty-six-mile trek with only a few hours' sleep.

Back on the *Elder*, they sailed deep into Prince William Sound, where they discovered a new arm of the waterway, promptly christened Harriman Fiord. Eventually they turned west into the treacherous, fogbound Bering Sea. There the outbound journey should have ended, but Mrs. Harriman had conceived a desire to set foot in Siberia. So they continued on, reaching a settlement known then as Plover Bay and today as Provideniya, where all the travelers disembarked for a few hours to pick flowers and buy trinkets from the local Eskimos. (More than four decades later, in September 1942, when Averell Harriman, Edward's elder son, was part of an Anglo-American mission to Moscow to discuss supplying the Soviet army against an invasion by Hitler, he confided to Joseph Stalin that he was making his second visit to Russia. The first, he explained, he had made without a passport as a seven-year-old during that stop at Plover

Bay. "Oh, that was under the Tsar," Stalin replied. "You couldn't do that now.")

The *George W. Elder* returned to Seattle on July 30, two months after its departure, laden with samples of six hundred species of flora and fauna previously unknown to science, five thousand photographs, and maps of four glaciers "never before seen by white men," as recounted in the *New York Times*. Upon the craft's landing, an Associated Press dispatch pronouncing the expedition "an entire success . . . both from a scientific and pleasure point of view" ran in newspapers coast to coast. The *Elder*, it reported, "resembled a floating curiosity shop, stocked with everything Alaskan from a totem-pole five feet through and sixty feet high, to the minutest insect."

The scientists immediately started sharing their findings with the public. Henry Gannett, a glacier expert from the US Coast and Geodetic Survey, expressed the view that "the glaciers of Alaska are gradually retreating, due . . . to climatic changes." Dr. George B. Grinnell, editor of *Forest and Stream*, passed along an observation from Alaska fishermen that "the salmon in the streams of the Territory are being rapidly exterminated" and advised that "some steps for the preservation of this fish should be taken before it is too late." For years, specialists in natural history and the natural sciences would mine the material, which was compiled into thirteen illustrated volumes. As for Edward H. Harriman, after nearly a decade of his rising renown in the railroad industry, the remarkable expedition had made him a household name.

HARRIMAN HAD BARELY settled back into his office routine after the Alaska expedition when he was forced to unwind the mess that Bet-a-Million Gates had made of the Kansas City Southern. This railroad had a colorful but dispiriting history—one to which Gates had been contributing prolifically.

The Kansas City Southern was originally the brainchild of a handlebar-mustached entrepreneur named Arthur Stilwell. The eccentric Stilwell was perennially in the grip of what he sometimes described as "hunches" and sometimes as ideas planted in his head by fairies or "brownies" visiting him in his sleep. Some of these intuitions were plausible enough, but they were invariably confounded by poor execution. That was the case with Stilwell's Kansas City, Pittsburg & Gulf Railroad, which ran 778 miles from Kansas City to the Gulf of Mexico at Port Arthur, Texas, a depot Stilwell built and named after himself on the site of a settlement that had been wiped off the map by a hurricane.

Stilwell's goal had been to capture some of the freight that was either being monopolized by the Illinois Central, the only north-south road in the region, or carried east directly to the Atlantic seaboard. This was a promising plan, initially well-capitalized thanks to Stilwell's adroit salesmanship. But Stilwell was fundamentally a real estate promoter. Rather than entering population centers his railroad skirted them, on his reasoning that the towns would expand toward the rail line, affording him lavish profits in land speculation. He not only saddled the railroad with uneconomical curves and unserviceable grades, but built it on the cheap — embankments too narrow, bridges and trestles too light, water supplies too meager. A venture that might have succeeded under different circumstances was unable to turn a profit, and in April 1899, when its trains had been running for only a few months, what was then known as the Kansas City Southern went bankrupt.

The struggling road's receivers had invited Harriman, who already possessed a reputation as someone who could manage a struggling railroad back to prosperity, to join the reorganization committee. He had accepted just before leaving for Alaska.

Strange doings went on in the Kansas City Southern while Harriman was away. After he returned, he discovered that Stilwell had sold a controlling interest in the railroad — or possibly his entire interest — to Gates. Several different versions exist of this transaction. From Harriman's point of view, Stilwell's sale to Gates behind his back was a "virtual breach of trust." Otto Kahn wrote later that he assumed this discovery would end Harriman's involvement with the line. Instead Harriman told him, "Not so fast! I am not through with this thing yet, by any means. I can't be played fast and loose with like this . . . I am in it to stay."

Stilwell's recollection is more colorful, if less plausible. In his 1912 memoir, *Cannibals of Finance*, he claimed that Gates and Harriman had conspired to rook him out of his interest. "I sometimes have wondered," he wrote, "if when Edward Harriman was dying it added one jot to his peace of mind to think that he had for years deprived me of my rightful place as the upbuilder of Port Arthur, of which I was the creator; or that he had for five years controlled the destinies of the Kansas City Southern Railroad, which he had helped seize from me and my stockholders just as the last spike was driven." (Harriman died three years before the memoir's publication.)

The reality is that Harriman tried to turn the Kansas City Southern into a going concern. According to Kahn, he refused to give up his position on the reorganization committee, and decided to wait for Gates and company to appeal to him for help. In time, they realized that as novices in the railroad business, their wisest course of action was to let Harriman run the line his own way—especially since the voting trust by which they all held power over the line would expire in April 1905.

The Kansas City Southern resembled the Union Pacific at the time of Harriman's takeover: a promising enterprise in need of drastic refurbishment. Like the UP, it had been hastily built, was desperately in need of new rolling stock and engines, wider embankments, fewer curves and smaller grades, and modern shops and machinery. Harriman did what he could to accomplish these tasks, spending nearly $5.6 million, but the railroad never generated enough revenue to finish the job and eventually time ran out. When the voting trust expired, the majority shareholders took over and removed Harriman and Gates. Neither fought to stay.

HARRIMAN'S FINAL COMPLETED deal of the nineteenth century was the biggest of his career: the acquisition of the sprawling Southern Pacific. His initial target had been the Central Pacific branch, the remnant of the western portion of the original transcontinental railroad. Originally constructed to only marginally better standards than the Union Pacific, like the old UP it was now hampered by unnecessary curves and grades and equipped with outdated rolling stock. In sum, the Central had aged into a bottleneck that prevented Harriman's UP from expanding its capacity to the full extent he desired.

The immovable obstacle to Harriman's quest to complete his line to the coast was Collis P. Huntington. At seventy-eight, the obstreperous old lion was one of the nation's last surviving railroad entrepreneurs from the era of transcontinental expansion. Huntington had outlived Mark Hopkins, Leland Stanford, and Charles Crocker, his three partners in the building of the Central Pacific. He had combined the Central Pacific with the Southern Pacific, which ran along the California coast before turning east along a southern route (known as the "Sunset Route"), creating the largest railroad line in the United States. Huntington's holdings of more than four hundred thousand shares of Southern Pacific stock accounted for only 20 percent of the total outstanding, but the combination of that single block and the shares held by his allies Edwin Hawley and James Speyer gave him unassailable authority over the enterprise. Many coveted the Southern Pacific, but Huntington had rebuffed them all. Harriman had offered to buy him out on at least three occasions.

Then, on August 13, 1900, Huntington died unexpectedly at his lodge in New York's Adirondack Mountains. His death removed the largest hurdle to the acquisition of the Central Pacific but erected another: To obtain the one railroad he wanted, Harriman would have to buy the entire enterprise—the Southern Pacific Company, which was valued at $100 million. The $40 to $50 million needed to acquire a controlling interest in the parent company seemed, superficially, well out of reach of the Union Pacific, which at the time had less than $4 million cash in its coffers.

Nevertheless, Harriman set his strategy in motion by starting to buy up SP shares soon after Huntington's death. The key to his acquisition plan was an audacious Union Pacific bond issue of $100 million paying 4 percent annual interest, secured by 1,135 miles of improved track and by the value of securities held by the Oregon Short Line and Oregon Railroad & Navigation Company—branches of the UP that had been foreclosed by creditors during its financial crisis, but which Harriman had bought back. The UP board had approved the bond issue that February. The borrowing overleveraged the railroad, but with a provision allowing the bonds' conversion into UP stock at par (that is, $100 per share) for five years, it was snapped up by investors when it went on the market in May.

Harriman approached Huntington's heirs with this immense war chest in hand, and promptly acquired their 475,000 shares. Schiff's firm acquired another 275,000 on the open market. Together, these purchases amounted to 38 percent of the outstanding stock of the Southern Pacific, which Harriman judged to be enough to discourage any competing bidders; later he would add 150,000 more shares of the common and 180,000 shares of preferred. (Preferred shares typically offer fixed dividends that must be paid before dividends on common shares, but have lesser ownership rights, usually not including shareholder votes.) Ultimately, the acquisition of the Southern Pacific cost about $40 million.

At the outset, Harriman's desire for the Central Pacific was widely assumed to be the driver of the huge transaction. The US Industrial Commission, examining the purchase later in 1901, parroted the standard version that "the Union Pacific purchased control of the Southern Pacific not because it needed the additional mileage, but rather that it might indirectly acquire the Central Pacific and a direct outlet to the Pacific Coast."

This indicates that the Southern Pacific was not generally seen in the financial community as an unalloyed treasure; while the Central Pacific offered access to the coast, the parent company was weighed down by the Sunset Route. A pet project of Huntington's, it had extended the Southern Pacific east to New Orleans, contributing negligible profit to the system while presenting a huge administrative burden. Otto Kahn would comment later that if the Southern Pacific could be broken up so that the UP could acquire the Central Pacific and leave the Sunset Route aside, "we would be getting rid of a nuisance."

The truth is, however, that while some parts of the Southern Pacific may have been more burdensome than others, bringing together the

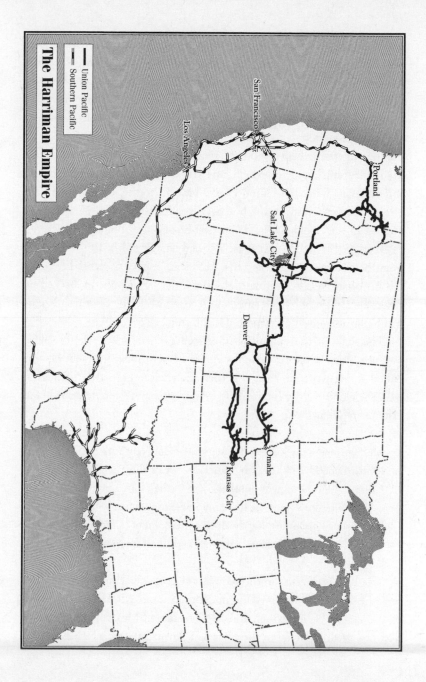

The Harriman Empire

Union Pacific
Southern Pacific

Portland

San Francisco

Los Angeles

Salt Lake City

Denver

Omaha

Kansas City

Union Pacific and the entirety of the Southern Pacific created a uniquely powerful combination that plainly fed Harriman's ambitions. With the Sunset Route included, the Southern Pacific owned the main line running between Portland, Oregon, and New Orleans via San Francisco, Los Angeles, Yuma, Arizona, and El Paso; numerous other lines in Texas and Louisiana; a monopoly road between Sacramento and Portland; a fleet of steamers operating between New Orleans and New York; and the Pacific Mail Steamship Company, which ran steamers from San Francisco to Asia and Panama. What the Union Pacific brought to the marriage were the Oregon Railroad, a steamship line between Portland and Asia, and a half interest in the Occidental and Oriental Steamship Company, which ran between San Francisco and Asia. The only major railroads in California were the Southern Pacific and the Atchison, Topeka & Santa Fe, but as UP historian Nelson Trottman observed, the latter railroad "lacked an extensive system of branch lines and feeders, while the Southern Pacific had built into almost every part of California."

The scale of the enterprise impressed even railroad veterans jaded by thirty years of daring ventures launched by courageous men. Having pulled these two companies together, Harriman's properties seemed to span the globe. As the Interstate Commerce Commission described Harriman's empire in 1907:

> Mr. Harriman may journey by steamship from New York to New Orleans, thence by rail to San Francisco, across the Pacific Ocean to China, and, returning by another route to the United States, may go to Ogden by any one of the three rail lines, and thence to Kansas City or Omaha, without leaving the deck or platform of a carrier which he controls, and without duplicating any part of his journey.

The ICC was less than thrilled with Harriman's acquisitiveness. "It is only the law which prevents the concentration into Mr. Harriman's hands of every railroad line lying between Canada and Mexico," the commission observed, referring to the Sherman Antitrust Act, which had been enacted in 1890. On the other side, General Grenville Dodge, who had led the Union Pacific to Promontory, Utah, in 1869, labeled the Southern Pacific purchase "a master stroke."

Harriman's fellow railroad tycoons viewed the purchase with suspicion and skepticism. "Some people also say that Harriman is posing as the Napoleon of Railways in New York," banker John S. Kennedy told his client James J. Hill of St. Paul, "but they think he has at last bitten off more than he can chew and that he ought to be checked."

Kennedy was unclear who should "check" Harriman or how, but his characterization of Harriman was not far wide of the mark. Contemplating his new possession, Harriman commented to a friend: "We have bought not only a railroad, but an empire."

Critics would never cease to see that empire as one devoted to crushing its rivals and profiteering from its customers. As it happens, long before Harriman acquired the Southern Pacific, indeed, it had earned Californians' antipathy. Still fresh in their minds was the Mussel Slough Tragedy of May 1880, when a simmering dispute with homesteaders convinced they had been defrauded by the Southern Pacific in sales of the railroad's government land grants erupted into a gun battle, resulting in seven deaths. Huntington and Stanford, not Harriman, were the Southern Pacific's bosses at the time, but that would be forgotten by 1901 when the muckraking novelist Frank Norris published his book *The Octopus*, a fictionalized account of the episode, whose title echoed what had already become a popular epithet for the Southern Pacific.

As a diversified transportation system, the Southern Pacific was well positioned to exploit all the freight traffic generated along the West Coast and between East and West—timber, grain, cotton, fruits and vegetables, and manufactured goods. By comparison, the Union Pacific on its own was a mere trunk line carrying through traffic along the transcontinental route—but, given Harriman's efforts, a glittering trunk line fully prepared for a doubling in its traffic. What was needed was to bring the old Central Pacific up to UP standards. The line was not exactly decrepit—it was in better shape than most other western railroads outside the Southern

THE CURSE OF CALIFORNIA.

By 1901, when Harriman acquired the Southern Pacific, the railroad had become known as "the Octopus." This 1882 cartoon from the *Wasp*, a San Francisco magazine, refers to its monopoly grasp on farming, mining, and finance, and to the 1880 Mussel Slough Tragedy in which a dispute between homesteaders and the railroad resulted in seven deaths. The figures in the eyes of the creature are Leland Stanford (left) and Charles Crocker (right), two of the Southern Pacific's original controlling shareholders.

Pacific system—but still needed to be straightened, leveled, and rebuilt with heavier rails and steel bridges.

To handle that task, Harriman tapped Julius Kruttschnitt, then serving as the Central Pacific's general manager. The portly, derby-hatted Kruttschnitt had met Harriman only once before, when he had hosted a reception in San Francisco for Harriman during the latter's grand tour in 1897. Now it was his turn to be dazzled by his new boss's preternatural intelligence and decisiveness.

SUMMONED TO NEW YORK, Kruttschnitt discovered that Harriman had already ridden the Central Pacific several times and had gained a working grasp of its inadequacies. Relying on Kruttschnitt's sixteen-year association with the railroad, Harriman assigned him to supervise the reconstruction.

After dinner one night at Harriman's home, the new boss "called for blue-prints, maps, and statistics covering the contemplated reconstruction work in Nevada and Utah," Kruttschnitt recalled. "He asked innumerable questions with great rapidity, always touching the crucial points." They covered the reconstruction needs of the entire road from Ogden to Sacramento in less than two hours. Harriman then dismissed Kruttschnitt with instructions to be on hand at Union Pacific headquarters the next morning for a meeting of the board.

"The plans called for an expenditure of $18,000,000, and I supposed that there would be no end of arguing and talking, which would result in the approval of only a part of the work," Kruttschnitt recalled. He was about to discover that Harriman could be as brusque with his board as with his engineers. Harriman outlined the general plan in a few words, outlining its cost and its rationale. The board gave its approval without a single dissenting vote. As Kruttschnitt wrote later,

> As I left for the West, I wondered what manner of man it was who in a few hours' talk could digest the details of an $18,000,000 reconstruction work along a thousand miles of railroad through a mountainous

country, expound the general principles of the plan to his executive associates in the course of a few minutes, and obtain the seal of financial approval.

Before departing, he met with Harriman one last time to ask how he should disburse his bounty of capital.

"Spend it all in a week if you can," Harriman replied.

It was a tall order, but at least Kruttschnitt knew where to begin. The weakest portion of the Central Pacific were the tracks between Ogden, Utah, and Reno, Nevada, a nearly 600-mile stretch of difficult topography that showed most vividly the haste of the original builders as they bulled their way through to the meeting with the Union Pacific at Promontory. Of that portion, the most demanding reconstruction involved 147 miles of track skirting the northern shore of the Great Salt Lake. The route crossed two mountain ranges and rugged country that forced the tracks into sharp curves and grades as steep as ninety feet of elevation in a mile. There seemed no alternative alignments that could appreciably straighten or level the track, so Harriman dusted off an old idea: Instead of going around the lake, he would cross it. The product of this decision would be the legendary Lucin Cutoff.

The cutoff had been a pet project of Collis Huntington, who had mapped out a causeway running almost on a straight line over the water and connecting Ogden and Lucin, a desert outpost located a few miles east of the Nevada state line. Huntington had delayed the project for years, doubting that his staff was up to the project's demanding engineering and uncertain that the railroad carried enough traffic to make the expenditure pay. Ultimately he approved the work, but died before construction could get underway.

To Harriman, the logic of shaving some forty miles off the railroad's route and circumventing the steep grades and tight curves of the original route was compelling. Engineering knowledge, he reckoned, had advanced sufficiently to overcome the challenges that had concerned Huntington, and given the growth in the transcontinental line's traffic

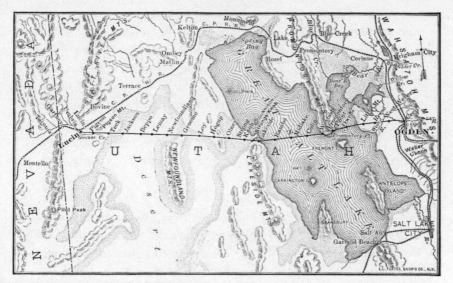

Bisecting the Great Salt Lake, the Lucin Cutoff, built as part of Harriman's massive reconstruction of the transcontinental railroad, shaved forty miles off the railroad's route and eliminated the steep grades and tight curves necessitated by its crossing of the Promontory Mountains.

he envisioned it was certain that rerouting the railroad would pay off. He ordered Kruttschnitt to build the cutoff without delay.

Harriman may have underestimated the obstacles facing the project, which ultimately would cost $9 million and take three years. The main problem was the lake itself. Huntington's construction engineers had warned of the frequently severe storms that lent demonic force to waves of the lake's heavy brine, endangering trestles and fills designed to conventional specifications. Local residents told stories of boats that had been "hammered to the bottom, . . . covered with soda by the spray until they sank under its weight." Some predicted that the winds sweeping across the surface would blow trains clear off the rails and into the water.

A major difficulty was the lake bottom. Although the maximum depth of the Great Salt Lake was thirty-two feet, the bottom itself was shifty and insubstantial, consisting of silt layered over a salt and mineral crust that would shatter like a pane of glass under the weight of railroad fill. Many times the builders would watch helplessly as an embankment painstakingly built up with rocks and gravel suddenly sank out of sight, often stranding a work train in open water. "The day on which there was not a sink somewhere along the job [was] crossed and starred and bordered with red on the calendars of the engineers in charge," wrote a participant. One stretch required the labors of twenty-five hundred men working day and night for more than a year before the embankment finally became stable enough to stay permanently dry.

The length of the cutoff would have made for a daunting construction job even under the best conditions. At thirty-two miles from shore to shore, it was longer than any span of causeway and trestle that had ever been built for a railroad. The work required a stupendous amount of equipment and supplies—twenty-five thousand piles each 125 feet long, pounded into the lakebed in search of a firm bottom by twenty-five pile drivers specially constructed in San Francisco and delivered to the work site in sections. To transport fill and deposit it in the lake, four hundred steel dump-cars were built, hauled by eighty locomotives in trains of twenty-five cars at a time. Workers were sequestered from the many temptations of camp life that might foment brawls or cause injuries that could only delay the project. No liquor was permitted in the work camp; all stores and packages for the workers were inspected and contraband alcohol confiscated. Occasionally an entrepreneur would set up a "groggery" on property outside the camp perimeters. Railroad guards had little trouble chasing most of them away; one established at Hogup, a few miles from the western shore of the lake, seemed dug in—until railroad engineers bored holes under the shanty and filled them with blasting powder, prompting the owner to flee ahead of the threatened blast.

The Lucin Cutoff was only one of several refurbishments Harriman dictated for his new acquisition, including a rebuilt approach into San Francisco from the south that also straightened, shortened, and leveled the tracks. This project required five tunnels to be bored on a stretch of only eleven miles.

On the whole, Harriman followed the practice that had raised the

Union Pacific from decrepitude: Invest heavily to modernize and improve. In its last eight years in charge of the Southern Pacific, the Huntington regime had spent about $58 million on construction, equipment, and upgrades; in the first eight years of his ownership, Harriman spent $242 million. But he now had a massive, economically viable empire to show for it.

And that empire was still expanding. Having devoted just over $40 million to the biggest acquisition of his career, Harriman still had $60 million in reserve to spend on his most audacious move yet. His quarry would be one of the most troubled railroads in the nation: the Northern Pacific.

15

THE QUEST FOR THE BURLINGTON

O N OCTOBER 3, 1898—just as he was beginning to contemplate his journey to Alaska the following spring—Harriman quietly but decisively blew apart a peace treaty that had bound the Union Pacific and two other railroads together in a division of traffic in the Pacific Northwest. His comments at a meeting in New York with Schiff, representatives of the House of Morgan, and the other roads' presidents would trigger a sequence of events leading to Harriman's cataclysmic confrontation with Pierpont Morgan two and a half years later. But that could not be predicted at the time.

The underlying issue on that October day was the competitive alignment of the Northern Pacific and its rival, the Great Northern Railroad. The latter was a strong, well-managed road of the northern prairie that had expanded to the West Coast, putting enormous pressure on the Northern Pacific, which after the collapse of Jay Cooke & Co. in the 1873 panic had entered a long period of stagnation and decline.

Still unfinished, routed across the prairie from Bismarck to Tacoma via a string of mostly vacant towns in Minnesota, Dakota, and points west, and bereft of Cooke's promotional vigor, the NP was derided as "a railroad from Nowhere, through No-Man's-Land to No Place." The extortionate 7.3 percent interest rate on its bonds had caused its red ink to rise by $2 million a year.

In 1874, the year after Cooke & Co.'s collapse, the Northern Pacific had been officially declared bankrupt. A reorganization effort was attempted, dependent on a proposal for Congress to bail out the line by guaranteeing its bonds in return for the surrender of its land grant. That effort failed. A subsequent attempt resulted in a dubious arrangement that largely exchanged the railroad's old obligations for a pledge of future profits.

The recovery in the national economy helped, for a time. In 1875 the road consisted of 550 miles of track; by 1893 it would be 5,400, reaching from St. Paul and Minneapolis to the Washington coast. In 1880 the road's president, Frederick Billings, had completed a traffic-sharing contract with the Oregon Railway & Navigation Company, which operated not only a rail line but a steamship fleet on the Columbia River. This secured for the Northern Pacific a connection to Pacific Ocean trade, via Portland.

The contract also brought the road into contact for the first time with Oregon Navigation's owner, Henry Villard, who would lead the Northern Pacific into its next phase— and start a chain of events that would eventually place Oregon Navigation in Harriman's hands. Villard was one of the most cultured, colorful, and imaginative railroad men of the era, though not an especially good manager and certainly not a successful one.

VILLARD WAS BORN Ferdinand Heinrich Gustav Hilgard in Bavaria in 1835 to a Lutheran judge and his Roman Catholic wife. His formative years coincided with a politically tumultuous period during which the French Revolution of 1848 spread to southern German duchies, including Bavaria, until finally extinguished by the Prussian army. At seventeen Heinrich Hilgard entered the University of Munich, complying with his father's directive to obtain a technical education. Heinrich, who preferred studying arts and letters, found the course of study dictated by his father "positively repugnant." Instead he fell among a fashionable set that spent its time in drunken carousing and saber dueling in the German student tradition.

Inevitably, Heinrich's father ordered him home and placed him in law school. Heinrich decided instead to flee abroad and booked steamship passage to America. To hide his tracks, he took the name of a classmate, Henri Villard, anglicized it, and landed in New York as Henry Villard. By his own account he arrived "with but a scanty wardrobe and an empty purse, ignorant of the English language, and without a friend to turn to in the American metropolis."

The presence of a family of distant relatives in Belleville, Illinois, lured him to the prairie, which railroad colonization campaigns were rapidly populating with middle-European immigrants. Soon he was editing a money-losing German-language newspaper, the *Volksblatt*, in Racine, Wisconsin, while perfecting his English. In 1858 he received an assignment from the *Staats-Zeitung*, the leading German newspaper in Chicago, to cover the debates between two candidates for the US Senate from Illinois, Democrat Stephen A. Douglas and Republican Abraham Lincoln.

With contracts in hand from several midwestern newspapers as well as Horace Greeley's *New York Tribune* and the competing *New York Herald*, Villard found himself in Washington during the Confederate bombing of Fort Sumter, which marked the beginning of the Civil War. He spent the next three years embedded, so to speak, with Union forces, starting at the First Battle of Bull Run.

After the war's end, Henry was approached by a group of German investors with stakes in West Coast railways. They were seeking his help in determining what had happened to their money, which amounted to nearly $11 million. "Such was the beginning of his business career," Villard wrote in his memoirs, in which he indulged the peculiar mannerism of referring to himself in the third person.

Villard went west to reconnoiter and made two discoveries. The first was that his countrymen indeed had been defrauded, for half their money had disappeared into the pockets of American promoters. A road that was to have stretched 375 miles from Portland to the California state line was still 200 miles short of its destination, and another line that was to have been financed with $3 million of the proceeds had not even been started. The second discovery was that Oregon Territory was ripe for development. All it needed to really thrive, he concluded, was a larger popula-

THE QUEST FOR THE BURLINGTON

tion. To that end Villard persuaded the investors to place him in charge of a bureau to lure German settlers to the territory.

What Villard possessed in abundance were charm and audacity, qualities he put to work in his new role. He also had absorbed some useful lessons from the railroad promoters who had cheated the German investors. One was how to load up an enterprise with liabilities far beyond its concrete assets—watering its stock, in other words. "As a stock-waterer he had, probably, no superior," wrote Henry Clews, the Wall Street banker and memoirist. Clews's judgment was based chiefly on Villard's creation of the Oregon Railway & Navigation Company, which he formed in 1879 to consolidate a fleet of steamboats with coastal shipping lines and short-line railroads to exploit the potential of the Far Western territory.

Villard successfully pitched Oregon Navigation to a clutch of railroad insiders, including George Pullman. As Clews recalled, Villard then listed the stock on the New York Stock Exchange, issued a sham financial report "showing immense and unprecedented earnings," and "had the stock bulled up to 200." Clews thought the entire project a chimera. "There is probably no instance in the whole history of railroad manipulation," he would write, "in which a man has presented to the public, and with such amazing success, such a specious appearance of possessing solid capital where so little existed in reality."

The Oregon flotation "was but the beginning of a series of like successes," Villard recounted. The most audacious of these was his "blind pool" of 1881, which he labeled a "unique financial feat, without precedent or parallel." Few on Wall Street could disagree.

The blind pool was designed to raise enough money to take over the Northern Pacific, which had emerged as a potentially ruinous competitor to Oregon Navigation. Villard would have to accumulate Northern Pacific stock quietly, for any hint of his interest would drive its price out of his reach. But he could hardly raise the capital to finance the purchases without divulging what the money was for . . . or could he? Villard issued a confidential prospectus to fifty backers, asking them to subscribe to a fund of $8 million for an enterprise "the exact nature of which he would disclose on or before May 15, 1881"—that is, ninety days hence.

The effect of this occult approach was electric. "The very novelty and mystery of the proposition proved to be an irresistible attraction," Villard wrote. "A regular rush for the privilege of subscribing ensured, and within twenty-four hours of the issue of the circular, more than twice the amount offered was applied for. . . . All wanted more." He easily raised enough to buy out the Northern Pacific, and then some.

Victory, achieved with truly Napoleonic bravado, brought Villard only pain, however. His great achievement on Wall Street merely proved to be the prelude to disaster in the field. Upon taking over the Northern Pacific, Villard found $34 million on its ledgers, the remains of a $40 million loan that had been made to its previous management by J. P. Morgan. But he also discovered the loan's punishing terms — the money would be disbursed by the bankers only at the rate of $25,000 per mile in sections of twenty-five miles at a time, and only after the completed sections had been inspected and approved by government officials. This would be a painfully slow process in the best of times, but it was made worse by the ten weeks of governmental paralysis following the assassination attempt on President James A. Garfield on July 2 (the very event that had threatened to sink Harriman's first purchase of Illinois Central bonds). Vice President Chester A. Arthur refused to take the reins of government as long as Garfield still clung to life, thus delaying the appointment of an inspection commission for the railroad. Before the wounded president's agony ended with his death on September 19, Villard had been forced to spend some $6 million from his own bank accounts.

Yet somehow he carried on, maintaining the confidence of the public and his investors via the occasional act of Villardian theatricality, as when he embarked on a headlong twenty-one-hundred-mile dash by rail from Chicago to fulfill a pressing appointment in Portland. The trip took less than half as long as regular trains on the route, which Villard turned into a claim that he had made the fastest rail journey in history.

The completion of the Northern Pacific's route to the coast in 1883 presented another opportunity for a public spectacle, this one designed as an "international celebration." There would be two weeks of galas as Villard's ceremonial train made its way across the continent from the East

Coast. Its ultimate destination was Montana, where Villard would drive a ceremonial spike to mark the conclusion of work. The cars carried leaders of the Senate and House of Representatives, governors of the seven states crossed by the line, more than a hundred newspaper reporters, former president Grant, and "the whole diplomatic corps . . . as well as several score of prominent Englishmen and Germans"—the latter representing Villard's foreign investors.

The procession was especially notable for a speech delivered on September 5 at Bismarck, North Dakota, by the Sioux chief Sitting Bull, only seven years after his tribe's victory over George Armstrong Custer at the Little Bighorn. The occasion was the laying of the cornerstone for the capitol of the Dakota Territory. Sitting Bull had been brought there "from his place of captivity," Villard recalled, to make an address "in the presence of a great multitude."

The event ranks as one of the most subtle acts of defiance in American history. The speech had been prepared jointly by Sitting Bull and a young US Army officer who understood the Sioux language, to be delivered by the chief in his native tongue while the officer offered a simultaneous translation. To the officer's horror, the words uttered by Sitting Bull bore no resemblance to the gracious message of amity they had written together. Instead, Sitting Bull declared, "I hate all white people." He paused for applause from the uncomprehending crowd, bowed and smiled at President Grant and the other dignitaries, and proceeded: "You are thieves and liars. You have taken away our land and made us outcasts." The officer continued to read out the original speech in English, resulting in a standing ovation for the Sioux chief. The impression that he had spoken up for friendship between whites and Indians gave Sitting Bull such popular standing that he was invited to join the Wild West show of William F. "Buffalo Bill" Cody, in which he soon became the lead attraction.

Yet even at the triumphal moment of completion, the Northern Pacific was in a state of financial collapse, staggered by a vast load of debt; Villard and his closest associates knew that his "last spike" ceremony was mere window-dressing to conceal the dismal condition of the railroad's books. "I cannot quite make up my mind," one of his investors had writ-

ten Villard while the event was still being planned, "whether it is you or
Barnum that has 'the greatest show on earth.'"

Villard had been counting on a surge of business on the NP now that it
was a through line all the way to the coast, but the traffic failed to appear.
The press, which had followed with such enthusiasm his breakneck trip to
the coast and the lavish completion ceremonies, now turned hostile, not
least because just as his railroad empire was collapsing he was erecting, on
Madison Avenue in New York, "a princely edifice" of brownstone in Ital-
ian Renaissance style, designed by the premier architectural firm McKim,
Mead & White. On the night of December 16 he was awakened there by
a delegation of investors and auditors and informed that he was bankrupt.
A syndicate had been formed to rescue the Northern Pacific, but only on
condition that he resign its presidency.

Villard and his family vacated their sumptuous Madison Avenue
palace, which encompassed six residences. (The building was sold to
Whitelaw Reid, who had succeeded Horace Greeley as editor and owner
of the *New York Tribune*, but it was known forever after as the "Villard
Houses.")

There would be one more turn of the wheel of fate for Henry Villard. Only three years after his eviction from the Northern Pacific he
was approached by a delegation from the Northern Pacific and Oregon
& Transcontinental, the holding company he had created for his railroad interests. The visitors appealed to him for a $5 million loan, which
he raised through his European connections. But he refused to pay the
money over unless he was again granted control of the Northern Pacific.
"He was hailed as the railroad king restored to his reign," Villard wrote in
his memoirs. "Congratulations by telegraph and mail at once poured in."

Villard's Northern Pacific joined in a new surge of overbuilding that
swept through the railroad industry in the late 1880s, and which once
again would bring the industry grief from rate cutting and overleveraging.
As before, Villard turned out to have greater skills as a visionary than as a
manager, but this time he was also guilty of loading down his railroad with
loans to himself at extortionate interest rates.

In August 1893 the Northern Pacific was placed in receivership for the

Railroad tycoon Henry Villard completed the so-called Villard Houses on New York's Madison Avenue, encompassing six sumptuous residences, in 1884, just as his financial empire was collapsing. Investors placed his Northern Pacific Railroad into receivership and evicted him from the mansion, which has since become incorporated into a high-rise hotel.

third time. Villard would write that he fully anticipated that the company's second collapse on his watch "would again mean for himself discredit, calumny, and abuse." He was correct. When the railroad board marked Villard's resignation with a pro forma letter of gratitude for his leadership, the *New York Times* erupted in fury, saying that the letter "seemed like a ghastly sarcasm. . . A more shameless disregard of the duties of Trustees and Directors have not been seen in the history of American railroads."

Given the history of rapine and plunder of the railroads over the previous forty years, this was surely too harsh. Like his fellow transportation tycoons, Villard aimed to become rich, but his chief fault was lack of managerial ability rather than a thirst for plunder. The former quality was what most strikingly distinguished him from his chief rival in the northern territory, James J. Hill.

Hill, like Villard, was cognizant of the traffic potential of the re-source-rich northern prairie and the Pacific Northwest. But he had moved cautiously, focusing on laying track for his Great Northern Railroad from St. Paul into the agriculturally rich Red River Valley of northern Dakota and southern Manitoba. By 1886, however, Hill had decided that the future of his enterprise lay in expanding it from a regional road into a transcontinental, encroaching on the territory crossed by the Northern Pacific. Hill's railroad and Villard's were now in open conflict.

JAMES J. HILL was the epitome of the self-made man of the late nineteenth century. Ten years Harriman's senior, he was born in the Canadian community of Rockwood about forty miles west of Toronto into a farming family that had migrated from County Armagh, Ireland, on his father's side and from Scotland, by way of Tipperary, on his mother's. His father's ambition had been for him to enter the medical profession, but at the age of nine a mishap with a handmade bow and arrow took out his right eye, ending that prospect.

At seventeen, Hill left home to seek his fortune. The following year, 1856, found him in St. Paul, Minnesota, then a riverfront trading settlement of fewer than five thousand souls that only recently had shaken off its original moniker of "Pig's Eye," which had been the nickname of its leading saloon-keeper. Like most well-sinewed young men in the community, he obtained his first employment on the levees of the Mississippi River waterfront, securing a job as a shipping clerk, a position that required him not only to manage the steamboat traffic that was St. Paul's only communication with the outside world (a rail connection to Chicago would not arrive for eleven more years) but oversee the brawling workforce that handled the steamboats' cargo. Hill was on hand when a locomotive named the *William Crooks* was offloaded from a Mississippi River barge one day in September 1861, joining the stevedores to haul the iron behemoth from the riverfront to the railroad tracks. It belonged to the St. Paul & Pacific, a puny road connecting the St. Paul steamboat landing with westward-reaching transportation at Breckenridge, on the Minnesota–North Dakota border, two hundred miles away. That could be taken as a foreshadowing of Hill's career, for the St. Paul & Pacific would be the first railroad he acquired when launching the defining project of his life, the creation of the Great Northern, in 1889. The acquisition set a pattern, for Hill built up his system by cobbling together smaller railroads he bought on the cheap when they were struggling or the industry was being shunned by the financial markets.

The St. Paul & Pacific had soon failed and the *Crooks* placed in storage. By 1877 the road was operating again, albeit unprofitably, and Hill offered to take it off the hands of its mostly Dutch investors. He calculated that he and his partners would need slightly more than $5.5 million to buy up its outstanding bonds and foreclose on its mortgages. In return for that outlay, they would acquire track he estimated to be worth $11.4 million, $800,000 in equipment, and a government land grant of more than 2.6 million acres, which he valued at some $6.7 million, based on the government's standard valuation of $2.50 per acre.

Hill's optimism about the wisdom of this transaction was not widely shared. As he recalled for Great Northern stockholders upon his retirement in July 1912, at the time "no individual or financial house in Europe or America, outside of those associated with us, would have taken the bargain off our hands. By a few it was regarded as a doubtful venture, by most as a hopeless mistake." But Hill was confident he could turn a profit from the growth in population and freight traffic destined to accompany the development of the Far Northwest. Immigrants already were flooding into the region, and the railroad would bring in even more settlers, whose crops it could bring to market. As for the government-granted land, ultimately it would bring the St. Paul $13 million, about twice Hill's initial estimate.

One characteristic that set Hill apart from his contemporaries was his vision of the railroad as a force for the improvement of the countryside. In his valedictory recollections, he observed that his railroad had "carried to market the products of the country at rates which have greatly developed the territory served by its lines." Had the Great Northern simply maintained its rates from 1881 through 1912, he said, it could have collected nearly $2 billion from shippers and passengers. But that would

The ferociously competitive James J. Hill, creator of the Great Northern and one of Harriman's chief adversaries in the battle over the Northern Pacific.

have sacrificed long-term growth for short-term profit. Instead, at its low rates it collected only about $700 million, but that endowed the territory served by the railroad with the economic fuel for "multiplying its wealth indefinitely" while "furnishing increasing and profitable tonnage for years to come" in a long-term symbiosis. "The Great Northern is now wrought so firmly into the economic as well as the corporate body of the land as to have fitted itself permanently into the natural frame of things," he said. "So far as any creation of human effort can be made, it will be proof against the attacks of time."

Hill's leadership of the Great Northern as it expanded across the northern plains to Puget Sound set a rare standard for conservative finance in the railroad industry. In addition to the seed capital provided by the federal land grant, the railroad's growth was funded by sales of shares and bonds carefully calibrated to the underlying value of the enterprise, without the torrents of water that rendered other railroads hopelessly overcapitalized. As a result, the Great Northern "never failed, never passed a dividend, never was financially insecure in any time of panic," he boasted in 1912. "The success and prosperity that attend the Company today have not been purchased either by any doubtful transactions in the stock market. . . . No emergency can surprise it."

Few of Hill's rival railroad presidents could match his knowledge of how best to build a road, where to build it, and how to operate what he built. "What we want," he remarked in 1890, "is the best possible line, shortest distance, lowest grades, and least curvature that we can build. We do not care enough for Rocky Mountain scenery to spend a large sum of money developing it."

In all these particulars, Hill sounded very much like Edward Harriman, who showed the same eye for efficiency and the recognition that plunder could never be more than a short-term strategy. With two such strong-willed tycoons building systems destined to compete with each other, a clash between them seemed preordained.

As an experienced railroad operator, Hill carefully routed his Great Northern and its branches from Minnesota to the West Coast through productive and populated territory capable of generating robust freight traffic. Villard, by contrast, heedlessly "threw lines across an inhospitable country, part of which was almost devoid of population," observed Julius Grodinsky, an astute chronicler of the railway expansions of the late nineteenth century. "While Hill was building carefully and checking his costs minutely Villard built in ignorance of costs." When the first bills arrived in 1883, Villard had been shocked to discover that the cost of building the Northern Pacific was twice what he expected. Nevertheless, he repeated the error nearly a decade later.

Hill's attention to costs gave him the latitude to undercut competitors' rates ruthlessly without sacrificing profits, while rivals with higher fixed costs were driven into the ground. He was able to wait out his competi-

tors, secure in the knowledge that in financial terms they were built on
sand, while his roads rested on firm ballast. Other railroads in the Pacific
Northwest might fear the Northern Pacific and its ambitious plans for
expansion. "But it had no terrors for Mr. Hill," reported his biographer
Joseph Gilpin Pyle. "He knew its financial condition. . . . He was in no
hurry or fret, because he knew that every day reduced the power of the
Northern Pacific to carry its own burdens, and hence minimized the danger of it as a competitor."

And once Hill knew that a competitor was on the ropes, he was ruthless in delivering the coup de grâce. He refused to join the pools or informal arrangements his fellow railroad men organized to fix rates, instead
forging ahead with relentless rate-cutting on his own. "Mr. Hill is a law
unto himself," a director of the Chicago, Burlington & Quincy, which
was soon destined to fall within Hill's gravitational field, wrote to its president, Charles Perkins. Hill had waited out the Northern Pacific, and now
he was poised to collect it as a prize. He did not know it yet, but his victory
would only set the stage for another battle.

In the late 1890s, the railroad situation in the Midwest resembled the
geopolitical landscape in place near the end of the Napoleonic period,
with duchies and great powers scrambling to make alliances crucial to
their survival. The railroad war would be fought with stocks, bonds, and
capital, not bullets and bombs, but it was ferocious enough for all that.

Four major systems were in play: the Great Northern, which ran from
St. Paul, Minnesota, to Seattle; the Northern Pacific, which ran roughly
along the same route; the Union Pacific, which ran from Omaha to San
Francisco and down the coast (after Harriman joined it with the Southern Pacific); and the Chicago, Burlington & Quincy, which was known
familiarly as the Burlington or the "Q." The first two were controlled by
Pierpont Morgan and James J. Hill; the third by Harriman; and the last
by the aging Charles E. Perkins, who had made the Burlington a road of
enviable quality, stability, and profitability.

Perkins's 7,911-mile railroad stretched lucratively west across the
plains from Chicago to Denver and Cheyenne, and from there north
to Billings, Montana, including the reach along the Mississippi River

between Quincy, Illinois, and Burlington, Iowa, from which it drew its name. The Burlington carried produce from Illinois, Iowa, and Nebraska, coal from Illinois and Iowa, and mineral ores from Colorado and the Black Hills of South Dakota and Wyoming. Thanks to its unbroken string of dividend payouts it was revered as a quintessential "widows and orphans" stock, widely held by some fifteen thousand small investors in blocks of twenty or thirty shares each.

The Burlington's misfortune, however, was that it possessed qualities that other big railroads wanted, and little financial capacity to hold them off. The Great Northern and Northern Pacific each coveted its access to Chicago, and the Union Pacific its branches in Kansas, Nebraska, and Colorado. In short, the Burlington's strategic position among these other railroads was not a strength but a weakness. "There can be no doubt about the value of C.B. & Q to any scheme for combining roads west of Chicago," Perkins wrote to a fellow director of his line as the nineteenth century was drawing to a close. For some reason he thought this was a guarantee of its survival, when in fact it presaged its eradication.

The threat to the Burlington's independence increased when Morgan brought the Great Northern and the Northern Pacific together under Hill's management in 1896. The consolidation was the consequence of Henry Villard's mismanagement of the Northern Pacific, which had culminated in its third bankruptcy. With failure staring its investors and bankers in the face, many perceived that the road's only hope of survival lay in turning it over to Hill. Among them was Jacob Schiff, who represented German investors in Northern Pacific bonds and was a director of Hill's Great Northern. The correct play, he wrote his friend Ernest Cassel, a well-connected British banker, was to bring the two lines under "close relationship" via joint management by Hill, in order to end their debilitating competition. Indeed, a bankrupt Northern Pacific would pose a threat to Hill's Great Northern; once a bankruptcy judge relieved it of the fixed expenses of bond interest and share dividends, it could cut rates to the nub.

Hill long had viewed the Northern Pacific with a contempt that only intensified in the aftermath of the Villard regime. The road "has not been run as a railway for years, but as a device for creating bonds to be sold," he wrote his friend Lord Mount Stephen, a Canadian railroad magnate. The chief goal of the Great Northern's acquisition of the Northern Pacific, Hill wrote, echoing Schiff, would be "mainly the freedom from competition."

In April 1895 the Great Northern agreed to acquire the Northern Pacific. The merger did not proceed smoothly. The deal was unpopular in Minnesota, where farmers contemplated unhappily the prospect of paying monopoly freight rates to send their produce to market. The state government sued to block the merger, citing a Minnesota law that barred railroads from taking control of any lines they paralleled within the state. Hill's elite lawyers at the New York firm of Simpson and Thatcher were confident that the law could not be applied retroactively to a railroad chartered in 1856. They were wrong. The Minnesota Supreme Court blocked the merger in a decision later upheld by the US Supreme Court. Searching for a new option, Hill and the Northern Pacific shareholders placed the matter in the hands of Hill's banker, Pierpont Morgan.

Morgan reorganized the Northern Pacific in what was seen at the time as an outstanding example of Morganization, involving the issuance of some $345 million in new shares and bonds. On all of this Morgan collected a commission of 10 percent. Morgan also established a voting trust to control the railroad that would remain in effect for five years, or until November 1, 1901, with himself as its chairman.

Morgan placed Hill in the indispensable role of the joint enterprise's operator, via an agreement reached quietly at Mount Stephens's London home and known accordingly as the "London memorandum." The document certified that the two railroads would "form a permanent alliance . . . with a view of avoiding competition." The Minnesota law was neatly circumvented by selling a controlling stake in the Northern Pacific to Hill personally, with the funds put up by Morgan—as the law prohibiting the sale of one railroad to another posed no obstacle to joint ownership by an individual.

Under Hill's supervision, the Great Northern and Northern Pacific prospered together. The likelihood that they would become even more powerful in the western United States concerned not only the Burling-

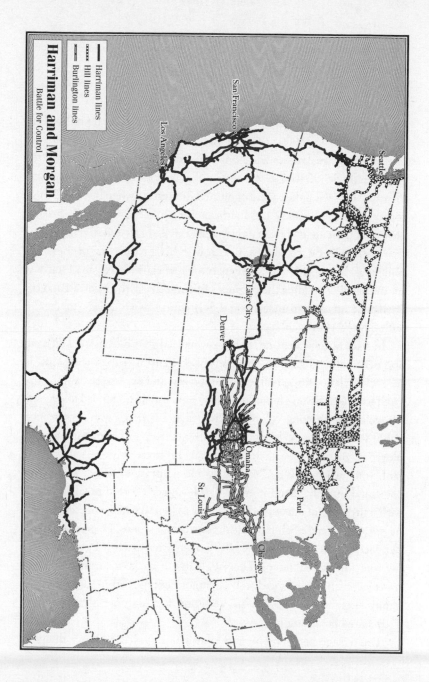

Harriman and Morgan
Battle for Control

— Harriman lines
░░░ Hill lines
||| Burlington lines

Seattle

San Francisco

Los Angeles

Salt Lake City

Denver

Omaha

St. Paul

St. Louis

Chicago

ton's Charles Perkins. The threat they now posed to the Union Pacific also made Edward Harriman uneasy.

AS HARRIMAN AND Hill moved into the front ranks of the railroad industry during the 1890s, they had circled each other warily, probing for one another's weaknesses like lions maneuvering to become king of the pride. Jacob Schiff, who served as a banker to both, struggled to mediate. He tried to develop their areas of mutual interest, as when he placed them together on the board of the Baltimore & Ohio. But it rapidly became clear that their areas of rivalry outweighed those of shared advantage, and that eventually he would have to throw in his lot with one or the other. Hill grew closer to Morgan and began to view Harriman as an obstacle to his own goal of building the premier railroad linking the Midwest and the Pacific; Schiff came to understand that his future as a railroad financier lay with Edward Harriman.

Indeed, as time went on, Schiff recognized that his business interests and personality aligned more closely with Harriman than with Hill. In his social relationships, Hill was bluff, breezy, and excessively familiar. Invited to dine at Schiff's home at 932 Fifth Avenue, Hill tended to overstay his welcome, chatting volubly, oblivious to his host's waning patience. Schiff's servant Joseph would materialize at 10 p.m. sharp with his employer's nightcap of orange juice, a signal Hill invariably overlooked. "Mr. Hill, your taxi is waiting," Joseph would whisper, to which Hill would command in reply, "Send it away!" Hill was accustomed to fidget noisily with a little bag of uncut precious stones as he talked; one evening, when he noticed Therese Schiff admiring one of the stones, he presented it to her. Jacob Schiff examined the gift disapprovingly. "Only I give jewels to my wife," he stated, telling Therese, "Give it back." Harriman, by contrast, was a chilly and taciturn companion, except within his immediate family circle. Otherwise, his conversation focused on business matters. That suited Schiff just fine.

The tension between Hill and Harriman revealed itself in a disagreement over the Oregon Short Line and the Oregon Railway & Navigation Company. These two roads had been controlled by the Union Pacific before its bankruptcy—Villard had lost control of the latter in 1883, and it was sold to the Union Pacific in 1889. The roads had been stripped from the UP by receivers, and then were reacquired by Harriman. Since they provided access to Portland, Oregon, via Wyoming and Idaho, they were crucial branch lines simultaneously for the Union Pacific, Hill's Great Northern, and the Northern Pacific.

Prior to the Union Pacific receivership, those three roads had negotiated shared access to Oregon Navigation, which was treated as a neutral connecting line. Schiff subsequently worked out a tentative deal with Morgan partner Charles Coster, a personal friend, in which the Northern Pacific and Great Northern each would own one-fourth of Oregon Navigation, with the other half held in joint trust by J. P. Morgan and Co. and Kuhn, Loeb. The banks would transfer their interests to the Union Pacific and the Oregon Short Line as soon as an agreement had been reached to secure "the permanent independence" of Oregon Navigation and the appointment of management committed to "the maintenance of rates, traffic at all times."

This proposed division of the spoils was the arrangement that Harriman torpedoed during that meeting on October 3, 1898. After listening to Coster and Schiff describe a plan for the Northern Pacific and Great Northern to share the traffic between the Twin Cities and the Pacific Coast, he interjected abruptly that he was no longer willing to cede rights to the ownership of Oregon Navigation to anyone else under any conditions. He knew that exclusive ownership of Oregon Navigation, with its access to Portland and points north, would effectively give the Union Pacific control of the northern transcontinental route, checking the expansion plans of both the Great Northern and Northern Pacific. Harriman's reading of the old contracts by which the Union Pacific had acquired Oregon Navigation stock was that the UP held sole ownership. "Nothing was said about any territorial division," he observed. Harriman was thereby unilaterally terminating a truce of long standing.

Hill was furious about what was effectively Harriman's declaration of war. To settle the disagreement, however, he offered to award Harriman joint ownership of Oregon Navigation by the Union Pacific, Northern Pacific, and Great Northern in return for his promise to give the Union Pacific the right to carry traffic between Seattle and Portland over Northern Pacific tracks. Hill also observed, in a letter to Harriman delivered via Schiff about six weeks after Harriman's return from Alaska, that the Great Northern could bring to Oregon Navigation "the valuable traffic of about 5,500 miles of railway in a new country which is very rapidly growing, and most of which the Navigation Company could not secure in any other way." Slipping the iron hand into the velvet glove, Hill warned that if Harriman refused to come to terms, he was prepared to build his own line to the coast in direct competition with Oregon Navigation. "I know that country fairly well," he wrote, "and I think that with five million dollars I could build a much better line from our road into Portland; and with, say, two million more, reach the most productive sections of the Navigation Company." The venture would cost a mere $300,000 a year in debt service, which he reckoned would be "much less than we would pay the Navigation Company for doing our business under such a plan as I have outlined."

Hill could scarcely have found a better formula for antagonizing Harriman than this truculent threat. Writing to Hill in September 1899, Schiff tried to describe Harriman's reaction in sugarcoated terms, but Harriman's anger leached out from between his lines. "Mr. Harriman has been much impressed by your suggestion," Schiff wrote, "though, frank as I am always with you, I should add that I think he felt somewhat irritated by the mandatory tone in which your letter to him was written."

Harriman himself never responded directly to Hill's proposition. Instead, he spent the next few months reintegrating the Union Pacific, Oregon Short Line, and Oregon Navigation into a single jointly functioning railroad. Negotiations with Harriman having broken down perhaps irretrievably, Hill focused on the urgent goal of securing for the Great Northern and Northern Pacific an entry into Chicago. That meant acquiring the Burlington. It was a goal Harriman was also pursuing.

———

HARRIMAN HAD TRIED to beat Hill to the Burlington via a direct approach to Perkins, meeting five times with Perkins to press his suit. Reflecting the Burlington's position as the belle of the midwestern railroad ball, Perkins chose to play hard to get. He informed Harriman that the Q was not for sale—but if it were, the price would be $200 per share. Even to a suitor as determined as Harriman, who was well aware of the danger to the Union Pacific should the railroad fall into his rival's hands, the price seemed ridiculously inflated. Over the next few months he offered Perkins cash and bonds in several different permutations, but never more than the equivalent of $150 per share. Rebuffed repeatedly, he withdrew from the contest—on the surface. In fact, he had formed a syndicate with Schiff, James Stillman, and George Gould to quietly purchase Burlington shares on the open market.

Perkins advised his board that Harriman was undoubtedly in the market for stock, but that with so many shares in "widows' and orphans'" hands, he doubted that control of the railroad could be achieved through piecemeal purchases on the open market. He was right. In the first six months of 1900 the Harriman syndicate acquired 70,000 shares, but then the well ran dry, with few shares available at prices they were willing to pay. By July 25, they had spent $10 million to accumulate 80,300 shares —less than 9 percent of the company, at an average price of more than $124. Just before the end of the year, Harriman gave in and liquidated the syndicate at a modest profit. Hill, who had been watching from the sidelines, chuckled at the syndicate's failure. Its members "found themselves up against a stone wall," he would remark later, adding that the small shareholders "resented [Harriman's] attempt to buy into their company." When his turn came, Hill decided, he would not bother with the small shareholders, but would go directly to the top.

Hill had thirsted for the Burlington for several years. The main obstacle in his way was Pierpont Morgan, who held the purse strings in their partnership. Morgan agreed with Hill that the Great Northern should have a direct link to Chicago, just as the New York Central, of which Morgan also was a director, should have its own link to Chicago. The best three candidates to carry the Great Northern into the hub were the

Chicago & Northwestern; the Chicago, Milwaukee & St. Paul; and the Burlington. Of those, the Northwestern was off the table, since it was affiliated with both the Union Pacific and the Vanderbilt interests, which would hardly want to turn it over to the Great Northern. As for the other two, a buyout of the St. Paul would cost $227 million, versus $255 million for the Burlington. Morgan pushed for the St. Paul as the better bargain. "Hill did not agree with me," Morgan testified later, "but he acquiesced."

Hill disagreed because he considered the Burlington a much better fit for his railroad. The Great Northern and Northern Pacific needed access to "the great provision centers" of Kansas City, St. Joseph, Omaha, Chicago, and St. Louis, he observed to Mount Stephen. "The Burlington lets us into all these districts and commercial centers over better lines and with better terminals than any other road." Hill also knew that if the Great Northern bought the St. Paul and left the Burlington to be acquired by Harriman, the latter's combination with the Union Pacific would become a mortal threat to the Great Northern and Northern Pacific by commanding freight traffic across the Northwest.

Fate intervened, in the form of a flat refusal by the St. Paul's owners to consider a sale at any price. "They would not even name terms," Morgan recalled. So he met again with Hill and said, "You can go ahead and see what you can do with the Burlington."

Negotiations with Perkins now moved quickly. Given the vigorous trading in Burlington shares, Perkins reckoned that "Wall Street would soon have had 51 per cent of the stock in spite of us. Then the question was, who to sell to." He decided that if his shareholders could get $200 per share for all their stock, "it was better than to let the *market* get 51 per cent, even if it paid more than $200."

Hill finally agreed to buy the Burlington for $200 per share in cash on April 9, with Morgan's assent. Under the terms of the deal, ownership of the Burlington would be held by the Great Northern and Northern Pacific on a fifty-fifty basis, though with both roads under Hill's control — the Great Northern directly, the Northern Pacific indirectly — this was a mere formality.

News of the pending merger left Harriman rattled and Schiff humiliated. Although Hill long would maintain that he kept Harriman and Schiff apprised of his talks with Perkins, they later insisted that they knew nothing of his interest. As Schiff would recall in a long, petulant letter to Morgan, Hill had told him flatly in late March that "neither directly nor indirectly was he interested in Burlington stock, nor did he have any intention to control the property."

"I accepted this statement on Mr. Hill's part," Schiff informed Morgan, "for I could not believe that a man whom I had known . . . for some fifteen years, whom I had never wronged, . . . and whom I believed to be my friend, would willingly mislead or deceive me." But deceive Schiff he did, flagrantly.

Learning of Hill's plans to travel from Washington to Boston to complete the Burlington purchase just prior to Easter Sunday, April 7, Schiff and Harriman staged one last-ditch attempt to block the transaction by intercepting Hill at his layover in New York. According to Schiff, he arranged in advance for financier George Fisher Baker to host an impromptu conference at his home for him, Hill, and Harriman. Schiff recalled dispatching his son Morti to waylay Hill as soon as he debarked from the Washington train and before he could transfer to the train for Boston. (Baker's own recollection was that he earlier had arranged to accompany Hill to Boston via the midnight train to meet the Burlington's directors and sign the acquisition papers, and had "inadvertently" mentioned within Harriman's earshot that he and Hill would be dining together that evening. Harriman tipped off Schiff and at 8 p.m., as the dinner was just concluding, the two of them showed up uninvited at Baker's front door.)

In any event, Schiff confronted Hill about his lie as soon as they set eyes on one another. According to Schiff, Hill apologized but explained that he had felt he had no choice, "knowing my relations to the Union Pacific." Schiff later told Morgan, "I expressed my mortification but did not further discuss this."

The reason for his forbearance may have been that Schiff and Harriman still hoped to salvage a compromise to avert the impending deal. Harriman was prepared to join the Burlington acquisition as a partner, putting up one-third of the purchase price, or about $65 million, in cash. Hill refused to give the proposal even a moment's consideration. The various participants described the tone of his response differently. Schiff recalled that Hill "replied with platitudes." Baker reported that the discussion proceeded with "increasing animation and fervor, not to say violence," and continued as Harriman and Schiff accompanied Baker and Hill to Grand Central Station for the train to Boston. They carried on their argument right up until the moment the train pulled away, Baker recalled, leaving Harriman and Schiff to watch forlornly from the empty platform.

Harriman's own recollection is certainly the most dramatic, and the one that has been most frequently repeated. He recalled that the conversation ended abruptly at Baker's home with Hill's curt refusal, just as Hill and Baker prepared to depart for the terminal. "Very well," Harriman said, rising to leave. "It is a hostile act and you must take the consequences." (Hill might well have savored the irony of Harriman, who high-handedly had refused to share Oregon Navigation with the Great Northern and Northern Pacific only two years earlier, now appearing at Baker's door to demand a similar accommodation from him.)

However the encounter unfolded, Schiff found the situation profoundly unnerving. The next morning he repaired to Morgan's office in the hope of finding a path for Harriman into the Burlington deal. But the banker, engaged in preparations for his annual voyage to Europe, granted Schiff only a few minutes' audience, during which he declined to make any promise other than that he would be willing to consider any plan that Schiff could contrive to bring Harriman into the Burlington deal; just send it to him in London, he said.

In truth, Morgan had no intention of letting Harriman through the door. Due to his distaste for Harriman, born of the battle for the Dubuque & Sioux City in which the low-born broker had outmaneuvered him, "he manifestly did not want Harriman as a partner or associate," Herbert Satterlee reported. Nor did he take seriously the veiled threat embodied in Harriman's assertion that the refusal was "a hostile act."

In any event, the Burlington deal was as good as final, as Schiff would discover when he took up the matter with Morgan's junior partner, Robert Bacon, in Morgan's absence. Schiff warned Bacon that placing the

Burlington under the exclusive control of the Northern Pacific and Great Northern would create an inherently menacing competitive situation for every railroad line crossing the Missouri, and "particularly . . . a constant danger to the Union Pacific." He repeated Harriman's offer to pay the one-third price of the Burlington, $65 million, in cash.

"It's too late," Bacon replied. "Nothing can be done."

The situation would be intolerable to the Union Pacific, Schiff warned. "The railroad will have to protect itself."

He would be as good as his word. Hill might have seized the Burlington in a lightning strike, but Harriman would deliver a lightning bolt of his own in return. He would move to take over not the Burlington itself, but its half owner, the Northern Pacific. What followed would be a defining moment for the financial community at the very outset of the new century.

PART III

---•᷉᷉•---

THE GHOST DANCE

16

PEACOCK ALLEY

THE 1800s DREW to a close with an entire generation of stock manipulators and buccaneers having passed away. Fisk, Drew, and Vanderbilt had died within a few years of one another in the 1870s—Fisk in 1872, Vanderbilt in 1877, and Drew in 1879. Jay Gould lasted a decade or two longer, dying in his bed of tuberculosis at the age of fifty-six in 1892.

The old guard had disappeared but their methods survived, taken up by a new generation of operators, some of whom were every bit as flamboyant as their predecessors. Figures like John "Bet-a-Million" Gates and the master stock trader James R. Keene, who worked his magic on behalf of such eminences as Pierpont Morgan, received the most voluminous press, but they were merely the center-ring acts in a big circus. After every trading day ended at 3 p.m., a select group repaired uptown to the Waldorf-Astoria to continue trading and to enjoy aftermarket conviviality. "To belong to the 'Waldorf crowd' meant that a man had arrived," recalled Bernard Baruch, an up-and-coming broker who had earned admission to the elite group by orchestrating the takeover of the tobacco company Liggett & Myers for the financier Thomas Fortune Ryan.

The vast Waldorf-Astoria extended west from Fifth Avenue between Thirty-Third and Thirty-Fourth streets (today the site of the Empire State Building). An Astor family dispute had prompted two cousins to open their own hotels at opposite corners of the same block, but eventually they combined the original Waldorf Hotel, completed in 1893, with the

Astoria, opened in 1897. The corridor connecting the two edifices became known as Peacock Alley, a thousand-foot-long promenade along which New York's elite and aspiring elite paraded in their most ostentatious finery. At the Waldorf end was New York's most exclusive restaurant, the Palm Room, where patrons were required to dine in full formal attire — men in white tie and tails, women in evening gowns.

The hotel's real attraction, however, was the opportunity to encounter celebrities face-to-face: famous writers, actresses, prizefighters, and those reigning stars of New York society, financiers. "On an afternoon or two at the Waldorf, one might brush elbows with Richard Harding Davis, Mark Twain, Lillian Russell, Gentleman Jim Corbett, Admiral Dewey, Mark Hanna, Chauncey Depew, Diamond Jim Brady, Edwin Hawley, and countless presidents of banks and railroads," Baruch reported. "Judge Elbert Gary, the head of U.S. Steel, lived there, as did Charley Schwab and James Keene. It was at a private dinner party in the Waldorf that I saw John W. Gates place a $1,000,000 bet on a game of baccarat." For those whose purpose extended beyond spending an hour or two in proximity to the great and near-great, there was always the prospect of putting over a business deal in the louche, smoky atmosphere of a Waldorf suite. It was as if all of Wall Street had become a moveable feast, more than two decades before Ernest Hemingway used the phrase as the title of his memoir of the Paris of the 1920s.

The most important characteristic of Wall Street at the end of the 1890s was that it was awash in money — euphorically so — for the country finally had shaken off the torpor that followed the Panic of 1893. The reserves of capital built up during the lean years were clamoring to be deployed. In 1896 came the presidential election in which the Republican William McKinley defeated William Jennings Bryan in part by promising to uphold the gold standard, signaling his determination to keep inflation in check. That was positive news for bankers and investors, whose holdings could only be drained of value by a general rise in prices, but bad news for farmers, who counted on inflation to buoy their income. McKinley had placed his thumb decisively on the scale for industry over agriculture, the city over the country.

The Palm Room of the Waldorf-Astoria was the epitome of Gilded Age elegance, in which patrons were required to wear formal attire; the hotel, assembled from two competing, adjoining hotels built by feuding members of the Astor family, served as the after-hours uptown refuge of Wall Street traders in the 1890s.

Ever creative, Wall Street bankers figured out exactly the right mechanism to put their torrent of capital to work: the industrial amalgamation, or the "trust." Notwithstanding the lessons provided by the collapse of the cordage trust in 1893, the years 1898 and 1899 saw new cartels founded in paper, copper, glue, elevators, and steel. Typically these assemblages involved issuing new securities well exceeding their industries' underlying values, but like a sick patient suddenly returned to health, America's economic prospects emitted a golden glow.

Some of these combinations and recombinations occurred at such a dizzying pace that their own promoters could not keep track of the money. That was the case with the series of mergers in the steel-wire industry masterminded by Gates, starting with the consolidation in 1897 of seven

Illinois factories into one corporation, the Consolidated Steel and Wire Company. A year later, Consolidated was acquired and combined with seven more mills by Gates's American Steel and Wire Company of Illinois, which issued $24 million in new stock. A year after that, Gates formed the American Steel and Wire Company of New Jersey, paid $33.6 million for the Illinois company's stock, bought eleven more plants, and issued $90 million in shares to cover it all. Somewhere along the line, $26 million in stock went missing.

"What became of it?" Gates was asked on the stand by a lawyer for a shareholder who had sued for an accounting.

"I don't know," Gates said.

"Have you got any of it?"

"No, I never got a cent's worth of it," Gates insisted.

Despite this evidence that Steel and Wire stock was so thoroughly watered that nearly a third of it could disappear without detection, the public did not seem to care. Over the first two months following the stock's issuance, its price more than doubled.

The clamor for stock and more stock fed and was fed by the bankers' inventiveness. Financial journalist Alexander Dana Noyes detected the signs of a speculative mania on every sidewalk and street corner. Especially worrisome was the popular conviction that the stock market was destined for a permanent rise. This was a period, Noyes wrote, in which punters and promoters comforted themselves with "the assumption that we were living in a New Era; that old rules and principles and precedent of finance were obsolete; that things could safely be done to-day which had been dangerous or impossible in the past." Such euphoria, the conviction that "this time it's different," is a familiar signpost of every major crash, right into the twenty-first century.

As the nation's leading industry, the railroads were also susceptible to the frenzy for combination—though as the financial commentator James Grant has observed, its mergers "were typically the result of distress, not prosperity." This is correct; Pierpont Morgan was working the magic of Morganization in part to wring from the railroads decades of stock watering, which had driven nearly two hundred rail lines into bankruptcy by

1894. In the following half decade, no business would undergo as much consolidation and transformation as the railroads. "At the beginning of the decade there had been innumerable great independent systems, . . . each competing against rival systems in the same regions," observed the railroad historian Edward G. Campbell. "At the end of the decade there were practically no independent systems; the various systems had been drawn into a few huge combinations which were dominated by a single man or a small group of men working in harmony with each other . . . The railroad industry had been transformed from one dominated by hundreds of competing leaders into one controlled by a small group of financiers" —Morgan and Harriman towering among them. The members of this group would soon be at each others' throats—at the same time that the American people and their elected leaders were attempting to drag them down by their lapels.

By the mid-1890s the railroads and their investors had been blamed for not one, but two economic crashes that cost millions of families dearly in lost savings and lost employment. Farmers and merchants complained that the railroads "have been exorbitant in their charges [and] have discriminated unjustly between localities," despite being gifted generously with power and money by state and federal lawmakers (to quote a bill of particulars issued by a national agricultural congress in 1873). Workers had wearied of the boom-and-bust employment cycle that saw them lured across the country en masse to build and operate new lines, only to have their wages ruthlessly slashed and their jobs eliminated when conditions deteriorated. It did not escape the notice of the boomers, who had helped the railroads expand during the fat years, that the lean years resulting in wage cuts and layoffs for themselves somehow left the fortunes of the owners and their protégés in Congress untouched. To the public at large, these capitalists had suborned the entire political structure of the country with graft.

Some hardened veterans of Wall Street grew wary of the market's unleashed animal spirits early in the boom. Among them was Jacob Schiff, who in September 1897 exchanged letters with a fellow banker, Robert Fleming, about the sudden upsurge in American economic fortunes after the McKinley election. "The revival which you and I have been looking for has come with a vengeance, and already at this early stage speculation is threatening to run away with good judgment," Schiff wrote uneasily. "The time appears not to be distant when almost any printed certificate, no matter what it represents, will command a market, and for this reason I believe it is already necessary to exercise considerable caution." Schiff was more in the right than he knew.

THE RAILROAD-DRIVEN SPECULATION and consolidation sweeping the US economy may have been bad for most ordinary Americans—but they had a peculiarly democratizing effect on Wall Street itself. It was a time when the word of a single individual or a cunning campaign of buying and selling could drive a stock higher or lower. Wall Street broker Roswell Pettibone Flower, for example: A former New York governor described as "the bull market incarnate," Flower had turned around a strong bear movement in early 1898 by declaring publicly that he was "a believer in American stocks and a buyer of American stocks." Investors hung on his every word, buying on his say-so just as later generations would follow the investment choices of Warren Buffett. In 1899 Flower had driven up shares of the Brooklyn Rapid Transit Company by repeatedly declaring that the trolley line was bound to rise—placing the target price at $75 when it was trading at $20, at $125 when it had reached $50, and eventually at $135. At that moment, however, Flower was struck down by a heart attack while fishing. The air instantly rushed out of BRT and other "Flower stocks," threatening to take down the entire market, until Morgan and other leading bankers stepped in with millions in capital to stem the downturn.

One manifestation of popular mania that brokers remarked on was the increasing presence of women among the investing throngs. Traditional club rooms and trading offices—not to mention the trading floor itself—were closed to women, but there was no dearth of entrepreneurs willing to give them access to the ticker in their own specialized rooms and to take their orders at the standard commission of twelve and a half cents per share. Condescension dripped from newspaper accounts of female trading habits. According to the *New York Sun*, women made money in the roaring bull market because they were always long (that is, they were exclusively buyers): "All she has to do is buy and the average woman who speculates in stocks can do that with as much éclat as she displays in dancing a cotillion or buying a spring bonnet." Many male bankers and traders were unsure what to make of the new customers. Investment banker Henry Clews regarded them with distaste and pity. "As speculators," he wrote, "women hitherto have been utter failures. They do not thrive in the atmosphere of Wall Street, for they do not seem to have the mental qualities required to take in the varied points of the situation upon which success in speculation depends. They are, by nature, parasites as speculators, and, when thrown upon their own resources, are comparatively helpless. . . . They have no ballast apart from men, and are liable to perish when adversity arises."

Clews's contemporary William Worthington Fowler had the exact opposite impression. "The female character is, in many respects, suited to a life of speculation," he wrote. "Speculation requires patience and fortitude, which are, or should be, both womanly virtues. Speculation derives its food from excitement, and women often feed on excitement." Fowler's conclusion was that women "are not only frequent, but daring speculators. They encounter risks that would appall the stoutest Wall Street veteran, and rush boldly into places where even a Vanderbilt would fear to tread."

The very structure of Wall Street also reflected the strange democratization of the stock market. There seemed to be a place for punters of every variety, for the investment business had coalesced into several strata. At the elite summit of the market, at least by its own estimation, was the New York Stock Exchange, which charged fixed commissions, required securities issuers to make financial disclosures (albeit meager ones, especially by comparison with the standards imposed under federal regulations after the crash of 1929), and maintained a huge trading floor inside its Victorian five-story edifice on Broad Street. The exchange's scrappy, not to say squalid, junior cousin was the "Curb," an unregulated gang of traders who gathered on the Broad Street sidewalk in rain or shine. There they traded securities unlisted on the Big Board, whether because the stocks were too "unseasoned" to win the New York Stock Exchange's imprimatur or they were issued by companies preferring to circumvent the exchange's disclosure rules. To the dismay of police, on heavy trading days the Curb brokers spilled onto the pavement, blocking traffic and frightening horses with the shouts and wild gesticulations by which they transmitted their orders to clerks hanging out of windows just overhead.

The Curb's brokers—indeed, all its employees—ran heavily to eastern European Jews and the Irish, ethnic groups shunned by many member firms of the Big Board thanks to perceptions of their lowly family backgrounds and less than elite educations. What the Curb's personnel lacked in gilded qualities they made up for in eccentricity and exuberance, pouring buckets of water over each other during the dog days of summer, dueling with water pistols, gifting each other with exploding cigars. Their investors, too, were typically shunned by the New York Stock Exchange, with its pretensions to aristocracy—though they were not necessarily poorer. Hetty Green, the heiress to a whaling fortune who haunted the byways of the financial district in frayed widow's weeds, could never gain entrée into the upstairs rooms of the New York Stock Exchange firms; but she was welcomed by the Curb, which handled the trades through which she turned her $6 million inheritance into an estimated $100 million at the time of her death in 1916. A figure of ridicule during her life, she died as reputedly the richest woman in the world.

At the lowest depths of Wall Street were the "bucket shops," which catered to the gambling blood of market players. To the solid citizens of the marketplace, the bucket shops were havens for "specious frauds," as Henry Clews put it. The New York Stock Exchange spent decades trying to get them eradicated. But others saw the shops as necessary relief valves for the speculation inherent in the buying and selling of shares. Bucket-shop customers would bet on a stock selected from a list posted on a chalkboard, posting 10 percent of its quoted price and theoretically borrowing the rest like an ordinary margin investor. The shop operator would record the transaction but not buy the stock. At the end of the day, players whose shares had risen would collect the closing price, less the 90 percent "loan" and a commission. Those whose shares had fallen typically allowed their positions to be liquidated, abandoning their stakes like losers discarding their worthless betting slips on a racetrack floor.

Legitimate traders were not above treating the bucket shops as prototypical options markets, using them to hedge their positions or making the equivalent of long or short investments in bulk without tipping off market rivals. But the tolerant oversight of bucket shops by law enforcement also gave free rein to thinly capitalized and thoroughly unscrupulous operators on Lower Broadway, where the shops proliferated. The shops that could not cover customers' winning streaks simply closed up and disappeared; in major panics, such as those of 1873 and 1893, bucket shops were wiped out by the hundreds. But once the economy regained its footing their operators would often reappear, sometimes under new names but at their old addresses.

Warnings like Clews's that "speculators who wish to make money in Wall Street . . . turn their backs on 'bucket shops'" tended to go unheeded by enough plungers to keep the shops in business. What really concerned the would-be aristocrats of the stock market was that the bucket shops placed all of Wall Street in bad odor. But by this point, they need not have worried—for the stench of the place, and the pools of stagnating wealth it had created, had already reached well beyond New York.

THE AMERICAN PUBLIC eyed the ostentation and excess of the late Gilded Age with a combination of disgust, fascination, and envy. Nothing brought those sentiments together in a bubbling emotional cauldron like the Bradley Martin Ball, almost literally a fin de siècle gala, held at the Waldorf on February 10, 1897, a snowy Wednesday evening in Manhattan.

The Bradley Martin Ball was, the newspapers said, a "once in a generation" affair, "an entertainment so stupendous in scope and sumptuous in detail that it makes an epoch in the history of society." Somewhere between six hundred and nine hundred guests attended, in costumes based on the garb of the European aristocracy dating back to the seventeenth century. Paintings by the old masters had been consulted to ensure that certain ladies were attired accurately, including one as "The Honorable Mrs. Thomas Graham," after a portrait by Gainsborough in 1777, and a debutante as the Infanta Margarita, princess of Spain, after a Velázquez work produced in 1659.

For fifteen years, Mr. and Mrs. Bradley Martin had been shouldering their way to the forefront of New York society via events such as this. Their wealth had come not from their own industriousness but as a bequest from Mrs. Martin's father, a merchant who had been thought to be modestly well-off but left his only child a fortune estimated at a robust $6 million. Mrs. Martin put the money to work by staging a series of increasingly notable society affairs. This would be the couple's most fabulous —and also their last. And it marked the very peak of Gilded Age society.

The timing of the Bradley Martin Ball was inauspicious, for the ostentation of the Gilded Age had already come into disrepute. The Panic of 1893 had ruined thousands of businesses and put tens of thousands of workers out on the street. Labor unrest was spreading, much of it aimed at that largest American industry, the railroads, and their barons, the Jay Goulds and George Pullmans of the world. The Bradley Martins may not have been tied up in the railroads, themselves—but before long, they would find themselves tarred with the same brush.

Mrs. Bradley Martin was not insensitive to the optics of staging the most lavish society ball in American history while in the real economy craftsmen and tradespeople were starving. She put it out that her true purpose was to provide an "an impetus to trade." For that reason, she explained, the invitations had gone out on short three weeks' notice—so the guests would not have time to order their costumes and finery from Paris and London but would be forced to patronize local couturiers and *bijouteries* instead. That seemed reasonable enough to some commentators. Dr. George Gunton, the president of the School of Social Economics on Union Square, sermonized against "the present state of the public mind, which is in a fever akin to an epidemic against wealth. . . . It is much better for the laboring people if the wealthy spend their money here instead of taking it to Europe." The Bradley Martins' spending "is bound to percolate down . . . to the humblest laborer," he concluded, voicing an early version of "trickle down" economic theory. "I don't want the man who is above me to get down to my level of living," Gunton declared. "I want to be helped up to his level."

This rosy view was not universally shared, however. Dr. William S. Rainsford, the rector of St. George's Episcopal Church, declared days before the ball that "lavish entertainments at this time by the rich are politically, socially, and ethically unwise." This was perilous ground for the rector of J. Pierpont Morgan's own church, and under pressure from his colleagues in the high-society pastorate, Rainsford backed down, assuring his flock that he had not been referring to any "entertainments" in particular. But his moment of candor triggered a debate in the press and pulpits across the city about what the social harvest might be from the accumulation of wealth in so few hands. "With all the people who have to lie awake nights contriving to spend their time and their money, and all the others who lie awake wondering how they may get food, there is danger in the air," remarked the Reverend Madison C. Peters. "All history teaches us that the concentration of wealth is the forerunner of social upheaval."

Such sermonizing failed to cause the Bradley Martins to cancel the ball or moderate its flamboyance. Sixty cases of French champagne were delivered to the Waldorf, and six thousand mauve orchids. The *New York Times* sniffed at the ostentation and scoffed at the turnout, which it judged to be disappointing. ("Twelve hundred invitations had been issued for the event, but little more than half the number of those invited were in attendance," the newspaper reported the following morning. "Of those that came, also, quite a number left early.") The *Times* might have reminded its readers that on almost every day the previous week it had published at least one article about the ball, and often two or more. On February 7, for example, the newspaper had devoted a full page to listing the most celebrated guests expected — Astors, Beekmans, Delafields, Harrimans, Rhinelanders, Van Cortlandts, Winthrops — along with detailed descriptions of their period costumes. This was accompanied in print by a Bradley Martin family biography and accounts of the couple's previous balls and cotillions. Over the following week, the *Times* continued to mine the event for gossipy articles, including an account of the security precautions, which involved the stationing of two hundred policemen outside the hotel under the personal supervision of New York's police commissioner, Theodore Roosevelt. After the ball, mortified by the obloquy showered upon them for hosting an event that was not much different from any other during that season except in its scale, the Bradley Martins fled New York for their estates in Britain; they would never return to the United States.

Discontent over the conspicuous spending of the nation's new industrial plutocrats had been building for years—the Bradley Martin Ball merely served as an exemplary target. It did not help that the source of much of the new wealth was railroads, for they had become transformed in the public mind from technological marvels and economic boons into rapacious, heartless juggernauts. Their builders and owners no longer were seen as industrial kings but buccaneers and cheats.

Storm clouds were on the horizon. For the time being, however, the "irrational exuberance" of that era persisted. It would continue for another four years after the 1897 ball. But Jacob Schiff never fully shed his disquiet, writing in March 1901 to his European friend Ernest Cassel, "To the cautious observer . . . it is almost terrifying to contemplate the way in which the market has risen, by leaps and bounds. The reaction must come; it is only a question of time."

During the first four months of 1901, the mania for stocks continued unabated. "Buying orders seemed to come from everywhere," Noyes reported. "Everyday conversation in clubs, business offices, social gatherings, trains, and ferryboats was largely made up of the 'good things' in the market, of successful 'turns in the market' which this or that individual had made, of 'tips' which acquaintances on the inside had privately communicated. The newspapers told of bootblacks, barbers, and hotel waiters who had got rich by following such pointers from an accommodating Wall Street patron."

It was the euphoria before the crash. Pierpont Morgan and Ned Harriman were about to knock this market for a loop. Years later, Bernard Baruch would recall the night "panic struck the Waldorf . . . and transformed it from the preening ground of all that was fashionable to a lair of frightened animals."

On April 30—a few days before Baruch witnessed his first market panic—volume on the New York Stock Exchange reached a once-unimaginable 3,303,017 shares. That would be the high-water mark of an age. The market would not touch that record again for twenty-seven years.

17

LIONS GUARDING THE WAY

ON APRIL 4, 1901, Pierpont Morgan boarded the White Star liner *Teutonic* in New York, bound for Europe and yet another of his annual forays into the art market.

The Gilded Age was reaching its zenith. The stock market was in the throes of a bullish frenzy. Exactly one month earlier, the Republican William McKinley, whose pro-business credentials were unassailable, had been sworn in for his second term as president. The most notable thorn in the side of establishment Republicanism, the progressive and unpredictable New York governor Theodore Roosevelt (the former New York police commissioner), had been quarantined impotently in the vice presidency. The only heavy weather confronting Morgan came from the stormy conditions on the high seas, which kept him imprisoned queasily in his cabin with only a solitaire deck for company.

Arriving in London on April 10, Morgan purchased Gainsborough's portrait of Georgiana, Duchess of Devonshire, which was celebrated not merely for the subject's physical beauty and scandalous lifestyle, but because it had been out of public sight for a quarter century, having been stolen from the art dealer William Agnew in 1876. The painting had been recovered only two weeks prior to Morgan's arrival in London, when it was returned for ransom by its thief, the criminal mastermind Adam Worth —later to become Arthur Conan Doyle's model for Sherlock Holmes's nemesis Dr. Moriarty. Morgan, aware that his father had hoped to acquire the work just before it disappeared, offered an astonishing 30,000 pounds sterling for it (then about $150,000), sight unseen. He refused at the time to divulge the price. "Nobody will ever know," he told a friend. "If the truth came out, I might be considered a candidate for the lunatic asylum." "The Duchess" would remain in the Morgan collection until 1994.

Morgan departed London for Paris on April 19, two days after turning sixty-four. There he continued stripping the continent of any treasures that caught his eye. "He received the art dealers at his hotel after breakfast each morning," Satterlee recorded, making "many mysterious trips to the jewelers on the Rue de la Paix and to collectors of antiques and pictures." At the end of April, having capped his raid with the acquisition of Raphael's *Colonna Madonna* and pieces by Rubens and Titian, he moved on to Aix-les-Bains for a rest cure.

The Burlington trade had been finalized, so as Pierpont Morgan went east, James J. Hill went west. Hill had business to transact in Seattle, where he headed by rail, escorting an advance guard of European investors over the Great Northern. But while Morgan was sating his appetite for art in London and Paris and wallowing luxuriantly in the South of France, and Hill was making his pitch to investors on the coast, matters at home were coming unglued.

JACOB SCHIFF HAD made one last effort to patch up his differences with Hill over the Burlington. He wrote Hill on April 8, shortly after the fraught meeting at the financier George Baker's house in New York, invoking their long friendship: "I feel it is too late in our lives to personally go apart. . . . Friendships have little value, if they are only determined by personal interest and go to pieces upon the first clashing of interest; on my part, I can assure you, this will never be the case, as far as my esteem and attachment for you are concerned." But he added that he thought Hill's purchase of the Burlington at $200 per share had overestimated its value to the Great Northern: "I am afraid you have permitted others to induce you, because of the personal advantage and profit they will get therefrom, to pay an exorbitant price." If this was a swipe at Morgan, the only individual who could have "induced" Hill to do anything, it was plainly misplaced, since Morgan himself had initially discouraged the Burlington purchase and it was Hill who had been determined to meet Perkins's price. Schiff closed his letter with a repeat of the warning he had delivered to Robert Bacon: "As to the Union Pacific, it must take care of itself, as it will be able to do."

Hill replied the next day to explain why Harriman's demand for a piece of the Burlington purchase could not have been accepted. The combination of the Union Pacific and Burlington, being two parallel lines, would have been illegal "west of the Mo. [Missouri] River," he asserted. Harriman's concern about the takeover of the Burlington by the Great Northern and Northern Pacific had been unnecessary, he added, because he had had no intention of competing with the four transcontinental lines already running between the East and Washington and Oregon or the two serving California. "We do not need any more through coast lines," he wrote. "Therefore, I was strongly of the opinion that a control of the CB&Q by the Gt. Northern & Nor. Pac. would remove any object for extending to the Pacific, and insure the greatest harmony." Thanks to Harriman's stubbornness, "I find myself mistaken."

He concluded in the same passive-aggressive tone that had antagonized Harriman in the past. "I like peace, and am not ashamed or afraid to work for it," he wrote. "On the other hand, I do not think the time has come when we must acknowledge that we have no rights which our neighbors claim for themselves, or such as we are willing to accord to them."

From Harriman's standpoint, Hill's rejection of his offer for a piece of the Burlington had made control of the Northern Pacific imperative. Notwithstanding Hill's assurances that he was a man of peace and had no intention of extending the Burlington west to the coast, it was crystal clear to Schiff and Harriman that its ownership by Hill posed a mortal threat to the Union Pacific. Accordingly, Schiff and his partners at Kuhn, Loeb had begun buying Northern Pacific stock almost immediately after the meeting at Baker's home.

As Schiff later confessed to Morgan, "the Union Pacific interests [i.e.,

Harriman and himself] held consultations and decided that, if the Burlington company had been so much of a factor for worriment and anxiety
while independent, how much more intensified these conditions would
necessarily become after the Burlington had passed into the hands of the
two powerful Northern roads." He wrote that "drastic measures" had been
called for, and in that vein "we thereupon, on behalf of Union Pacific
interests, set to work to accumulate Northern Pacific stock." The goal
was not to acquire control of the railroad itself, but merely to move into
position to "exercise a potent influence upon the management . . . and
thereby obtain also an influence upon the management of the Burlington."

Schiff undoubtedly felt safe outlining his strategy to Morgan after the
matter had been resolved. He knew he could count on Morgan's discretion as a fellow financier—plus, they still had business to transact with
one another related to the Northern Pacific and Great Northern. In public, however, Schiff would be cagey to the point of flagrant deception.
Interrogated in court more than a year later by M. H. Boutelle, a Minneapolis lawyer representing the government in its attempt to break up the
Northern Securities trust—the corporate device concocted to settle the
Morgan-Harriman battle—Schiff flatly denied that Kuhn, Loeb had ever
"represented the interests" of the Union Pacific or Oregon Short Line in
its purchases of Northern Pacific stock. (Asked if he had represented *Harriman's* interests, he declined to answer.) He portrayed his firm's purchases
of Northern Pacific shares and their subsequent transfer to the Union
Pacific and Oregon Short Line as separate transactions—as if Kuhn, Loeb
had first bought the shares for itself, and then just happened to sell them
to the UP and Oregon line weeks later.

Whether Schiff was deliberately trying to conceal a strategy that had
come under legal attack by the federal government or was resisting questions that he genuinely considered impertinent—he told Boutelle on
several occasions that he would "decline to discuss the business of Kuhn,
Loeb" unless "directed by the court," which chose not to force the issue
—he was spinning a yarn that was transparently implausible. By the time
he had finished transferring all the firm's holdings of Northern Pacific to

Harriman, they came to $78 million. That was an enormous investment for even the best-capitalized banking firm to make on its own account, without a solid understanding that the assets would be promptly taken off its hands. The true nature of the dealings was so obvious to everyone in the courtroom and the marketplace that Boutelle did not bother to follow up.

Schiff's traders at Kuhn, Loeb managed to accumulate a large portion of Northern Pacific common and preferred shares all throughout April without arousing suspicion, even as NP common rose from $101 to $109. The run-up seemed almost natural, given the likely enhanced value of a Northern Pacific owning half the Burlington under the leadership of the eminently capable Jim Hill. The traders were also beneficiaries of luck, for their large block purchases of "Nipper," as the Northern Pacific was known in Wall Street shorthand, were buried within the general frenzy that had seized stock market investors.

The volume of transactions on the stock exchange throughout April took traders' breaths away. Experts struggled to explain it. "Early theories that adroit manipulation was alone or even chiefly responsible for current record-breaking accomplishments must be abandoned," the *New York Times* counseled. "Pools and cliques and operators 'making a turn' have in times past been able to give the market impetus and for a time maintain it; but no such market as the present has ever been so developed or supported. The Stock Exchange trader is a pigmy in this movement, his skill, his orders, and his influence being insignificant compared with the forces that are actually dominating." Since the previous autumn, the *Times* observed, the judgments of market sages that the run-up was "illogical" and bound to lead to disaster were confounded; every bear trend was outpaced by a subsequent bull run. "Scant sympathy will be wasted in or out of Wall Street upon over-clever traders who have been guessing and betting wrong" by selling short, the newspaper gloated.

One could find plausible explanations for the surge in certain stocks. United States Steel, cobbled together as a giant conglomerate by Morgan, had recently begun trading. The flotation drew considerable attention not merely for the optimism the huge issue betokened for the US economy, but for the skill of Morgan's master trader, James R. Keene, in placing the securities on the market. The flotation of US Steel would be judged Keene's greatest triumph, for the steel trust organized by Pierpont Morgan was the largest stock issuer ever to come to market, with an inventory of a half-billion dollars each of common and preferred shares. Few thought that the market could absorb the full billion dollars without driving the steel shares or even the general market lower, absent a huge capital commitment by the Morgan bank. "But Keene had an uncanny ability to mix orders to buy and sell so that the market would respond to his control," Bernard Baruch recalled. Using market-making techniques that eventually would be outlawed, Keene placed the shares so skillfully that "all that the Morgan firm had to put up was $25,000,000. The public supplied the rest."

Yet in general the buoyant stock market seemed to be nothing more than what the nation deserved, given its manifest virtues and the leadership of its bankers and financiers. "The existing financial situation is remarkable," declared a prominent broker interviewed by the *Times*, "but it is not more remarkable than the foundation upon which it rests. . . . The master minds of trade and finance enjoy public confidence to a greater degree, perhaps, than any similar number of men of business in this country."

The truth was, however, that much of the trading volume in that period stemmed from Harriman's campaign to undo Hill's acquisition of the Burlington. As Hill's biographer, Joseph Gilpin Pyle, described Harriman's strategy, "He would buy the mare to get the filly."

The Northern Pacific was the mare; the Burlington, of which it was half owner, the filly. The secret stock transactions that Pyle described in horse-trading terms, however, would create a maelstrom in the securities markets in April and May of 1901, culminating in a catastrophic crash that would bring ruin to thousands of innocent investors.

Pyle felt obliged to doff his hat to the sheer daring of Harriman's plan to wrest control of the Northern Pacific from Hill and Morgan: "From those two grim old lions who guarded the way, the quarry was to be snatched before they sensed the presence of an enemy." Harriman's execution was "so swift, so unsparing, so successful, that but for a single oversight his stroke would have gone home." He was right, in that the single oversight would cost Harriman millions of dollars and a new empire.

TRADERS FINALLY TOOK notice of the steady gain in Northern Pacific shares in late April, though they saw it as an opportunity to take profits by selling—not a good development for Hill, as it would turn out, for he would need every available share to be assured of control. The complacency extended to Hill's friends and Morgan's own traders, whose sales of Nipper sent their shares directly into the accounts of Kuhn, Loeb and thence into Harriman's hands. When the truth became known, mortification would be widespread. "I cannot tell you how sorry I am," Charles Ellis, a crony of Lord Mount Stephen's, wrote Hill late in May. "I sold all my N.P. shares thinking this was nothing but a mad gamble . . . But of course we were all in the dark . . . I would sooner have thrown the money into the sea than look as if I had sold away for the sake of profit." Another investor who had sold thirty-five thousand shares, or $3.5 million at par value, confessed that he would have "burned his stock" had he known the consequence of his action.

The greatest embarrassment may have been felt by Edward D. Adams, the US representative of Deutsche Bank. Even though he was a member of the Northern Pacific's executive committee, Adams dumped a large block of Deutsche Bank's holdings onto the market and sold short another seven thousand shares on the assumption that NP was about to top out as its price neared $100. He was wrong, exposing his bank to a loss of as much as $6 million as the shorted stock kept rising. When that tally was made, however, he was out of communication on the high seas, sailing for Europe. Morgan, it would be reported, was "deeply incensed by the disclosure that an officer of the Northern Pacific had so sold, and thus perhaps contributed to a change in the control of the company."

The complacency even reached Hill himself. When he was queried by a Great Northern director in the early spring about the chance that the Northern Pacific might pass into hostile hands,

I answered that, with what my friends held at that time, and what Morgan & Co. held, we would have somewhere in the neighborhood of 35 or 40 millions of the stock out of a total of 155 millions, which is larger than is usually held in any of the larger companies. I did not think, at the time, that it was at all likely that anybody would undertake to buy in the market the control of 155 millions of stock.

He was not alone in thinking so, for his holdings combined with Morgan's indeed seemed out of the reach of mere financial mortals. He soon would learn differently.

Toward the end of the month, Hill realized that something other than the market's general euphoria must be driving Northern Pacific shares higher. His reaction has been inflated into one of Wall Street's great historical legends — a mad cross-country dash from Seattle to New York to get his arms around the crisis, with all rail traffic shunted out of his way and the transcontinental trip completed in two and a half days. But legend it almost certainly is: The best evidence indicates that Hill left Seattle on April 18 and dallied at home in St. Paul.

But a week later his journey east at last became invested with a sense of urgency. On Friday, April 26, he learned that Northern Pacific had advanced three points that day on astonishing volume of 106,500 shares. Plainly, an attempt to corner the stock was unfolding, and equally plainly, Harriman was behind it.

No one could have been more aware than Hill of the threat this posed to the Great Northern. His entire life's work hung in the balance. Control of the Great Northern rested securely in the hands of himself and his friends, but ownership of Northern Pacific was spread among a fragmented, aging, and none too dependable cadre of small investors. "Some of them were 86 years old, others are more than 80, and so on," Hill testified later. With a well-financed Edward Harriman in the field, "they might have concluded that they would sell their stock, and it might have made a difference as to the majority of the common stock." And if control of the Northern Pacific passed to the Union Pacific, control of the Great

Northern would follow almost inevitably. "We would not have held it a day longer than we could have sold it," he said. "You can see readily that we didn't want to hold a line from Lake Superior and the Twin Cities to Puget Sound, with all the rest of the roads in the United States in a position to fight us and without power to fight back."

Hill boarded an express to Chicago on Saturday, April 27, and was in New York by Monday morning, April 29. Here the chronology of Hill's travels becomes murky. By some accounts, he headed downtown immediately after disembarking in New York and marched through the front doors of 27 Pine Street, an edifice that housed the headquarters of both the Great Northern and Kuhn, Loeb. According to Schiff, the visit did not take place until Friday, May 3. Schiff based his recollection on the fact that the meeting preceded a dinner at Schiff's home at which Hill, typically, overstayed his welcome until after midnight even though the Jewish Sabbath, which Schiff observed rigorously, had begun at sundown.

What all agree on was that Schiff took this opportunity to inform Hill that he had been buying Northern Pacific on the Union Pacific's behalf.

"But you can't get control," Hill exclaimed, reminding Schiff that he and his friends held as much as $40 million of Northern Pacific, and that as far as he knew, "none of it has been sold."

"That may be," Schiff replied, "but we've got a lot of it."

In fact, by then his camp owned at least $60 million, on their way to a total of $78 million.

Hill as yet was unaware of the selling by his friends, heedless as they were of the threat posed by Harriman's purchases. Hill later would recall that Schiff and Harriman applied pressure on him to allow the Northern Pacific to be swallowed up by the Union Pacific. He recounted to Lord Mount Stephen that Harriman had poked his head into his meeting with Schiff to offer him administrative authority over the combined lines— "You are the boss," Harriman supposedly told him. "We are all working for you. Give me your orders." This sounds unlikely, especially since Hill did not mention it to Mount Stephen until July 1904, more than three years later; possibly it reflected an effort by Hill to paint himself as a man who resisted even this alluring blandishment in the name of protecting the interests of his minority shareholders.

Monday, April 29, was an extraordinary day for the New York Stock Exchange in several respects. For one thing, it was the exchange's first session in its temporary quarters at the New York Produce Exchange, a cavernous landmark overlooking Bowling Green at the foot of Broadway. The stock exchange was renting the south end of the building for $25,000 a year while a new building was constructed for its traders at Broad and Wall, two city blocks north. Workmen had labored through the weekend, tearing tickers and trading posts out of the old stock exchange "by the roots," leaving a gutted building to be razed. Crews at the Produce Exchange finished installing the "annunciator," a wall of five hundred signboards that notified brokers they were needed at the door or on the telephone; 450 telephones were wired and tested for the opening of trading. Western Union had installed six cables of fifty wires each, and tested these by sending sample dispatches to Chicago and San Francisco.

At nine thirty the next morning, McPherson Kennedy, the Stock Exchange chairman, stood on the floor, dubiously eyeing a rostrum "perched high on the Whitehall-St. side like a swallow's nest on a cliff," from which he would gavel open the trading day a half-hour hence. Brokers swarmed around him, trying to find trading posts that were not quite situated in the same places as they had been in their old digs, since the old configuration could not be precisely replicated. The floor was unusually congested, for dozens of senior traders who normally would have worked from their offices had decided to join the throng on this inaugural day.

Finally, at 10 a.m., Kennedy brought the gavel down from his swallow's nest. Pandemonium instantly spread wall-to-wall. Wires were crossed and phones went dead. The annunciators failed to work. The stock trading floor was separated from the corn and wheat pits only by a low partition, and the open outcry of the commodities brokers mixed with the stock traders' calls in a cacophonous babel. But that was merely the physical environment. From the moment trading began, the entire financial world seemed to be seized by insanity.

Before the first hour of trading had passed, 739,870 shares had been traded—a figure that would have surpassed the entire day's volume on all but a handful of sessions in the previous year, generally by two- or threefold. By noon the volume had reached 1,138,000 million shares, and by the end of the day a new record of 2,760,000 was set. Fully one-third of the total volume was accounted for by trading in only seven stocks: Union Pacific common and preferred, Northern Pacific common and preferred, Southern Pacific, and United States Steel common and preferred —all companies associated with Harriman or Morgan. Union Pacific and Northern Pacific had gained a stunning eleven and ten and a half points, respectively. The next day would bring even more frenzied trading, ending with a volume record that would stand for decades.

The trading in Union Pacific reflected rumors that Harriman's control of the railroad was slipping. The prevailing story was that a consortium of Chicagoans had caught him by surprise by buying up shares of UP, purportedly with the connivance of William K. Vanderbilt, the Commodore's grandson and current head of the family. The newspapers took the bit in their teeth and ran with it. "Union Pacific Control Lost By E.H. Harriman," the *Times* declared in its editions of May 1. "The story of how the control of this great property was lost by E.H. Harriman and his associates, who are credited as being among the shrewdest railroad men and financiers in the country, is one of the most interesting in the long chapter of remarkable incidents which have filled the history of American Railway management and financiering," the *Times* reported.

This supposed contest for control of the Union Pacific was nonexistent, but reporters found irresistible the concept of Harriman "caught napping," as the *Times* put it. "Representatives of Harriman interests . . . say they know nothing, and, although they will not admit that they have lost control, they will not deny that someone else has secured it." The *Times* struggled to find credible sources, eventually reporting from Grand Central Station, the nerve center of Vanderbilt's rail empire, that "every one from the porters up seemed to believe that Mr. Vanderbilt had secured control of the property [that is, the Union Pacific], though everybody denied having any specific reason for this belief."

From Harriman's standpoint, the market's preoccupation with the fate of the Union Pacific was heaven-sent camouflage for what he was really up to, the securing of control of the Northern Pacific. He would wait until Thursday, May 2, to quash the rumors about the Union Pacific. "I certainly have not let go of anything that I have had," he told reporters then. With that, the air promptly began leaking out of Union Pacific stock, which would fall as low as $76 in the ensuing week. But the frenzy in other railroad issues continued, underscoring Morgan's later assertion that at the time "it was a common story . . . that nearly every day, somebody was negotiating for some line or buying, or trying to buy, a railroad."

AT NOON ON Tuesday, April 30, the cream of New York Jewish financial society gathered at the home of Mr. and Mrs. Sigmund Neustadt at Sixty-Ninth Street and Fifth Avenue to witness the wedding of Miss Adele Gertrude Neustadt to Mortimer Leo Schiff, Jacob Schiff's son. This was another dynastic intermarriage within the Jewish financial community, for Neustadt was the son of a founder of the prominent securities brokerage Hallgarten & Co. The event warranted a lengthy notice in the *New York Times*. Though not easily impressed, the *Times* remarked that "not since the Vanderbilt wedding have such costly and handsome presents been seen at any wedding" and counted one hundred valued at more than $1,000 each — a prize hoard that was displayed, in accordance with society custom, only to the relatives and most intimate friends of the couple. (The *Times*'s reference was to the lavish 1899 wedding of William K. Vanderbilt II, the Commodore's great-grandson, to Virginia Fair, heiress to the Comstock Lode.)

Among the guests were the Harrimans, the William A. Rockefellers (erroneously identified by the *Times* as the "William D." Rockefellers) but not James J. Hill, even though a few years earlier he had employed Mortimer Schiff, known as Morti, at the Great Northern offices in St. Paul at Jacob's request. Jacob and Therese, who had moved three blocks uptown to 965 Fifth Avenue at Seventy-Seventh Street, gave Morti and Adele the old family town home at 932 Fifth Avenue as a wedding present. "It's nice to own a house in which I got so many spankings," Morti, who had been something of a family black sheep and a disappointment to his father, was said to have remarked.* After the ceremony, the wedding party repaired to the opulent Sherry's restaurant at Fifth and Forty-Fourth for a 3 p.m. reception.

While the ceremony was still ongoing, the stock market was continuing the frenzy of the previous day. The *New York Sun* calculated the value of trading that Tuesday at "a million every minute"—based on $1 million in par value (that is, the $100 face value of a stock share in that era) traded per minute. Not all the trading of 3,303,017 shares was on the upside, for Northern Pacific and Union Pacific both gave up some of their gains from the previous day, Union Pacific in part because Vanderbilt was rumored to have prevailed in his attempt to control the road. Exhaustion swept across the exchange, where the floor brokers, or "specialists," staggered under the onslaught of orders. "The strain has affected the health of some of the specialists," the *Sun* reported, "and they said that they were going to give up business for a time at any cost rather than risk a permanent breakdown."

The trading surge continued unrelentingly over the next several days. Meanwhile, in the offices of the Great Northern and of the House of Morgan a few blocks from the Produce Exchange, a crisis of a different sort was developing.

Hill's conversation with Jacob Schiff on April 29 had brought home the point that even if Hill still had control of the Northern Pacific, his position was deteriorating rapidly. The selling into what appeared to be an unwarrantedly buoyant market for Nipper had taken on a life of its own. Hill began to wire his friends to stand fast, but insiders' sell orders already in the pipeline were still being executed as if his control was secure. On May 2, J. P. Morgan & Co. sold ten thousand shares of Northern Pacific,

---

* The entwined fortunes of the Schiffs and Harrimans would continue into the next generation, though not entirely happily: The elder daughter of Morti and Adele, Dorothy Schiff, who reigned as doyenne of New York liberal politics for decades as owner of the *New York Post*, would cause a furor in 1958 by withdrawing her newspaper's endorsement of Averell Harriman, Edward's son, for governor the day before the election. Her action was widely regarded as having helped swing the election to Nelson Rockefeller—William Rockefeller's grand-nephew.

a cool million dollars' worth, "in the ordinary course of business." The same day, the treasurer of one of the railroad's own subsidiaries unloaded thirteen thousand more shares. What was uncertain was whether control already had passed to the Harriman clique. A counterstrike was imperative, Hill agreed with Robert Bacon, the senior partner at Morgan's firm in New York. They dispatched a wire to Aix-les-Bains with a request for Pierpont's permission to take it.

Around that time, John S. Kennedy encountered Pierpont at Aix, where they were sharing the waters. Morgan informed him apropos of Northern Pacific that "there were parties evidently purchasing the stock in New York, and he seemed to think it was with a view of getting control." Ostensibly without prompting, Kennedy volunteered a pledge not to sell any of his own holdings of the stock. Kennedy claimed that Morgan did not mention Harriman's name, nor what steps he intended to take. But his next move would become clear soon enough. The battle was now on, and the New York Stock Exchange was about to experience the wildest week in its history.

18

"A GOOD-SIZED PANIC"

Bernard Baruch made a habit of arriving at the stock exchange an hour or two before the opening, hoping to glean some intelligence that might allow him to repeat his 1899 triumph in Liggett & Myers. On Monday morning, May 6, the ambitious thirty-year-old broker was hanging out at the arbitrage desk, keeping an eye on incoming cables from London. Next to him stood Talbot Taylor, the son-in-law of James Keene, Pierpont Morgan's ace trader. Baruch companionably pointed out that Northern Pacific was trading in London several points below its closing price in New York.

Taylor fixed him with a level stare. "Bernie, are you doing anything in Northern Pacific?"

"Yes," Baruch replied. "And I'll tell you how to make some money out of it: Take an arbitrage profit." In other words, buy in London at the lower price and sell in New York simultaneously at the higher.

To any experienced broker, this was an obvious strategy. Taylor seemed to have doubts. He pondered the idea, thoughtfully tapping his lips with the blunt end of his pencil. Then he said: "If I were you, Bernie, I wouldn't arbitrage Nipper."

Baruch did not need to hear another word to know that something was up with Northern Pacific, and J. P. Morgan must be at the center of it. He told Taylor that he already had acquired some NP and would let him have the shares if he needed them. At that, Taylor took him by the arm and led him to a quiet spot.

"Bernie," he whispered, "there is a terrific contest for control and Mr. Keene is acting for J.P. Morgan. Be careful, and don't be short of this stock." He explained that the contest would be won by whoever had the most shares actually in hand. There was no point in buying shares in London, for the week or more needed to ship the stock certificates across the Atlantic meant they would be useless in a situation that was likely to come to a climax within days. "What I buy must be delivered now," Taylor said. "Stock bought in London will not do."

Baruch was determined to keep Taylor's words to himself, but their import could not be ignored. With Morgan and Harriman both in the market for Northern Pacific, every available share was likely to be snapped up in a strongly rising market. This posed a mortal threat to unsuspecting shorts—traders who had sold borrowed shares in the expectation that Nipper's elevated price would collapse, at which point they could buy back the shares cheaply and return them to the lenders at a profit. Short sellers merely reversed the order of the Wall Street mantra to "buy low, sell high"—they sold high first, and bought low later. The practice required ready capital and intestinal fortitude, for a short who reckoned wrong was exposed to a theoretically infinite loss if the shares he had sold kept rising in price; he would have sold high and been forced to cover his positions by buying even higher.

Baruch knew that the shorts had been betting big on Nipper's fall. If trading proceeded as Taylor hinted, they would have to raise millions to cover their Nipper shorts—almost certainly by dumping all their other stocks at fire-sale prices. "A corner in Northern Securities," he reflected, "would produce a general collapse in the market."

Accordingly, Baruch made two decisions on that fateful Monday morning. The first was to avoid any trading in Northern Pacific, for when behemoths were trampling each other, the only safe place to be was the sidelines. The second was to go short in several leading stocks in the market, anticipating the crash. Over the next four days, these resolutions enabled him to witness events "as if I were a spectator, and not one of its hapless victims."

And spectacle it was—one of the great panics of Baruch's career.

OVER THE WEEKEND of May 4–5, both sides in the battle over Northern Pacific had assessed their positions and found the results unnerving.

At their meeting that week, Jacob Schiff had assured James J. Hill that Harriman's buying had not been aimed at driving Hill out of the Northern Pacific, but rather at bringing about "the harmony and community of interest which other means and appeals to him [that is, the proposal to share the Burlington] had failed to produce." Hill was not comforted. After assessing his portfolio he warned the Morgan partner Robert Bacon that he and his associates held only $20 million of Nipper. Combining that with Morgan's $8 million, they were still well short of a majority of the $80 million outstanding in Northern Pacific common and therefore had their flanks exposed to Harriman's raid.

Bacon wired these figures to Morgan at Aix-les-Bains and asked him for permission to buy another 150,000 shares, or $15 million at par value, to put them over the top. His message did not reach Aix until after the stock market closed for the weekend at noon on Saturday, New York time. And when he received it, the wire rattled Morgan—not least because he considered his role in the reorganization of the railroad to be on a more elevated plane than the merely financial. "We had reorganized the Northern Pacific," he recounted later. "I feel bound in all honor when I reorganize a property and am morally responsible for its management to protect it." His reply telegram, bearing authorization to acquire 150,000 shares, was in Bacon's hands by midday Sunday.

Harriman, meanwhile, had lain abed Friday night tormented by the thought that a loophole might have left his own position less than airtight. Thanks to assiduous buying by Kuhn, Loeb, the Union Pacific now controlled more than $78 million in Northern Pacific stock—a majority of all the $155 million in outstanding shares. But $42 million of the total was in preferred shares. The remainder was in common, but short of a majority in the common by about forty thousand shares.

The common and preferred shareholders had equal voting rights, but as Harriman knew, the corporate bylaws allowed Northern Pacific's board to retire the preferred at par, or $100 per share, effective the following January 1. The rules gave the common shareholders the right to buy up the preferred shares and convert them to common, but no reciprocal right was afforded the preferred—its holders could not convert to common, but could receive only cash. This "bothered me somewhat," Harriman reflected later, "and I felt that we ought not to leave open to them any chance of retiring our preferred stock and leaving us with a minority interest in the common stock."

This was not a new concern. Aware of the bylaw provisions, Harriman and the partners at Kuhn, Loeb had polled five experts in corporate law about whether a majority of both classes together was tantamount to majority control of the company. The experts "agreed unanimously" that it was, Otto Kahn recalled. "On the strength of these legal opinions . . . Mr. Harriman was convinced at the time and ever afterward that he held, beyond any question of doubt, the winning hand."

Yet the situation was not so clear-cut. It was true that Harriman's majority holding of all shares would allow him to elect his own board at the annual shareholders meeting, which was to take place in October. Morgan and Hill, however, planned to hold an early board vote in May to retire the preferred as of January. They also proposed to postpone the annual meeting until after January 1. These two actions together would allow the majority of common stockholders—that is, the Morgan and Hill camp—to extinguish Harriman's preferred holdings before he could elect his own board to block the move. Whether the sitting Northern Pacific board had the power to retire the preferred that far in advance and to postpone the annual meeting was unclear. Harriman's lawyers answered in the negative, but as long as control remained in question, litigation—prolonged, expensive, and uncertain—threatened. Surely, Harriman reasoned, it would be better to make the issue moot by acquiring an undisputed majority of the common shares.

Rising on that Saturday morning from his sickbed—most likely from the recurrence of a bronchial condition plaguing him regularly—Harriman reached out to Schiff's partner Louis Heinsheimer at the Kuhn, Loeb office and asked the firm to close up the forty-thousand-share shortfall in common shares. Heinsheimer agreed. Harriman returned to bed confident, as he would recall, "that, come what might, I had control of Northern Pacific, common stock and all."

He was wrong. Spending the more than $4 million required for a forty-thousand-share purchase vastly exceeded Heinsheimer's authority. He needed Schiff's approval, but on Saturday mornings Schiff could be found only at his synagogue. Steeling himself to interrupt his senior partner at worship, Heinsheimer traveled uptown to Fifth Avenue and Forty-Third Street, the location of Temple Emanu-El, an elegant landmark built in Moorish style in 1868 to mark the rising prominence of the city's German Jewish elite. Summoned from his pew, Schiff heard Heinsheimer out and brusquely countermanded Harriman's order. Secure in his belief that owning a majority of all the capital shares, preferred and common, cemented control of the Northern Pacific, Schiff reckoned that acquiring another forty thousand common shares would be a waste of money—especially since the shares had closed the previous day at a stratospheric $115. That was far more than Schiff thought reasonable to pay, notwithstanding his client's fretfulness. (The stock would close on Saturday at $110.) Schiff sent Heinsheimer home with the assurance that he would take the responsibility for the rejected order, and returned to the sanctuary.

To paraphrase an ancient adage, Schiff's unwise decision was the nail by which the battle for the Northern Pacific was lost. It may have been difficult to fully execute Harriman's order on that Saturday morning in the scant hours before the exchange closed at noon, even if Harriman were well enough to deliver the order to Schiff in person. But precious time was squandered; Harriman did not learn that his instructions had been ignored until trading was already underway on Monday, when he called Heinsheimer to ask why he had not received a trade confirmation.

By then, Northern Pacific was enveloped in a bull frenzy. For while Schiff had resisted making the last investment necessary to control the railroad, Morgan's floor brokers had been instructed to acquire the necessary shares for victory at any price. The moment the opening gavel sounded on Monday morning, they swung into action. Trading started with a powerful bound upward and scarcely paused for the entire five-hour session. Northern Pacific opened at $114, a nearly unheard-of advance of four points from its Saturday close, and promptly rose another two and a half points.

As was their habit, the Morgan bankers had placed the task of managing their purchases in the hands of their master stock trader. Keene was known for his immaculate dress and impeccably trimmed beard, which earned him the nickname "the silver fox." He was never seen on the floor of the New York Stock Exchange, for he was not a member, but preferred to work from his office and the Waldorf-Astoria. He called the hotel his "home . . . from Monday to Friday night," in the words of the *New York Sun*, which further reported that brokers gathered there every evening "with the hope of getting an inkling of what Mr. Keene is to do next." More to the point, his generalship was flawless: "Keene took more care in preparing a financial campaign, and was quicker and surer in its execution, than any man I know," Baruch attested.

Keene delegated the floor trading of Northern Pacific chiefly to Eddie Norton of the Street & Norton brokerage firm. Street & Norton would end Monday's session with total purchases of 200,000 shares of NP, a new record for purchases of a single stock by a single firm in a single day; its buying and selling accounted for more than half of Nipper's total trading volume of 370,000 shares that day. Anyone with knowledge of Norton's role could have discerned Morgan's hand in the trading, for Street & Norton was widely known as Morgan's favorite brokerage. But gaining that knowledge was not easy, for Norton carefully camouflaged his trading by interspersing large block sales of the shares within his even larger purchases. Yet at the end of the day Norton was still shy of the 150,000 shares needed by Hill.

What was uncertain even to those who detected a hint of Morgan's involvement was its purpose. Rumors swept across the floor. The *New York Tribune* asserted that Morgan had been infuriated by the discovery that

Hill and his cronies had sold Northern Pacific short during the previous week. Morgan, according to this version, had enlisted William K. Vanderbilt in a buying splurge "to catch Mr. Hill and his friends napping" and thereby "[add] the control of Northern Pacific to that of Union Pacific, which Mr. Vanderbilt secured last week." The *Tribune* thus managed to allow two erroneous reports to lead it to a single utterly misguided conclusion. Cornered by reporters during the afternoon, Hill said he had "no explanation at all for the rise of Northern Pacific," a statement that was disingenuous at best and deceitful at worst.

Some observers continued to view the action in Nipper as an artifact of the broader frenzy for stocks. "The wonderful advances in prices have been altogether too alluring to the outside public longer to resist," reported the *New York Times*, citing "many signs . . . that this public was coming more and more into the market." Among them was that sure signal to an almost exclusively male profession of a market becoming irrational: "Brokers reported that the craze had spread mightily to women, and that many orders had been received from women, rich and in only moderate circumstances alike — women, some of them, who would be the last in the world to be suspected of such a thing. . . . The speculative fever is on; where and when it will end nobody can know."

The remarkable rise in Northern Pacific remained the center of attention all day. With the stock being bought in blocks of hundreds, even thousands, of shares, its price rose to $117, then $120, topped out at $133 and closed at $127.50. It looked like the crest of an elemental torrent of buying. But it was only the beginning.

When the market opened on the morning of Tuesday, May 7, Eddie Norton resumed buying. He had been instructed to buy up to a price of $125, but the market was running ahead of him — by the time the price reached $120 he had yet to fill half his order. There he paused, perhaps hoping that the apparent slowdown in trading would provoke the bulls to take profits by selling down. But that had not happened. The reason was that the shorts were beginning to panic.

"There was virtually no Northern Pacific stock that anyone wanted to sell," Baruch recalled. Under exchange rules, all stock bought or sold in New York had to be delivered the following day; if a short seller could not buy shares or borrow them to make good on his trades, any investor to whom he had sold phantom stock had the right to buy on the market at any price, and demand compensation from him. Given the scarcity of Northern Pacific shares, the shorts faced catastrophe.

The result was a melee. Any trader suspected to have access to Northern Pacific shares risked being virtually assaulted on the floor. Baruch witnessed one unwitting broker being pressed flat against a railing by a baying crowd. "Let me go, will you?" he cried. "I haven't a share of the damned stock—do you think I carry it in my clothes?"

A young broker for Kuhn, Loeb named Al Stern strode through the crowd, blithely offering to lend out a block of Harriman's stock. As Baruch recollected:

The first response was a deafening shout. There was an infinitesimal pause and then the desperate brokers rushed at Stern. . . . Strong brokers thrust aside the weak ones. Hands were waving and trembling in the air. Almost doubled over on a chair, his face close to a pad, Stern began to note his transactions. He would mumble to one man, "All right, you get in," and then complain to another, "For heaven's sake, don't stick your finger in my eye." . . . Soon Stern had loaned the last of his stock. His face white, and his clothes disheveled, he managed to break away.

No one could yet be sure what was driving the maelstrom. "The Control of N.P.: Wall Street Still Guessing Who Has It," blared the *Tribune*'s headline on Wednesday morning. The *Sun*, more confident in its guesswork, if not especially accurate, declared Hill the loser in his "stock duel" with Harriman. Closer to the truth, the *Sun* also reported that "the tremendous buying demand of the rival Harriman and Hill interests [had] absorbed the entire floating supply" of Northern Pacific. In the aftermarket, where loans of needed stock were negotiated broker-to-broker, the "money rate" hit 7 percent, meaning that for every 100-share lot a broker borrowed, he had to pay interest of $700—per day. The ferocious bidding for borrowable shares suggested that "every Stock Exchange house must be short of Northern Pacific," the *Sun* reported. Estimates of stupendous losses circulated—the eminent trader Louis Wormser was said to be short sixty thousand shares, for a potential loss of $6 million. A member of his firm was seen entering the office of Kuhn, Loeb late that afternoon, possibly to plead for mercy.

NP rose by as much as twenty points on Tuesday, reaching $149.75 before closing at $143.50, up sixteen points on the day and more than thirty-three points higher than it had closed on that distant Saturday, four days earlier. May 8 promised only more madness.

On that Wednesday morning, indications emerged that the public was becoming perturbed by the goings-on of the plutocrats on the stock exchange. Observing that the machinations of Street & Norton would have required some $25 million in capital, the *Sun* editorialized, "At first the public were unable to account for transactions so enormous on any other theory than that vast and serious schemes of consolidation were the cause of them." But no: In its view the truth was more frivolous. "Wall Street believes now that these astounding changes instead of signifying a revolutionary remaking of the railroad map, are simply speculation. They do not mean investment . . . but stock 'manipulation.'" The speculators "are venturing into schemes of market twisting as staggering in their boldness as the United States Steel Corporation was among industrial enterprises . . . , with a blind and prosperous public plunging after. . . . It is a good thing for ordinary men to let alone."

Sure enough, as Wednesday wore on, the market began to crack. With Northern Pacific still rising—it would peak at $180 that day, an incredible seventy-point gain in three trading sessions—the shorts' desperation reached a fever pitch. Neither the Harriman nor Morgan camps were buying that day, for both had become confident that they held the necessary majority. Wednesday's action was all from the speculators. In fact, the holdings claimed by the Harriman and Morgan camps taken together exceeded the Northern Pacific shares actually in existence by one hundred thousand, possibly two hundred thousand, shares. Whatever the true figure, there were no Nipper shares to be found in the market.

Northern Pacific had been "cornered," in market parlance. But it was a corner unlike any other the market had seen. Corners deliberately staged to squeeze shorts for the benefit of speculators were a common occurrence; in this case, however, Morgan and Harriman were not trying to squeeze shorts in Northern Pacific—they were genuinely bidding for control of the railroad. It was the frenzied buying and selling by onlookers that created this corner. The Northern Pacific corner would be the largest ever known up to that point, but it was entirely accidental.

That was not to say that its effects were illusory. "Panic Reigns," the *New York Times* declared, judging the lunacy to be even greater than what had followed the death of Roswell P. Flower two years before, previously the preeminent example of the stock market in full stampede. "Brokers acted like insane men," the *Times* reported from the Produce Exchange. "Big men lightly threw little men aside, and the little men, fairly crying with indignation, jumped anew into the fray, using hands, arms, elbows, feet—anything to gain their point . . . It was something incomprehensible, almost demoniac—this struggle, this Babel of voices, these wild-eyed, excited brokers, selling and buying, buying and selling." In the brokerage offices blocks away, the tickers "ticked out fortunes, easily made, being more easily lost."

Unnerved by the storm, Schiff and his partners tried to quell the speculation in Northern Pacific. Asked by reporters that afternoon if it was true that the "Harriman syndicate" now had control of the railroad, Schiff replied levelly, "We think that we have." An unnamed spokesman for Morgan was somewhat more reserved, but also signaled that his side's buying was at an end. "Mr. Schiff, himself, told me to-day that they controlled the Northern Pacific," he said. "Mr. Schiff is a truthful man and I suppose I must believe him."

AFTER THE MARKET'S 3 p.m. close on Wednesday, May 8, the insanity moved uptown to the Waldorf. The vast hotel's bars and hallways were dense with tobacco smoke and redolent of stale whiskey. Brokers huddled in clumps to negotiate borrowings of Northern Pacific stock at prices that threatened ruin—money rates reached 85 percent, meaning that a borrower would have to pay $8,500 for the loan of one hundred shares for only a few hours. To onlookers, it seemed that a well-deserved comeuppance was at hand. "For several months," crowed the *Sun,* "the brokers and the professional room traders and even their clerks have turned up at the Waldorf-Astoria for dinner . . . All were in evening clothes and all lolled and waggled their heads, and proclaimed, 'The world is mine.' Last night very few of the brokers and none of the professional room traders and no clerks appeared in evening clothes."

The rumor mill continued to grind at top speed, with spectacular losses by major players still the prime grist. Bet-a-Million Gates was said to be in a $6 million hole on his short position in Northern Pacific. Mobbed by newspaper reporters at the Waldorf, he denied the calumny.

"Do I look like it?" he barked. "No, I have not lost a cent. But even if I had it would not interest the public; it would only concern my heirs."

"But the public believes that you sold 60,000 shares of Northern Pacific short."

"If anyone can prove that I have sold 6,000 shares short I will give him 60,000 shares as a present."

("Nevertheless," commented the *Sun,* "Mr. Gates was not as frisky and not in as genial a mood as usual.")

Exasperation with the turbulent market was plainly spreading. James Hill watched bemusedly what he later referred to as "a good-sized panic in New York." Unlike Schiff, Harriman, and Morgan, he was not a habitué of Wall Street and found the goings-on unseemly and thoroughly inexplicable. He reached back to his experience on the western frontier for his judgment. "All I can do is liken it to a ghost dance," he told reporters.

The Indians begin their dance and don't know why they are doing it. They whirl about until they are almost crazy. It is so when these Wall Street people get the speculative fever. Perhaps they imagine they have a motive in that they see two sets of powerful interests which may be said to be clashing. Then these outsiders, without rhyme or reason, rush in on one side or the other. They could not tell you why they make their choice, but in they go, and the result is such as has been seen here for the past few days.

The other rumors consuming the Waldorf crowd concerned the possibility of a settlement allowing the short sellers to escape with their shirts, which would require an agreement between the Harriman and Morgan camps. Both sides were inclined to find a solution—desperate, in fact —for it served no one's interest to have a major panic roiling Wall Street and ruining brokers and shareholders.

Stories circulated that representatives of both sides had been seen entering the Morgan offices at six thirty that evening; others heard that Keene had been seen at the Waldorf in conference with his principals at 10 p.m., with a deal bruited about to allow the shorts to cover their positions at anywhere from $150 to $250 per share.

But by the end of the night no settlement had been announced. As dawn broke on Thursday, May 9, Wall Street steeled itself for a final paroxysm.

19

EXHAUSTION

Long before the 10 a.m. market open, traders had been arriving at the Produce Exchange drenched from a morning downpour, shaking out and furling their sodden umbrellas, only to confront the deeper gloom indoors. For a brief period before the open on May 9, the traders took heart from a rumor that Morgan and Harriman had settled their struggle over control of the Northern Pacific. But the battle of titans no longer had much to do with events on the floor, for a full-scale convulsion was brewing.

The gavel came down, and an expectant calm fell momentarily on the exchange. A few stocks were up, a few were down. Erie preferred advanced a point; the Baltimore & Ohio retreated a point. Northern Pacific opened up ten points to $170 on the very first sale, vaulted higher to $210, and fell back to $170—all in the first few minutes. Then the storm erupted, violently. Northern Pacific leaped ahead to $320, $400, $650, and $700. At that point the exchange formally declared a "corner" in Nipper; all subsequent sales would have to be in cash. Only one hour had passed. Within the next fifteen minutes, three hundred shares were sold at $1,000 each. It was the high point for Northern Pacific, "an incident putting every railroad stock quotation record of the world to rout," the *Times* reported.

In Albany, Sam Hessberg, a resourceful branch manager for the brokerage house J. S. Bache & Co., found a way to make his clients a quick buck. Hessberg reckoned that his customers had deposited five hundred NP shares in his branch's vault, most of them purchased a year earlier for as little as $20. The shares would lay fallow while money rates for lending them out reached to the stratosphere — unless they could be transferred to New York. The problem was that the certificates were secured behind time locks set to open at 9 a.m.

Within an hour after the locks had sprung Hessberg could be found speeding south with the shares toward Wall Street on a special train made up by the New York Central, his aim to reach New York by 2:15 p.m., the exchange's deadline for share deliveries. The train beat its scheduled arrival time of 1:45 by seven minutes. At Grand Central Station a messenger boy was waiting. He collected the shares and came sprinting into the Bache office at two o'clock, with fifteen minutes to spare, enabling Hessberg's clients to reap their bounty.

While everyone on the floor seemed to be short Northern Pacific and anxious to buy, investors desperate to raise cash were dumping every other stock they owned — "Not slowly, as on the day previous, but with fearful, heart-breaking rapidity," the *Times* reported. The price gap between sales widened from a point or two to ten points, then twenty. "It was more than a complete demoralization," the *Times* reported; "it was a general destruction of values, a mad, ungovernable selling movement." US Steel came down twenty-two points on the day, representing a decline of $100 million in its market value. The Delaware & Hudson lost fifty-nine points, more than one-third of its value. Bernard Baruch's prediction was coming true.

Floor brokers were agitated by the sheer physical disorder of the trading floor, not to say the collapse of decorum, with traders mauling each other to get an order in. "The thing was so sudden that conservative men lost their heads," one broker complained to the press, "and language was heard from reputable church-going members of society that would not bear repetition under ordinary circumstances in a barroom of even the second class."

Anecdotes of calamity and ruin were exchanged on every street corner. "Ruin, pitiless, desperate ruin," declared the *New York Times*. "Throughout the entire country men, women, and children alike had been tempted into the whirl of speculation by the promises of fortunes to be made over night." From brokerage offices came bathetic accounts of clients reduced to tears upon learning of their losses. "An elderly woman drove to the Exchange in a cab just before noon and was helped into the building by a colored servant," reported the *Tribune*. She inquired of a doorkeeper the price of US Steel preferred, which had topped out on Monday at over $101. "Eighty-three," came the reply.

"'God help me!' exclaimed the woman. 'I am ruined!' She was helped back to her cab, sobbing violently."

In Troy, New York, the body of Samuel Bolton Jr., a prominent brewer, was recovered from a vat of hot beer, with his hat, coat, watch, and wallet found nearby. Police concluded that he had committed suicide, having "lost heavily in stocks lately." More gratifying news was associated with the prominent broker Arthur A. Housman, who was rumored to have dropped dead at his exchange post at midday; instead, he materialized on the trading floor during the afternoon session, offering to lend buyers $1 million at a market rate of 6 percent, as if to proclaim his health via generous financing terms.

Even some of the canniest investors were caught unawares by the velocity of the trading. The panic marked one of the few stock market crashes from which the legendary stock trader Jesse Livermore failed to make a profit. But he was only twenty-three at the time, and had not yet learned to mistrust stock tickers in a fast market. As would be recounted by the author Edwin Lefèvre in *Reminiscences of a Stock Operator*, a thinly fictionalized biography of Livermore based in part on interviews with the trader, he had bought one thousand shares of Northern Pacific early in its bull run that spring and unloaded it on Saturday, May 4, at $110, for a thirty-point profit that brought his brokerage balance up to $50,000. For Livermore, who would experience many cycles of spectacular gains and complete losses in a career of nearly five decades but was then still a fairly small plunger, this was a high-water mark. On Thursday morning, reckoning that the Northern Pacific panic was peaking and a market break was imminent, he placed an order to short US Steel at $100 and the Atchi-

son, Topeka & Santa Fe at $80, expecting to cover the first at $80 and
the second at $65, for gains of twenty and fifteen points respectively. His
instincts were dead-on and his brokers expert, but they could not outrun
the collapsing market. His order to sell US Steel short got filled at $80 and
the order for Atchison at $65. Instead of capturing a profit, he had sold at
the prices he expected to buy, and was now exposed to huge losses if the
market recovered.

"The tape double-crossed me," laments Larry Livingston, Lefèvre's
stand-in for Livermore. His error was to trust the ticker, not realizing that
the pace of trading had delayed its quotes by thirty to forty minutes, so
that the prices he had sought were long past before his orders could be
filled. When his order slips returned with the disastrously low prices, he
decided to cover his shorts immediately—but just as the short orders were
delayed, so were his buy orders. He lost $25,000 on Steel and $25,000 on
Atchison, and ended the day busted.

By then, the panic had ended. Shortly after 2 p.m., Morgan & Co.
and Kuhn, Loeb jointly announced that they would not demand delivery
from the shorts that day. Around the same time, a consortium of fifteen
banks led by Morgan & Co. assembled a financing pool of $20 million at
a reasonable interest rate, thus putting a brake on the frenzied run-up in
rates that brokers had been charging each other for overnight loans.

The most important initiative was an agreement by Morgan & Co.
and Kuhn, Loeb to take delivery of all shorted stock at $150 per share.
This was a recognition that more was at stake in the stock market than the
possibility of making a killing from the destruction of dozens of brokerages
and the ruin of thousands of investors. The two contesting banks issued
bulletins expressing confidence that a settlement would hold "at what
will generally be considered a fair market price." There would be plenty
of time for finger-pointing later. Morgan & Co., for its part, made sure to
communicate that "this difficulty is not of our making, and we wish to do
all in our power to see it remedied." Hill, whose need for a firm majority
of shares in the Northern Pacific had helped trigger the week's events, did
his best to distance himself from the consequences. "I am a plain farmer
from Hazelbright, Minnesota," he told reporters disingenuously. "I'm not

causing any panics or helping to cause them. A farmer fights shy of panics like he does of measles."

What about the conferences held that afternoon and night to craft a settlement for the shorts? he was asked.

"I don't know what there is to confer about. It looks to me like as if this whole situation would straighten itself out when some folks get some sense. I expect before long that people will stop selling that which they haven't got and can't get, and then we'll get down to a satisfactory business basis."

Those who were not directly touched by the carnage, whether rich or not so rich, could view it with relative dispassion. Disembarking Thursday morning from the Hamburg America Line's steamship *Deutschland* at the Hoboken piers, William K. Vanderbilt and sugar tycoon Henry O. Havemeyer were besieged by reporters baying for their views on the panic raging just across the harbor. "I am not in the habit of talking for publication," Vanderbilt said, "but I am willing to say that I regard the condition of things in Wall Street as silly." To Havemeyer, it sounded as if "there had been a pretty lively shindig in Wall Street."

For humorist Finley Peter Dunne, speaking through his alter ego Mr. Dooley, the crash was an occasion for bittersweet ridicule. "Well, sir, I see th' Titans iv Finance has clutched each other be th' throat an' engaged in a death struggle," Mr. Dooley observed, in his deep brogue, to his friend Mr. Hennessey in *Harper's Weekly* on June 1.

'Twas a fine spree while it lasted, Hinnissey. Niver befure in th' history iv th' wurruld has so manny barbers an' waiters been on th' verge iv a private yacht. . . . But it's all past now. Th' waiter has returned to his mutton an' th' barber to his plowshare. Th' chorus girl has raysumed th' position f'r which nature intinded her, an' th' usual yachtin' will be done on th' cable cars at eight a.m. and six p.m., as befure. The jag is over. . . . But crazy come, crazy go.

For all the talk of barbers and waiters staking their little all on the exchange, the majority of Americans watched the goings-on in the stock market from afar. Yet for many small investors, the damage from the Panic of 1901 would be lasting. Nest eggs representing the savings of a lifetime vanished in a flash. These were ordinary people who had been suckered into investing on Wall Street by the transformation of the securities markets into a cultural monument and the elevation of its grandees into celebrities.

The popular press had begun to cover the tycoons' daily lives, their mansion-building and sojourns at international watering spots, in sedulous detail to slake the growing appetite of their growing middle-class readership for glimpses of the rich and famous. On the surface this popular interest reflected the ambitions of the masses to share this lifestyle, but at its core it amounted to a happy delusion, like the adulation later generations would harbor for film stars, that anyone could move into this rarefied world, if only luck smiled upon them.

By the time of the 1901 panic, reporting on Wall Street had spread from the financial news sheets to the pages of general-interest newspapers. The peculiarities of stock market buying and selling were normalized for the average reader in columns entitled "Wall Street Talk" and "Financial Affairs" in the *New York Times*; and *Harper's Weekly* assured its readers of the safety of securities trading in its regular feature "The World of Finance." These publications were soon retailing pearls of received wisdom from Wall Street bankers — that competition was ruinous, stock market speculation was virtuous, and the markets were an instrument for spreading wealth to the ordinary workingman and -woman.

The investment world's would-be populists, like Henry Clews, had been working hard to counter the public's wariness about stock market risks by preaching the gospel of prosperity for all. They cursed the naysayers who pointed to the markets' recurrent crashes as warnings to the wise. Instead, Clews would write, the boom-and-bust cycle was an indicator of the underlying vigor of the American experiment, which was destined for a triumph all should share. "Risks and panics are inseparable from our vast pioneering enterprise," Clews had asserted in 1888. (The same sentiment would emerge after notable crashes of later decades, such as the dotcom craze of the 1990s and the housing bubble of the 2010s.) The public needed only to trust to the astuteness of its business leaders. "All depends on the calmness and wisdom of the banks. . . . They have largely succeeded in combining self-protection with the protection of their customers; and the antecedents they have established will go far toward breaking the force of any future panic."

Clews was writing a mere four years after one major panic (in 1884) and five years before the next. Three more would occur in the first two decades of the next century, followed by the great crash of 1929, which would put to shame every assurance of the market makers' wisdom and integrity. But while the panic raged in 1901 the conviction still reigned on Wall Street that the market would be put right by its masters, represented chiefly by Pierpont Morgan. Asked at midweek what had provoked the break, the speculator Jefferson Monroe Levy ascribed it to Morgan's absence in France. "It looks as if the little boys had commenced while the big boy was away," Levy opined. "If Mr. Morgan had been here this never would have happened."

The Panic of 1901 shattered the conviction that the market's leaders were committed to keeping it orderly for the benefit of all Americans, not just those who worked on a few blocks of Lower Manhattan and their partners. Opportunistic financial promoters instantly began to exploit the 1901 crisis by steering customers away from stocks. The morning after the May 9 crash, readers turning to the financial pages of the big New York newspapers were confronted with a quarter-page advertisement placed by the Equitable Life Assurance Society, headlined "A Policy of Life Assurance Never Declines in Value." The ad promised that "it is always worth its face value at maturity. It may be worth more. It can never be worth less . . . And there are many good companies, but *The Equitable is the Strongest in the World.*" (Emphasis in the original.) The Equitable and other such promoters knew their market: Lying just under the surface of the public's fascination with empire builders such as Morgan and Harriman was the suspicion that the stock market was still haunted by scoundrels and mountebanks, best to be given a wide berth by the prudent man and woman.

Away from Wall Street, moreover, faith in the nation's business leadership was already distinctly on the wane. The image of the robber barons had developed over decades, starting with Commodore Vanderbilt's charging monopoly fares on his steamships and trains; then through the steel magnate Henry Clay Frick's violent (and lethal) 1892 assault on strikers at the Homestead Steel Works in Pennsylvania; and Pullman's refusal to reduce his workers' rents while slashing their wages, thereby fomenting a monumental strike in 1894.

But the piece of evidence that has lasted longest and most vividly as marking Wall Street bankers as amoral, heartless profiteers is Pierpont Morgan's statement to a reporter for the *New York World* who bearded him in London and asked if "some statement were not due the public" as an explanation of a panic that has "ruined thousands of people and disturbed a whole nation." Morgan's ineradicable reply: "I owe the public nothing."

Morgan's most recent biographer, Jean Strouse, has ably argued that the quote itself may be apocryphal, and its common interpretation as signifying Morgan's utter disregard for the public interest exaggerated. As Strouse documents, the episode was popularized by the financial writer Matthew Josephson in his 1934 book *The Robber Barons*. Josephson got it from Lewis Corey's critical 1930 biography, *The House of Morgan*, and Corey from the *New York World* edition of May 12, 1901. In the *World's* version, however, the quote appears in a shirttail datelined London attached to a story datelined Paris, where the reporter ostensibly caught Morgan relaxing on a park bench in the Bois de Boulogne and received a surly brush-off.

It is no secret that Morgan deeply detested impromptu encounters with newspersons; one of the most famous images of the plutocrat shows him raising a cane in fury at a photographer on a street in 1910 (possibly out of sensitivity about his grotesquely inflamed nose, the product of a skin condition and an irresistible target for cartoonists). Corey reports him threatening one inquisitive reporter with "murder." Even if inauthentic, the quote does at least hint at the vantage point from which Morgan viewed the world. He saw himself as an agent of the public interest. But he defined that interest paternalistically, as the preservation of a functioning economy and a functioning fiscal environment for government.

Public curiosity, sentiment, opinion—those were features of the rabble. To Morgan, they were beneath notice, and in any case obstructions to what Herbert Satterlee called "Morgan leadership," which of course was always exercised for the public good.

Morgan saw economic progress as the proverbial tide lifting all boats. "A few men in this country are charged with the terrible offense of being very rich," he told the *New York Times* in 1903. "The fact is that the wealth of this country is less 'bunched' than at any time in its history . . . Wealth is more equally distributed among the people than ever before."

This early version of the "trickle down" theory, however, was demonstrably untrue. "The recent growth of the great class who seem destined to remain lifelong wage-workers in the employ of mammoth concerns, would tend toward less uniform distribution," commented Willford Isbell King, a pioneering statistician and economist. King was writing in 1922, but upon reviewing the previous three decades, he identified "the greatest force . . . making for income concentration [to be] the successful organization of monster corporations." The chief agent of this phenomenon was,

Fiercely defensive about his economic influence and sensitive about images showing his bulbous nose, J. Pierpont Morgan threatened a news photographer with bodily harm in this famous 1910 shot on a New York sidewalk.

of course, J. Pierpont Morgan, creator of US Steel and consolidator of the railroads.

Still, as the smoke dissipated from a weeklong panic, Wall Street's leaders felt justified in concluding that they and the nation as a whole had come unscathed through the fiery furnace. Russell Sage, a former partner of Jay Gould, told the *New York Times*, "There's been no wreck, and the feeling is quieting down . . . There is at the close of the market a general feeling of confidence and that the worst of the crisis has passed and that the fine condition of National affairs will be a big factor in adjusting the situation."

And why not? The national government was in the hands of the pro-business Republican president William McKinley, who had defeated that radical populist William Jennings Bryan twice, in 1896 and 1900.

Yet discontent only grew at the spectacle of railroad tycoons wrestling with each other for business primacy to the disadvantage of countless innocent men and women. Panics such as the one in 1901 and its predecessors had sown seeds that were beginning to yield bitter fruit. The harvest would not be long in coming.

20

THE TRUSTBUSTER

WALL STREET'S COMPLACENCY about the state of the national economy ended with gunfire at 4:07 p.m. on September 6, 1901, when an anarchist named Leon Czolgosz shot President William McKinley twice point-blank at the Pan-American Exposition in Buffalo, New York.

When the news of McKinley's wounding reached New York, Pierpont Morgan was preparing to leave his office for the day. He was scanning a ledger with his hat on and cane in hand when a newspaper man burst in.

"Well?" Morgan snapped.

"An attempt has been made on the life of the President," came the reply.

Despite the suddenness of the news, Morgan seemed to grasp its implications immediately. He sat down heavily at his desk, "gazing steadily at the carpeted floor." Another reporter arrived waving a printed "extra," which drew Morgan's attention for uncomfortably long minutes. Very slowly he uttered the words, "This is sad, sad, very sad news. . . . There is nothing I can say at this time." Then he shuffled silently out the door.

McKinley's followers were aware that national policy might be suddenly upended. The Republican establishment, exasperated with what they saw as Theodore Roosevelt's antibusiness regulatory bent as governor of New York, had thought to neutralize him by placing him in the notoriously powerless position of vice president. That left McKinley free to implement the pro–Wall Street policies that so contented Morgan and his ilk. Now an assassin's bullet threatened to give Roosevelt almost unlimited scope to turn his inclinations into action. The threat became real on September 14, eight days after the attack, when McKinley succumbed to his wound and Roosevelt was sworn in at a friend's mansion on Buffalo's fashionable Delaware Avenue.

Wall Street bankers were not the only Americans steeling themselves for the advent of the Roosevelt administration. Henry Adams fretted about the new president's temperament. "Power when wielded by abnormal energy is the most serious of facts," he would reflect in his autobiography, *The Education of Henry Adams*, "and all Roosevelt's friends know that his restless and combative energy was more than abnormal. . . . He was pure act."

On the surface, Roosevelt was willing to mollify the financial community. He seemed to accept the counsel of Mark Hanna, the Republican senator from Ohio who had been widely regarded as the power behind McKinley's throne, to "Go Slow. . . . You will be besieged from all sides . . . *Hear* them all patiently but *reserve* your decision."

Roosevelt's first annual address to Congress, delivered on December 3, offered glimmers of the passive-aggressive approach he would pursue in dealing with Wall Street. In its opening passages he lionized the slain McKinley and appeared to endorse his predecessor's hands-off business policies: "During the last five years business confidence has been restored, and the nation is to be congratulated because of its present abounding prosperity," Roosevelt declared. "Such prosperity can never be created by law alone, although it is easy enough to destroy it by mischievous laws." He praised "the captains of industry who have driven the railway systems across this continent, who have built up our commerce, who have developed our manufactures."

He bowed to the profit motive, which he acknowledged to be the spark of successful enterprises. The creation of great business fortunes, he observed, "has aroused much antagonism, a great part of which is wholly without warrant. . . . The mechanism of modern business is so delicate that extreme care must be taken not to interfere with it in a spirit of rashness or ignorance. Many of those who have made it their vocation to denounce the great industrial combinations which are popularly, although with technical inaccuracy, known as 'trusts,' appeal especially to hatred and fear."

Then, so smoothly it may have eluded his listeners at first, Roosevelt endorsed those very same denunciations. The "widespread conviction in the minds of the American people that the great corporations known as trusts are in certain of their features and tendencies hurtful to the general welfare" was not to be dismissed, for it was based not on envy or ignorance, but upon "the sincere conviction that combination and concentration should be . . . supervised and within reasonable limits controlled; and in my judgment this conviction is right."

Roosevelt called for a higher standard of disclosure—a concept that was anathema to trust barons who customarily kept the financial details of their businesses concealed even from their own directors and shareholders. "The first requisite is knowledge, full and complete—knowledge which may be made public to the world." He demanded federal supervision and regulation over all corporations engaged in interstate commerce, especially of any deriving any portion of its profits from "some monopolistic element or tendency in its business"—the railroads, for instance. His words presaged vigorous enforcement of the Sherman Antitrust Act's prohibition of any such combinations "in restraint of trade of commerce" for the first time since its enactment a decade earlier.

Roosevelt placed the welfare of wage earners front and center in administration policy and pledged to protect workers' rights to act "in combination or association with others [through] associations or unions of wage-workers."

The details of these proposals and pledges were vague. But there could be no doubt that the address represented not Republican Party orthodoxy but a specifically Rooseveltian worldview. "The President has written every word of it himself," John Hay, who would serve Roosevelt as secretary of state as he had served McKinley, told journalist Joseph Bucklin Bishop, Roosevelt's authorized biographer. Under McKinley, Hay explained, the annual message had been a composite of statements from cabinet departments; this one was Roosevelt's alone. "It is the most individual message since Lincoln." (Hay would know; he had served as Abraham Lincoln's private secretary.)

The vigor of Roosevelt's speech won praise on Capitol Hill and in newspaper editorial offices around the country. But Wall Street bankers who reviewed its words carefully could not have been comforted by the signs that the White House was shifting from unquestioning support of business toward a broader concept of the public interest, including a tilt toward labor that sharply diverged from White House policy dating back to Grover Cleveland. Plainly, Roosevelt intended to make it his business to disrupt economic power if he thought its concentration led to abuses against the public good. Whom he would target first, however, remained to be seen.

MORGAN MIGHT WELL have thought his life's work to be especially vulnerable to the new president's reformist agenda, for only a month earlier —weeks after Roosevelt's accession to the presidency—he had put the finishing touches on a solution to the chaos unleashed by the battle over the Northern Pacific. This was the creation of a new trust, the Northern Securities Company.

Following the crash of early May and the joint decision of Kuhn, Loeb and Morgan & Co. to allow the Northern Pacific shorts to cover at $150 per share, the principals in the dispute showed little taste for prolonging hostilities. Hill, who habitually kept Wall Street and its machinations at arm's length, was even jaunty about the end of the fight. On May 12, three days after the climactic panic, he had wandered into the Kuhn, Loeb offices for a companionable chat with Jacob Schiff, who was out. Instead he stopped by Felix Warburg's desk.

"How is Schiff?" he asked.

"Not very happy," Warburg replied.

Hill shrugged. "He takes these things too seriously," he said.

Morgan had wanted to end the conflict over the Northern Pacific as much as anyone else, but he constructed the peace settlement exactingly. Concerned with finding a way to block any new battle for control of the

Northern Pacific, he dusted off a structure that had been conceived years earlier by Hill for the consolidation of the Northern Pacific and Great Northern, but had been shelved after the state of Minnesota blocked the merger: a holding company to which the shares of both railroads would be contributed by their owners, to be managed as a unified enterprise.

Hill and Morgan—along with Harriman and Schiff—would testify later that the idea of eliminating competition between the two northern roads never entered their heads, though it obviously would be the inevitable result of unified management. Morgan put the case succinctly that the Northern Securities trust reflected the higher imperative of averting another takeover effort, since that would interfere with the future he envisioned for the Northern Pacific, and which NP shareholders ostensibly endorsed.

"We didn't want convulsions going on," Morgan explained. His goal was to protect the reorganization plans he had made for the railroad, "for the carrying out of which we were morally responsible. . . . It was not a question of control. It is a moral control."

The idea was to quarantine the shares in an entity whose very size placed it beyond the grasp of hostile attackers. "I wanted to put it in a company that nobody could ever buy," Morgan testified. Northern Securities, as he conceived the trust, would have a capitalization of some $400 million, mostly comprising the shares of Northern Pacific and the Great Northern. That would create what Morgan described as "the only investment or trust company that I knew of where the stock was large enough so that in all human probability I felt that if it was not safe there it was not safe anywhere . . . There is no interest that I know of to-day that can control the Northern Securities Company."

For the scheme to work, however, almost all the shares of Northern Pacific had to be contributed. That meant bringing Harriman into the tent.

Still combative in public, Harriman understood that he had little choice but to join up. For the record, he continued to question whether the majority holders of Northern Pacific common—that is, the Hill and Morgan camp—had the right to retire the preferred shares for cash, which would render him powerless despite his owning a majority of all shares, preferred and common. But practically speaking, his sole option was to exchange his Northern Pacific shares for stock in the new Northern Securities Company. This forced exchange, he observed, "was a foregone conclusion unless we were prepared to commence litigation, which would be protracted and which would probably be detrimental to the value of all railroad securities in view of the panic of May 9."

Jacob Schiff, desperate to end the hostilities between his current and former clients, importuned Harriman to accept the peaceful resolution by depicting it as a boon to his extensive holdings. He reassured Harriman that his reputation as a master dealmaker was undiluted and "a great 'stock in trade,' which you and we must be very careful not to imperil" through willful obstruction of the trust. "Although the Union Pacific is in the minority in this holding company, it will nevertheless exercise a potent influence upon the management of the two Northern lines," Schiff promised. The Union Pacific, after all, had already reached an agreement with the Northern Pacific and Great Northern protecting it from competition for traffic to the Pacific Northwest. "I believe the whole arrangement," Schiff remarked, "justifies in every way our attempt last spring to preserve the Union Pacific from damage."

By the end of May, Harriman had agreed to hand over his Northern Pacific shares and to grant authority to Pierpont Morgan to name the directors of the new company, trusting Morgan to apportion the board seats fairly. In the event, the fifteen-member board named by Morgan included Harriman, Schiff, and Stillman; Morgan's own associates Daniel S. Lamont, Robert Bacon, and John S. Kennedy; and Hill and several of his lieutenants. Whether Morgan had made a formal undertaking to give Harriman seats on the Northern Securities board is unclear, but it must have been understood that shutting out the Harriman camp entirely would have been an affront to the principles of comity and cooperation he regarded as his personal contribution to the railroad industry. Morgan said his purpose was to show that Northern Pacific management and the Morgan firm "were acting under what we know as a community of interest principle, and that we were not going to have that battle on Wall Street.

There was not going to be people standing up there fighting each other."
(He testified later that "the people that were more than surprised that they
were put on [the board] were the Union Pacific interests themselves.")

Morgan failed, however, to reckon with one individual spoiling for a
fight: Theodore Roosevelt.

IT WAS INDISPUTABLE that ordinary Americans shared the new president's skepticism about the increasing concentration of economic power,
to which he had alluded in that maiden address to Congress. Public discontent with economic imperialism was stirred by magazines such as Mc-
Clure's, which had been publishing investigative articles by journalists
Ida Tarbell, Lincoln Steffens, and Ray Stannard Baker, all of whom had
trained their gun sights on big corporations. Theodore Roosevelt was
about to take up the muckrakers' cause in his own inimitable way.

On September 19, 1902, just after the securities markets closed for the
day, Attorney General Philander Knox made good on Roosevelt's threat
to regulate big business, announcing that the president had directed him
to file suit to dissolve the Northern Securities Company as a violation of
the Sherman Antitrust Act of 1890.

Roosevelt's sudden initiative thrilled Morgan critics like Henry Adams, though Adams's relish was tempered with disquiet about where "our
stormy petrel of a President" might turn his attentions next. "Suddenly,
this week, without warning, he has hit Pierpont Morgan, the whole railway interest, and the whole Wall Street connection, a tremendous whack
square on the nose," Adams wrote to his friend Elizabeth Cameron. Observing that Roosevelt had given his orders to Attorney General Knox
without consulting anyone else in his cabinet, Adams added, "the Wall
Street people are in an ulcerated state of inflammation." To underscore
his umbrage at Roosevelt's action, Morgan even had "declined the White
House dinner" for Prince Henry of Prussia, Kaiser Wilhelm's brother, an
important diplomatic event with commercial and high-society overtones.
(Morgan eventually attended after all.) Roosevelt "has knocked the stock

market silly, and made enemies of pretty much every man in Congress," Adams commented. Adams was right about Wall Street's reaction: "Not since the assassination of President McKinley has the stock market had such a sudden and severe shock," observed the *New York Tribune*.

Morgan, perceiving the Northern Securities lawsuit to be the opening salvo of a war on his corporate mergers, including the creation of US Steel, promptly booked a train to Washington to remonstrate with the president in person. The encounter seemed only to increase the president's delight in having struck the plutocrat "square on the nose." When Morgan complained about the president's having acted without warning him in advance, Roosevelt replied, "That is just what we did not want to do."

"If we have done anything wrong," Morgan said, "send your man [Knox] to my man [presumably Francis Lynde Stetson, Morgan's chief legal counselor] and they can fix it up."

"That can't be done," Roosevelt shot back. Added Knox, who was in the room, "We don't want to fix it up, we want to stop it."

Finally, Morgan asked if the Northern Securities suit presaged an attack on US Steel.

Roosevelt's reply was less than comforting. "Certainly not," he said, adding mischievously: "Unless we find out that in any case they have done something that we regard as wrong."

After Morgan departed, the president reveled in having bested the banker in hand-to-hand combat. "That is a most illuminating illustration of the Wall Street point of view," he told Knox. "Mr. Morgan could not help regarding me as a big rival operator, who either intended to ruin all his interest or else could be induced to come to an agreement to ruin none."

The federal lawsuit and a companion case filed by the state of Minnesota wended their way through the federal courts until fetching up at the Supreme Court for oral arguments on December 14, 1903. The court issued its ruling three months later, to the day: a narrow 5–4 decision finding the Northern trust illegal and ordering its breakup.

The majority opinion by Justice John Marshall Harlan addressed two questions: whether the Sherman Act extended to railroads even though it seemed to apply strictly to businesses engaged in the manufacture or production of goods or commodities; and if so, whether the Northern trust operated in "restraint of trade or commerce," which would violate the act. Harlan answered both questions in the affirmative, thus not merely endorsing Roosevelt's campaign against concentrated economic power but broadening its potential reach.

Harlan was not persuaded by Morgan's statements about the "moral" imperatives underlying the creation of the trust, or his goal of fulfilling the simple desire of aging shareholders to see that their hopes for their railroads would survive them. Harlan found that the trust organizers' intention was "to destroy competition between two great railway carriers engaged in interstate commerce in distant States of the Union." This goal, he observed, "was concealed under very general words that gave no clue whatever to the real purposes of those who brought about the organization of the Securities Company."

The decision in *Northern Securities Co. v. United States* solidified the federal government's jurisdiction over corporate behavior, giving Roosevelt a legal cudgel he would continue to wield as the nation's "trust-buster." But it is perhaps most noted among legal historians for the ringing dissent lodged by Justice Oliver Wendell Holmes, whom Roosevelt had appointed to the court in the first month of his presidency. "Great cases, like hard cases, make bad law," Holmes wrote in his pithy fashion. Northern Securities was a "great case" merely because of the "accident of immediate overwhelming interest" that placed it on the political front burner — that is, popular discontent with the concentration of economic power. That circumstance distorted the legal reasoning underlying the case, which Holmes wrote should have been decided in favor of the company. He felt that the majority had interpreted the language of "restraint of trade" improperly; the phrase did not apply to business combinations merely because they might be big enough to cause public "anxiety," but to those that actively interfered with competition from outside. In other words, the Great Northern and Northern Pacific should be free to combine in order to limit their competition with each other; only if they prevented competition from *outsiders* would they be in violation of the law. Otherwise, Holmes concluded, "I can see no part of the conduct of life with which on similar principles Congress might not interfere."

Roosevelt was not the first president to have his expectations confounded by his own appointee to the Supreme Court (and would not be the last). But he certainly felt the sting of Holmes's dissent deeply and personally. "I could carve out of a banana a judge with more backbone than that," he exclaimed to a friend. Holmes later acknowledged that his dissent in *Northern Securities* "broke up our incipient friendship," since Roosevelt looked upon the dissent "as a political departure (or, I suspect, more truly, couldn't forgive anyone who stood in his way)."

Yet the Supreme Court's *Northern Securities* decision was not to be the last word. Although the justices had ordered the trust broken up, they were silent on how to do so. That was left to the Northern Securities board—and here Pierpont Morgan's apportionment of only three seats to the Harriman camp, which seemed at the time to be fair, gave Hill and his majority group a significant advantage. For the board voted to distribute the company's assets pro rata to the contributors, rather than to return to the shareholders the shares they had originally contributed.

For Harriman, the distinction was not trivial. If he got back his original shares, he would emerge with a controlling interest in the Northern Pacific. Under the terms of a pro rata distribution, however, he would have no more than minority interests in both the Northern Pacific and the Great Northern and no effective influence over either. Hill would be in charge.

Within days of the board's decision, Harriman filed suit to block the breakup. The lawsuit utterly wrecked Schiff's already quixotic effort to bring Harriman and Hill together. Hill maintained that Harriman had assented to the pro rata plan at least tacitly, during a meeting shortly after the Supreme Court ruling. Harriman's position to the contrary now, Hill fumed, was "a piece of conscienceless lying" that left him unwilling to be "associated with [the Harriman camp] in any business. All they want to make them crooked is the opportunity to cheat some one." (According to

Harriman's biographer George Kennan, Harriman had sent an intermediary to the meeting, and when the proposed terms were described to him afterwards he objected at once.)

Resolving the dispute took nearly another year, until the Supreme Court upheld the pro rata distribution on March 6, 1905. In legal terms this was a clear victory for Hill and Morgan. In financial terms, however, being force-fed Northern Pacific and Great Northern shares eventually produced for Harriman "a veritable bonanza," Kennan observed. Over the following year, the stock market and particularly railroad shares boomed, allowing Harriman to sell off his holdings in both roads at a profit conservatively estimated at $58 million and possibly as much as $80 million. Asked by a magazine writer in 1906 to identify Harriman's most notable achievement, the railroad economist Thomas F. Woodlock replied: "I think it was this, to get licked in a fight and pull out of it with a colossal fortune as a result."

But the money was not to look at; it was to use. Harriman would do so with his typical energy, albeit in a way that would cast a shadow over the final chapter of his life.

21

"MALEFACTORS OF GREAT WEALTH"

Harriman's closest advisers were uneasy about how he set about spending the immense cash hoard the Union Pacific had accumulated. Among other bounties, he was sitting on the profits from the Northern Securities stock sales and $60 million remaining from the $100 million bond issue floated to buy the Southern Pacific in 1901. Now he began using the money to buy up shares of other railroads, many of them direct competitors of the Union Pacific.

Otto Kahn later called the spending of this money a "difficult and complex problem," even though the investments in railroad stocks were likely to yield a large profit for UP shareholders. Kahn acknowledged that the timing of the purchases, given that Harriman was already saddled with the public image of a railroad robber baron, was unwise. Kahn, generally one of Harriman's most consistent defenders, called the stock purchases "the one serious mistake of his management of Union Pacific affairs." He pointed to a particular problem: The purchases helped exacerbate the cooling of the relationship between Harriman and Theodore Roosevelt into a clean break—what Kahn called "the crisis in Mr. Harriman's career."

The deterioration in this relationship unfolded while Roosevelt expanded and intensified his attacks on the banking and investment communities, especially after he won election as president in his own right in 1904. His victory brought about more talk of bringing the railroads under federal regulation, and more antitrust lawsuits. Wall Street felt the pressure increasing even as Roosevelt offered superficial reassurances that he was targeting not corporate behemoths or individual tycoons, but only wrongdoing—as he did in a speech at Philadelphia's upper-crust Union League on January 31, 1905.

"We are not trying to strike down the rich man," he said. "On the contrary, we will not tolerate any attack upon his rights. We are not trying to give an improper advantage to the poor man because he is poor . . . but we are striving to see that the man of small means has exactly as good a chance, so far as we can obtain it for him, as the man of larger means." But he warned that "the great development of industrialism means that there must be an increase in the supervision exercised by the government over business enterprises."

Wall Street's relations with the White House were destined to darken as the bankers continued to resist Roosevelt's calls for "supervision" and given the clash of personalities between the president on one side and figures like Morgan and Harriman on the other. "His war on Pierpont Morgan has been wholly personal," Henry Adams wrote Elizabeth Cameron. "And you know, as well as I do, what Wall Street does when men try to kick."

There seemed to be no common ground among the principal figures. Roosevelt expected blind obedience and thrived on flattery. Morgan considered himself the master of any economic or financial situation, as long as the government and small investors kept out of his way. Harriman was confident in his own rectitude and judgment, and obstinate in dealing with challenges whether they came from individuals or conditions in the natural world.

"The big New York capitalists seem to me to have gone partially insane in their opposition to me," Roosevelt wrote the liberal Republican Carl Schurz in December 1903; "but I have long been convinced that the men of very great wealth in too many instances totally failed to understand the temper of the country and . . . attack the very men who, by doing justice, are showing themselves the wisest friends of property."

But Roosevelt was not above appealing to the bankers by hinting at quid pro quos for political contributions. For his 1904 campaign he extracted more than $2 million from George Gould, Morgan, the Rockefellers, and other leaders of the money center, though he left them feeling conned after the fact. "Roosevelt fairly went down on his knees to us in his fear of defeat," steel tycoon Henry Clay Frick recounted later, "and said that he would be good and would leave the railroads and the corporations alone if we would only give him this financial help. We did, but he didn't stay put in his second term. We got nothing for our money."

Harriman, at least, did not have this problem — for he was not among Roosevelt's reelection donors. It was another sign of how far apart the men had drifted, and a harbinger of the showdown to come.

WHAT MADE THE break between Roosevelt and Harriman especially notable was that the two had been political allies and personally close for a decade. They originally came to know each other as twin pillars of the New York State Republican Party in the 1890s — Roosevelt as its rising young flag-bearer, Harriman as an important financial backer. After Roosevelt's accession to the presidency, Harriman was a frequent visitor to the White House and enjoyed what his biographer George Kennan described as "cordial and harmonious, if not intimate," relations with the president. As late as 1906 they were still friendly enough for the Harrimans to be among the invited guests at the wedding of the president's daughter, Alice, to Nicholas Longworth, the outstanding social event in Washington that year.

A distinct chill could be felt in the air, however. The first signs of a change in the relationship between Roosevelt and Harriman had emerged prior to the 1904 election, linked to two factors. One was the convoluted internal politics of the New York Republican Party, which was in dire financial straits. The party's appeals to Harriman for relief went unanswered, in part because Harriman felt that Roosevelt had reneged on a commitment to provide a political appointment for a Harriman friend. The second issue was Harriman's wish that Roosevelt tone down his antitrust campaign against the railroads.

In Roosevelt's mind, the two issues were inextricable—he assumed
that Harriman's rebuff to the party in its hour of financial need was aimed
at applying pressure on him politically. That led to a series of misunder-
standings related to the scheduling of a meeting between Roosevelt and
Harriman—which of the two had proffered the first invitation, what was
to be on the agenda, and so on. Letters pertaining to their plans crossed
in the mail, and at least on Roosevelt's part were suspiciously vague, as
though the president was creating a written record for public consumption casting himself in the best light. A few courtiers did their part to
curry favor with Roosevelt by undermining Harriman; one told Roosevelt
of a conversation in which Harriman purportedly claimed to care little
about who presided in Albany or Washington, since he had the ability
to "buy Congress" or "buy the judiciary" to get his way. The words later
were flatly denied by a witness to the conversation, but by then Roosevelt
was in a fury, grousing to Senator Henry Cabot Lodge that Harriman had
displayed "a perfectly cynical spirit of defiance throughout, his tone being
that he greatly preferred to have in office demagogues rather than honest
men."

In Otto Kahn's view, the anti-Harriman whispering campaign originated with malcontents whom Harriman had bested in financial combat,
or "unknowingly offended, or who were merely envious of his success."
As Kahn would write after Harriman's death: "The Harriman Extermi-
nation League—if I may so call it—played its trump-card by poisoning
President Roosevelt's mind against Mr. Harriman . . . by gross misrepre-
sentations, which caused him to see in Mr. Harriman the embodiment
of everything that his own moral sense most abhorred and the archetype
of a class whose exposure and destruction he looked upon as a solemn
patriotic duty."

Roosevelt launched his most direct attack on Harriman's business empire via the Interstate Commerce Commission, which voted on November 15, 1906, to open an investigation of transactions the Union Pacific
had made under Harriman's leadership, some dating as far back as 1899.
Although the ICC was nominally an independent body, Harriman's par-
tisans considered the timing of the probe suspect to the point of being

conclusive. "It may be only a chronological coincidence," Kennan wrote in 1916, but it was "immediately after the rupture of friendly relations between the President and Mr. Harriman" that the ICC began its investigation, "acting either on its own initiative or upon suggestion."

Harriman's ability to fight back was at a low ebb, for he had been suffering from a complex of illnesses, including his recurrent bronchial condition (friends attributed his poor health to relentless overwork). "He told me later," Kahn reported, "that during the year 1906 there was not a day in which he was not tormented by severe pain." Yet Kahn also acknowledged that, whether it was illness, hubris, or ambition that impaired Harriman's judgment, his own spending of the Union Pacific's cash gave the regulators the pretext they needed to open their investigation.

Harriman's testimony before the ICC did not help his cause. Kahn was braced for the worst when Harriman took the stand. "He always made an indifferent witness," Kahn recalled, "being impatient and rather resentful and defiant under examination, reluctant to explain so as to make things plain, . . . and disdaining to defend himself against accusations or innuendo."

As it happened, Harriman made it clear in the commission's hearing room that he would buy even more railroads if he could, and all but taunted the ICC to stand in his way.

"If you let us, I will go and take the Santa Fe tomorrow," Harriman said.

"You would take it tomorrow?" he was asked.

"Why, certainly I would. . . . It is a pretty good property."

". . . Then after you had gotten through with the Santa Fe and had taken it, you would also take the Northern Pacific and Great Northern, if you could get them?"

"If you would let me."

"And your power, which you have, would gradually increase as you took one road after another, so that you might spread not only over the Pacific coast, but spread out over the Atlantic coast?"

"Yes."

Placed in the public record verbatim by the ICC, these remarks "lent color to the impression that Mr. Harriman was aiming at a gigantic illegal monopoly of the railroad industry" in flagrant violation of the Sherman Act, Kahn recalled. The result was "a veritable cyclone of criticism, condemnation and defamation."

Roosevelt heatedly denied that he had anything to do with the timing, much less the existence, of the ICC investigation. Speaking of the five commissioners, he stated that "the suggestion that these men would listen to, or that I would make, a request that they proceed against a railroad president because of my personal disagreement with him, is monstrous in its iniquity, and equally monstrous in its absurdity." Yet he took a personal interest in the investigation and was not at all shy about trying to exploit its result. Upon receiving an advance copy of the ICC's investigative report in July, he demanded that its public release be timed to coincide with the announcement of a federal lawsuit against Harriman based on its findings — and then complained bitterly to Attorney General Charles J. Bonaparte, who had succeeded Knox, when the commission barged ahead and released the report on its own. By doing so, he wrote Bonaparte, "they have given the impression that they have made rather a milk-and-water report."

Roosevelt instructed Bonaparte to meet him at his home at Sagamore Hill, Long Island, to draft a joint statement announcing a lawsuit. But the litigation was not filed until the following January, possibly because the ICC's criticism of Harriman was, as Roosevelt observed, less than full-throated. To be sure, its report was not exactly kind to Harriman, for it harshly denounced some of Harriman's financial maneuvers: "Purchasing and controlling stocks in competing lines," it reported, "must mean suppression of competition." Harriman's control and restructuring of the Chicago & Alton in particular was rife with "indefensible financing" that benefited Harriman and his business partners.

The commission acknowledged, however, another aspect of Harriman's management — its effectiveness.

> It has been . . . no part of the Harriman policy to permit the properties which were brought under the Union Pacific control to degenerate

and decline; as railroads they are better properties to-day, with lower grades, straighter tracks, and more ample equipment than they were when they came under that control. Large sums have been generously expended in the carrying on of engineering works and betterments which make for the improvement of the service and the permanent value of the property.

Nor did the ICC call explicitly for a breakup of the Union Pacific. Its recommendations were largely prospective and conditional—"The function of a railroad corporation should be confined to the furnishing of transportation" rather than playing the stock market, for example.

Roosevelt's hand may have been stayed even more by his fear that suing Harriman would fuel Wall Street's inclination to blame his policies for an economic slowdown and stock market slump in 1906–7.

Wall Street bankers had been ascribing emergent economic shudders to the president's antibusiness campaign virtually since the election of 1904. As Roosevelt repeatedly groused to his friends, this was unfair. The causes of what blossomed into a major economic crisis in 1907 were global. They included worldwide competition for capital generated by prosperity across Europe, in the Far East and South America, and further with demand for funds by Britain, which was still paying bills from the Boer War of 1899–1902, and by Russia and Japan, which had run up expenses of nearly $1 billion each during the Russo-Japanese War of 1904–5.

The well of capital was running dry. The production of gold for a global economy based on the gold standard could no longer keep up with demand. Structural weaknesses had manifested themselves in the banking, credit, and currency systems of the developed countries, including the United States. Among those who feared that America's system of monetary oversight had become badly outdated was Jacob Schiff, who warned in a speech to the New York Chamber of Commerce in January 1906 that unless America's decentralized, unregulated monetary system were reformed, "we will get a panic in this country compared with which the three which have preceded it would only be child's play."

Although the stock market was unnerved by all these factors, Wall

Street tended to point its finger at Roosevelt and his associates such as
Bonaparte, the attorney general. After the market broke severely on
March 14, 1907, with Union Pacific shedding more than twenty points to
$120—a drop almost as steep as on the calamitous panic day of March 9,
1901—Harriman was besieged by reporters outside his Lower Manhattan
office. "I would hate to tell you to whom I think you ought to go for the
explanation of all this," he said, his implication crystal clear.

The drumbeat of blame only increased in early August, after federal
judge Kenesaw Mountain Landis imposed a fine of more than $29 million
on John D. Rockefeller's Standard Oil of Indiana for illegal rebating, in a
case brought by the government. "Everyone is frightened to death by the
action of people like our fool Attorney General," J. Pierpont "Jack" Morgan Jr., the House of Morgan's heir apparent, told his London partners.
Charles S. Mellen, president of the New York, New Haven & Hartford
Railroad—who was so close to the Morgan bank that critics derided him
as its "hired megaphone"—likened Roosevelt's attack on corporations to
"a drunken man's debauch."

Roosevelt put it about that he was unmoved by these brickbats, even
proud to be their target, but that is not to say that he ignored them. In a
missive to the Boston banker Henry Lee Higginson in early August, he
referred to a letter from a voter who warned that "if hard times come they
will be due to Rough Rider methods," a reference to the volunteer cavalry
regiment that Roosevelt had led with such élan in Cuba during the Span-
ish-American war. Of such complaints Roosevelt commented, "All strike
the same note; a note of lunacy."

Roosevelt then turned the tables on the bankers, speaking loudly
while also brandishing a figurative big stick. The occasion was the August
20 cornerstone ceremony for the Pilgrim Monument in Provincetown,
Massachusetts, where the Mayflower Compact had been signed after the
Pilgrims' first landfall in 1620.

He alluded in his talk to the "world-wide financial disturbance" touching Paris, Berlin, and London, but then implied that Wall Streeters were
deliberately undermining the US markets to strike at him personally. "It

Theodore Roosevelt's campaign against "malefactors of great wealth" captivated editorial cartoonists such as Samuel Ehrhart of *Puck*, who depicted the president bidding farewell to a troupe of tycoons including Morgan and Harriman at the front and John Jacob Astor, John D. Rockefeller, Russell Sage, and Andrew Carnegie trailing behind.

may well be that the determination of the government (in which, gentlemen, it will not waver), to punish certain malefactors of great wealth has been responsible for something of the trouble," he said, employing a phrase he had scribbled onto the typescript of his speech prepared earlier. He accused the bankers of having "[combined] to bring about as much financial stress as possible, in order to discredit the policies of the government . . . so that they may enjoy unmolested the fruits of their own evil-doing."

The bankers may not have thought highly of Roosevelt's speech, but his own impression, perhaps inevitably, was that it was a roaring success. "My speech told, I believe," he wrote his son Kermit the next day. "Of course it did not suit Wall Street, but I did not expect that it would."

The president did not name any individual "malefactors" in his speech,

but he hardly needed to be explicit. Any members of the public attentive
to current affairs knew that the administration was in the throes of battle with Harriman and the Rockefellers, with Morgan not far removed
from Roosevelt's gun sights. Roosevelt's associates had even less cause for
doubt, as he had been disparaging Harriman in private; in a typical tirade,
he called Harriman "at least as undesirable a citizen as Debs, or Moyer,
or Haywood" in a letter to New York Republican Congressman James S.
Sherman. The references were to the socialist Eugene V. Debs and the
radical union leaders Charles Moyer and William "Big Bill" Haywood,
both of whom were about to go on trial for the murder of a former Idaho
governor. (Haywood, who was defended by Clarence Darrow, would be
acquitted and the charges against Moyer dropped.)

Still, throughout this period Roosevelt was not above turning again to
his wealthy targets for assistance when crisis beckoned. In October, the
markets broke down decisively; the trigger was a failed attempt by a pair
of financial adventurers to corner copper stocks, provoking depositor runs
on the trust companies that had backed them. These trust companies were
shadow banking institutions — as overleveraged and lightly supervised as
the "non-bank banks" in the market crash of 2008, a century later. Their
activities threatened to bring down the entire financial community, and
with it the US economy. The October crash brought together Morgan
and George B. Cortelyou, Roosevelt's treasury secretary, for a series of
all-night meetings in New York that resulted in Cortelyou's commitment
of $25 million in government funds to shore up the tottering banks, in
return for Morgan's raising millions more from the banking community to
halt the stock market plunge.

The spirit of cooperation shown by the ever-opportunistic Morgan
did more to temper Roosevelt's trust-busting campaign than any amount
of public blustering by bankers. After Morgan helped the government
weather the crisis, Roosevelt began to soft-pedal his attacks. Partially in
recognition of Morgan's services, Roosevelt even allowed Morgan's US
Steel to acquire yet another steel company, Tennessee Coal & Iron, ostensibly to rescue a large brokerage firm endangered by its investments
in the failing TC&I. A debate would rage well into the administration

of Roosevelt's handpicked successor, William Howard Taft, over whether the trustbuster had been duped into approving the merger or yielded to necessity with his eyes wide open. Roosevelt's version, naturally, was the latter: "We were in the midst of the most intense crisis of the panic," he said later, explaining that failing to rescue the brokerage would have precipitated "such a crash as we saw in 1893." The TC&I deal would cast a long shadow, however. Taft would lose a lawsuit to break up US Steel in 1911 partially on the grounds that Roosevelt had implicitly approved the steel trust by waving the TC&I merger through.

PERHAPS BECAUSE THEY once had had a warm personal relationship, Roosevelt's treatment of Harriman continued to be distinctly chillier than his relations with Morgan. That was especially evident in Roosevelt's high-handedness during a catastrophic break in a Colorado River canal that threatened permanently to inundate California's Imperial Valley, then as now one of the nation's most productive agricultural regions. Harriman's Southern Pacific had made a $200,000 loan in June 1905 to the California Development Company, which had incompetently built the canal. (Harriman thought he was investing in an expansion of the valley's irrigation, which would produce more freight for his railroad—but in an uncharacteristic moment of absent-mindedness, failed to learn of the canal builders' ineptitude in time.) Roosevelt chose to interpret this modest investment as evidence that the railroad owned the canal company and was therefore responsible for the break.

In an exchange of testy telegrams, the two tried to saddle each other with the cost of repairing the damaged canal and restoring the valley. With icy formality, Harriman on December 13, 1906, tallied all the money the railroad had spent in its fruitless attempt to control the river—roughly $2 million, by his reckoning—on behalf of the valley's settlers and the federal government. "It does not seem fair," he wrote, "that we should be called upon to do more."

Roosevelt replied to Harriman with condescending terseness: "I assume you are planning to continue work immediately on closing break

A poorly constructed canal cut into the Colorado River produced a devastating flood over California's Imperial Valley, wiping out farms and railroad tracks until the Southern Pacific, at Harriman's direction and Roosevelt's insistence, muscled the unruly river back into its natural course.

in Colorado River. I should be fully informed as to how far you intend to proceed in the matter." Harriman offered to contribute his tracks and crews and to allow use of the Southern Pacific's quarries for gravel, but he asked that the labor be performed by men employed by the government's Reclamation Service. "Can you bring this about?" he asked Roosevelt.

The president refused the bait. He promised Harriman to ask Congress to reimburse the railroad for the repair work when it reconvened in the new year. But he told Harriman on December 20, "This is a matter of such vital importance . . . that there is not the slightest excuse for the California Development Company [that is, the Southern Pacific] waiting an hour for the action of the Government." That very day Harriman wired Epes Randolph, his on-site engineering chief: "Close that break at all cost." The job would take seven attempts over eighteen months, and cost the railroad more than $3.2 million.

Roosevelt would exploit the great flood to his own advantage. On January 12, 1907, even before the Southern Pacific closed the breach, he delivered to Congress his personal vision of a vast western desert reclaimed for agriculture. He proposed a monumental program of "diversion dams and distribution systems in the arid West," summing it all up as "a broad comprehensive scheme of development for all the irrigable land upon [the] Colorado River . . . so that none of the water of this great river which can be put to beneficial use will be allowed to go to waste." (More than a quarter century later, Theodore Roosevelt's distant cousin Franklin would preside over the dedication of the first great Colorado River project built in response to his call for action: Hoover Dam.)

The ICC investigation and Roosevelt's relentless attacks had severely eroded Harriman's reputation by 1907. "Very few there were who remained loyal to him," Kahn would recollect, "and still fewer who dared believe that he would ever recover his old position of prestige and influence." His friends advised him to resign from his companies and quarantine himself in Europe for a year or more. Yet "amidst all this terrifying din, this avalanche of vituperation, misrepresentation, threatening and assault, amidst the desertion of some friends, the lukewarmness of others, amidst the simultaneous strain and stress of a financial panic, . . . Mr. Harriman stood firm as a rock. . . . He never for one moment took his hand off the helm — and thus he rode out the storm."

Circumstance brought him a chance to regain his "prestige and influence," in the form of that old financial harlot, the Erie Railroad. In the spring of 1908, the Erie was again on the verge of insolvency. A bond issue of $5.5 million was due to mature on April 8, with no money or credit available for redemption. In Morgan's library on the afternoon of April 7, an emergency meeting was convened of the Erie board, including Harriman. Morgan himself was in Europe, but his partners made clear that they would not finance the redemption, and indeed already had prepared legal papers to place the road in receivership.

Harriman listened silently to the dispirited discussion, smoking and staring into the fire. In his mind, receivership portended disaster — not only for the Erie, but for the still-nascent recovery from the 1907 panic. If the Erie defaulted, so too would every other company still struggling to work its way out of the post-panic economic doldrums. The depression would be indefinitely prolonged. Finally he spoke up. He would advance the entire $5.5 million, he said, if the other directors would lend him the money on his collateral. The deadline for redemption was 3 p.m. on April 8. The deal was done before noon.

Harriman's venture to rescue the Erie by placing his own assets at risk transformed him into the hero of the hour. "He has taken a heavy load from off the market and ought to receive the gratitude of the public," asserted the *Commercial and Financial Chronicle*. The *New York Times* contrasted Harriman's bold action with his longtime adversary's timidity: "Harriman Cash Saves the Erie," its headline read the next day; "Morgan Plan a Failure."

But this would be Harriman's last major financial deal. The following spring, his health failing, he sailed to Europe for a rest cure — after a preliminary trip west to Mazatlán to inspect the Mexican branch of the Southern Pacific, which had just been completed. The full roster of his medical ailments has not been documented, but they certainly included chronic bronchitis, ulcerative colitis, and physical exhaustion. At the end of August, when he disembarked from his return voyage at Jersey City, he insisted on meeting personally with the throng of reporters, as though to demonstrate his haleness. It was a bad idea, for the reporters instead witnessed the gaunt tycoon, his skin a waxy yellow, collapsing several times into the arms of an associate. "I'm feeling fine," he gasped out. "It's only that seasickness again." Commented the *New York Tribune*, with a solicitude that would have been unthinkable only two years earlier, "E.H. Harriman will go down in Wall Street history as the gamest little man that ever lived."

He was game almost to the last breath. After leaving the waterfront on August 24 he was taken directly to Arden House, the country home

Showing the ravages of multiple infirmities and what friends considered the rigors of overwork, a gaunt Harriman pays one of his final visits to his Manhattan headquarters before heading home to Arden, where he passed away on September 9, 1909, at sixty-one.

he had built north of New York City some twenty years before, on the outskirts of a community now known as Harriman, New York. He never left Arden again. The end came on September 9, at the age of sixty-one. Jacob Schiff recalled for a friend his last conversation with Harriman, days before his death. "He did not believe for a moment that his last hour was near . . . He talked so confidently about his plans! . . . I myself almost believed he would recover."

MORGAN OUTLIVED HARRIMAN by more than three years, but his final years were trying psychically and physically. His particular burden was the congressional investigation of Wall Street in which Representative Arsène Pujo, Democrat of Louisiana, placed Morganization in the dock.

Morgan spent a day and a half on the witness stand starting Wednesday, December 18, 1912, getting politely but relentlessly interrogated by Samuel Untermyer, Pujo's counsel. Untermyer bore down on the intricate threads tying together the country's banks and industrial enterprises, all of which seemed to run through Morgan's hands. Morgan's denial that he had any real power rang transparently false.

"Your firm is run by you, is it not?" Untermyer asked.

"No, sir."

"You are the final authority, are you not?"

"No, sir."

"You have never been?"

"Never have."

Untermyer then asked, "You do not think you have any power in any department of industry in this country?"

"I do not."

"Not the slightest?"

"Not the slightest. . . . I am not seeking it, either."

When the ordeal was over, Pierpont accepted the plaudits of his family and partners for having seemingly bested Untermyer with his resolute circumspection and oracular mien. Pierpont's daughter Louisa confided to her diary: "Father made a magnificent showing. Untermyer *nowhere*."

Yet the experience had left the seventy-five-year-old financier profoundly rattled. "The long preparation and the inimical atmosphere of the committee room had offended him deeply and wearied him extremely," reported that assiduous chronicler, Herbert Satterlee. Morgan spent the last months of his life haunted by the experience. A doctor treating him in Cairo, where he took respite in March, diagnosed him as having been laid low by "nervous depression and insomnia," which were manifestations of "prolonged excessive strain." Biographer Jean Strouse reported that his visitors found him "thin, exhausted, terrified of losing his mind, obsessed with the idea that he was about to be subpoenaed or cited for contempt of court, and that he was dying." Never fully regaining his equilibrium, he died in Rome on March 31, 1913, after suffering through bouts of delirium possibly caused by a series of strokes.

Pujo had released his report on the "money trust" one month earlier, on February 28, and it became clear from its 258-page text that Morgan had not pulled the wool over his interrogator's eyes at all. The committee laid out in pitiless detail all the interrelationships and financial maneuvers of a small group of powerful men, which Morgan had tried to obscure. The report devoted special attention to "our archaic, extravagant, and utterly indefensible procedure for the reorganization of insolvent railroads"—one of the capstones of "Morganization"—concluding that these arrangements had furnished to the interconnected banking groups "opportunities of which they have not been slow to avail themselves, of securing the dominating relation that they now hold to many of our leading railroad systems." Pujo acknowledged that Morgan and his ilk had "added to the prosperity of the country" in some ways, but nonetheless concluded that they had broken the law to the extent they aimed "to throttle the competition upon which they had thrived. . . . Whilst they were struggling against one another for supremacy they were a valuable asset to the country; since they have pursued the opposite policy they have become a menace."

The Pujo Report would provide grist for financial reformers for decades, perhaps none so august as a Boston lawyer named Louis Brandeis, presently to be appointed to the Supreme Court by Woodrow Wilson. A few weeks after the report appeared, Brandeis pored over it line by line with Untermyer, and soon produced a deconstruction of the report for the general reader, published as a series of articles in *Harper's* and in book form under the title *Other People's Money, and How the Bankers Use It.*

Here Brandeis set forth the themes that would undergird his jurisprudence during his twenty-three years as one of the court's outstanding progressive figures. These included a deep skepticism of "bigness" in government and business, especially when it placed inordinate power in too few hands: "Big railroad systems, Big industrial trusts, Big public service companies; and as instruments of these[,] Big Banks and Big trust companies." He scoffed at Morgan's rationalization before the Pujo Committee that financial concentration was demanded by "the needs of Big Business." Those ostensible needs were merely justifications for law-breaking.

Brandeis argued that the bankers' power over capital allocation put the economic cart before the horse. Morgan and his colleagues portrayed themselves as crucial players in the creation of great industries; Brandeis argued that they should be seen instead as rent-seeking exploiters of spadework done by others. He ridiculed Morgan's claim that "practically all the railroad and industrial development of this country has taken place initially through the medium of the great banking houses," writing,

> On the contrary nearly every such contribution to our comfort and prosperity was "initiated" *without* their aid. The "great banking houses" came into relation with these enterprises, either after success had been attained, or upon "reorganization" after the possibility of success had been demonstrated but the funds of the hardy pioneers, who had risked their all, were exhausted. This is true of our early railroads, of our early street railways, and of the automobile; of the telegraph, the telephone and the wireless; of gas and oil; of harvesting machinery. . . . The *initiation* of each of these enterprises may properly be characterized as "great transactions"; . . . But the instances are extremely rare where the original financing of such enterprises was undertaken by investment bankers, great or small. [Emphasis in the original.]

Of the hundreds of millions of dollars that Morgan cited as the investment-banking community's capital contribution to American industrial progress, only a small fraction was applied to improvements of the enterprises and the rest to the trading of securities, Brandeis charged. The financings "served, substantially, no purpose save to transfer the ownership of railroad stocks from one set of persons to another." In the process, competition was extinguished and a goodly portion of the wealth siphoned into the coffers of firms such as Morgan & Co.

Brandeis questioned this system not merely because it gave so much power to such a small circle of individuals, but because it also burdened those individuals with more responsibility than they could handle. His Exhibit A was Edward Harriman, who had "succeeded in becoming director in 27 railroads with 39,354 miles of line [extending] from the Atlantic to the Pacific; from the Great Lakes to the Gulf of Mexico." The legacy of this concentration, Brandeis argued, was equivocal at best, for the global reputation Harriman had earned as rescuer of the Union Pacific was frittered away by the shortcomings of his subsequent performance. "It was not death only that set a limit to [Harriman's] achievements," he wrote, but "the multiplicity of his interests."

As if to prove Brandeis's point, in 1910 a major scandal erupted at the Illinois Central, which Harriman had served as chairman until his death. As recently as 1908 Harriman had exercised paramount control over the Illinois, forcing his old friend Stuyvesant Fish out of his posts as president and director over allegations of financial improprieties (and amid countercharges from the Fish camp that Harriman was plotting to make the IC subservient to the Union Pacific). Harriman's handpicked successors in management were accused of a scheme in which repair bills on IC cars were padded by a contracting firm in which several of them held stock. Meanwhile, Harriman's ever-controversial restructuring of the Alton & Chicago came under renewed scrutiny; as Brandeis observed, the road "never regained the prosperity it enjoyed before [Harriman] and his associates acquired control" in 1899. Due to blunders like these, Harriman's iron empire began to show signs of corrosion. But its ultimate collapse would result from the handiwork of his most determined enemy, Theodore Roosevelt.

ROOSEVELT WAS MORE than three years out of office—and Harriman more than three years in the grave—when his attack on Harriman's empire finally bore fruit. On December 2, 1912, the Supreme Court decided that the Union Pacific's acquisition of the Southern Pacific some eleven years earlier had violated the Sherman Antitrust Act, and ordered the merger unwound.

Business experts have debated ever since whether the two roads truly had been competitors and therefore whether their combination truly restrained interstate trade. But the court, for its part, explicitly rejected the railroads' defense — that the roads had engaged in negligible competition at most. "It is urged that this competitive traffic was infinitesimal when compared with the gross amount of the business transacted by both roads, and so small as only to amount to that incidental restraint of trade which ought not to be held to be within the law," Justice William Rufus Day — a Roosevelt appointee — wrote for a nearly unanimous court. (Justice Willis Van Devanter, who had been a member of the lower court majority that had approved the merger, recused himself.) Although the competitive business was only a small part of the total traffic of the combined roads, Day observed, "nevertheless such competing traffic was large in volume, amounting to many millions of dollars. . . . It was by no means a negligible part, but a large and valuable part, of interstate commerce."

The court-ordered breakup of the Union Pacific proved to be as messy as the breakup of Northern Securities nine years earlier. It soon became evident that, for all his domineering authority, Harriman had failed to construct an integrated empire out of his disparate acquisitions. Although many top executives of Harriman's imperial Union Pacific had come from the Southern Pacific, resentments seethed between the two camps; in the course of the corporate divorce, many chose to return to the Southern Pacific, among them Julius Kruttschnitt, Harriman's skilled and trusted right-hand man, who would be named chairman of the newly independent Southern Pacific.

The Union Pacific attempted to return to the original merger plan plotted out by Harriman and Otto Kahn — keep the Central Pacific and shed as much of the Southern Pacific as they could. But they ran into resistance from the newly independent Southern Pacific, whose managers knew that losing the Central Pacific would subordinate it like a slave to a

UP holding a virtual stranglehold over traffic into and out of California. They mustered local shippers and state officials to agitate in favor of their keeping the Central Pacific, and after nearly a decade of further litigation and regulatory proceedings, finally won approval from the ICC.

But even that was not a permanent condition, and eventually the two systems would return to the mold Harriman had laid. Faced with new challenges in a competitive world, the Union Pacific and Southern Pacific would merge again in 1996. This time, the merger stood.

Epilogue:
The End of an Epoch

I N THE FIRST years of the twentieth century, the direct influence of E. H. Harriman and J. Pierpont Morgan over the railroad industry waned. In part this was because the industry had achieved a maturity that absorbed and then outpaced Harriman's and Morgan's reforms. But even more it was because their role in the American economy came under penetrating public scrutiny. The power of the tycoons begat suspicion, and that suspicion was manifested in Theodore Roosevelt's campaigns to dismantle the trust structures created by these "malefactors of great wealth"—first by breaking up the Northern Securities trust, and then by severing the Union Pacific from the Southern Pacific.

Roosevelt's efforts, and those of the US Congress and the courts, launched a period of decline for what had been a towering industry. The 1880s and 1890s, when Harriman and Morgan rose to preeminence in the railroad world, were the high-water mark of American railroad building. In those two decades more than 107,000 miles of track were added to the national network. Never again would America's railroad builders come close to that pace. Only 62,000 miles would be added from 1901 through 1920; after that, construction continued to fall off.

The mistrust generated by the great railroad combinations at the turn of the twentieth century would cast a shadow over the industry for decades. Government regulators refused to allow the railroads to charge rates that later scholars judged not only warranted but essential to promote maintenance and upkeep. The consequences became inescapably clear after the United States entered World War I in 1917. The government had effectively nationalized the railroads in order to muster troops and equipment for transport to Europe, only to discover that the roads were so derelict and disorganized that chaos ensued at the docks. After the war, there was reason to hope that the experience would prompt the industry to reorganize and regulators to treat their rate requests more responsibly, if not indulgently. But by then the railroads were facing a new crisis: competition from a resurgence of shipping over water and the growth of air transport and highway trucking.

After further decades of deterioration, the only apparent option for preserving this crucial mode of transport was to reconsolidate systems that had been broken up by judges and regulators. In 1970 the federal government allowed the Great Northern, Northern Pacific, and the Chicago, Burlington & Quincy to merge into what was dubbed the Burlington Northern; in 1996 the Burlington Northern acquired the Atchison, Topeka & Santa Fe and was eventually renamed BNSF Railway. (As of this writing BNSF is owned by Warren Buffett's Berkshire Hathaway Inc.) In 1996 the government permitted the Union Pacific and Southern Pacific to re-create the merger between them that had been broken apart in 1912. At the time of the new merger, railroad historians Robert E. Gallamore and John F. Meyer observed, "much was made of the historical antecedents and how these mergers were just putting things back the way they might have been all along."

That was cold comfort, for the railroad industry had irreversibly changed in the intervening years. By the end of the twentieth century the mileage of America's railroads had shrunk by a third compared to their length in 1900. Once the prime employers of American labor, in 2000 they accounted for more than ten times the freight ton-miles (that is, a ton of freight carried one mile) as they had in 1900, but with a workforce only 16.5 percent of its size one hundred years earlier. The almost despotic role the railroads had played in American life in the last half of the nineteenth century, driving the nation westward, creating and then serving towns and cities, fostering agricultural and industrial development from the Atlantic to the Pacific, had become little more than a cultural memory, consigned to history books and museum exhibitions.

As the new century wore on, the consequences of underfunded maintenance and slipshod operational standards grew exponentially, along with unrelenting pressure from the new transport competitors in the air and on land and water. The pattern of consolidation continued from the nineteenth century into the twentieth, but often the mergers were prompted and managed by government in a desperate effort to keep the railroads relevant in America's multimodal transportation grid. They were still important, even crucial, for moving goods and produce, but as Gallamore and Meyer observed in 2014, in the twentieth century the railroad industry "survived more than it prospered."

YET THE HANDIWORK of the pioneering iron imperialists of the nineteenth century is still visible, if sometimes in skeletal form. It can be seen in the crosshatching of rail across the American continent, much of which still follows the routes laid down during their dominion. The remnants of the great railroads of their time still traverse America's prairies, span its canyons, climb its mountains or burrow beneath them. Passengers on the nation's remaining transcontinental trunk lines or its short lines or its commuter networks today can still thrill to the sensation of the landscape rushing past their windows at close range, an experience that cannot be replicated by air travel.

In the second decade of the twenty-first century, the nation's railroads still recorded more than 527 million passenger trips (about the same figure as in 1890). The railroads carried some 1.7 trillion tons of freight in 2017, far outstripping the 79 billion tons they were carrying annually at the close of the nineteenth century, but that accounted for only about one-third of America's freight, overtaken by highway and water shipping.

No political or economic history of the United States can fail to come to grips with the role of the railroads in the late nineteenth and early twentieth centuries, or the complex and sometimes contradictory role that the railway kings played in their story.

"The reasonable man adapts himself to the world: the unreasonable one persists in trying to adapt the world to himself," George Bernard Shaw wrote in *Maxims for Revolutionists*. "Therefore all progress depends on the unreasonable man."

The leading figures in this book were "unreasonable" men determined to shape the world into which they were born. For all their faults and flaws, they succeeded in doing so.

Their railroads defined the American economy of the period. Almost every business cycle "turned on the roads and was either created or conditioned by them, and large-scale financing found its main object in them," political economist Joseph Schumpeter wrote in the 1920s.

The railroads were the physical embodiment of the march of modern technology—and also of "the unexampled ruthlessness of economic power," the historian Alan Trachtenberg has written. "In railroad monopolies, combinations, conspiracies to set rates and control traffic, lobbies to bribe public officials and buy legislators, the nation had its first taste of robber barons on a grand scale."

Yet the story is more complex, for the railroads also gave the nation a glimmer of the limitations of the robber barons' power. The railroads were the dominant businesses in boom years, but also the first to collapse during the great busts of the 1870s and 1890s: "During the 1880s more miles of track were built than in any other decade in American history," Alfred Chandler observed, "and in the 1890s more mileage was in bankruptcy than in any decade before or since."

These factors help explain why the legacy of America's nineteenth-century railroad titans is mixed. That is perhaps inevitable, for in the forty-eight years between the driving of the golden spike and America's entry into World War I, the railroads and American capitalism grew and matured together—and rose and fell together.

American capitalism and its railroads were born together, reached adolescence together, and attained maturity together. They both went through a long period of what Schumpeter called "creative destruction." In some respects the financiers at the center of this story were agents of this process, destroying the railroad industry as it existed when they arrived on the scene, but turning it in the long run into what it had to become. Schumpeter saw this process as "the essential fact about capitalism," the process of "industrial mutation . . . that incessantly revolutionizes the economic structure from within, incessantly destroying the old one, incessantly creating a new one."

The business leaders whose careers are traced in this book came into the industry with divergent goals and skills. Daniel Drew and Jim Fisk were speculators to their bones, preoccupied with the trading of investment securities with little concern about the commerce underlying the paper they were buying and selling. Cornelius Vanderbilt and Jay Gould married their speculative impulses to their empire-building ambitions, but those ambitions were aimed fundamentally at creating personal fortunes. It fell to Edward H. Harriman and J. Pierpont Morgan to yoke the vision of railroad empires devoted to the public good to their quests for personal wealth and influence. In the process, they bequeathed us new methods of managing enormously complex businesses that inform management practices to this day. Harriman and Morgan were not the first to conceive of the necessity of sophisticated corporate management for railroads — the credit often is given to Albert Fink, a German-born engineer for the Baltimore & Ohio and later the Louisville & Nashville road, who developed systems of information sharing that, as Chandler observed, "made possible the 'control through statistics' that has become an essential hallmark of modern corporate administration." But they applied those systems to even larger systems than Fink had, making them efficient, profitable, and, as Chandler wrote, modern.

Whether Harriman and Morgan were motivated chiefly by public or personal interest can be endlessly debated. The question certainly was raised during their lifetimes and in the years immediately following their deaths. Their careers motivated Louis Brandeis's critical assessment of the role of capitalists in the railroad industry. His judgment that American capitalists' "financiering" amounted chiefly to moving paper securities from one hand to the other, taking a commission for each step, was not entirely unfair, if perhaps too one-sided. The drawbacks of Morgan's and Harriman's systems of anticompetitive consolidation were manifest, as

Brandeis outlined them. But their contributions were unique and important.

Whatever the motivations of these tycoons, efforts like theirs are necessary for the development of any innovative and disruptive technology. Pioneers of new technology contribute their inspiration, but they tend to be better at inventing than managing; they are often incapable of making the transition from creator to industrial leader. In the late 1800s the railroads were in unmistakable need of discipline, rationalization, and modernization. In that respect they were no different from steam power, the wireless, the telegraph, and in our own time personal computing and the internet.

Even Brandeis acknowledged that the great bankers stepped into the railroad business only after "the funds of the hardy pioneers . . . were exhausted." He did not hold that those who contributed the capital and business management that created thriving industries out of disorganized businesses were wholly undeserving of the public's gratitude, only that they did not deserve *all* the credit — they were "entitled to share, *equally with inventors*, in our gratitude," he wrote. His disagreement was with their profiteering from a process he agreed was, in truth, indispensable.

It is unlikely that the railroads could have survived the transition from the nineteenth century to the twentieth without the transformation that Vanderbilt and Gould helped to launch and Harriman and Morgan completed.

The differences between the railroad empires of J. P. Morgan and E. H. Harriman reflected their leaders' particular strengths and proclivities. Morgan was a pioneer in financial modernization whose perception that "the scrambled disorder of the railroad business in the unregulated and financially profligate eighteen-seventies and -eighties," in the words of Frederick Lewis Allen, would stand as an insurmountable obstacle to growth unless it could be made to yield to organization. Morgan brought about order by tying operating companies together with investment companies through interlocking corporate directorships and stockholder syndicates, with his own firm and banks he controlled at the center and railroads (and other industrial companies) orbiting them, like moons held in their thrall by gravity and by what Morgan biographer Lewis Corey called "the personal dictatorship of J. Pierpont Morgan."

Frederick Allen noted that the influence Morgan and his partners exercised was "pretty much limited to finances," for "they knew little about practical railroad operation and didn't need or want to know more."

The man who did know about practical railroad operation, for he had taught himself the science, was Edward H. Harriman. That is what made him as necessary a figure as Morgan in the evolution of the railroad industry. Harriman was unique in his ability to straddle the worlds of finance and operations. Morgan imposed order on the railroads from the outside; Harriman imposed it on his roads from the inside, learning the intricacies of his roads' operations with a granularity that Morgan could never hope —nor did he wish—to achieve.

Harriman's approach produced his signal contribution to the modernization of the American railroad industry: his acquisition and rehabilitation of the Union Pacific—the one major trunk line that Morgan had so carelessly shunned.

The name of Edward Harriman carries less weight for Americans today than Morgan's. The main reason is that Morgan, through the partners he trained and the financial foundations he built for his firm, created a dynastic institution that has maintained its global influence over business and finance without a break from his time to ours. Harriman's legacy is harder to detect. His Wall Street firm was not a partnership as Morgan's was, but an expression solely of his vision, determination, and skill. His name lives on today in the nameplate of Brown Brothers Harriman, one of the nation's largest private banks, but that firm is the product of a merger between the Brown Brothers merchant bank and W. A. Harriman & Co., which was founded in 1922 by Averell Harriman, Edward's son, with the fortune he was left by his father.

But Harriman's legacy is deeply embedded in the Union Pacific, the great line that remains part of the steel spine of America's railroad network to this day. In the words of Maury Klein, the official historian of the Union Pacific, it was Edward Harriman who bequeathed the railroad "the leadership and the principles to ensure continuity through rapidly changing times."

In a way, while rivals, Morgan and Harriman ultimately were complementary competitors—opponents who, together, remade America in their image and brought it into the modern era.

Acknowledgments

As a chronicle of bygone times, this book is necessarily the product of much solitary research amid dusty tomes and files dispersed coast to coast. But I could not have finished this work or brought the story to life without the indispensable assistance of many others.

I owe gratitude to the staff of the Morgan Library and Museum, which provided me with the time and assistance to mine its records for crucial primary documents, not least the handwritten journals kept by Frances Louisa ("Fanny") Morgan during her family's trip across the United States by rail in the summer of 1869, at the very dawn of the era of transcontinental rail travel.

Sabina Beauchard of the Massachusetts Historical Society helped unearth crucial pages from the personal memorabilia of Charles Francis Adams Jr. in which he describes firsthand the meetings in 1888 and 1889 at which Pierpont Morgan attempted to fashion a "community of interest" out of a herd of obstreperous railroad presidents. Greg LeRoy provided invaluable insights into the business of George Pullman and the Pullman Strike of 1894. Archivists at the Chicago History Museum, the Pullman State Historic Site, the Smithsonian Institution, the Wyoming State Archives, and the New York Public Library helped to turn up pertinent images to illustrate this story.

I offer particular thanks to the staff of the Langson Library of the University of California, Irvine, which—as has been the case with several of my previous books—functioned as my bibliographic home away from home during the research stage of *Iron Empires*.

Every book presents its own unique combination of problems to solve. In this case, I was fortunate to have the help of Alexander Littlefield of Houghton Mifflin Harcourt, whose grasp of the themes and advice on shaping the myriad narratives of this book made him a full partner in its creation. My agent, Sandra Dijkstra, as always, brought to this project the enthusiasm, advocacy, and confidence on which I long ago came to rely, along with the assistance of her very able staff.

Finally, but most importantly, this book could not have been researched and written without the love, forbearance, and support of my wife, Deborah, or the inspiration of my sons, Andrew and David.

Notes

Introduction:
Agents of Transformation

page

ix   *"the power of healing"*: James B. Hedges, "The Colonization Work of the
      Northern Pacific Railroad," *Mississippi Valley Historical Review* 13, no. 3 (Dec.
      1926), 315.
      "prosperity, freedom": Oberholtzer, vol. 2, 128.

x   *"a $50 lot"*: Josephson, *The Robber Barons*, 98.
      "shed but a dying": Quotes from Stevenson regarding his journey are from
      Across the Plains, 3–77.

xi   *"Here," he wrote*: Charles Francis Adams and Henry Adams, *Chapters of Erie*,
      335.

xiii *from fewer than*: See Department of the Interior, Census Office, *Report on
      Transportation Business in the United States at the Eleventh Census, 1890*, vol. 1
      (Washington, DC: GPO, 1894–95).
      America's largest industrial: Chandler, *The Railroads*, 97.

xiv *"The railway kings"*: Bryce, vol. 2, 1314.

xv   *"before a spadeful"*: See Anthony Trollope, *The Way We Live Now*, chap. 9.
      "Your *roads*": Strouse, 196. The emphases appear to be Strouse's.

xvi *"The question might"*: Larrabee, 205.

xvii *"They are but . . . upon us"*: Thoreau, 19, 33.
      "excessive freight . . . extortionate charges": Chandler, *The Railroads*, 188–90.
      "A great change": Henry George, "What the Railroad Will Bring Us," *Over-
      land Monthly*, October 1868, 297–306.

xviii *The historian Frederick Jackson Turner*: See Turner, "The Significance of the

Frontier in American History," in *Proceedings of the State Historical Society of Wisconsin*, 41st Annual Meeting, Dec. 14, 1893 (Madison, WI: Democrat Printing, 1894), 10.

xix *"domestic values"*: Richter, 32.
    "thirty-three women": Dall, 19.
 xx *"but two or three"*: Quoted in Richter, 45.
    "a squealing pig": *New York Times*, Mar. 30, 1882.
xxi *"He tried to"*: Wells, 18–19.
    "A Darky Damsel": Ibid., 19.
    "alike in every respect": Ibid., 19–20.
xxii *"a rustic"*: Croffut, 2.
    "I see over": Whitman, *Complete Poems*, 430.

1. Uncle Daniel and the Commodore

3 *"dreadfully mangled"*: See Massachusetts Historical Society, Diaries of John Quincy Adams: A Digital Collection, vol. 39, 178–79, http://www.masshist.org/jqadiaries/php/diaries (accessed July 16, 2017). The description of Vanderbilt's injuries is taken from the testimony of his personal physician, Jared Linsly, at the surrogate court's proceeding after Vanderbilt's death, reported in the *New York Sun*, Nov. 14, 1877. Croffut incorrectly dates the accident as October 1833.
    Now he was lying: Stiles, 90.
4 *"I'm a steamboat man"*: Croffut, 71.
    "a mere plaything": Ibid., 28.
5 *"when I stepped"*: Ibid., 18.
    The conflict between: See Gibbons v. Ogden, 22 US 1 (1824).
    "No one who has not": Rev. J. McClintock, "Daniel Drew, Esq., of New York," *Ladies' Repository*, Sept. 1859.
    ruthless mutual fare-cutting: Browder, 36.
6 *"About the only"*: Croffut, 95.
7 *"You have no business"*: McClintock, "Daniel Drew, Esq." See also Browder, 36.
    "relax in each other's": Browder, 66.
    "shrewd, unscrupulous": Charles Francis Adams and Henry Adams, *Chapters of Erie*, 5.
    "a believer in the doctrine": James Medbery, "The Great Erie Imbroglio," *Atlantic Monthly*, July 1868.
    "a country deacon": Clews, *Twenty-Eight Years*, 156.
9 *"dull and commonplace"*: Croffut, 39.
    "was not blessed": Ibid., 20.

"*a wharf rat*": Sobel, *Panic*, 124.

"*to the great terror*": Ibid., 45.

"*You have undertaken*": Croffut, 49.

10 *By the time Vanderbilt*: Ibid., 43.

"*wealth and obvious soullessness*": "Commodore Vanderbilt," *Harper's Weekly*, March 5, 1859.

A proposal by: Moody, *The Railroad Builders*, 4.

11 "*There was a road*": Ibid., 10.

America of that era: Gordon, 35.

the crop accounted: Sven Beckert, "Slavery and Capitalism," *Chronicle of Higher Education*, Dec. 12, 2014.

12 "*in fact America's*": Ibid.

having only about 9,800: Douglas, 96.

made the South: Ibid.

"*Railroads are the greatest*": *Cincinnati Commercial*, Feb. 4, 1854, cited in Johnson, 127.

"*I considered*": Douglass, 385.

13 *according to a famous map*: See Charles O. Paullin and John K. Wright, *Atlas of the Historical Geography of the United States* (1932), Digital Scholarship Lab, University of Richmond, http://dsl.richmond.edu/historicalatlas/ (accessed May 28, 2017).

The outbound and return: For Whitney's China trip, see Bain, 6ff.

14 "*Time & space*": Diary of Asa Whitney, quoted in Thomas, 1.

"*Memorial*": H.R. Doc. No. 72, 28th Cong., 2nd Sess. (1845).

"*silly and chimerical*": Robert S. Cotterill, "Early Agitation for a Pacific Railroad 1845–1850," *Mississippi Valley Historical Review* 5, no. 4 (March 1919), 398.

15 *Whitney withdrew*: Bain, 46.

"*We have drawn*": Ibid, 115.

16 "*1, buy your railroad*": Croffut, 75.

17 "*People who had never*": Taylor, 75.

"*The stock was the favorite*": Fowler, 204.

"*The Commodore did not*": Croffut, 71.

18 "*Something was in the wind*": Ibid., 207.

19 *Vanderbilt let the*: Stiles, 377.

"*When any one desired*": Ibid., 208.

Among those: Ibid., 393. Stiles casts doubt on the assertion, which evidently originated with Henry Clews, that Drew betrayed Vanderbilt in the Harlem corner. The confusion may arise from the fact that there were two Harlem corners managed by Vanderbilt, which followed closely upon one another; Stiles accepts that Drew sold Harlem shares against Vanderbilt's interests in the second corner.

Put simply: For an explanation of Drew's call strategy and its outcome, see Fowler, 350–56.

20   *"These contracts":* Ibid., 356.

      "No more through": Croffut, 82.

      "I was at home": Ibid., 83.

2. Chapters of Erie

22   *The founders also opted:* Mott, 48.

23   *"jerkwater affair":* Holbrook, 55.

      "I tell Billy": Croffut, 81.

24   *By November 1867:* Ibid., 84.

      "between the ocean": The line is the title of Mott's chronicle.

      "The great Vanderbilt": Mott, 56.

      had been "milked dry": Nation, June 5, 1866.

      "The road was acting": Croffut, 88.

26   *"one-stringed Chinese lyre":* Fowler, 439.

      "at once a good friend": Charles Francis Adams, chap. 5.

      "conducting his roads": "Erie Campaigns in 1868," *Fraser's Magazine*, May 1869, 571–72.

      "more fiction than fact": Browder, 144.

27   *"small, cadaverous":* Harper's Monthly, April 1870.

28   *"a large burly":* Ibid.

29   *in "fancy suits":* Swanberg, 2.

      "beggary staring him": Croffut, 89.

31   *"all enjoining or commanding":* Charles Francis Adams, "The Erie Railroad Row," *American Law Review* 3, no. 1 (October 1868), 51.

      "impossible to keep": Ibid., 52.

      "If this printing press": Croffut, 91.

      "a police officer": Browder, 164.

32   *Drew: I'm sick:* Swanberg, 58.

      On one occasion: Browder, 184.

      one Sunday: It was March 29, according to ibid., 185.

33   *"Vanderbilt tole me":* Croffut, 95.

      "The full and true history": Charles Francis Adams and Henry Adams, *Chapters of Erie*, 52. Charles Francis Adams identifies Gould's Albany hotel as the "Develin," but this is almost certainly wrong. The premier hotel in the city at this time was the Delavan House, and there is no record of a "Develin."

34   *"to control elections":* New York State Assembly, Select Committee to Investigate Erie Railway Company, *Report of the Select Committee to Investigate Alleged Mismanagement on the Part of the Erie Railway Co.*, May 16, 1873, p. xix.

"*I have no details*": Ibid., 556.

"*Gould wanted to wait*": Croffut, 96.

35   "*You should be*": Clews, *Twenty-Eight Years*, 145.

"*an empty shell*": Grodinsky, *Jay Gould*, 100.

"*The iron rails have broken*": Memos quoted in Mott, 156ff.

"*never have anything more*": Croffut, 97.

36   "*His face, sir*": *New York Sun*, Nov. 27, 1872.

"*With his deep-set*": Ibid., Nov. 28, 1872.

38   "*It is sun*": Richardson, *Garnered Sheaves*, 288.

3. Pierpont Morgan's Grand Tour

41   *the escapade*: Chernow, 20–21, and Sinclair, 16–17.

42   "*from farmers, merchants*": Chandler, *The Visible Hand*, 90.

By 1865: See Strouse, 131.

helping to manage: Ibid., 135.

43   "*Such comfortable rooms*": These and other quotations from Fanny Morgan's journals are drawn directly from the journal books held in the collection of the Morgan Library in New York.

44   "*into the hot sun*": Humason, 40.

"*It was necessary*": Sarah Chauncey Woolsey, "A Few Hints on the California Journey," *Scribner's Monthly*, May 1873.

46   *by some reckonings*: Mormon scholarship differs on how to define "wife"; some of Young's marital relationships were designated "for eternity," others only for life, and not all Young's marriages involved conjugal relations or even cohabitation. The figure used here treats all such "sealings" as marriages.

48   "*two rusty streaks*": The phrase was coined by Charles Francis Adams to describe what would be left of the Union Pacific if speculators and looters had their way with the road. See Trottman, n. 274.

49   "*a difficult and sequestered*": Charles Francis Adams and Henry Adams, *Chapters of Erie*, 138–39.

"*carrying things*": Strouse, 136.

"*losing their power*": Ibid.

50   "*entirely and absolutely*": Satterlee, 138.

"*where he was not averse*": Josephson, *The Robber Barons*, 153. See also Charles Francis Adams and Henry Adams, *Chapters of Erie*, 153.

51   "*A more unwieldy*": Charles Francis Adams and Henry Adams, *Chapters of Erie*, 163.

"*heartily sick of running*": *New York Times*, Sept. 8, 1869.

52   "*knocked off his feet*": Satterlee, 142.

family legend: See Chernow, 31. Chernow attributes the yarn to Herbert Satterlee, Morgan's son-in-law, but Satterlee's published version of the confrontation merely places Pierpont at the head of the stairs with Ramsey, and states only that "something happened very quickly." (Satterlee, 142.)

"arrayed in his": New York Times, Sept. 8, 1869.

53 *"a ruthless destroyer"*: Satterlee, 133.

4. The King of Frauds

56 THE KING OF FRAUDS: New York Sun, Sept. 4, 1872. Capitalization as in original.

57 *"A new piece"*: C. F. Adams Jr., "Railroad Inflation," North American Review 108, no. 222 (January 1869), 147.

58 *"Did this road"*: United States Congress, House, Select Committee on Credit Mobilier and Union Pacific Railroad, and Jeremiah M. Wilson, Report of the Select Committee of the House of Representatives, Appointed Under the Resolution of January 6, to Make Inquiry in Relation to the Affairs of the Union Pacific Railroad, the Credit Mobilier of America, and Other Matters Specified in Said Resolution and in Other Resolutions Referred to Said Committee (Washington, DC: GPO, 1873), 167. (Hereafter, Wilson Report.)

59 *"Mr. Blaine"*: New York Sun, Sept. 10, 1872.

60 *"the most malignant"*: New York Times, Sept. 16, 1872.

61 *"the most dramatic"*: Ibid., Feb. 2, 1885.

on February 18: All quotations come from United States Congress, House, Select Committee on Alleged Credit Mobilier Bribery, Report of the Select Committee to Investigate the Alleged Credit Mobilier Bribery, Made to the House of Representatives, February 18, 1873 (Washington, DC: GPO, 1873). (Hereafter, Poland Report.)

"There is no": Poland Report, 46.

"Those of us": Ibid., 16.

62 *"not subject to"*: Ibid., viii.

"forbidden by the letter": Ibid., xiii.

63 *"contempt and disgrace"*: Ibid., xiv.

"when it was worth": Ibid., xviii.

"manifest injustice": New York Sun, Feb. 22, 1873.

"shed tears": Ibid., Feb. 26, 1873.

"It's like the man": Bain, 700.

64 *"(Stifled, O days!"*: Whitman, Complete Poems, 604.

"become an established": Trottman, 78.

65 *"This country is"*: Poland Report, x.

66 *"Instead of gaining"*: Daggett, 224.

"The 'Credit Mobilier'": Union Pacific Railroad Company, Report of the Government Directors of the Union Pacific Railroad Company for the Year 1874.

On the day: Trottman, 54.

67   *If not for:* Wilson Report, 396.
      "is now helpless": Ibid., xxii.

5. The Northern Pacific Panic

68   *"numerous, powerful, and entirely savage"*: "Memorial of Asa Whitney: praying
      a grant of public land to enable him to construct a railroad from Lake Mich-
      igan to the Pacific Ocean; Feb. 24, 1846," S. Doc. No. 161, 28th Cong., 1st
      Sess., 1846, p. 8.
70   *"People's Pacific Railway"*: See Smalley, 97ff.
71   *having failed miserably:* Smalley, 129.
      Eleutheros Cooke: Oberholtzer, vol. 1, 7.
      "Old Ogontz": Cooke memoirs, cited in ibid., 10.
73   *"with an absolutely"*: Ibid., 89.
      "Most of the members": Congressional Globe, Dec. 10, 1860, 42.
      "It is regarded": Oberholtzer, vol. 1, 111.
74   *"filled full"*: Ibid., 233.
      "all United States bonds": Ibid., 532.
      "it required": Cited in ibid., 536.
75   *"The manner in which"*: Hamilton A. Hill to Cooke, Feb. 11, 1871, in Ober-
      holtzer, vol. 2, 99.
      "Like Moses and Washington": Jay Cooke's memoir, 2; cited in Lubetkin, 13.
76   *"The appearance"*: Oberholtzer, vol. 1, 106.
      "If successful": Ibid., 113.
      "the capitalists of Europe": Jay Cooke, "A Decade of American Finance," *North
      American Review* 175, no. 552 (Nov. 1902), 583.
      "increase his income": Oberholtzer, vol. 2, 108.
77   *"a perfect storm"*: *Walla Walla Standard,* cited in Oberholtzer, vol. 2, 119.
      "salmon are not caught": Ibid., 120.
      One article: Ibid., 127–28.
      "one uninterrupted field": W. B. Hazen, "The Great Middle Region of the Unit-
      ed States, and Its Limited Space of Arable Land," *North American Review* 120,
      no. 246 (Jan. 1875), 1, 3.
78   *"orange groves and monkeys"*: Oberholzer, vol. 2, 120.
      "Jay Cooke's banana": Josephson, *The Robber Barons,* 94.
      "I have hundreds": Cooke to Moorhead, Aug. 13, 1869, in Oberholtzer, vol. 2,
      147.
      "the bad odor": Ibid., 151.
79   *"I was stunned"*: Cooke, "A Decade of American Finance," 584.
      "emigration across": Oberholzer, vol. 2, 155.
      "I flung my hat": Ibid., 157.
      "No extraordinary foresight": Smalley, 170.

80　*"with some pleasing"*: Oberholtzer, vol. 2, 165.

　　"It is not seen": Hancock to Cooke, Jan. 11, 1870, in ibid., 170.

81　*"Our force was"*: "A Brush with Indians," *New York Times*, Sept. 30, 1872.

　　"Mr. Cooke resisted": Oberholtzer, vol. 2, 171.

　　"Do you think": Cooke to Drexel, Feb. 17, 1869, in ibid., 134.

　　"since the celebrated": Ibid., 190.

82　*"rather sneering"*: Ibid., 220.

　　"I tell you": Banning to Cooke, Sept. 23, 1870, in ibid., 246.

　　"The present actual": Ibid., 381.

83　*"even if signed"*: Ibid., 418.

84　*Junius Morgan was unhappy*: See Strouse, 151.

　　Farmers and railroad: Sobel, 159.

85　*He turned his face*: Oberholtzer, vol. 2, 422.

　　"like a thunderclap": Ibid.

　　"one or two gentlemen": Strong, 493.

　　"I'll tell you": *New York Herald*, Sept. 19, 1873.

86　*The collapse had*: Stiles, 537.

　　"The kinds of bonds": Ibid., 533.

87　*The economy shrank*: See Sobel, *Panic*, 192.

　　Railroad construction: The figures are from the National Bureau of Economic Research database: NBER Macrohistory: II. Construction, "U.S. Miles of Railroad Built, Bureau of the Census—Railway Age 1830–1952," at http://www.nber.org/databases/macrohistory/contents/chapter02.html (accessed Sept. 2, 2019).

　　Grant made a pilgrimage: McFeely, 393–94.

　　"the corridors and parlors": *Harper's Weekly*, Oct. 11, 1873.

88　*"prostration in business"*: Grant, State of the Union address, Dec. 7, 1874.

　　"With the increasingly": Chandler, *The Visible Hand*, 136.

89　*"robber barons"*: John Tipple, "The Anatomy of Prejudice: Origins of the Robber Baron Legend," *Business History Review* 33, no. 4 (Winter 1959), 511.

　　"insinuation that pernicious conduct": Ibid.

　　had "more wealth": Clews, *Twenty-Eight Years*, 449.

　　"admirably adapted": McAllister, 181.

90　*"Money-getting"*: Charles Francis Adams, 190.

　　The pace of: Sobel, 192.

91　*Having detected*: See Strouse, 151–52.

6. Jay Gould Returns

92　*"sent an order"*: Testimony of Jay Gould, *Report of the United States Pacific Railway Commission*, 10 vols. (Washington, DC: GPO, 1887–88), 446. (Hereafter, USPRC.)

"*factually correct*": Grodinsky, *Jay Gould*, 118.

93 A *rather different*: See Klein, *Union Pacific*, vol. 1, 308.
    "*various have been*": *New York Times*, Mar. 15, 1874.

94 "*a transaction worthy*": Charles Francis Adams and Henry Adams, *Chapters of Erie*, 118.

95 "*to have nothing*": Julia Dent Grant, 182.
    "*saw the whole*": United States Congress, House of Representatives, Committee on Banking and Currency, *Gold Panic Investigation*, March 1, 1870, p. 12. (Hereafter, *Gold Panic*.)

96 "*damned old scoundrel*": *Gold Panic*, 175–76.
    "*Of course matters*": Ibid., 176.
    "*Hundreds of firms*": Ibid., 19.

97 "*produced an impression*": Ibid., 334.
    "*Messrs. Gould and Fisk*": Charles Francis Adams and Henry Adams, *Chapters of Erie*, 133.

98 *Irked that Durant*: Trottman, 47.
    "*Fisk had told us*": Wilson Report, 48.
    "*the most infamous*": USPRC, vol. 1, 441.
    Another $50,000: Wilson Report, 295.

99 "*was in rather*": *The Story of Mr. Jay Gould, as Told by Himself*, 11. This volume, published by the American News Company of New York, comprises selections from the transcript of Gould's testimony before the US Senate Committee on Education and Labor on Sept. 5, 1883.

100 "*without justification*": Union Pacific Railroad Company, *Report of the Government Directors of the Union Pacific Railroad Company for the Year 1874*.
    "*with farms and villages*": Union Pacific Railroad Company, *Report of the Government Directors of the Union Pacific Railroad Company for the Year 1876*.
    The population: See Trottman, 102, for figures drawn from the US Census.
    a record grain harvest: Grodinsky, *Jay Gould*, 122.

101 "*Commodore Vanderbilt*": *New York Times*, Jan. 1, 1877.

102 "*Can any sane person*": *New York Evening Mail*, June 3, 1881, cited by Trottman, n. 200.
    few maneuvers: This description of the Kansas Pacific affair is based chiefly on Trottman, 147ff; Daggett, 220ff; and USPRC. Except where indicated, direct quotations are from USPRC testimony by Jay Gould, Henry Villard, Frederick Ames, and Oliver Ames II. Other sources consulted are Grodinsky, *Jay Gould*, and Klein, *The Life and Legend of Jay Gould*, an energetic but ultimately unconvincing defense of Gould's machinations in the affair.

103 "*while the Kansas Pacific*": Grodinsky, *Jay Gould*, 178.

104 "*the Union Pacific had reported*": Daggett, 229.
    "*He had his war paint*": USPRC, 704.
    "*It would have destroyed*": Ibid., 509.

105   *"According to"*: Ibid.
       Later analysis: Another source estimates Gould's profit as $5 million: see
       Klein, *Union Pacific*, vol. 1, 415. Klein's admiration for the intricacies of
       Gould's maneuvers may have desensitized him to the fact that Gould had
       mustered his undeniable manipulative skills for an attack on an enterprise of
       which he was, for most of that period, an officer.
106   *"old, and had lost"*: Charles Francis Adams, 192.

7. Year of Upheaval

107   *"In the space"*: Select Committee on Existing Labor Troubles, Investigation of
       Labor Troubles in Missouri, Arkansas, Kansas, Texas, and Illinois, H.R. Rep.
       No. 4174, 49th Cong., 2nd Sess., 1887, p. 394. (Hereafter, Curtin Report.)
       "The organization": F. W. Taussig, "The South-Western Strike of 1886," *Quarterly Journal of Economics* 1, no. 2 (January 1887), 185.
       "Traffic Throttled": Case, 152.
       "the great upheaval": The same phrase has also been applied to a strike on the
       Baltimore & Ohio in 1877.
       "extreme in its magnitude": Taussig, "The South-Western Strike," 184.
108   *"the most imposing"*: Ware, xi.
109   *the only national*: Ibid., 3.
       "defend [labor] from degradation": Carroll D. Wright, "An Historical Sketch of
       the Knights of Labor," *Quarterly Journal of Economics* 1, no. 2 (January 1887),
       7.
       "short and slight": New York Sun, Mar. 28, 1886.
110   *Once the organization shed*: Donald L. Kemmerer and Edward D. Wickersham,
       "Reasons for the Growth of the Knights of Labor in 1885–1886," *Industrial
       and Labor Relations Review* 3, no. 2 (January 1950).
       "Capital has now": Quoted in Foner, 7.
       "long hours": Dubofsky and Dulles, 170.
111   *"The power of money"*: New York Times, Jan. 31, 1874.
       Although in 1870: Gordon, 53.
       "The aim of the Knights": Quoted in Chandler, *The Railroads*, 130.
       "the big impersonal": Ibid., 129.
112   *"Knowing that amid"*: George, 164.
113   *"the farms were first"*: Josiah Strong, 157.
       "The final culmination": See Whitman, *Complete Prose Works*, 300.
       the historian C. Vann Woodward: See, generally, Woodward's *Reunion and Reaction*.
114   *"steal or starve"*: Baltimore Sun, July 14, 1877, cited in Loomis, 54.
       "a rifle diet": Hyndman, 109.
       "It is wrong": Dubofsky and Dulles, 109.

115 *"This enemy"*: William M. Grosvenor, "The Communist and the Railway," *International Review* 4 (September 1877), 585.
     According to a compilation: The list can be found at Yellen, 33.
     "in the hands": *New York Times,* July 26, 1877.
116 *"prosperous and powerful"*: Klein, *The Life and Legend of Jay Gould,* 346.
117 *"Work enough?"*: Curtin Report, 449.
     "by laundering clothes": Cited in Case, 88.
     "Who put the Wabash": Ibid., 93.
118 *"one of the most eloquent"*: Buchanan, 144.
     "No such victory": Cited in Ware, 144.
119 *"alarming fact"*: Powderly, *The Path,* 120.
     "five men": Powderly, *Thirty Years,* 494.
120 *"eleven hours"*: Curtin Report, 452.
     "We saw very plainly": Ibid., 553.
     "the settlement so far": Case, 139.
     "The whole system": Curtin Report, 468–69.
121 *"if men and"*: Powderly, *The Path,* 114.
     "Precious lives were": Ibid., 115.
     "There are people": Bureau of Labor Statistics and Inspection of Missouri, *The Official History of the Great Strike of 1886 on the Southwestern Railway System* (Jefferson City, Mo.: Tribune), 94. (Hereafter, *Official History.*)
     "reported every move": Powderly, *The Path,* 117.
122 *Powderly himself only learned:* Ibid., 118.
123 *The railroads:* Taussig, "The South-Western Strike."
     "masterly inactivity": Ibid., 202.
     "will force merchants": *Official History,* 55.
124 *It carried:* Taussig, "The South-Western Strike."
     "You shall be": Gould to Hoxie, cited in Klein, *The Life and Legend of Jay Gould,* 359.
     "We see no objection": *Official History,* 68.
125 *"In short"*: Ibid., 79–81.
     One Sunday night: The account of this meeting comes from Powderly, *The Path,* 134ff.
     "essentially a pedagogue": Ware, 145.
127 *"in the throes"*: Ibid., 375.

8. The Rise of Ned Harriman

131 *"controlled fifty thousand"*: William Z. Ripley, "Federal Financial Railway Regulation: The Alton as a Test Case," *North American Review* 203, no. 725 (April 1916), 538.
132 *"the last figure"*: Kahn, 13.

"He fairly revelled": Muir, 6.

133　*"the loving-kindness"*: Ibid.

134　*"the best"*: Kahn, 49.

　　"Then we have the satisfaction": Kennan, vol. 2, 171–72. For a fuller accounting of the Southern Pacific's battle with the Colorado River see Hiltzik,
42–50.

135　*"never fully recovered"*: Kennan, vol. 1, 3.

　　"Cold and austere": Ibid., 4.

　　A pay dispute: C. M. Keys, "Harriman: The Man in the Making," *The World's
Work*, 13, no. 3, (January 1907), 8460.

136　*"compromised at $250"*: Ibid.

　　"hangs a heavy": Ibid.

　　"I am going": Kennan, vol. 1, 11.

137　*"Not one man"*: Edwin Lefèvre, "Harriman," *American Magazine*, June 1907,
118.

　　Yet he must: See John Moody and George Kibbe Turner, "The Masters of
Capital in America: The Inevitable Railroad Monopoly," *McClure's Magazine*,
January 1911, 335.

　　"extraordinary 'nose for money'": Ibid.

　　Two years later: Kennan, vol. 1, 15. An alternate version of the source of
Harriman's seed money is that he had sold the market short and profited from
the collapse of the attempt by Gould and Fisk to corner gold, which triggered
a marketwide panic in 1869. Kennan's version has the advantages of greater
plausibility and the biographer's authority.

138　*"I am dead tired"*: Kahn, 14.

　　"simply brought to bear": Ibid.

139　*"at a moment"*: Keys, "Harriman," 8461.

　　"the depravity of the business": Whitman, *Complete Prose*, 13. His broadside
Democratic Vistas, from which these words are taken, was written in mid-1870
and published the following year.

140　*"When I first came"*: *New York Times*, Dec. 3, 1892. Numerous versions of
this monologue exist of various degrees of frankness; see, for example, Sobel,
Panic, 165.

141　*"I can't lose much"*: Moody and Turner, "The Masters of Capital in America,"
335.

　　"Any biography": The quotation is from R. S. Lovett, general counsel for the
Harriman railroads, and appears in Persia Campbell, 6.

　　Arriving at the Ogdensburg: Kennan, vol. 1, 61.

142　*had been appointed*: For the history of the Ogdensburg railroad, see Klein, *The
Life and Legend of E. H. Harriman*, chap. 3.

　　Over the next year: *Commercial & Financial Chronicle*, May 24, 1879, and June

12, 1880.

"tall, blond, leonine": Eckenrode and Edmunds, 38.

"big-hearted, hand-shaking chap": George H. Cushing, "Hill Against Harriman: The Story of the Ten-Years' Struggle for the Railroad Supremacy of the West," *American Magazine* 63, no. 5 (September 1909).

143   *"It is a common thing"*: *New York Times*, Oct. 29, 1906.

"badly managed": Kennan, vol. 1, 61.

"two crippled locomotives": Moody and Turner, "The Masters of Capital in America," 336.

"had great strategic": Quoted in Kennan, vol. 1, 65–66.

Harriman's brother-in-law: Klein, *The Life and Legend of E. H. Harriman*, 51.

145   *"I knew that"*: Kennan, vol. 1, 66.

The "importance of": Ibid.

9. The First Skirmish

147   *"The road will be"*: Quoted in Stover, 21.

Advertisements placed in East Coast: A sample newspaper ad can be found in ibid., 47.

149   *"a monument"*: Charles Francis Adams and Henry Adams, *Chapters of Erie*, 5.

"Little Egypt": This nickname for a region of southern Illinois is thought to have originated with a Baptist minister and early settler who compared it to the fertile "Land of Goshen," a part of Egypt referred to in the Bible.

"the 'Egyptians' turned out": William K. Ackerman, 85.

150   *By 1854*: Ibid., 36.

At the urging: Klein, *The Life and Legend of E. H. Harriman*, 56.

"the assistance of rich": Moody and Turner, "The Masters of Capital in America," 338.

151   *"It's the best"*: Ibid.

"twisted rails, burned ties": Stover, 145.

"a train composed": Reid, 28.

"shipped by steamboats": Osborn to IC board, Dec. 30, 1882, in Ackerman, 115.

152   *"bluest of blue"*: Klein, *The Life and Legend of E. H. Harriman*, 54.

"I don't like": Moody and Turner, "The Masters of Capital in America," 338. The authors misspelled William H. Osborn's name as "Osborne" throughout their account, possibly confusing him with C. J. Osborne, a prominent Wall Street speculator of the period.

"How much of it": *Commercial and Financial Chronicle*, March 1, 1884.

153   *"Somehow or other"*: Kahn, 13.

They founded the Chicago: See Kennan, vol. 1, 72.

154 *At 9 a.m.*: Stover, 204.

  "When Harriman had": Ibid., 209.

155 *Immigrants were pouring*: See "Illinois Central Railroad Company: Report of the Directors to the Stockholders," *Commercial and Financial Chronicle*, Mar. 6, 1886.

  That was a huge: For a sample of contemporary share prices, see *Commercial and Financial Chronicle*, Dec. 5, 1885.

  "who had previously been a broker": Satterlee, 243.

  "There is no doubt": *Commercial and Financial Chronicle*, Feb. 19, 1887.

157 *"a prejudice against"*: Satterlee, 244.

  the "Bismarck": For Morgan's ambition in this direction, see Strouse, 239ff.

158 *Industrialists and economists*: Strouse, 407.

10. A Community of Interests

159 *On the surface*: USPRC, vol. 1, 3.

  "almost valueless": Ibid., 20.

  "perfect and absolute": Ibid., 9.

160 *"two rusty streaks"*: Trottman, n. 274.

162 *"With a good deal"*: Charles Francis Adams, 193.

  "upon the principle": Union Pacific Railroad Company, *Report of the Government Directors of the Union Pacific Railroad Company for the Year 1884*, p. 7.

163 *"Everything in Colorado"*: USPRC, vol. 1, 47.

  "have done away": Quoted in Trottman, 216.

  "devoted itself honestly": USPRC, 50.

164 *"my first experience"*: Charles Francis Adams, 192.

165 *"has been wholly selfish"*: *Commercial and Financial Chronicle*, Jan. 12, 1889.

  "struck me as a somewhat": *Report of the Senate Select Committee on Interstate Commerce, 49th Congress, 1st Session, Submitted to the Senate January 18, 1886* (Washington, DC: GPO, 1886), 1207–8.

166 *"For forty years"*: Moody, *Masters of Capital*, 29.

  Billy decided in 1879: See Strouse, 197ff.

  "the largest ever": *New York Tribune*, November 27, 1879.

  60,000 shares: Klein, *The Life and Legend of Jay Gould*, 242.

168 *This was a road*: Strouse, 246–47.

  "I look on": *New York Tribune*, July 20, 1885.

169 *It was not a relaxing*: See Corey, 152–53, for an account of the meeting on board.

  "Mr. Roberts was not": Satterlee, 224.

170 *"That is not"*: Ibid., 226.

  an intricate sequence: Strouse, 249.

171 *"solely on the spoken"*: Ibid., 236.

"*made it easy*": Ibid., 241.

"*join in any*": New York Tribune, Dec. 16, 1888.

172 "*the representatives of capital*": Hovey, 139.

"*dreadfully sick*": Journal of Charles Francis Adams Jr., Dec. 23, 1888, collection of Massachusetts Historical Society. Satterlee places this meeting on December 21, but according to Adams it was a two-day meeting that began on Thursday, December 20.

"*to cause the*": Hovey, 139–40.

"*I object*": Ibid., 140.

"*the old story*": Adams journal, December 23, 1888.

173 "*but in so*": Ibid.

174 *signed by twenty-two*: Kolko, 59.

"*When the party*": Commercial and Financial Chronicle, Jan. 12, 1889.

"*barely enough time*": Kolko, 61.

175 "*Think of it*": New York Tribune, Dec. 17, 1890.

"*I have the utmost*": Ibid.

The "*cordage trust*": Dewing, 23ff.

176 "*Cordage has collapsed*": Commercial and Financial Chronicle, May 6, 1892.

178 *In the panic year*: Sobel, Panic, 258.

179 "*Myself!*": Edwin Lefèvre, "Harriman," American Magazine, June 1907.

"*the court should*": Kennan, vol. 1, 101.

"*Harriman always wanted*": Satterlee, 272.

11. Savior of the Union Pacific

181 "*I was receiving*": Josephson, The Robber Barons, 311.

"*a revival of the old*": Quoted in Commercial and Financial Chronicle, Nov. 15, 1890.

182 "*Under his direction*": New York Times, Nov. 12, 1890.

"*There is nothing strange*": New York World, Nov. 27, 1890.

"*ejected by Jay Gould*": Charles Francis Adams, 198.

183 *Adams had also spent*: Kennan, vol. 1, 115.

But then opportunity: Trottman, n. 238.

184 *Gould was flush*: Grodinsky, Jay Gould, 577.

"*had a talk*": New York Times, Sept. 27, 1891.

185 "*After his death*": Grodinsky, Jay Gould, 593.

between November 1, 1895: Daggett, 239.

186 "*Not . . . nearly as bad*": Commercial and Financial Chronicle, April 28, 1894.

"*All, unfortunately, have had*": Davis, 230.

187 "*a position which*": Schiff to R. L. Strauss, June 12, 1865, in Adler, Jacob H. Schiff: His Life and Letters, vol. 1, 4–5.

188 "*He was a*": Adler, Life and Letters, vol. 2, 340.

"That's Morgan's affair": Kennan, vol. 1, 119.

189　"He was so disgusted": Ibid., 120.

190　"would have to paint": Klein, The Life and Legend of E. H. Harriman, 110.

191　"It's that little fellow": Kennan, vol. 1, 123. The description of the subsequent encounter between Schiff and Harriman is based on ibid., 124ff.

192　"If you prove": Ibid., 126.

"Mr. Harriman was a newcomer": Kahn, 26.

"Ned Harriman!": Ibid., 14.

193　"the greatest reservoir": Burr, 121.

"a very prominent": Ibid., 124.

12. The Reconstruction

194　"if he didn't think": Dodge, 75.

Shortly after taking office: Klein, The Life and Legend of E. H. Harriman, 110.

195　"the physical condition": Kennan, vol. 1, 140.

"even by reputation": W. H. Bancroft, "Impression of E. H. Harriman," unpublished manuscript reproduced in part in Kennan, vol. 1, 141–42.

196　"It's the size": Kennan, vol. 1, 278.

197　"The depots were": Park testimony, United States of America v. the Union Pacific Railroad Co., et al. (Washington, DC: GPO, 1909–10), vol. 9, 4280ff.

"All its feeders": Ripley, 501.

"Never before has there been": Commercial and Financial Chronicle, Sept. 16, 1893.

198　"If it was called": Kennan, vol. 1, 145.

"the great tracts": Ibid., 146.

"pretty wild talk": Kahn, 32.

199　"he clearly discovered": Ibid., 29.

200　"the chisel and the straightedge": Quoted in Kennan, vol. 1, 156.

"We heard": Quoted in ibid., 163.

201　"The mention of goats": United States of America v. the Union Pacific Railroad Co., et al., vol. 9, 4284–85.

202　"The contractors uncovered": Spearman, 65.

"ejecting men": Kennan, vol. 1, 158.

the tunnel completed: Railroad Gazette, Dec. 6, 1901.

203　record time: See Kennan, vol. 1, 167.

"East or West": Ibid., 166–67.

"had long been a Mecca": William Park, "Recollections of E.H. Harriman in Connection with the Union Pacific," unpublished manuscript reproduced in part in Kennan, vol. 1, 171ff.

They would be immortalized: The film is best regarded as a pastiche of fact and fantasy. It is true that the Union Pacific suffered from a surfeit of robberies and that Harriman established a private constabulary. The ultimate fate of the two outlaws, as the film implies, was never fully established, and sightings of one or the other were reported throughout North and South America for years.

204   *"The expense was"*: Park quoted in Kennan, vol. 1, 173–74.
205   *"on all of the American"*: *United States of America v. the Union Pacific Railroad Co., et al.,* vol. 2, 781.
      During Harriman's first: Kennan, vol. 1, 160.
      "Fortune favored": Ripley, 502.
206   *"the most discussed"*: E. G. Campbell, 233.
      "archaic, extravagant": US House, *Report of the Committee to Investigate the Concentration of Control of Money and Credit,* Feb. 23, 1913, 148. (Hereafter, Pujo Report.) The Pujo Committee was a precursor to the better-known Pecora Investigation of Wall Street, launched by the US Senate during the Great Depression; by then the Morgan in the hot seat was J. Pierpont "Jack" Morgan Jr.
207   *"They say it is the most"*: *Railway World,* Mar. 21, 1896, quoted in E. G. Campbell, 321.
      Morgan's typical fee: E. G. Campbell, 323.
      "it is in the railroad": Moody, *The Truth About Trusts,* 492.
210   *It was no longer possible*: See E. G. Campbell, 327–28.
211   *"Five years ago"*: Charles A. Prouty, "National Regulation of Railways," American Economic Association, Dec. 26–29, 1902, in ibid., 334.

13. "A Pig-Headed Affair"

212   *"all-pervading air"*: Richard T. Ely, "Pullman: A Social Study," *Harper's New Monthly Magazine,* February 1885, 457.
      "a pampered millionaire": Cobb, 125.
213   *"Last summer"*: Carwardine, 77–78.
214   *"The Social Palace"*: "The Social Palace at Guise," *Harper's New Monthly Magazine,* April 1872.
      "The Pullman car": Carwardine, 15.
215   *"As seen from the railway"*: Ibid., 16.
216   *make do on as little*: United States Strike Commission, *Report on the Chicago Strike of June–July, 1894* (Washington, DC: GPO, 1895), xxxiv. (Hereafter, Strike Report.)
      twelve thousand: Carwardine, 23.
      library enrolled only: Strike Report, xxi.
      "from which all": Carwardine, 19.
217   *"No private individual"*: Ely, 460.

218   *"the corporation trims"*: Peter Quinion of the *Pittsburgh Times*, quoted in Car-
       wardine, 24.
       The company employed: Strike Report, xxii.
       "This is a corporation": Carwardine, 24–25.
       "each new superior": Ely, 463–64.
       The job of porter: Kelly, 99–100.
219   *"a manifestly inadequate"*: Strike Report, 580.
220   *"a most unfortunate thing"*: Ibid., 579.
       "because they only got": Ibid., 426.
       From July 1893: Ibid., xxi.
221   *"There may have lived"*: Darrow, 68.
222   *"we concluded that"*: Strike Report, 129.
223   *"The great trouble"*: Quoted in Eggert, 214.
       "Today there is": The article was entered into the record of the strike commis-
       sion by Debs; *Strike Report*, 132.
224   *"all grades"*: Strike Report, xxxviii.
       On June 15: Kelly, 102. Kelly and others, including the US Strike Commis-
       sion, report Curtiss's last name as "Curtis," but Carwardine, who reprinted her
       letter in his published account of the strike, has it as "Curtiss."
225   *Cleveland himself*: For the railroad connections of the Cleveland cabinet, see
       Eggert, 137–38.
226   *"legal time bomb"*: Eggert, 151.
       On June 27: Ginger, 122.
       The Chicago Tribune: Ibid., 126.
       "aid in the repression": Milchrist to Olney, June 30, 1894. The source of this
       and all other communications among Olney, Milchrist, Walker, and Arnold
       referred to in this section is the appendix to the *Annual Report of the Attor-
       ney-General of the United States for the Year 1896* (Washington, DC: GPO,
       1896), 55–102.
228   *"Probably every man"*: Strike Report, 228.
       "The trouble at Chicago": Speech at Cooper Union, New York City, Oct. 27,
       1896, in Altgeld, 656.
229   *"I realized my anomalous"*: Darrow, 58.
230   *"I did not regard"*: Ibid., 61.
       "If there are still": Ibid., 47.
       unanimous Supreme Court: The decision is In re Debs, 158 US 564 (1895).
231   *"The A.R.U. was destroyed"*: Darrow, 48.
       "the strike never": Chandler, The Railroads, 131.
       only his arrest: Debs's testimony is in *Strike Report*, 143. Debs recalled that his
       arrest took place on July 7, but that is contradicted by other evidence, includ-
       ing a communication from Arnold to Olney on July 10 stating that the arrest

had taken place that day. A communication from Walker to Olney on July 9
indicates plainly that the indictments allowing for the arrest had not yet been
handed up.

He recounted: Kelly, 221–22.

"We have been brought": Eggert, 172.

232 *Wages fell:* For an outline of the decline of labor power in the years after Pullman, see Dubofsky and Dulles, 169.

233 *"It would be impossible":* Ibid., 567.

14. The Empire Builder

234 *"unassuming, matter-of-fact":* Merriam's unpublished "Reflections and Impressions of E. H. Harriman" is reproduced in Kennan, vol. 1, 186ff.

235 *"had a grand time":* Satterlee, 332.

236 *"had not added":* Statement by J. H. McClement, cited in Kennan, "The Chicago & Alton Case: A Misunderstood Transaction," *North American Review*
203, no. 722 (January 1916), 36.

"you and Mr. Harriman": Schiff to Hill, Sept. 25, 1899, in Adler, *Jacob H.
Schiff: His Life and Letters*, vol. 1, 145.

237 *"a summer cruise":* Burroughs, Muir, and Grinnell, xxi. The quote is from
Harriman's preface.

His youngest son: Harriman, 3.

Clinton Hart Merriam: Wilfred H. Osgood, "Biographical Memoir of Clinton
Hart Merriam," *National Academy of Sciences*, 1944.

238 *"a man of means":* Merriam, "Reflections," in Kennan, vol. 1, 186.

"He thought there": Ibid.

"unwilling to accept": Muir, 8.

239 *"Pray for me":* Worster, 359.

"no more distinguished": Kennan, vol. 1, 187.

"abloom with wild": Ibid., 193.

240 *"of the blessed ministry":* Muir, 35.

"I soon saw": Ibid., 10.

241 *"fairy tale":* Merriam, "Reflections," in Kennan, vol. 1, 197–98.

242 *"Oh, that was under":* See Alton A. Lindsey, "The Harriman Alaska Expedition of 1899," *BioScience*, June 1978. Averell Harriman's recollection appears
in his introduction to the article.

"never before seen": *New York Times*, July 29, 1899.

"an entire success": *New York Times* and *New York Tribune*, July 31, 1899.

"resembled a floating": *Los Angeles Times*, Aug. 1, 1899.

"the glaciers": Ibid.

243 *"virtual breach of trust":* Kennan, vol. 1, 219.

"*Not so fast*": Kahn, 16.

244   "*I sometimes have wondered*": Stilwell, 24.

245   *set his strategy*: For details of the acquisition transactions, see Kennan, vol. 1, 234ff.

246   "*the Union Pacific purchased*": Ibid., 235.

"*we would be getting rid*": United States of America v. the Union Pacific Railroad Co., et al., vol. 10, 4731.

248   "*lacked an extensive system*": Trottman, 283.

"*Mr. Harriman may*": Interstate Commerce Commission, *In the Matter of Consolidations and Combinations of Carriers*, Report No. 943, July 11, 1907, in *Decisions of the Interstate Commerce Commission of the United States, November 1906 to December 1907*, vol. 12 (Washington, DC: GPO, 1908).

249   "*a master stroke*": Dodge, 76.

"*Some people also say*": Kennedy to Hill, Feb. 6, 1901, cited in Klein, *The Life and Legend of E. H. Harriman*, 219.

"*We have bought*": Kennan, vol. 1, 241.

251   "*called for blue-prints*": Ibid., 244.

252   *ninety feet*: See Ibid., 246.

253   "*hammered to the bottom*": Oscar King Davis, "The Lucin Cut-Off," *Century Illustrated Monthly*, Jan. 1906, 461.

254   "*The day on*": Ibid., 467.

15. The Quest for the Burlington

256   *On October 3*: Klein, *The Life and Legend of E. H. Harriman*, 149.

"*a railroad from Nowhere*": Smalley, 204.

257   *In 1875 the road*: Daggett, 270.

"*positively repugnant*": Villard, vol. 1, 7.

259   "*As a stock-waterer*": Clews, *Twenty-Eight Years*, 211.

"*showing immense*": Ibid., 213.

"*There is probably*": Ibid., 214.

261   "*I hate all white people*": There is some confusion about the date of Sitting Bull's speech. Among others, Dee Brown, in *Bury My Heart at Wounded Knee*, 494, places it at the "last spike" ceremony on September 8. Contemporary accounts of that event do not mention Sitting Bull and identify Evarts as the main speaker; nor is Grant mentioned among the attendees (see *New York Times*, Sept. 9, 1883). Villard, in his own memoirs (vol. 2, 311), is among the sources who more credibly place it at the Bismarck cornerstone laying, which occurred on September 5, though Villard makes no mention of the discrepancy between Sitting Bull's speech and the prepared text.

"*I cannot quite*": Grodinsky, *Transcontinental Railroad Strategy*, 206.

262 *"a princely edifice"*: Villard, vol. 2, 316.
     "He was hailed": Ibid., 324.

263 *"would again mean"*: Ibid., 365.
     "a ghastly sarcasm": New York Times, Aug. 17, 1893.

264 James J. Hill was the epitome: Details of Hill's early life are from Pyle, vol. 1,
     3ff, and Albro Martin, 7ff.
     a rail connection: Albro Martin, 33.
     Hill was on hand: Ibid., 45–46.

265 *In return for*: Ibid., 131.
     But Hill was confident: See Hill, letter to Great Northern stockholders, July 1,
     1912, in Bruchey, 1.

267 *"What we want"*: Albro Martin, 366.
     "threw lines across": Grodinsky, Transcontinental Railroad Strategy, 292.

268 *"But it had no terrors"*: Pyle, vol. 1, 334.
     "Mr. Hill is a law": Grodinsky, Transcontinental Railroad Strategy, 293.

269 *"There can be"*: Overton, 247.
     "has not been run": Hill to Mount Stephen, Oct. 20 and 25, 1894, in Albro
     Martin, 442.

270 *Hill's elite lawyers*: Ibid., 446.
     "London memorandum": Ibid., 453.
     "form a permanent": Ibid.

272 *Invited to dine*: Birmingham, 192.
     "Only I give": Ibid.

273 *agreement had been reached*: The arrangement was outlined in Schiff to Hill,
     Feb. 9, 1897, in Adler, Jacob H. Schiff: His Life and Letters, vol. 1, 88–89.
     "Nothing was said": Albro Martin, 484.

274 *offered to award*: Pyle, vol. 2, 42.
     "Mr. Harriman has been": Schiff to Hill, Sept. 25, 1899, in Adler, Jacob H.
     Schiff: His Life and Letters, vol. 1, 89–90.
     Harriman himself never: See Klein, The Life and Legend of E. H. Harriman,
     158.

275 *By July 25*: Kennan, vol. 1, 291. See also Overton, 249–50.
     "found themselves up": Pyle, vol. 2, 139.
     The best three: See Ibid., 113.

276 *"Hill did not"*: Morgan testimony, United States of America v. Northern Securi-
     ties Co. et al., vol. 1, 328.
     "The Burlington lets us": Ibid., 120.
     "Wall Street would soon": Overton, 252.

277 *"neither directly nor indirectly"*: Schiff to Morgan, May 16, 1901, in Adler, Jacob
     H. Schiff: His Life and Letters, vol. 1, 102–7.
     "I accepted": Ibid.

Baker's own recollection: Paine, 201ff.

278   *"replied with platitudes":* Schiff to Morgan, May 16, 1901, in Adler, *Jacob H. Schiff: His Life and Letters,* vol. 1, 102–7.
      "Very well": Kennan, vol. 1, 296.
      "a hostile act": Satterlee, 354.

279   *"particularly . . . a constant":* Schiff to Morgan, May 16, 1901.

16. Peacock Alley

283   *"To belong to":* Baruch, 135.
284   *"On an afternoon":* Ibid. 136.
286   *"What became of it?":* New York Daily Tribune, Mar. 19, 1902.
      "the assumption that": Noyes, *The Market Place,* 195.
      "were typically": Grant, 39.
287   *"At the beginning":* E. G. Campbell, 331–32.
      "have been exorbitant": "Resolutions of the Second National Agricultural Congress," in Chandler, *The Railroads,* 188.
288   *"The revival":* Schiff to Fleming, Sept. 1, 1897, in Adler, *Jacob H. Schiff: His Life and Letters,* vol. 1, 32.
      "the bull market incarnate": James Grant, 56.
289   *"All she has":* New York Sun, May 2, 1901.
      "As speculators": Clews, *Twenty-Eight Years,* 437.
      "The female character": Fowler, 450.
290   *What the Curb's:* For a picture of the Curb at the turn of the twentieth century, see Sobel, *The Curbstone Brokers,* 107ff.
      "specious frauds": Clews, *Twenty-Eight Years,* 20.
291   *"once in a generation":* New York Sun, Feb. 11, 1897.
292   *"an impetus to trade":* "The Party of the Century," *Quest,* February 1997.
293   *"lavish entertainments":* New York Times, Jan. 24, 1897.
      "With all the people": Ibid., Jan. 23, 1897.
      "Twelve hundred invitations": Ibid., Feb. 11, 1897.
      On February 7: Ibid., Feb. 7, 1897.
294   *"To the cautious":* Schiff to Cassel, Mar. 20, 1901, in Adler, *Jacob H. Schiff: His Life and Letters,* vol. 1, 34.
      "Buying orders seemed": Noyes, *The Market Place,* 194–95.
      "panic struck": Baruch, 136.

17. Lions Guarding the Way

296   *Morgan boarded:* For Morgan's crossing and subsequent art purchases see Satterlee, 350ff.

297 *"Nobody will ever"*: Satterlee, 353.

   escorting an advance: Albro Martin, 498.

   "I feel it is": Schiff to Hill, April 8, 1901, in Adler, *Jacob H. Schiff: His Life and Letters,* vol. 1, 100.

298 *Hill replied:* Hill to Schiff, April 9, [1901], in Albro Martin, 498.

   "the Union Pacific interests": Schiff to Morgan, May 16, 1901, in Adler, *Jacob H. Schiff: His Life and Letters,* vol. 1, 105.

299 *"represented the interests"*: Schiff testimony, *United States of America v. Northern Securities Co., et al.,* vol. 1, 260ff.

300 *"Early theories"*: *New York Times,* April 7, 1901.

301 *"But Keene had"*: Baruch, 156.

   "He would buy": Pyle, vol. 2, 141.

302 *"I sold all"*: Ellis to Hill, May 9, 1901, in Haeg, 136.

   Another investor who: Pyle, vol. 2, 146. The same transaction was reported by Satterlee, 354–55.

   "deeply incensed": *New York Times,* May 28, 1901.

303 *"I answered that"*: Pyle, vol. 2, 143–44.

   His reaction: For an authoritative debunking of the legend, see Albro Martin, 499.

   "Some of them": Hill testimony, *United States of America v. Northern Securities Co., et al.,* vol. 1, 84.

304 *based his recollection:* Schiff to Morgan, May 16, 1901, in Adler, *Jacob H. Schiff: His Life and Letters,* vol. 1, 106.

   "But you can't": Kennan, vol. 1, 304.

   "You are the boss": Hill to Mount Stephen, July 22, 1904, in Albro Martin, 500.

305 *"by the roots"*: *New York Tribune,* April 28, 1901.

   "perched high": Ibid., April 30, 1901.

306 *Before the first hour:* For volume statistics, see *New York Sun* and *New York Tribune,* April 30, 1901.

   "Union Pacific Control": *New York Times,* May 1, 1901.

307 *"I certainly have not"*: *New York Sun,* May 3, 1901. Harriman's words were reported with slight variations by different newspapers. See *New York Times,* May 3, 1901: "I have not let go of any of my holdings."

   "it was a common": *United States of America v. Northern Securities Co., et al.,* vol. 1, 335.

   "not since the Vanderbilt": *New York Times,* May 1, 1901.

   "It's nice to own": Birmingham, 298.

308 *"a million every minute"*: *New York Sun,* May 1, 1901.

309 *"in the ordinary"*: Pyle, vol. 2, 147.

   "there were parties": *United States of America v. Northern Securities Co., et al.,* vol. 1, 188.

18. "A Good-Sized Panic"

310   *Bernard Baruch made a habit:* Baruch, 141.
312   *"the harmony and community":* Schiff to Morgan, May 16, 1901, in Adler,
        Jacob H. Schiff: His Life and Letters, vol. 1, 106.
        "We had reorganized": United States of America v. Northern Securities Co., et al.,
        vol. 1, 338.
        Harriman, meanwhile: Kennan, vol. 1, 305.
313   *"bothered me somewhat":* Ibid.
        "agreed unanimously": Kahn, 45.
314   *Harriman returned:* Kennan, vol. 1, 306.
        especially since the shares: For the prices of Northern Pacific from May 3
        through May 10, see *Commercial & Financial Chronicle,* May 4 and 11, 1901.
315   *"the silver fox":* Baruch, 156.
        "home . . . from Monday": New York Sun, May 7, 1901.
        a new record: New York Times, May 7, 1901.
316   *"to catch Mr. Hill":* New York Tribune, May 7, 1901.
        "The wonderful advances": Ibid.
        He had been instructed: New York Times, May 12, 1901.
317   *"The first response":* Baruch, 144.
        "The Control of N.P.": New York Tribune, May 8, 1901.
        "stock duel": New York Sun, May 8, 1901.
319   *"Panic Reigns":* New York Times, May 9, 1901.
320   *"For several months":* New York Sun, May 9, 1901.
        "Do I look": New York Times, May 9, 1901.
        "a good-sized panic": United States of America v. Northern Securities Co., et al.,
        vol. 1, 48.
        "All I can do": Kennan, vol. 1, 316.

19. Exhaustion

322   *"an incident putting":* New York Times, May 12, 1901.
        In Albany: New York Tribune, May 10, 1901; New York Times, May 10, 1901.
323   *"Not slowly":* New York Times, May 10, 1901.
324   *"lost heavily in stocks":* Ibid.
        As would be recounted: Lefèvre, 30. Lefèvre's version of Livermore's blunder
        has entered Wall Street lore but has not been conclusively questioned by any-
        one, including by Livermore, who later published his own book about stock
        trading.
325   *His order to sell:* Smitten, 46–47.
326   *"I am not in the habit":* New York Sun, May 10, 1901.
327   *The peculiarities:* Fraser, 258.

"Risks and panics": Clews, *Twenty-Eight Years*, 160–61.

328 *"It looks as if"*: *New York Times*, May 9, 1901.

    "A Policy of Life": See, for example, *New York Sun*, May 10, 1901, p. 5; and *New York Tribune*, May 10, p. 3.

329 *"some statement"*: See Josephson, *The Robber Barons*, 441.

    Morgan's most recent: Strouse, xi.

    Josephson got it: See Corey, 301.

330 *"A few men"*: See ibid., 366.

    "The recent growth": King, 218.

331 *"There's been no wreck"*: *New York Times*, May 10, 1901.

20. The Trustbuster

332 *He was scanning*: *New York Times*, Sept. 7, 1901.

333 *"Power when wielded"*: Henry Adams, 417.

    "Go Slow": Bishop, vol. 1, 154.

    "During the last": Teddy Roosevelt's first annual address is at https://miller center.org/the-presidency/presidential-speeches/december-3-1901-first-annu al-message (accessed September 1, 2019).

334 *"The President has written"*: Bishop, vol. 1, 160.

335 *"How is Schiff?"*: Adler, *Jacob H. Schiff: His Life and Letters*, vol. 1, 108.

336 *"We didn't want"*: *United States of America v. Northern Securities Co., et al.*, vol. 1, 345.

    "I wanted to put": Ibid., 356.

337 *"was a foregone"*: Albro Martin, 509.

    "a great 'stock'": Schiff to Harriman, Sept. 11, 1901, in Klein, *The Life and Legend of E. H. Harriman*, 238.

    "Although the Union": Schiff to Ernest Cassel, Nov. 11, 1901, in Adler, *Jacob H. Schiff: His Life and Letters*, vol. 1, 110.

338 *"the people that"*: *United States of America v. Northern Securities Co., et al.*, vol. 1, 1343.

    On September 19: See, for example, *New York Tribune*, Sept. 20, 1902.

    "Suddenly, this week": Adams to Cameron, Feb. 23, 1902, in Ford, 374.

339 *"Not since the"*: *New York Tribune*, Sept. 21, 1902.

    "If we have done": Bishop, vol. 1, 184–85.

    The court issued: *Northern Securities Co. v. United States*, 193 US 197 (1904).

341 *"I could carve"*: Harbaugh, 162.

    "broke up our": Holmes to Sir Francis Pollock, Feb. 9, 1921, in Howe, vol. 2, 63–64.

    "a piece of conscienceless": Klein, *The Life and Legend of E. H. Harriman*, 313.

    According to Harriman's: Kennan, vol. 1, 389.

342   *"a veritable bonanza"*: Ibid., 394.
      "I think it was": Carl Snyder, "Harriman: 'Colossus of Roads,'" *American
      Monthly Review of Reviews*, January 1907, 48.

21. "Malefactors of Great Wealth"

343   *"difficult and complex"*: Kahn, 54.
      "the crisis": Ibid., 51.
344   *"We are not"*: New York Tribune, Jan. 31, 1905.
      "His war on": Adams to Elizabeth Cameron, April 19, 1903, in Ford, 405.
      "The big New York": Roosevelt to Schurz, Dec. 24, 1903, in Morison, vol. 3,
      679.
345   *"Roosevelt fairly"*: Corey, 371.
346   *"a perfectly cynical"*: Roosevelt to Lodge, Oct. 8, 1906, in Bishop, vol. 2, 32.
      "The Harriman Extermination": Kahn, 52.
347   *"It may be only"*: George Kennan, "The Chicago and Alton Case," *North
      American Review*, Jan. 1916.
      "He told me": Kahn, 53.
      "He always made": Ibid., 55.
      "If you let": Interstate Commerce Commission, *In the Matter of Consolidations
      and Combinations of Carriers*, Report No. 943, July 11, 1907, in *Decisions of the
      Interstate Commerce Commission of the United States, November 1906 to Decem-
      ber 1907*, vol. 12 (Washington, DC: GPO, 1908), 280–81.
348   *"a veritable cyclone"*: Kahn, 56.
      "the suggestion that": Roosevelt to William Z. Ripley, Jan. 19, 1916, in Ripley,
      "Federal Financial Railway Regulation."
      Upon receiving: See Roosevelt to Bonaparte, July 10, 1907, and July 13, 1907,
      in Morison, vol. 5, 710, 716.
349   *"we will get"*: New York Times, Jan. 5, 1906.
350   *"I would hate"*: Ibid., Mar. 15, 1907. Other versions of this quote were more
      ambiguous; see, for example, *New York Tribune*, Mar. 15, 1907. ("I'd hate to
      tell you who could give you correct information on the situation.")
      "Everyone is frightened": Strouse, 574.
      "hired megaphone": Ibid., 616.
      "a drunken man's": New York Times, Nov. 14, 1907.
      "if hard times": Roosevelt to Henry Lee Higginson, Aug. 12, 1907, in Morison,
      vol. 5, 746.
      The occasion was: Address of President Roosevelt on the Occasion of the Laying of
      the Corner Stone of the Pilgrim Memorial Monument (Washington, DC: GPO,
      1907).
351   *"My speech told"*: Roosevelt to Kermit Roosevelt, Aug. 21, 1907, in Morison,
      vol. 5, 760.

352 *"at least as"*: See Bishop, vol. 2, 61.

353 *"We were in"*: Roosevelt to William Dudley Foulke, Oct. 24, 1908, in Morison, vol. 6, 1317.

In an exchange: S. Doc. No. 212, 59th Cong., 2nd Sess., Jan. 12, 1907. See also Hiltzik, 41–51.

355 *"diversion dams and"*: Roosevelt's message can be found in *Congressional Record*, vol. 41, (Senate, January 12, 1907), 1028-29.

"Very few there were": Kahn, 56.

356 *Harriman listened*: Kennan, vol. 2, 315.

"He has taken": *Commercial and Financial Chronicle*, April 11, 1908.

"Harriman Cash": *New York Times*, April 9, 1908.

The following spring: Kennan, vol. 2, 345.

"E.H. Harriman will go": *New York Tribune*, Aug. 25, 1909.

357 *He never left*: Kennan, vol. 2, 346.

"He did not believe": Schiff to Ernest Cassel, Sept. 12, 1909, in Adler, *Jacob H. Schiff: His Life and Letters*, vol. 1, 117.

358 *"Your firm is"*: Pujo Report, part 15, 1053–54, 1061.

"Father made a": Strouse, 671.

"The long preparation": Satterlee, 560.

"nervous depression": Strouse, 676.

"thin, exhausted": Ibid.

359 *"our archaic"*: Pujo Report, 148.

"Big railroad systems": Brandeis, 162.

360 *"practically all"*: See ibid., 135.

"served, substantially": Ibid., 167.

361 *"succeeded in becoming"*: Ibid., 169.

As recently as: Stover, 242.

362 *On December 2*: United States v. Union Pacific Railroad Company, 226 US 61 (1912).

Epilogue: The End of an Epoch

366 *The consequences*: See Gallamore and Meyer, 60.

"much was made": Ibid., 55.

Once the prime: The statistics in this section come from ibid., 396ff.

367 *"survived more"*: Ibid., 401.

368 *"The reasonable"*: The author is indebted to Andrew Roberts (*Churchill: Walking with Destiny*) for exhuming this epigram.

"turned on the": Schumpeter, *Business Cycles*, 383.

"the unexampled": Trachtenberg, 57.

"During the 1880s": Chandler, *The Visible Hand*, 147.

369 *"the essential fact"*: Schumpeter, *Capitalism, Socialism and Democracy*, 83.

"made possible": Chandler, *The Visible Hand*, 99.

370   *"hardy pioneers"*: Brandeis, 135.

"entitled to share": Ibid., 136.

"the scrambled disorder": Frederick Lewis Allen, "The Great Pierpont Morgan," *Harper's Magazine*, December 1948, 28.

371   *"the personal dictatorship"*: Corey, 357.

372   *"the leadership"*: Klein, *The Life and Legend of E. H. Harriman*, 446.

Bibliography

Ackerman, Kenneth D. *The Gold Ring: Jim Fisk, Jay Gould, and Black Friday, 1869.* New York: Dodd, Mead, 1988.

Ackerman, William K. *Historical Sketch of the Illinois-Central Railroad.* Chicago: Fergus, 1890.

Adams, Charles Francis. *Charles Francis Adams: An Autobiography.* Boston: Houghton Mifflin, 1916.

Adams, Charles F., Jr., and Henry Adams. *Chapters of Erie, and Other Essays.* Boston: J. R. Osgood, 1871.

Adams, Henry. *The Education of Henry Adams.* Boston: Houghton Mifflin, 1918.

Adler, Cyrus. *Jacob Henry Schiff: A Biographical Sketch.* New York: American Jewish Committee, 1921.

———. *Jacob H. Schiff: His Life and Letters.* 2 vols. Garden City, NY: Doubleday, Doran, 1928.

Altgeld, John P. *Live Questions.* Chicago: Geo. S. Bowen & Son, 1899.

Armstrong, Margaret. *Five Generations: Life and Letters of an American Family, 1750–1900.* New York: Harper & Brothers, 1930.

Bain, David Haward. *Empire Express: Building the First Transcontinental Railroad.* New York: Viking, 1999.

Barron, Clarence W. *They Told Barron: Conversations and Revelations of an American Pepys in Wall Street.* New York: Harper & Brothers, 1930.

Baruch, Bernard. *Baruch: My Own Story.* New York: Henry Holt, 1957.

Birmingham, Stephen. *"Our Crowd": The Great Jewish Families of New York.* New York: Open Road, 2015.

Bishop, Joseph Bucklin. *Theodore Roosevelt and His Time Shown in His Own Letters.* 2 vols. New York: C. Scribner's Sons, 1920.

Brandeis, Louis D. *Other People's Money, and How the Bankers Use It.* New York: Frederick A. Stokes, 1914.

Browder, Clifford. *The Money Game in Old New York: Daniel Drew and His Times.* Lexington: University Press of Kentucky, 1986.

Brown, Dee. *Bury My Heart at Wounded Knee.* New York: Henry Holt, 1970.

———. *Hear That Lonesome Whistle Blow: Railroads in the West.* New York: Holt, Rinehart and Winston, 1977.

Bruchey, Stuart W., ed. *Memoirs of Three Railroad Pioneers.* New York: Arno, 1981.

Bryce, James. *The American Commonwealth.* 2 vols. Philadelphia: John D. Morris, 1906.

Buchanan, Joseph R. *The Story of a Labor Agitator.* New York: Outlook, 1903.

Burr, Anna Robeson. *The Portrait of a Banker: James Stillman, 1850–1918.* New York: Duffield, 1927.

Burroughs, John, John Muir, and George Bird Grinnell. Preface by E. H. Harriman. *Alaska.* Vol. 1, *Narrative, Glaciers, Natives.* New York: Doubleday, Page, 1901.

Campbell, E. G. *The Reorganization of the American Railroad System, 1893–1900.* New York: Columbia University Press, 1938.

Campbell, Persia. *Mary Williamson Harriman.* New York: Columbia University Press, 1960.

Carnegie, Andrew. *The Autobiography of Andrew Carnegie.* New York: PublicAffairs, 2011.

Carwardine, Rev. William H. *The Pullman Strike.* Chicago: Charles H. Kerr, 1894.

Case, Theresa Ann. *The Great Southwest Railroad Strike and Free Labor.* College Station: Texas A&M University Press, 2010.

Chandler, Alfred D., Jr., ed. *The Railroads: The Nation's First Big Business.* New York: Harcourt, Brace & World, 1965.

———. *The Visible Hand: The Managerial Revolution in American Business.* Cambridge, Mass.: Belknap Press, 1977.

Chernow, Ron. *The House of Morgan: An American Banking Dynasty and the Rise of Modern Finance.* Boston: Atlantic Monthly Press, 1990.

———. *Titan: The Life of John D. Rockefeller, Sr.* New York: Vintage, 1998.

Clews, Henry. *Twenty-Eight Years in Wall Street.* New York: Irving, 1888.

———. *Fifty Years in Wall Street.* New York: Irving, 1908.

Cobb, Stephen G. *Reverend William Carwardine and the Pullman Strike of 1894.* Lewiston, NY: Edwin Mellen, 1992.

Cohen, Naomi W. *Jacob H. Schiff: A Study in American Jewish Leadership.* Hanover, NH: Brandeis University Press, 1999.

Coit, Margaret L. *Mr. Baruch.* Boston: Houghton Mifflin, 1957.

Corey, Lewis. *The House of Morgan: A Social Biography of the Masters of Money.* New York: Grosset & Dunlap, 1930.

Croffut, W. A. *The Vanderbilts and the Story of Their Fortune.* London: Griffith, Farran, Okeden & Welsh, 1886.

Daggett, Stuart. *Railroad Reorganization.* Boston: Houghton Mifflin, 1908.

Dall, Caroline H. *My First Holiday, or Letters Home from Colorado, Utah, and California*. Boston: Roberts Brothers, 1881.

Darrow, Clarence. *The Story of My Life*. New York: Charles Scribner's Sons, 1932.

Davis, John P. *The Union Pacific Railway: A Study in Railway Politics, History, and Economics*. Chicago: S. C. Griggs, 1894.

Debs, Eugene V. *Debs: His Life, Writings and Speeches*. Chicago: Charles H. Kerr, 1908.

Dewing, Arthur S. *A History of the National Cordage Company*. Cambridge, Mass.: Harvard University Press, 1913.

Dodge, Grenville M. *How We Built the Union Pacific Railway*. Council Bluffs, Iowa: Monarch Printing, [1910?].

Douglas, George H. *All Aboard! The Railroad in American Life*. New York: Paragon, 1992.

Douglass, Frederick. *The Complete Autobiographies of Frederick Douglass*. Radford, Va.: Wilder, 2008.

Dubovsky, Melvyn, and Foster Rhea Dulles. *Labor in America: A History*. Wheeling, Ill.: Harland Davidson, 1999.

Ducker, James H. *Men of the Steel Rails: Workers on the Atchison, Topeka & Santa Fe Railroad, 1869–1900*. Lincoln: University of Nebraska Press, 1983.

Eckenrode, H. J., and Pocohontas Wight Edmunds. *E. H. Harriman: The Little Giant of Wall Street*. New York: Greenberg, 1933.

Eggert, Gerald G. *Railroad Labor Disputes: The Beginnings of Federal Strike Policy*. Ann Arbor: University of Michigan Press, 1967.

Elmer, Isabel Lincoln. *Cinderella Rockefeller*. New York: Freundlich, 1987.

Foner, Philip S. *The Great Labor Uprising of 1877*. New York: Monad Press, 1977.

Ford, Worthington Chauncey, ed. *Letters of Henry Adams (1892–1918)*. New York: Houghton Mifflin, 1928.

Fowler, William Worthington. *Ten Years in Wall Street*. Hartford, Conn.: Worthington, Dustin, 1870.

Fraser, Steve. *Every Man a Speculator: A History of Wall Street in American Life*. New York: HarperCollins, 2005.

Gallamore, Robert E., and John R. Meyer. *American Railroads: Decline and Renaissance in the Twentieth Century*. Cambridge, Mass.: Harvard University Press, 2014.

George, Charles B. *Forty Years on the Rail*. Chicago: R. R. Donnelly & Sons, 1887.

Ginger, Ray. *The Bending Cross: A Biography of Eugene Victor Debs*. New Brunswick, NJ: Rutgers University Press, 1949.

Gordon, John Steele. *The Scarlet Woman of Wall Street: Jay Gould, Jim Fisk, Cornelius Vanderbilt, the Erie Railroad Wars, and the Birth of Wall Street*. New York: Weidenfeld & Nicholson, 1988.

Grant, James. *Bernard M. Baruch: The Adventures of a Wall Street Legend*. New York: John Wiley & Sons, 1997.

Grant, Julia Dent. *The Personal Memoirs of Julia Dent Grant*. New York: G. P. Putnam's Sons, 1975.

Grodinsky, Julius. *Jay Gould: His Business Career 1867–1892*. Philadelphia: University of Pennsylvania Press, 1957.

———. *Transcontinental Railway Strategy, 1869–1893: A Study of Businessmen*. Philadelphia, University of Pennsylvania Press, 1962.

Haeg, Larry. *Harriman vs. Hill: Wall Street's Great Railroad War*. Minneapolis: University of Minnesota Press, 2013.

Harbaugh, William Henry. *Power and Responsibility: The Life and Times of Theodore Roosevelt*. New York: Farrar, Straus and Cudahy, 1961.

Harriman, E. Roland. *I Reminisce*. New York: Doubleday, 1975.

Harris, Neil. *Cultural Excursions*. Chicago: University of Chicago Press, 1990.

Hiltzik, Michael. *Colossus: Hoover Dam and the Making of the American Century*. New York: Simon & Schuster, 2010.

Holbrook, Stewart H. *The Story of American Railroads*. New York: Crown, 1947.

Hovey, Carl. *The Life Story of J. Pierpont Morgan: A Biography*. New York: Sturgis & Walton, 1911.

Howard, Ernest. *Wall Street Fifty Years After Erie*. Boston: Stratford, 1923.

Howe, Mark DeWolfe, ed. *Holmes-Pollock Letters: The Correspondence of Mr. Justice Holmes and Sir Frederick Pollock, 1874–1932*. Cambridge, Mass.: Harvard University Press, 1961.

Humason, William Lawrence. *From the Atlantic Surf to the Golden Gate*. Hartford, Conn.: Press of William C. Humason, 1869.

Hyndman, H. M. *The Chicago Riots and the Class War in the United States*. London: Swan Sonnenschein, Lowrey, 1883.

Johnson, Walter. *River of Dark Dreams: Slavery and Empire in the Cotton Kingdom*. Cambridge, Mass.: Harvard University Press, 2013.

Josephson, Matthew. *The Politicos*. New York: Harcourt, Brace & World, 1938.

———. *The Robber Barons*. New York: Harcourt, Brace, 1934.

Kahn, Otto H. *Our Economic and Other Problems: A Financier's Point of View*. New York: George H. Doran, 1920.

Kelly, Jack. *The Edge of Anarchy: The Railroad Barons, the Gilded Age, and the Greatest Labor Uprising in America*. New York: St. Martin's, 2019.

Kennan, George. *E. H. Harriman: A Biography*. 2 vols. Boston: Houghton Mifflin, 1922.

King, Willford Isbell. *The Wealth and Income of the People of the United States*. New York: Macmillan, 1922.

Klein, Maury. *The Life and Legend of E. H. Harriman*. Chapel Hill: University of North Carolina Press, 2000.

———. *The Life and Legend of Jay Gould*. Baltimore: Johns Hopkins University Press, 1997.

———. *Union Pacific*. Vol. 1, *1862–1893*. New York: Doubleday, 1987.

Kolko, Gabriel. *Railroads and Regulation, 1877–1916*. Princeton, NJ: Princeton University Press, 1965.

Larrabee, William. *The Railroad Question*. Chicago: Schulte, 1893.

Lefèvre, Edwin. *Reminiscences of a Stock Operator*. New York: George H. Doran, 1923.

Loomis, Erik. *A History of America in Ten Strikes*. New York: New Press, 2018.

Lubetkin, M. John. *Jay Cooke's Gamble: The Northern Pacific Railroad, the Sioux, and the Panic of 1873*. Norman: University of Oklahoma Press, 2006.

Martin, Albro. *James J. Hill and the Opening of the Northwest*. New York: Oxford University Press, 1976.

Martin, Frederick Townsend. *The Passing of the Idle Rich*. Garden City, NY: Doubleday, Page, 1911.

Matz, Mary Jane. *The Many Lives of Otto Kahn*. New York: Macmillan, 1963.

McAllister, Ward. *Society As I Have Found It*. New York: Cassell, 1890.

McFeely, William S. *Grant: A Biography*. New York: W. W. Norton, 1981.

Medbery, James K. *Men and Mysteries of Wall Street*. New York: R. Worthington, 1878.

Moody, John. *The Masters of Capital: A Chronicle of Wall Street*. New Haven, Conn.: Yale University Press, 1919.

———. *The Railroad Builders: A Chronicle of the Welding of the States*. New Haven, Conn.: Yale University Press, 1919.

———. *The Truth About Trusts*. New York: Moody, 1904.

Morison, Elting E., ed. *The Letters of Theodore Roosevelt*. Vols. 3, 4, and 5. Cambridge, Mass.: Harvard University Press, 1951–52.

Morris, Lloyd R. *Incredible New York: High Life and Low Life from 1850 to 1950*. Syracuse, NY: Syracuse University Press, 1996.

Mott, Edward Harold. *Between the Ocean and the Lakes: The Story of Erie*. New York: John S. Collins, 1900.

Muir, John. *Edward Henry Harriman*. Garden City, NY: Doubleday, Page, 1912.

Nasaw, David. *Andrew Carnegie*. New York: Penguin, 2006.

Norris, Frank. *The Octopus: A Story of California*. Garden City, NY: Doubleday, 1901.

Noyes, Alexander Dana. *Forty Years of American Finance*. New York: G. P. Putnam's Sons, 1909.

———. *The Market Place: Reminiscences of a Financial Editor*. New York: Greenwood, 1938.

Oberholtzer, Ellis Paxson. *Jay Cooke, Financier of the Civil War*. 2 vols. Philadelphia: George W. Jacobs, 1907.

O'Connor, Richard. *Gould's Millions*. Garden City, NY: Doubleday, 1962.

Orsi, Richard J. *Sunset Limited: The Southern Pacific Railroad and the Development of the American West, 1850–1930*. Berkeley: University of California Press, 2005.

Overton, Richard C. *Burlington Route: A History of the Burlington Lines*. New York: Alfred A. Knopf, 1965.

Paine, Albert Bigelow. *George Fisher Baker: A Biography*. New York: G. P. Putnam's Sons, 1933.

Papke, David Ray. *The Pullman Case: The Clash of Labor and Capital in Industrial America*. Lawrence: University Press of Kansas, 1999.

Powderly, Terence Vincent. *The Path I Trod: The Autobiograpy of Terence V. Powderly*. Edited by Harry J. Carman, Henry David, and Paul N. Guthrie. New York: Columbia University Press, 1940.

———. *Thirty Years of Labor, 1859–1889*. Columbus, Ohio: Excelsior, 1889.

Pyle, Joseph Gilpin. *The Life of James J. Hill*. 2 vols. New York: Peter Smith, 1936.

Reid, Whitelaw. *After the War: A Southern Tour*. Cincinnati, Ohio: Moore, Wilstach & Baldwin, 1866.

Richardson, Albert D. *Beyond the Mississippi: From the Great River to the Great Ocean*. Hartford, Conn.: American, 1867.

———. *Garnered Sheaves from the Writings of Albert D. Richardson*. Hartford, Conn.: Columbian, 1871.

Richter, Amy G. *Home on the Rails: Women, the Railroad, and the Rise of Public Domesticity*. Chapel Hill: University of North Carolina Press, 2005.

Ripley, William Z. *Railroads Finance & Organization*. New York: Longmans, Green, 1915.

Satterlee, Herbert L. *J. Pierpont Morgan: An Intimate Portrait*. New York: Macmillan, 1939.

Schumpeter, Joseph A. *Business Cycles: A Theoretical, Historical, and Statistical Analysis of the Capitalist Process*. Vol. 1. New York: McGraw-Hill, 1923.

———. *Capitalism, Socialism and Democracy*. New York: Harper & Brothers, 1942.

Sinclair, Andrew. *Corsair: The Life of J. Pierpont Morgan*. Boston: Little, Brown, 1981.

Sklar, Martin J. *The Corporate Reconstruction of American Capitalism, 1890–1916*. Cambridge, UK: Cambridge University Press, 1988.

Smalley, Eugene V. *History of the Northern Pacific*. New York: G. P. Putnam's Sons, 1883.

Smitten, Richard. *Jesse Livermore: World's Greatest Stock Trader*. New York: John Wiley & Sons, 2001.

Sobel, Robert. *The Curbstone Brokers: The Origins of the American Stock Exchange*. New York: Macmillan, 1970.

———. *Panic on Wall Street*. New York: E. P. Dutton, 1968.

Spearman, Frank H. *The Strategy of Great Railroads*. New York: Charles Scribner's Sons, 1913.

Stein, Leon, ed. *The Pullman Strike*. New York: Arno, 1969.

Stevenson, Robert Louis. *Across the Plains, with Other Memories and Essays*. New York: Charles Scribner's Sons, 1917.

Stiles, T. J. *The First Tycoon: The Epic Life of Cornelius Vanderbilt*. New York: Alfred A. Knopf, 2009.

Stilwell, Arthur Edward. *Cannibals of Finance: Fifteen Years' Contest with the Money Trust*. Chicago: Farnum, 1912.

Stover, John F. *History of the Illinois Central Railroad*. New York: Macmillan, 1975.

Stromquist, Shelton. *A Generation of Boomers: The Pattern of Railroad Labor Conflict in Nineteenth-Century America*. Urbana: University of Illinois Press, 1987.

Strong, George Templeton. *The Diary of George Templeton Strong*. Edited by Allan Nevins and Milton Halsey. Vol. 1, *The Postwar Years 1865–1875*. New York: Macmillan, 1952.

Strong, Josiah. *Our Country: Its Possible Future and Its Present Crisis*. New York: Baker & Taylor, 1885.

Strouse, Jean. *Morgan: American Financier*. New York: Random House, 1999.

Swanberg, W. A. *Jim Fisk: The Career of an Improbable Rascal*. New York: Charles Scribner's Sons, 1959.

Taylor, George Rogers. *The Transportation Revolution 1815–1860*. New York: Rinehart, 1957.

Thomas, William G. *The Iron Way: Railroads, the Civil War, and the Making of Modern America*. New Haven, Conn.: Yale University Press, 2011.

Thoreau, Henry David. *Walden and Civil Disobedience*. New York: Signet, 2012.

Trottman, Nelson. *History of the Union Pacific*. New York: Ronald, 1923.

Urofsky, Melvin I. *Louis D. Brandeis: A Life*. New York: Pantheon, 2009.

Van Rensselaer, Mrs. John King. *The Social Ladder*. New York: Henry Holt, 1924.

Villard, Henry. *Memoirs of Henry Villard*. 2 vols. Boston: Houghton Mifflin, 1904.

Warburg, Frieda Schiff. *Reminiscences of a Long Life*. New York: privately printed, 1956.

Ware, Norman J. *The Labor Movement in the United States, 1860–1895: A Study in Democracy*. Gloucester, Mass: Peter Smith, 1959.

Warne, Colston E., ed. *The Pullman Boycott of 1894: The Problem of Federal Intervention*. Boston: D. C. Heath, 1955.

Wells, Ida B. *Crusade for Justice: The Autobiography of Ida B. Wells*. Chicago: University of Chicago Press, 1970.

Wendt, Lloyd, and Herman Kogan. *Bet a Million! The Story of John W. Gates*. Indianapolis: Bobbs-Merrill, 1948.

Whitman, Walt. *The Complete Poems*. New York: Penguin, 2004.

———. *Complete Prose Works of Walt Whitman*. Vol. 2. New York: G. P. Putnam's Sons, 1902.

Whitney, Asa. *A Project for a Railroad to the Pacific*. New York: George W. Wood, 1849.

Wolff, Kurt H., and Barrington Moore Jr. *The Critical Spirit: Essays in Honor of Herbert Marcuse*. Boston: Beacon, 1967.

Woodward, C. Vann. *Reunion and Reaction: The Compromise of 1877 and the End of Reconstruction*. New York: Oxford University Press, 1966.

Worster, Donald. *A Passion for Nature: The Life of John Muir*. New York: Oxford University Press, 2008.

Yellen, Samuel. *American Labor Struggles, 1877–1934*. New York: Harcourt, Brace, 1936.

List of Illustration Credits

Page 6: Courtesy of The New York Public Library.

Page 8: Wood engraving by Matthew B. Brady, 1867. Photo courtesy of Library of Congress.

Page 13: Monograph series no. 401: *Atlas of the Historical Geography of the U.S. 1932* by Charles O. Paullin. Courtesy of Carnegie Institution of Washington.

Page 27: Photo from Bain News Service, c. 1909. Courtesy of Library of Congress.

Page 28: Granger Historical Picture Archive.

Page 30: *The Great Race for the Western Stakes 1870,* first published by Currier & Ives. Courtesy of Library of Congress.

Page 37: *East and West Shaking Hands at Laying Last Rail* by Andrew Russell. Courtesy of the Beinecke Rare Book and Manuscript Library, Yale University.

Page 40: Photo taken by Edward Steichen, c. 1903. Courtesy of Library of Congress.

Page 72: Photo from *Jay Cooke: Financier of the Civil War* by Ellis Paxson Oberholtzer (Philadelphia: G. W. Jacobs & Co., 1907).

Page 133: Photo from Bain News Service, 1908. Courtesy of Library of Congress.

Page 144: Photo from Bain News Service, c. 1900. Courtesy of Library of Congress.

Page 148: Photo from *Investors' Supplement of the Commercial & Financial Chronicle,* Vol. L (William B. Dana & Co. Publishers, May 31, 1890).

Page 161: Courtesy of Library of Congress.

Page 189: Photo from Bain News Service, c. 1915–20. Courtesy of Library of Congress.

Page 204: Courtesy of Wyoming State Archives Photo Collection, Sub Neg 19324 deriv.

Page 215: Photo taken by Carleton Watkins, c. 1870–75. Courtesy of the Open Content Program of The J. Paul Getty Trust.

Page 217: Courtesy of Chicago History Museum; ICHi-021195.

Page 237: Courtesy of Smithsonian Institution Archives.

Page 250: *The Curse of California* by George Frederick Keller, tinted lithograph, first appeared on pp. 520–521 of *The Wasp*, vol. 9., no. 316, published August 19, 1882.

Page 253: *Map of the Lucin Cut-Off* from *The Century Illustrated Monthly Magazine*, vol. LXXI (The Century Co., 1905–1906).

Page 263: Courtesy of Library of Congress.

Page 266: Photo taken by the Pach Brothers, 1902. Courtesy of Minnesota Historical Society.

Page 285: Photo taken by Geo. C. Boldt, c. 1902. Courtesy of Library of Congress.

Page 330: Photo from Montauk Photo Concern, c. 1910. Courtesy of Library of Congress.

Page 351: *The poor man's candidate* by Samuel D. Ehrhart from *Puck*, vol. 56, no. 1437 (J. Ottmann Lith. Co., Sept. 14, 1904). Courtesy of Library of Congress.

Page 354: Photo courtesy of the archival website of Salton Sea Museum.

Page 357: Photo from Bain News Service, c. 1900. Courtesy of Library of Congress.

Index

Page numbers in *italics* indicate illustrations.